BECOMING AMERICA

BECOMING AMERICA

*The Revolution
before 1776*

JON BUTLER

HARVARD UNIVERSITY PRESS
Cambridge, Massachusetts
London, England

Copyright © 2000 by the President and Fellows
of Harvard College
All rights reserved
Printed in the United States of America
Third printing, 2001

First Harvard University Press paperback edition, 2001

Library of Congress Cataloging-in-Publication Data

Butler, Jon, 1940–
Becoming America : the revolution before 1776 / Jon Butler.
p. cm.
Includes bibliographical references (p.   ) and index.
ISBN 0-674-00091-9 (cloth)
ISBN 0-674-00667-4 (pbk.)
1. United States—History—Colonial period, ca. 1600–1775.
2. United States—Civilization—To 1783. I. Title.
E188 .B97 2000
973.2—dc21   99-054646

Designed by Gwen Nefsky Frankfeldt

FOR MY MOTHER
GENEVIEVE VIRGINIA SORENSON BUTLER
AND IN MEMORY OF MY FATHER
HAROLD JASON BUTLER
1912–1998

"You can see things on the Minnesota prairie
that you can't see anywhere else."

CONTENTS

ILLUSTRATIONS

BECOMING AMERICA

INTRODUCTION

Each summer, for more than two hundred years, Americans have clambered across the eastern seaboard searching for "the colonies" and "olden times." The trek is fun but doubly ironic. The homes, public buildings, and churches they tour generally represent only the last half of the colonial era, that is, the years between 1680 and 1770. They see very little from the seventeenth-century colonies established between 1607 and 1680 except through modern reconstructions, such as those at Plimoth Plantation in Plymouth, Massachusetts, and at Jamestown Settlement in Jamestown, Virginia. And however odd it may seem, the buildings that look so quaint and so "colonial," such as the famous House of Seven Gables in Salem, Massachusetts, through which Nathaniel Hawthorne symbolized a crabbed seventeenth-century Puritanism, actually exemplify the first flowering of modernity in America. Taken together, these buildings embody a revolution that utterly transformed the original seventeenth-century British colonies, marking the creation of the first modern society in Britain's colonies before independence. This transformation, which emerged with unplanned force in Britain's mainland colonies between 1680 and 1770, pointed to the future far more than it pointed to the past. It shaped the Revolution of 1776, including the social and political upheaval unleashed by independence, although it cannot be said to have precipitated the Revolutionary War.

This book traces the enormous social, economic, political, and cultural changes that created a distinctively modern and, ultimately, "American" society in Britain's mainland colonies between 1680 and 1770. By 1770 Britain's mainland settlements contained a polyglot population of English, Scots, Germans, Dutch, Swiss, French, and Africans, although in 1680 most European settlers were English. By 1770 slavery had profoundly reshaped colonial life everywhere, whereas it cast only curious shadows in the mainland colonies as late as 1670. As early as 1720 cities of real urban complexity emerged from the meanest and simplest of towns. Modest as well as prosperous farmers increasingly thrust themselves into international market economies, some happily, some less so. Eighteenth-century colonial merchants and planters created and inherited wealth so vast that their predecessors scarcely could have comprehended it. Complex, sophisticated politics replaced the rudimentary political mechanisms typical of the seventeenth-century colonies. New patterns of production and consumption accompanied the rise of refined crafts and trades. A vigorous religious pluralism overran the old orthodoxy of the Puritans in Massachusetts and the Anglicans in Virginia. Here, then, was an America already modern in important ways.

Britain's eighteenth-century mainland colonies were not completely modern, of course. Two characteristics of modern society never appeared in the colonies. Britain's mainland settlements never were overwhelmingly urban, and they were not driven by or beset with the massive technological change that transformed nineteenth-century America and Europe. But the colonies emerged as surprisingly modern in five other important ways. They became ethnically and nationally diverse, not homogeneous. They developed transatlantic and international economies that supported a vigorous domestic trade and production. Their politics looked ahead to the large-scale participatory politics of modern societies. They exhibited the modern penchant for power, control, and authority over both humanity and nature that brooked few limitations or questions about their propriety. And they displayed a religious pluralism that dwarfed the mild religious diversity found in any early modern European nation.[1]

The "modern" features of Britain's eighteenth-century colonies were not fully developed even on the eve of the Revolution. Ethnic and national diversity did not obviate a strong British dominance in government and culture; regional disparities and increasing stratification of wealth typified colonial economic development; patronage and status inflected colonial politics; and even in the 1760s not everyone accepted religious pluralism as legitimate in principle, even if it was present in fact. Yet the changes were so pronounced that most foreign observers had long since described the colonies as profoundly different from modern Europe. The America of the British mainland colonies had come to mean a new kind of society even if strong remnants of older societies still persisted past the American Revolution.

The transformation of the colonies between 1680 and 1770 exhibited the settlers' increasing fascination with power and authority, a determination to make the world anew in yet untested images. Men and women of all kinds pressed on to control their own destiny, sometimes collectively, sometimes individually as America's population, economy, secular life, and religion became more complex and variegated. Colonists created a far more independent economy than their "colonial" status might have suggested was desirable or possible. Most European settlers extended and enlivened traditional religious expression in the New World. Africans and American Indians shaped new cultures and modes of living under extraordinarily difficult conditions. Provincial politics gave European settlers persuasive control over colonial affairs. A vigorous secular life emulated European models yet moved to New World rhythms and concerns.

Modernity could also support and even create new problems that would afflict America and much of the modern world for decades, even centuries. Most spectacularly, the slaveholding that overwhelmed Spanish America and the British Caribbean by the 1650s was perfected in the British mainland colonies after 1680, where it overwhelmed the feeble, informal slave practices first cobbled together in British America in the 1650s and 1660s. The result by the mid-eighteenth century was an institution of exceptional power that exemplified modernity's capacity and inclination to control human lives. It set the British mainland colonies dramatically apart from Britain itself, but not necessarily from other New World societies, even though British slaveholding was different from that of other New World colonies.

Eighteenth-century America thus underwent a twofold transformation. One change created a new society with a distinctive economy, politics, secular life, and religion. Another change, more subtle and more difficult to elicit, created a new public and even private culture, simultaneously aggressive and willful, materialistic as well as idealistic, driven toward authority and mastery.

The result was America in its aspirations, its character, its flaws, and its achievements—a surprising America that seventeenth-century immigrants never imagined. The transformations occurring between 1680 and 1770 made the term "America" increasingly indelible. They made the direction of American history unmistakable, even if they did not make it inevitable.

These views run counter to three different historical interpretations, one old, two more recent. The older interpretation focused on the first European settlements before 1650, the American Revolution, and New England and sometimes Virginia. In this history the middle period of the colonial era, between 1680 and 1770, and the "middle colonies" of New York, New Jersey, and Pennsylvania and the southern colonies beyond Virginia won relatively little attention. This attention to the beginning and the end of the colonial period, plus the continuing emphasis on New England, obscured the crucial decades between 1680 and 1770 and the larger America beyond New England and Virginia.[2]

Fortunately, these habits shifted in the 1970s. A widening stream of historical studies revealed fascinating decades and regions largely ignored earlier. One group of scholars concentrated on the Chesapeake region of both Maryland and Virginia and used new quantitative methods that threw open the doors of previously obscure economic and social history.[3] Other scholars revised the histories of the middle colonies, focusing especially on religion and politics, but also on immigration and ethnicity.[4] Still others turned to the Carolinas, perhaps the colonies least well treated in previous histories, where they located fascinating models for understanding early American patterns in race, politics, and economics.[5] Even scholarship on the Puritans changed. New England historians increasingly concentrated on social life rather than intellectual history, theology, and the Puritan elite, and they turned greater attention to the eighteenth century.[6]

This book also rebuffs more recent interpretations that stress the "Europeanization" of eighteenth-century America and the "deferential," monarchical character of prerevolutionary society. By "Euro-peanization," historians have meant a growing fascination for and de-pendence on European society and material goods.[7] By "deferential," they have meant a growing emphasis on the privileges of class, on the power of a developing colonial aristocracy, and on the sense of obliga-tion and dependence upon superiors that was determined at least as much by ascription and reputation as by demonstrable personal achievement.[8] If these characteristics are considered together, eigh-teenth-century America sometimes appears more "colonial" than does its seventeenth-century predecessor. The first settlements might seem crude and peculiarly independent in their relative simplicity and isola-tion; eighteenth-century America appears sophisticated yet necessarily more dependent, more classically "colonial" in its lusting after Euro-pean convictions and things on the peripheries of Western culture.

The view here contests many if not all of these arguments. European imports increased substantially in eighteenth-century America, and colonists looked to Europe for culture and status, Britain especially. But imports did not outstrip the rise in the colonial population, and the European goods and ideas fit into a society not at all like Europe. America never wholly refashioned these goods and ideas, but neither did these goods and ideas transform the New World colonies into Euro-pean imitations. Moreover, although colonists frequently deferred to their betters, it is a mistake to see eighteenth-century America as a deferential society. In an aggressive authority-driven culture, deference was endemic, perhaps even necessary. But it was one of several recipro-cal relations in a complex web of early modern colonial politics and social connections that allowed numerous modes of interpersonal rela-tionships. These ranged from deference to acceptance to condescension to wariness to antiauthoritarianism to simple orneriness. In eighteenth-century America these relationships veered toward an unusual asser-tiveness that affected every aspect of prerevolutionary life.

Finally, the book implicitly contests the recent stress on a "market revolution" in antebellum America. In this view, the colonial era's local-ized, subsistence, and community-focused lifestyle gave way to a postrevolutionary "market" economy whose profit orientation and en-thusiastic entrepreneurialism reshaped American culture, politics, and religion as thoroughly as it transformed the economy from agriculture to manufacturing. Between 1810 and 1850 major transformations indeed overtook America. Whether, how, and to what extent they constituted a "market revolution" is a matter of considerable debate. Yet whatever the verdict on that subject, *Becoming America* locates the origins and early progress of many crucial changes not in the early nineteenth century but in the subtle and dramatic alterations that created a new society in British America before 1776. Whether we label these changes a "market revolution" or use some other expression, the complicated process of creating a distinctive, even "modern" America stretched across seven to eight decades on either side of the American Revolution. *Becoming America* describes the stages that occurred before 1776. What happened later is described in other books by other historians.[9]

In all, then, this book centers on the transformation of colonial America between 1680 and 1770—its extraordinary heterogeneity of peoples; its rapid economic transformation; its energetic provincial and local politics; its evolving secular and material culture; its rapidly expanding pluralistic religions; its regionalism and sometimes unwilling creation of vigorous subsocieties within the larger culture; and a widespread drive for authority to shape individual and collective destinies.

Of course, America would become far more "modern" after the American Revolution. New theories of genetics and "race" made slavery even more devastating in the nineteenth century than it had already become in the eighteenth century. Politics quickly transcended its colonial heritage after 1776, not merely in the state constitutions and Federal Constitution of 1789 but in regional and national parties and an aggressive, enthusiastic pursuit of democracy in the antebellum era. Urbanization, industrialization, and technological advance brought canals, steamships, railroads, and electricity, all of which soon transformed the nation physically in ways not even Benjamin Franklin anticipated. Still, the transformations between 1680 and 1770 carried a unique importance. They created the America that fought the Revolution of 1776 and gave the new nation much of its essential identity.

The book is not a general account of colonial or prerevolutionary America. Many things happened there between 1680 and 1770 that aren't discussed here. Instead, the book stresses those features that dramatically reshaped the seventeenth-century colonies. Nor does the book discuss the "American character." A favorite of historians in the past, the search for the American character has long faltered on its inability to extend particular findings to the colonies generally. The argument here is simple—that an American society emerged before an "American character" could be found in any of its residents. The origins of an American character are better located in the consequences of independence in 1776 and the rise of American nationalism in the next half century, a character Americans then tested in the Civil War.[10]

The book also concentrates on the past, not on historians. I have rejected the increasingly common practice of naming historians in the text when discussing interpretive conflicts—"as Smith says," "as Allen argues," and so forth. This is a self-obsessive habit that I have employed myself. But it leaves many readers gasping for air, and I have confined historians' names, if not their arguments, to the notes, which I hope will guide readers to deeper studies of interesting, sometimes heavily debated topics. After all, every topic discussed here is the subject of many varied and often different historical studies. Finally, to readers who might have wanted a longer, more expansive book, I can only respond that I preferred a shorter one.

The book comes out of more than two decades of my own studies in the colonial era's "dark ages," usually on religious themes away from New Englanders and Virginians. It was written to answer two questions. One was posed by a friend—"How do you synthesize colonial history after the Puritans?" The other has long bothered early American historians—when Hector St. John de Crèvecoeur asked his famous question, "What then is the American, this new man?" was he correct in his answer: "He is an American, who leaving behind him all his ancient prejudices and manners, receives new ones from the new mode of life he has embraced, the new government he obeys, and the new rank he holds."

I have addressed these questions by exploring how, why, and to what effect the first modern society came into being in Britain's mainland American colonies between 1680 and 1770.

One

PEOPLES

The next wish of this traveller will be to know whence came all
these people.

J. HECTOR ST. JOHN DE CRÈVECOEUR (1782)

O N Monday morning, April 7, 1712, New Yorkers gasped at the
bodies strewn about town after a night of unprecedented violence. Auguste Grasset lay dead with "severall wounds about his Neck
and head and fingers." The corpse of Henry Brasier bore a grotesque ax
chop to the neck. Adrian Hooghlandt died after being stabbed in the
back. William Asht's attacker thrust a knife through his throat and
"under his right Breast." A gunshot killed Joris Marschalck. Adrian
Beekman died from a knife to the chest. The coroner ascribed no causes
of death to Lieutenant John Corbett and Johannes Lauw, who also
perished the same night. Seven men wounded April 6 and 7 later recovered—David Coesart, Johannes Dehonneur, George Elsworth, Jr.,
Adrian Hooghlandt, Jr., Lawrence Reade, Thomas Stewart, and John
Troop.[1]

Within only two weeks, New York's magistrates doubled the number
of the dead in the town. They determined to their own satisfaction that
the murders of April 6 and 7 stemmed from a "Negro plot" to spirit
freed slaves to Africa, and they moved swiftly to suppress additional
disturbances. Six Africans committed suicide as the magistrates interro-
gated New York's slaves. By April 20, only two weeks after the murders, the magistrates had not only convicted nineteen persons for the
crimes—three women and sixteen men, all captured Africans—but according to the *Boston Weekly News-Letter,* had already executed seven-

teen of them, "one burnt, a second broke upon the wheel, and a third hung up alive." (They delayed the executions of two pregnant African women until the women delivered their babies, careful to extricate their owners' anticipated property.) Governor Robert Hunter, an otherwise urbane and sophisticated man who wrote the first English play in America—a ribald satire entitled *Androboros* (1714)—protested the verdicts and punishments as hasty and unprincipled. But in an ominous tone, Hunter also called them the "most exemplary that could be possibly thought of."[2]

New York's 1712 carnage symbolized many things: African anger over enslavement, the violence already endemic to America, the demand for authority in a society that beckoned freedom, the willful determination that motivated so many in America, and the tenacious colonial stress on property, including a human property that might strike at its owners. It also revealed the population diversity of New York even by 1700. The slain Europeans included three Englishmen, three French Huguenots, two Dutch men, a French-speaking Walloon from the region of modern Belgium, and a German. The executed Africans, more difficult to identify because English records only occasionally described their birthplaces, probably included Ibos from the area of modern Biafra, Cormantines from the so-called Gold Coast, and Bakongo and Mbundu from the area of modern Angola. Here, then, were not merely "English colonists," but an array of unalike peoples never before gathered together in the English experience on either side of the Atlantic.[3]

This heterogeneity did not surprise contemporaries. Although in 1670 Dutch, Africans, Germans, Walloons, and Portuguese and Spanish Jews all lived in New Amsterdam, the Dutch dominated both the population and the culture. That changed by 1703. A decade before the 1712 slave revolt, New York already bore one crucial element of its modern identity: immigrant minorities dominated its population. The 1703 New York census documented a city population of no national, ethnic, or religious majority: 42 percent Dutch, 30 percent English, 18 percent African, 9 percent French, and 1 percent Jewish. Only the town's Dutch residents were likely to have been born in America. Most others, whether Europeans or Africans, arrived from the Old World as children and young adults. In short, J. Hector St. John de Crèvecoeur's description of Americans in *Letters from an American Farmer* (1782) already applied to New York in 1703: "They are a mixture of English, Scotch, Irish, French, Dutch, German, and Swedes," Crèvecoeur wrote, as well as enslaved Africans.[4]

Crèvecoeur actually underestimated eighteenth-century British colonial heterogeneity. Not even New England remained New *England,* at least not exclusively. Crèvecoeur described New Englanders as "the unmixed descendants of Englishmen." But by 1760, 30 percent of New Englanders came from outside England. Africans, Scots, Scots-Irish, and Irish made up about 15 percent of Massachusetts's people, 25 percent of Connecticut's, and 35 percent of Rhode Island's. Even Massachusetts knew substantial numbers of minorities, although it indeed remained the most homogeneous colony in New England. Its 5,000 Africans and 4,000 Scots, Scots-Irish, and Irish constituted a sufficient "critical mass" to support burgeoning group identities, and English settlers acknowledged their presence warily, in part because they knew how prominently these non-English residents figured in the other mainland colonies.[5]

An unprecedented jumble of peoples typified the colonies from New York to Georgia in 1760. Most colonies from New York south could form a cultural majority only by grouping together all white settlers, and then sometimes only barely. In the "middle" colonies of New York, New Jersey, Delaware, and Pennsylvania, English settlers constituted only 30 to 45 percent of all residents (45 percent in New York, 40 percent in New Jersey, and about 30 percent in Pennsylvania). New York's 1760 population clustered into four principal groups: English (about 52,000), Germans and Dutch (22,000), Africans (16,000), and Scots, Scots-Irish, and Irish (15,000). In Pennsylvania, German and Dutch settlers roughly equaled English residents (approximately 63,000 each), while Scots, Scots-Irish, and Irish accounted for about 42,000 residents; Africans numbered about 4,500 persons.[6]

The southern colonies proved equally heterogeneous, but in different ways. In 1760 Africans constituted the region's most numerous people, slightly outnumbering the English; Scots, Scots-Irish, and Irish made up another 15 percent of the population. Even in Maryland and North Carolina, the least diverse southern colonies, English settlers comprised only about 45 percent of the population, while in Virginia they comprised about 35 percent of the population. Africans outnumbered the

English in South Carolina by a ratio of 2–1 in 1760, and this ratio climbed to 10–1 in South Carolina's rural counties. Africans then dramatically outnumbered overseers and neighboring yeoman farmers—a configuration unparalleled in any other mainland colony. South Carolina never typified colonial America, but its population peculiarities did suggest how much colonial America could differ from Europe, much less from the America Indians once possessed alone.[7]

W HEN Crèvecoeur described Nantucket in the fourth of his *Letters from an American Farmer,* he included a simple and stark judgment about Nantucket's Indians: "They are hastening towards a total annihilation." The process was already so advanced that Crèvecoeur could not determine the Indians' origins. He did not know if they descended from "the ancient natives of the island, or whether they are the remains of the many different nations which once inhabited . . . the peninsula now known by the name of Cape Cod." Crèvecoeur blamed some Indian troubles on their quarrelsomeness, which he allowed was a "disposition of man." But he also noted how Indians throughout Britain's colonies also had been decimated by "the smallpox and the use of spirituous liquors, the two greatest curses they have received from us." British attacks only added to the dangers, and among Indians "whole nations have disappeared." "What is become of those numerous tribes which formerly inhabited the extensive shores of the great bay of Massachusetts . . . without mentioning those powerful tribes which once dwelt between the rivers Hudson, Connecticut, Piscataqua, and Kennebec?"[8]

Between 1680 and 1760 many American Indian cultures disappeared altogether or merged with other cultures, almost always quite involuntarily. Inaccurate and confusing seventeenth- and eighteenth-century reports make it difficult to identify distinct American Indian cultural groups after 1600, as British settlement began. But in the territory of the British mainland colonies, roughly 160 such groups that existed in 1680 had been reduced to about 75 by 1800. In the southern colonies, for example, the Indian population fell from about 200,000 in 1685 to fewer than 60,000, while the European and African population rose from 50,000 to more than 900,000.

This radical population decline and cultural homicide in the mainland British colonies was the second of several stages in a tragic process that started in the sixteenth century and that continued into the twentieth. The first major contraction began in the 1550s and stemmed from the ravages of European diseases and European conquest. Relatively isolated from far-flung foreign disease environments, American Indians fell before the onslaught of European sicknesses. War proved equally devastating, including wars begun by Indians to stem European conquest. For example, when New England's Wampanoags began Metacom's War in June 1675 (the English called it "King Philip's War"), they hoped to end fifty years of English incursion and, perhaps, even eject the English altogether. The Wampanoags, aided by other Indians nearby, burned and destroyed Deerfield, Northfield, and Springfield in Massachusetts and killed almost one in sixteen European men then living in New England. But Metacom's death in 1676 and superior English armament soon turned the destructiveness on the Indians. The English destroyed numerous Wampanoag, Narragansett, and Abenaki villages. Ultimately, Metacom's War confirmed the English domination of New England.[9]

The period from 1680 to 1760 sealed the massive reductions of Indian populations begun in the late sixteenth century from disease and conquest. Everywhere along the eastern seaboard, minuscule numbers of Indian survivors occupied ever smaller geographical pockets surrounded by ever more Europeans. In New England, epidemics reduced Massachusett and Patuxet societies from about 25,000 people in 1600 to less than 300 people by 1700 while the European population rose to nearly 90,000. The 3,000 Indians living on Nantucket Island in 1642 had been reduced to about 1,500 in 1674, then to 20 in 1790. By 1700 the 20,000 Indians who once lived in tidewater Virginia had been reduced to fewer than 2,000, by which time the European and African slave population had reached 60,000.[10]

The experience of the Lenni Lenapi or Delaware Indians in Pennsylvania reflected the devastation wrought after 1680 even in a colony with a reputation for "fair" treatment of Indians. The Lenni Lenape, "original people" in the Algonkian language they spoke, sold substantial land to William Penn between 1682 and 1684. They quickly found themselves engulfed by the swarms of European immigrants settling there and ravaged by the diseases the Europeans brought. The pamphleteer Gabriel Thomas wrote in 1698 that "the Indians themselves say that two of them die for every one Christian that comes in here." The Lenni Lenape also experienced degradation from the uncontrolled liquor trade. Then, in the infamous 1737 "walking purchase," James Logan and the Pennsylvania government swindled them into deeding even more land to the government. Government agents cleared trails and used trained runners to "walk" the boundaries of a territory far greater than the Delaware ever intended to sell. The colonial government set aside towns for the Delaware Indians as early as 1708—Okehocking in Chester County, for example. But when the Lenni Lenape found themselves surrounded by Europeans, they moved farther west into the Susquehanna Valley. There they had to compete with the Susquehannock, Conoy, and Iroquois for land and wilds. Like the Delaware, they all occupied smaller land tracts every decade and found themselves forced to accommodate one another and the Europeans simultaneously.[11]

Whole Indian cultures disappeared in all the mainland colonies. Groups that had existed for hundreds, even several thousand years, died out or joined with other threatened groups throughout the seventeenth and eighteenth centuries. Those who disappeared included the Chilucan, Oconee, Pensacola, Pohoy, Potano, Saturiwa, Surruque, Tekesta, Timucua, Tocobaga, and Yustaga of Florida; the Tacatacuru, Yufera, and Yui, of Georgia; the Chawasha of Mississippi; the Cape Fear, Chowanoc, Coree, Hatteras, Machapunga, Neusiok, Pamlico, and Pedee of North Carolina; the Sewee, Shakori, and Waxhaw of South Carolina; and the Manahoac, Monacan, Moneton, Nahyssan, and Occaneechi of Virginia. Some, like the Ais, Guacata, and Jeaga Indians of Florida, fled to Cuba about 1763, where native groups absorbed them. This process continued across the continent into the early twentieth century. The destruction of Indian groups in Florida was easily matched in California, as its 250 distinctive cultural groups were reduced to fewer than 50 by 1900. The lonely Ishi, "the last Yahi," captured in a northern California mining camp in August 1911, exemplified the devastation. Ishi became a human exhibit in Alfred Kroeber's Anthropology Museum at the University of California at Berkeley, where he died in March 1916. But the Yahi culture that patterned his individuality and forged his identity had effectively disappeared decades earlier.[12]

Some eighteenth-century Indian groups created new cultures from the remnants of old ones in a process that signaled a crucial drive for survival among Indians not done in by European disease and arms. For example, between about 1710 and 1740 more than a dozen separate peoples of the Carolinas, among them the Cape Fear, Cheraw, Santee, Winyaw, and Woccon Indians, formed a new "Catawba" nation that has endured into the twentieth century. The term "Catawba" was a largely English invention that predated the actual emergence of a cohesive Catawba nation; family, village, and clan allegiances that crisscrossed larger "tribal" identities in early America further complicated Catawba culture. Still, a distinct Catawba culture emerged that demonstrated the Indian capacity for adaptation and accommodation in the face of massive change. The task was difficult. Some Indians who joined the Catawbas in the 1720s had left them a decade later, and a German observer described the Catawbas as late as 1745 as "an Irregular people" with indifferent leadership.[13]

Yet between 1700 and 1750 the Catawbas developed an effective political leadership. Conflict with the English and other Indians, especially the Tuscaroras and their Iroquois allies to the north, sharpened Catawba diplomatic and military skill. Catawbas became well known, if not renowned, for their taunting, treachery, warrior skills, and bravery, attributes that strengthened their internal cohesion and stature among enemies. The six or seven Catawba villages of the mid-eighteenth century reflected a material culture common in its diversity. Catawbas used both native and European defenses and placed dwellings inside circular fortifications of vertical timbers covered with bark. They mixed clothing. Some men dressed in largely European attire, while other men and most women wore a combination of blankets and deerskins. They employed both European and traditional Indian names, the latter largely disappearing in the nineteenth century.[14]

Trade underwrote the Catawbas' cultural survival, their own "modernization," as well as their subjection to the English. Having traded with other Indians for centuries, the Catawbas and their constituent groups quickly traded with the English as well. The Indians offered highly valuable skins, especially deerskins, which attracted English traders, and they sometimes traded agricultural produce with nearby settlers. The English traders offered beads, cloth, weapons, and ammunition. Trade could be perplexing. English traders did not always appreciate arbitrary Indian aesthetics: why did some Indians refuse beads and cloth when others found them ideal? Trade produced tensions among Indians and stimulated open, sometimes violent, conflict with the English. Discontent over trade sparked the so-called Yamasee War of 1715, whose rapid Indian victories were followed by a disastrous defeat in June. When trade resumed, as it quickly did, Catawbas moved ever more resolutely within the world of English commerce, goods, and technology. The transit quietly shaped their villages, produced ever more hybrid modes of living, and underwrote the Catawbas' emergence as an independent people. But the emerging Catawba and the English never competed as sovereign nations. The Catawba people came into being, survived, and even prospered in eighteenth-century South Carolina; the English moved around them to the western Carolinas and beyond.[15]

The Catawba experience of adaptation, accommodation, and survival typified surviving Indian responses to English advances in the eighteenth century, even if the Catawbas offered an unusually complex illustration of the process. More powerful Indian groups learned to use alternating strategies of threat and compromise with the English who, in turn, increasingly understood better the Indians' strengths and weaknesses. The Iroquois or Five Nations, consisting of the Mohawks, Oneidas, Onondagas, Cayugas, and Senecas, maintained fierce reputations as warriors even though they lost numerous battles with the English and French. Still feared, they adopted European goods and technology, including weapons, and in New York they became almost economically dependent on selling land to the English. Smaller groups, like the Mahicans, persevered in tiny villages, such as the settlements at Stockbridge and Shekomeko in western Massachusetts. They lived as traders, laborers, and farmers but left a decidedly mixed record on religion, pleasing Moravian missionaries but disappointing Congregationalists such as Jonathan Edwards.[16]

This persistence among surviving Indians had important implications for prerevolutionary American society. It meant that between 1680 and 1770 Indians and Europeans lived side by side almost everywhere in rural eighteenth-century America, where they sustained innumerable encounters under circumstances new for each. Certainly exceptions existed. Tidewater Virginia was almost bereft of Indians by the 1720s, as was far eastern Pennsylvania, New Jersey, and some sections of New England. But throughout most of the Carolinas, backcountry Virginia, western Maryland, Pennsylvania, and New York, and western and northern New England, Indians remained a regular presence among Europeans, sometimes feared, sometimes loathed, occasionally admired, everywhere changed. The era of greater segregation would come in the nineteenth century as the European and African-American population boomed and the Indian population declined further, often forcibly. Yet in the prerevolutionary era, Indians solidified new ways of dealing with the European challenge, with each other, and with the natural world that they had previously claimed for themselves.[17]

WHEN Judith Giton, fleeing Catholic attacks on Protestants, left Languedoc in southern France in 1682, she expected and hoped to remain in Europe. She and her family had endured "eight months [of] exactions and quartering" by soldiers "with much evil" and finally fled "France by night." After a tense journey to Lyon and Dijon, Giton, her mother, and her brothers Pierre and Louis arrived in Cologne, on the Rhine River. There Judith hoped to settle with a third brother who had settled thirty miles from Cologne after leaving France earlier. Such foreign refugeee communities were not uncommon in Europe. Men and women escaping religious persecution, Jews moving between still circumscribed urban ghettos, and other Europeans simply seeking better land in new places created pockets of alien settlements across the Continent, and this pattern extended into the eighteenth century, especially in eastern Europe from Poland to Hungary, which received immigrants from as far as England and Scotland.

Yet Judith Giton never settled near Cologne nor in expanding Huguenot refugee communities in Germany, the Netherlands, or England. Instead, her brother Pierre had read a pamphlet advertising a place called South Carolina in America and "had nothing but Carolina on his thoughts." Within months the Giton family was living with Huguenot refugees in London while seeking passage to Carolina. Their success was not without costs. Judith Giton's mother died during the passage to America, Louis Giton died after only eighteen months in South Carolina, and Judith found the colony distasteful, choked with "sickness, pestilence, famine, poverty, [and] very hard work." Only after marrying a Huguenot refugee named Pierre Manigault—by the 1770s their grandson Peter may have been the richest man in the colonies—could she proclaim that "God has had pity on me, and has changed my lot to one more happy. Glory be unto him."[18]

Clearly, late-seventeenth-century Europe was not homogeneous. London, Paris, and Rotterdam had known resident "strangers" for hundreds of years. The newly independent Netherlands possessed a more diversified and variegated population than did many others, including England. Alsace divided French- and German-speaking Europeans. On the site of the former Yugoslavia, multiple languages, religions, and cultural identities produced bitter territorial contests in the eighteenth century as in the twentieth. And England enjoyed Old World possessions it kept by force. The English settled Scots in northern Ireland, where an English elite dominated the remainder of the country, all to create territorial and hierarchical beachheads in a land that had resisted English conquest for centuries.[19]

Still, European population diversity proved modest, certainly compared with the variety of peoples who transformed Britain's mainland colonies between 1680 and 1760. The foreign traders in early modern London, Paris, Amsterdam, and Rotterdam seldom expanded into large, muscular immigrant communities. If substantial numbers of foreigners lived in lands other than their "own," it usually was because they were religious exiles. Religious tension, bigotry, and war often sent thousands of refugees into nearby territories seeking safety. After France's Louis XIV banned Protestantism in 1685, for example, the country's beleaguered Huguenots fled to Prussia, Switzerland, the Netherlands, and England, with some finally settling in America.[20]

The British colonization of Ireland and the Caribbean never attained the heterogeneous population present in the mainland American colonies after 1680. Both Ireland and the Caribbean became strikingly bifurcated societies under English rule. In Ireland, English and Scottish settlers dominated the Irish Catholic population for centuries. In the Caribbean, the English dominated captured Africans through a horrific slavery. In the British mainland colonies, however, interrelationships among peoples emerged as far more complicated, in part because so many different peoples came to the mainland colonies from so many diverse sources, some freely, many under coercion.[21]

Tradition and new opportunities turned Europeans toward America in rising numbers after 1680. European migration to America built on frequent population movement within and throughout early modern Europe, contrary to nineteenth- and twentieth-century myths that Europeans seldom moved until they left for America. For example, Scots emigrated to many places throughout Europe long before they moved to America. Before 1700 Scots settled in England, Ireland, Scandinavia, the Netherlands, and even Poland, where some thirty thousand Scots lived by the 1620s.[22]

Early modern political primitiveness—euphemistically called "fluidity"—sometimes compensated for the crude transportation and limited technology that otherwise impeded population movement. Borders were vaguely drawn and poorly guarded. Most governments allowed "foreigners" sufficient privileges to cushion the immigrants' lack of status as subjects protected by the Crown. Although many governments often failed to enforce antiforeign strictures, they regularly made scapegoats of immigrants and foreigners during domestic upheavals. Jews felt discrimination more frequently than any other group. Jews not only were non-Christian but often were foreign, and in many European countries they were living models for discrimination exercised against others, such as anti-Protestant prejudice in Catholic France.[23]

The difficulty of emigration throughout the seventeenth and eighteenth centuries demonstrated the determination that motivated emigrants. In both Europe and America, roads were little more than mud trails. Progress was slow and seldom exceeded more than twenty or thirty miles a day. Lodgers slept seven to ten in a room with no privacy. Emigrants passed diseases to one another, picked them up as they moved through one town after another, then met new diseases in new habitats. Ironically, then, migration often shortened rather than lengthened life spans, even though most migrants hoped their journeys would better their lives.[24]

Europeans faced immense challenges as they turned Old World migration into New World adventure. Information about the New World came through chance and accident as much as through advertising and systematic inquiry. Immigrants acted on rumors, the experiences of kinsmen or acquaintances, propaganda from entrepreneurs (like Pennsylvania's William Penn), and the enticements of ship captains. Was the captain reliable? Was a ship safe? Was food ample or sparse? These were not idle questions; voyages to America took six weeks to three months and luck all too often rested on the skill and integrity of the captain. An optimistic ship owner of the 1770s described spaces for adults in the upper hold as only "six feet long & 20 inches or two feet broad." Poorer emigrants traveling in steerage below the main deck were "crowded together four in a bed, and those beds one upon another three deep, with not so much room betwixt each as to admit even the smallest person to sit up on end."[25]

The immigrant contour changed as its flow widened after 1680. Immigrants paid for their New World passage through indentures and redemption bonds. Indentures gave ship owners and their agents the right to use immigrant labor for limited terms, usually between four and seven years, in exchange for paying their passage to America. Indentures fueled English migration to the Chesapeake between 1610 and 1660, but declined in the next decades and never were common in New England immigration. After about 1720, however, indentures increased in popularity again among English immigrants, including skilled tradesmen, workers, and former apprentices. Redemption bonds gave immigrants a specific amount of time to "redeem" the cost of ship passage, usually by selling their own labor on the local American market. Indentured and "redemptioner" immigrants took major risks: they contracted to labor for utter strangers in order to live on a continent where freedom seemed unlimited.[26]

The migrants' identity changed as well. After 1680 Scottish, Scots-Irish, French, German, and Swiss immigrants constituted about three-fourths of all European immigrants to the British mainland colonies, where before 1680, English immigrants constituted 85 to 90 percent of European settlers in the English colonies. A lack of registration records or detailed census records makes it impossible to chart this change accurately. But a combination of admittedly imperfect materials establishes the general contours of the change with little doubt: after 1680, the British mainland colonies became a haven for non-English Europeans. Britain's mainland colonies became unique in this regard. The colonies established by France, Spain, and Portugal simply never developed the mixtures of Europeans common in British America.[27]

Four groups—Huguenots, Scots, Jews, and Germans—typified the European immigrant experience in America between 1680 and 1760. None was fully "representative." The eighteenth-century immigrant experience proved as varied as its nineteenth- and twentieth-century successors, and some contemporaries found in its anomalies and eccentricities more than modest amusement. Lewis Morris, sometime governor of New Jersey, wrote in the 1730s,

> from Dane, from Hollander, and Swede,
> from Wales, and from the north of Tweed
> our first Supply's came o'er,
> from france a band of refugees,
> and from fair Ireland rapparees,
> came crowding to this Shore
> a mungrell brood of canting Saints,
> that filled all Europe with complaints
> came here to fix their stakes.[28]

THE story of the Huguenots—French Protestants—offers intriguing insights into the process and result of migrations by religious refugees to America. Huguenots were the first substantial continental European immigrants to arrive in British America, the first to form identifiable "immigrant" communities within the English colonies, and the first to assimilate thoroughly. Although the Huguenots' experience ultimately proved atypical, it spoke to the special openness of America to European immigrants in the late seventeenth and early eighteenth centuries.

The Huguenots' route to America linked continental European population mobility and American emigration. Huguenots came to America in a second, unanticipated stage of a bitter and forced exile from France. The first stage occurred between 1675 and 1690 as 100,000 French Protestants fled France when Louis XIV revoked the Edict of Nantes that had guaranteed limited Protestant worship in Catholic

France since 1592. This stream of emigrants, called *le refuge* by Protestant historians, sent French Protestants pouring into Prussia, Switzerland, the Netherlands, and England—men, women, and children, young and old, rich and poor.[29]

The second stage emerged as refugee Huguenots took up American colonization to alleviate their miserable exile in Europe. The Huguenot exodus had occurred just as a late-seventeenth-century colonization boom was beginning in America, and colonial entrepreneurs quickly advertised among the Huguenot refugees. Agents for William Penn and the proprietors of the Carolinas circulated pamphlets in the Huguenot refugee centers advertising their colonies, and their pamphlets proved intriguing in one special regard: even to the Huguenots they appealed more to their material than their spiritual interest in America. Penn and the Carolina proprietors touted their commitment to religious toleration. But most of their pamphlets also stressed the material gain possible across the Atlantic.[30]

Huguenot immigrants to America looked very much like many later European immigrants to America. Aid records document their poverty in London: for example, Laurent Corniflau received money for "stockings and shoes," Charles Faucheraud received a straw bed, and Pierre Cante received money for food and clothing. By 1695 all three men were in America. Huguenot immigrants to America also were overwhelmingly young, although many old people and children had fled France. A 1697 naturalization list from South Carolina and a 1698 census of the Huguenot village of New Rochelle in New York profile settlers who were between twenty-five and forty when they arrived in America and who traveled with few older immigrants and very few children. Clearly, the decision to emigrate to America was quite separate from the decision to leave France, and it produced a far younger, largely childless group of immigrants to the New World.[31]

Huguenots settled in surprising and selective places in America. Pennsylvania received almost no Huguenots despite William Penn's advertising. Instead, most of the 2,000 to 2,500 Huguenots who arrived in America between 1680 and 1700 headed for South Carolina and New York, with smaller numbers going to New England. In South Carolina, most settlers farmed, though many of the Huguenots who settled there were identified in the London aid records as craftsmen and tradesmen. In New York, Huguenots split between settlers who farmed (mainly on Staten Island and in the town of New Rochelle) and settlers who pursued trades (mainly in New York City). And in New England, most congregated in Boston, especially after early agricultural settlements at Oxford in Massachusetts and in the "Narragansett country" of Rhode Island collapsed (as in New York City, most of Boston's Huguenots were merchants and tradesmen). In America, agriculture attracted Huguenots who had been skilled craftsmen in France and who had already been prevented from exercising their traditional crafts during their European exile.[32]

Huguenots quickly disappeared as a cohesive religious and "ethnic" group in America. Their small congregations never established the denominational institutions—associations, presbyteries, or synods—that English, Scottish, and German religious groups developed. Huguenots increasingly joined non-Huguenot congregations or followed none at all. By the 1740s, New York City's Huguenot congregation recorded fewer than 10 baptisms per year. In Charleston, former Huguenots accounted for more than 60 marriages, 40 baptisms, and 90 burials at the Anglican St. Philip's Church. The two fragile yet still independent Huguenot congregations in New York City and Charleston depended on charitable contributions from former Huguenots to sustain their services; most third-generation Huguenots had long since become Anglicans, Presbyterians, Baptists, and even Quakers. Not surprisingly, the New York City and Charleston Huguenot congregations closed during the Revolution.

Intermarriage paralleled, reinforced, and speeded the Huguenots' religious fissure. Huguenots sought out non-Huguenot spouses, and other colonists seemed eager to reciprocate. As early as 1700, fewer than twenty years after most Huguenots first arrived in the colonies, almost half of Boston and New York Huguenots—women and men alike—took English, Dutch, and Scots-Irish spouses. This Huguenot pattern became the archetype for patterns that would come to be regarded as indelibly American, even if few other groups yet followed them. Crève-coeur, himself French and a convert to Protestantism, described the pattern in his *Letters from an American Farmer*:

What then is the American, this new man? He is either an European or the descendant of an European, hence that strange mixture of blood, which you will find in no other country. I could point out to you a family whose grandfather was an Englishman, whose wife was Dutch, whose son married a French woman, and whose present four sons have now four wives of different nations.[33]

S COTS constituted a second major non-English European immigrant population in colonial America, coming from Scotland itself and from northern Ireland ("Ulster"), where they had been part of an English effort to "protestantize" Ireland. Scottish immigration was long-lived and massive. Scots began arriving in the colonies in small numbers in the early seventeenth century, and their numbers rose slowly after 1670, then exploded after 1730. Only about 4,000 Scots-Irish emigrated from Ulster to America between 1700 and 1730. But more than 60,000 arrived between 1730 and 1770. Similarly, immigrants from Scotland itself likely numbered only 1,500 between 1700 and 1730, but then rose to perhaps 35,000 between 1730 and 1775. Here, then, were almost entirely new colonial peoples whose numbers, unlike the Huguenots', grew ever larger until, between 1730 and 1775, they became a veritable flood.[34]

Complex, interrelated causes brought the Scots to America. As with refugee Huguenots, the most obvious causes were material, meaning land. The Scots and Scots-Irish were overwhelmingly agricultural peoples hobbled at home by extremely scarce farmland, intense poverty, and resilient fecundity. In northern Scotland the climate was cold, the soil poor and riddled with rocks, and the available acreage small and usually rented or leased, not owned. The lowlands, to the south of Scotland, were more diverse and prosperous but poverty prevailed nonetheless. As Daniel Defoe wrote, "The common People all over the Country not only are poor, but look poor."[35]

Scots in northern Ireland fared little better. Parliament restricted exports from Ireland to prevent competition with English manufactured goods, principally woolens. The Anglican church in Ireland won restrictions on Presbyterian political activity, ironically oppressing men and women sent to curb Irish Catholicism. And major famines in 1727 and 1740 reinforced the urge for Scottish immigration, which proved particularly strong at four special points: 1717–1718, 1727–1728, 1740–1741, and 1771–1773.[36]

Fully half of the Scottish and Scots-Irish immigrants were agricultural workers and general laborers, quite unlike the Huguenots. For example, in a group of 89 Scottish men emigrating to the Carolinas in the early 1770s, 25 were simple laborers and 24 were farmers or husbandmen. Only a few were skilled: tailors (7), merchants (6), spinners (6), clerks (5), joiners (4), weavers (3), shoemakers (2), coopers (2), plus a clothier, shipmaster, seamstress, maltster, and jeweler.[37]

At the same time, women provided about 40 percent of the Scottish immigrants to America, a figure that compares favorably with the division among Huguenots, Germans, and even captured Africans but, as we shall see, differs sharply from that for English emigrants. Moreover, the women were relatively well distributed across the age spectrum, a different pattern than that for immigrant Huguenots. In short, Scots of all kinds sought escape from the barren material and social conditions of early modern Scotland and northern Ireland.[38]

Although a few Scots were deported to America, such as prisoners of war in the 1650s and some "covenanters" who lost the Scottish rebellion against England of 1745, most emigrated voluntarily. In the late 1760s and early 1770s (we do not know about earlier years), roughly 80 percent of the Scots who emigrated to America paid their own passage. Fewer than 20 percent came as indentured servants. Yet those who used indentures came from a broad spectrum of Scottish society and included artisans, tutors, clerks, and farmers. Indentures allowed those Scots to emigrate with capital rather than spend their assets on ship passage. Thus, while most Scots paid their own passage to America— they heeded rumors about greedy shipmasters "who may sell them like cattle in a market"—the indentures used by the remaining Scots revealed how widely the American appeal surged through eighteenth-century Scotland.[39]

Perhaps the freedom and frequency of Scottish and Scots-Irish emigration to America accounts for these newcomers' broad dispersal across so many mainland colonies, more so than any other immigrant group except the English. By 1770 Scots and Scots-Irish immigrants could be found in New Hampshire, Massachusetts, New York, New Jersey, Pennsylvania, Maryland, Virginia, North and South Carolina, and Georgia. Their relative freedom allowed them to settle in a variety of circumstances. East New Jersey became, in effect, a Scots' colony at its founding in 1683, when a diverse range of Scottish merchants invested in it and furnished its early settlers. Several shiploads of Highland Scots arrived in New York in the 1730s, drawn by promises of land that went unfulfilled. Some immigrants returned to Scotland; others remained. And after 1680 Scottish merchants moved to America with such frequency that if the term "merchant" carried ethnic connotations, it usually meant Scottish merchant (even if the single wealthiest merchants in the eighteenth-century colonies were Boston's Faneuils, who were Huguenots).[40]

Scots shaped a distinctive ethnic and religious identity in America, despite their dispersal and unlike the Huguenots. It could even be said that for the Scots, a considerable degree of their modern ethnic identity was created in America. Their history predicted the role and nature of ethnic commitment in nineteenth- and twentieth-century America. Scots emigrating to America between 1680 and 1740 came from a wide variety of religious backgrounds that ranged from the Church of Scotland (Anglican) to Presbyterianism and Quakerism. But by the 1740s most Scots were uniquely—and narrowly—Presbyterian. The contrast with the Huguenots could not have been stronger. Scots possessed a superiority of numbers Huguenots never enjoyed, since 100,000 Scots arrived by the time of the Revolution compared with only 2,000–2,500 Huguenots. Scots could more easily turn to other Scots for marriage and appear to have done so down to the Revolution, while those who married "out" married English settlers.[41]

Scots created an institutional culture that fostered a "Scottish" ethnic identity and predicted the growing importance of ethnicity in America. By fashioning the Presbytery of Philadelphia in 1707, then turning it into the Synod of Philadelphia in 1717, with constituent presbyteries spread out across an ever-expanding countryside in the 1720s and 1730s, Scottish and Scots-Irish Presbyterians created institutions that ultimately nourished distinctive "Scottish" spiritual sensibilities. In religion these centered on Calvinistic revivalist culture, imported from home and then redeveloped in America. In culture they centered on "classic" Scottish frugality, clarity of purpose, quiet drive, and feisty temperament. Here was a "Scottish" personality shaped as much in the process of getting to America and making a success as in northern Ireland or Scotland.[42]

THE settlement of Jews in the British mainland colonies, like that of the Huguenots, further bolstered colonial diversity even if the Jews' numbers remained small. From the 1650s through the 1770s most Jews in the colonies were Sephardic or Spanish and Portuguese Jews, spin-offs from Jewish refugee communities in the Caribbean and South America that were themselves the product of the Spanish and Portuguese Inquisitions. Only slowly did Ashkenazic Jews representing the Yiddish-speaking tradition of central Europe arrive in colonial America, most of them also coming from the Caribbean, not directly from Europe. The first Jews on the eastern seaboard arrived in New Amsterdam in 1654, refugees from the Portuguese conquest of the Dutch in Brazil. Most had left by the mid-1660s, and little wonder. Governor Peter Stuyvesant described them as a "deceitful race . . . hateful enemies and blasphemers of the name of Christ," and he expelled them as too poor to remain without burdening the struggling colony. The directors of the Dutch West India Company reversed Stuyvesant's expulsion and the tiny Jewish population actually won permission to establish a separate cemetery in 1656, but no Jews lived in New Amsterdam at the English conquest in 1664.[43]

Permanent Jewish settlements increased in the mainland colonies only after 1680. These earliest communities remained small, mobile, and still largely derived from the Caribbean. But reasonably stable communities began to emerge in the 1690s. By 1695, for example, almost 100 Jews lived in New York. Newport, Rhode Island, which tolerated a handful of Jews from 1658 forward, witnessed a sudden influx in 1693 with the arrival of more than 90 Jews fleeing an epidemic in Curaçao, though a third or less actually remained in Newport. Jews first appeared in Charleston in 1697 but they probably numbered fewer than 10 through the 1740s, and Jews did not settle in Philadelphia until after 1706 despite Pennsylvania's reputation for religious toleration, at least for Christians. By the 1720s perhaps 100 Jewish families lived in the mainland British colonies, almost exclusively in Newport, New York City, Philadelphia, and Charleston, and by 1770 the colonies contained perhaps 250 Jewish families.[44]

Jews followed traditional occupations more closely than other European immigrants. Most immigrant Jews were merchants and shopkeepers, ranging from poor butchers to prominent merchants such as Newport's Aaron Lopez or New York's Moses Levy and Jacob Franks, although a few were artisans, such as the New York City silversmith Myer Myers. Even Jews who settled in rural areas made their living as merchants. Unlike Huguenots, few Jews took up farming, perhaps because the occupational change would have necessitated a complete withdrawal from the already fragile Jewish communities of the colonial cities.[45]

Communities of shared feelings, resources, and loyalties emerged among colonial Jews despite their tiny numbers. Although in 1685 New York's aldermen rejected a request that would have allowed Jews to worship publicly in the town, worship proceeded anyway without any known incident; like other colonial towns, New York tolerated Jews in practice but did not honor toleration in principle. New York Jews rented a building for use as a synagogue by at least 1692, possibly earlier, and they rented a larger structure from the late 1690s to the 1720s that housed the congregation finally known as Shearith Israel, the oldest Jewish congregation in the British colonies. In 1728 Shearith Israel constructed its own synagogue, a very small building serving the city's twenty-five or fewer Jewish families. By 1760 New York's Jews also supported a school, synagogue office, school, schoolmaster, shammash (a synagogue employee who announced prayer and managed the synagogue building), and hazan or cantor who conducted services for a congregation of no more than fifty Jewish families. A parallel situation existed in Newport, where even fewer Jews lived, and in 1763 Newport's Jewish congregation constructed the jewel-like synagogue that still stands today as the oldest synagogue in the United States.[46]

The Jewish laity managed community life free from—or without the benefit of—the clerical leadership characteristic of other European immigrants. The tiny population lacked the financial resources to support rabbis, who led congregational and community life in the European Jewish ghettos or even on Curaçao. No mainland colony congregation employed a rabbi until the 1830s, and rabbis did not visit until the 1760s. A vivid community life emerged nonetheless. Newport and New York Jews worked hard to observe kashruth, the dietary laws, and certified products as kosher, or produced according to the religious law. Elders managed synagogue life by restricting nonobservant Jews from services and allowing others to attend. In both New York City and Newport, authority devolved into the hands of the more powerful merchant families, just as it did among Protestants in colonial cities. Tensions between Sephardic and Ashkenazic Jews persisted, but did not cripple community life. Both groups supported the construction of the New York and Newport synagogues in 1728 and 1763, and New York's Ashkenazic Jews accepted Sephardic ritual for years even though they most likely outnumbered Sephardic Jews at least by the Revolution.[47]

Tensions over marriage and intermarriage could fracture Jewish cohesion and stemmed from two sources: conflicts between Sephardic and Ashkenazic Jews, and the tiny size of the colonial Jewish population that encouraged Jews to find spouses among Christians, despite Christian anti-Semitism and strong Jewish prohibitions against intermarriage. Tensions between Sephardic and Ashkenazic Jews in European Jewish refugee communities followed into the New World as well. New York's Portuguese or Sephardic Jews were scandalized by Isaac Seixas's proposal to marry an Ashkenazic Jew, Rachel Levy, in 1740. But Seixas and Levy married anyway and exemplified an increasingly common pattern of Sephardic and Ashkenazic intermarriage. Marriage to a Christian was a parental calamity. In 1743 Phila Franks married Oliver DeLancey, wealthy son of the former Huguenot and now Anglican merchant Stephen DeLancey. Phila Franks's marriage devastated her mother, Abigail Franks. After Phila eloped, her mother wrote, "My Spirits Was for Some time Soe Depresst that it was a pain to me to Speak or See Any one . . . I Shall Never have that Serenity[,] nor Peace within[,] I have Soe happyly had hitherto[.] My house has bin my prisson." Yet most colonial Jews—between 80 and 90 percent—married Jews, despite the Sephardic-Ashkenazic tension and the small number of eligible potential spouses. Newly arriving European Jews of the 1830s thus found well-established Jewish communities in America that traced their origins back to the 1680s, not unlike the Scots, Germans, and other non-English settlers in America.[48]

G ERMANS constituted the largest continental European immigrant group in colonial America and the one most different from the English. When colonists thought about "immigrants" by 1760, they thought most commonly about Germans, since Huguenots had long disappeared, Scots were, seemingly, at least partially "English," Jews were few in number, and Africans were neither "immigrants" in any customary meaning of the term nor free. In America, Germans were both widespread in the middle and southern colonies and the most obviously "ethnic" of all non-English settlers.

Two causes—a classic "push" and "pull"—prompted Germans to set out for America after 1710. One centered on conditions at home. Scarce land combined with war, religious turmoil, and political dislocations induced Germans to look for new homes in many places, including America. In 1732 Peter Iskenius, whose sister and two sons had already emigrated to New York, described the effect of constant war and high taxes to support garrisoned troops: "People everywhere would be oppressed and brought to poverty, so that at the moment they ask urgently about America." This was the other cause—the pull—that impelled so many Germans toward America. John George Käsebier could hardly believe how good things were after he arrived in Philadelphia in 1724: "A reaper earns a florin a day in the summer plus 'wedding meals' along with it, and the work is not nearly so hard as in Germany. . . . The freedom of the inhabitants is indescribable. They let their sows, cows, and horses run without a keeper." Pennsylvania was, to many Germans, simply the "best poor man's country." No wonder Germans at home begged for news of America. Peter Iskenius wrote to his sister in 1737, "My beloved sister, I think almost every day of you, if only I might hear word from America. . . . The cry goes out yet again into the wilderness to hear whether there might once be an echo or an answering sound."[49]

German immigration to America, once it began to accelerate in the 1710s, continued steadily to the Revolution. German immigrants after 1710 thoroughly outstripped the small numbers who had arrived earlier. Some 3,700 Germans emigrated in the 1710s, 13,000 in the 1730s, and 30,000 in the 1750s. By 1770 the flow of immigrants begun in the 1710s had deposited at least 85,000 Germans into the British mainland colonies, fully half of them arriving in the 1740s and 1750s alone.[50]

German immigration centered heavily on Pennsylvania. Germans settled elsewhere—rural New York, the backcountry of Maryland, Virginia, the Carolinas, and the newest British colony, Georgia. But between two-thirds and perhaps three-fourths of the eighteenth-century German immigrants came to Pennsylvania. This reflected three important developments: advertising, shipping, and general immigrant happiness with Pennsylvania. William Penn's early advertising for immigrants stimulated an informal network of personal contact and letter writing that drew prospective German immigrants ever more strongly toward Pennsylvania. By word of mouth, Pennsylvania became the place for Germans to go. The contrast with New York was striking. New York did not advertise, Germans experienced substantial troubles in New York, including difficulties with the entrepreneurs who brought them there, and Germans therefore steered clear of the colony after 1730.[51]

German immigrants proved to be quite different from other Old World immigrants. First, Germans often came in family groups, rather like the seventeenth-century English Puritans who settled New England. Relatively few Germans—probably no more than 20 percent—sailed alone, even at the height of German immigration in the 1740s and 1750s. This pattern sharply separated German immigration from seventeenth-century English migration to the Chesapeake or much eighteenth-century Scottish immigration, where autonomous individuals prevailed. Second, the German families were seldom impoverished, and many possessed property in the Old World, usually very small farms. For these Germans, New World migration was another step—certainly a long one—toward greater material accumulation.[52]

Third, most German immigrants used contracted servitude to get to America despite their modest property-holding. The earliest German immigrants used the familiar indenture system to finance their American passages. But when Philadelphia shippers invented the "redemption" contract in the 1720s, Germans turned to it almost exclusively for the next half century. Through it, they borrowed passage fees and money for provisions from shippers whom they agreed to repay several weeks after arriving in America. Once in the New World, immigrants then negotiated labor contracts with American merchants or farmers who "redeemed" their loans in exchange for the immigrants' contracted labor, usually for three to four years. Shippers liked the redemption system because it gave them a chance to redeem their loans more profitably in an expanding colonial economy. And immigrants—now called "redemptioners"—liked the redemption system because they could negotiate their own contracts directly with prospective American masters and thereby achieve greater control over their New World destiny. Thus most German immigrants arrived in family units and spread out across the Pennsylvania countryside to serve the terms of their redemption contracts, then, if they were lucky, purchased or leased farms substantially larger than they could have expected to acquire at home.[53]

German immigration also included an exceptional variety of religious groups. These included sectarian groups, such as German Baptist perfectionists settling at Ephrata (the twentieth-century novelist, Thomas Mann, wrote about the Ephrata leader, Conrad Beisel, in his novel *Doctor Faustus*); Mennonites, followers of Menno Simons, the sixteenth-century Protestant reformer; and Moravians, who settled both in the Carolina backcountry and near what is now Bethlehem, Pennsylvania, and were led by the famous Count Nikolaus Zinzendorf. At the same time, although Lutheranism and German Calvinism (the German Reformed Church) accounted for the formal religious background of most German settlers, immigrants often paid these churches relatively little attention. Church attendance and baptism remained relatively low among both, and Lutheran and Reformed church leaders worked hard to shape even modestly sized congregations despite a burgeoning immigrant population.[54]

Rural isolation, density of population, and, to an extent, English resistance and even prejudice strongly molded German community life and group identity, a sharp contrast to the Scottish experience. Although our knowledge of German marriage patterns is relatively thin, it seems to have been markedly endogamous despite some surprising signs of marriage to non-Germans. Even in Germantown, just outside early Philadelphia, some 18 percent of eighteenth-century German marriages were contracted with English spouses, usually German women marrying English men. Still, despite the choice available to German women and men—choices seldom available in the more exclusively German areas of rural Pennsylvania—80 percent of Germans in and around Philadelphia took German spouses until after 1800.[55]

Germans were also the first major European Christians to feel a sharp pinch of ethnic prejudice. Neither Huguenots nor Scots experienced substantial discrimination, though minor incidents certainly occurred.

As German immigration mounted, however, aided by its heavy concentration in Pennsylvania, English prejudice against Germans grew. The xenophobic, almost nativist, even vaguely racial rhetoric formed a type that became all too familiar in the next century; Benjamin Franklin gave it special venom:

> Why should the Palatine boors be suffered to swarm into our settlements, and, by herding together, establish their language and manners, to the exclusion of ours? Why should Pennsylvania, founded by the English, become a colony of aliens, who will shortly be so numerous as to Germanize us, instead of our Anglicizing them, and will never adopt our language or customs any more than they can acquire our complexion?

Franklin was not alone. William Smith, head of the College of Philadelphia, called Germans "ignorant" and "stubborn Clowns" in a 1755 pamphlet, and proposed a scheme of Charity Schools to Anglicize German children that Franklin backed.[56]

In fact, the Charity Schools won little support among Pennsylvania's English settlers, and the movement failed. English settlers might not embrace Germans, but neither were they prepared to force assimilation, drive the Germans out, or even worry much about their presence. Most Germans lived far from English settlers in a very large colony. And most Germans realized that even the ugliest colonial rhetoric—vigorously protested by German printers like Christopher Sauer—paled before the legal discrimination and open oppression that German sectarians faced at home, nor did it compare to the horrors of constant war that Germans faced in Europe. Finally, nowhere at home could German farmers till the rich soils found throughout Pennsylvania, and certainly not in the acreage so cheaply available in America. In this context, Pennsylvania and America were not only the "best poor man's countries," but the best countries for European immigrants of all means.[57]

SURPRISINGLY, much of English migration remains a mystery between 1680 and 1770, except at the very beginning and close of the era, despite the fact that about 200,000 English men and women left home for America in this period. Although historians have uncovered incredible, intimate detail about the earliest English immigration to the

Chesapeake and New England between 1610 and 1650, they have all but ignored English immigration from 1660 to about 1760. One interesting exception between 1680 and 1710, Quaker immigration to early Pennsylvania from Wales and northern England, offers a fascinating comparison with both continental European immigration and with English immigration on the eve of the American Revolution.[58]

Quaker immigration demonstrated how forcefully religious persecution could move men and women far beyond their traditional residences and how collective religious motivations also encouraged family emigration rather than the emigration of single men and women. William Penn's acquisition of Pennsylvania in 1681 opened the possibility of a new life for Quakers persecuted in both England and Wales, and they eagerly took up the opportunity. Between four thousand and six thousand English and Welsh Quakers emigrated to Pennsylvania between 1681 and 1710. Even contemporary observers noted that the most persecuted Quakers often moved to Pennsylvania—those who had been fined for holding unauthorized religious meetings, for preaching at "conventicles," or for refusing to attend Anglican worship. These Quakers not only left northern England and Wales but typically settled with their families, including wives and children. Pennsylvania solved two problems for them. There would be no fines and harassment over religion, since Penn promised freedom for Protestants, and land would be cheap, less than three shillings per acre. The response was so deep and swift that in some sections of northern England the Pennsylvania migration stripped Quaker meetings of both members and their best local leaders, who backed the Pennsylvania migration vigorously after years of persecution. Little wonder that in 1698 the Quaker Yearly Meeting in Wales protested the "unsavory proceedings and runnings into Pennsylvania" that caused "weakening, if not total destroying of some meetings [here] in . . . Wales."[59]

One other English group united by behavior and perhaps even beliefs also emigrated to eighteenth-century America in far greater numbers than Quakers, though at a direction other than their own: convicts, usually men and sometimes women convicted of grand larceny, but some petty thieves and occasional murderers who had escaped the gallows. The English transported as many as 50,000 convicts to America between 1718 and 1776, almost a quarter of total English emigration to

America in these years. The motivation was simple and selfish. Believing Britain was suffering a major crime wave, British politicians campaigned to rid Britain of dangerous felons, and the 1718 Transportation Act empowered magistrates to order felons transported to America. About 36,000 English, 13,000 Irish, and 700 Scots were transported to America in the next six decades, 80 percent of them young men between sixteen and twenty-five, most from poorer backgrounds with few artisan or craft skills. At mid-century, Maryland received as many as 700 deported convicts a year, and they quickly constituted as much as 10 percent of the adult population.[60]

The convicts' experience in America was not always uplifting, though it was usually law-abiding. If their deportation was official, commercial prospects determined their destination. Ship captains took them to markets that would bring the highest prices for their seven-year labor contracts, and more than 90 percent of the convicts ended up in the Chesapeake, where they supplemented an already strong demand for slave labor. They proved tame in America. In Kent County, Maryland, for example, deported convicts accounted for only 41 of 601 criminal prosecutions between 1732 and 1746, a proportion most likely below their proportion of the population. This low crime rate may have been dictated from another fact of immigrant convict life: many escaped back to England to ply their craft in more familiar territory, sometimes for gangs who secretly engineered their passage home. Those who stayed in America remained relatively pacific but seldom prospered. In Virginia they were not awarded "freedom dues" at the completion of their labor (indentured servants received £3 10s). Most worked as laborers for the remainder of their lives, and few ever owned farms or possessed substantial estates at their deaths. The convicts' relative impoverishment demonstrated how powerfully the aid of friends, kinfolk, and religious compatriots affected material success in America. Men and women who sought success in America without resources beyond their own skill and labor did not often succeed.[61]

Quakers and convicts aside, the general English emigration to America between 1680 and 1770 remains largely unclear, although English emigration between 1760 and 1776 provides clues to earlier patterns. Certainly, more than Quakers and convicts emigrated to America after 1680. English immigration to America between 1680 and 1700 was fairly substantial, stimulated by the founding of Pennsylvania and the Carolinas and early English settlement into New Jersey and New York. English immigration then fell back, ranging from fewer than 500 in the 1700s to fewer than 3,000 in the 1720s. But it rose rapidly after 1730, from 5,000 in the 1730s to 12,000 in the 1760s. As a result, almost 45,000 English men and women emigrated to the mainland colonies between 1700 and 1770 alone, and two-thirds of them arrived after 1730. On the very eve of the Revolution, between 1770 and 1775, the 7,000 English immigrants who arrived placed third among European immigrants behind only the Scots (15,000) and the Scots-Irish (13,200), and substantially ahead of the Germans (5,200) and Irish Catholics (3,900).[62]

If the 1760–1775 British immigrants typified British immigration as a whole, then English emigration generally looked considerably different from the migration of others, including Scots, for example. It looked more like the forced transportation of convicts. Single young men predominated, almost all of whom got to America through indenture, the pattern typical of the seventeenth-century Chesapeake rather than of early New England. Slightly more than half of the English immigrants after 1760 were between fifteen and twenty-four years of age, although this age group constituted only a fifth of the English population. In contrast, the 41 percent of the immigrants who were between twenty-five and fifty-nine all but matched exactly their proportion in the English population at home (39 percent). At the same time, few children or old people emigrated to America from England between 1760 and 1775. Moreover, men dominated this late-eighteenth-century English immigration in sharp contrast to the Huguenot, Scottish, and German immigration. Only 16 percent of the post-1760 English immigrants were women. It was, then, an immigration that approximated Thomas Hobbes's state of nature: unrelated men bringing no wives, no parents, no children, and precious few friends.[63]

It also was an emigration of the well skilled. These English emigrants frequently were trained artisans, quite different from the Scots and Germans and rather like the Huguenots. Fully half of the English emigrants were artisans and craftsmen, who produced sophisticated goods such as watches, jewelry, and furniture, while others were skilled construction, food, and service trade workers. Here then were well-trained men looking for even better opportunities in America than they possessed at home, where a sluggish economy hindered their prospects.[64]

Their American experiences are more difficult to trace. Like the Scots, English immigrants dispersed widely across the English colonies, from Georgia to New Hampshire. Yet unlike the continental European immigrants or the Scots, they seldom formed distinctive new social or religious institutions in America. Some certainly helped fill Church of England congregations that expanded greatly between 1730 and 1770. But whom and when they married, where they worked, and how quickly or sluggishly they joined in colonial politics remain unknown in a society where the welter of English surnames make them difficult for historians to trace. However much they expanded the colonial population, their very commonness in an English-dominated society has hidden them from view, especially when they fail to possess the religious commitments borne by Puritans and Quakers or the social stigma carried by deported convicts.[65]

T HE history of Africans in America differs dramatically from the history of Europeans in America. Where the African experience in America centered on themes of capture, enslavement, and coercion, the history of Europeans in America centered on themes of choice, profit, and considerable freedom. The African and European experiences never duplicated and seldom paralleled each other. Yet Africans and their experience in America powerfully intersected the decline of the Indian population and the outpouring of non-English immigrants to America to recast the seventeenth-century colonies and become the American future.

In 1680 slavery was uncommon, strange, and even exotic in the British mainland colonies. British colonists certainly knew what it was. They knew it meant ownership of other human beings. They knew it gave owners untrammeled power to buy, sell, and compel labor from the enslaved and to own their offspring. As the eighteenth century progressed, they tightened slaveholding and treated bonded men and women with ever greater severity. They consistently corralled Africans' behavior and wrung from them every conceivable advantage of labor and creativity, often through unimaginable mental and physical cruelty.

The principal impetus for this action was simple: profit. Slaveholding attracted European colonists intent on realizing the dreams that brought them to America even when it subjected others to horrific suffering.

As late as 1680 the English mainland colonies knew few Africans and little slavery. In the Chesapeake colonies of Maryland and Virginia, Africans accounted for only 5 percent of the population in 1680, and English indentured servants comprised more than 90 percent of the hired labor force. Between 1650 and 1680 the minor slavery that existed in the Chesapeake remained loose and relatively informal. Its legal articulation was sparse, and its social leakage substantial. The Maryland and Virginia legislatures passed few laws enunciating a comprehensive slave "code" before 1690, and from the 1650s into the 1680s, surprising numbers of Africans lived as free residents, completing labor terms more akin to those of indentured servants, after which they were freed by their owners. Some free Africans farmed land they owned, and a few, like Anthony Johnson of Accomack County, Virginia, owned African slaves themselves. Yet by 1700 the free Africans had disappeared—fled or been reenslaved, no one knows—probably because the English settlers' sudden turn to extensive slaveholding after 1680 made them a threat, a preview of the ways that increased slaveholding would transform seventeenth-century colonial society almost beyond recognition.[66]

Why the rush to slaveholding after 1680? Complex causes created the change. First, the supply of British and continental European indentured servants declined as the colonial demand for labor continued and accelerated, especially after 1680. English officials complained less about overcrowding at home, and rumors of mistreatment of indentured servants in America abounded. As a result, the immigration of servants from England to America declined in the last quarter of the seventeenth century and failed to satisfy the rising labor demands of colonial farmers, especially in the Chesapeake and the Carolinas. The immigration statistics for the first decade of the eighteenth century reflect the result: between 1700 and 1709, only 1,500 indentured English, Scottish, and continental European indentured servants arrived in America, while imported Africans numbered 9,000. By the first decade of the eighteenth century, then, captured Africans outstripped indentured servants by a ratio of at least 6–1 and established a pattern of colonial labor consumption not broken until the American Revolution.[67]

Second, captive Africans consistently became easier to obtain. The Royal African Company, which had been granted a monopoly for the British slave trade in 1672, eagerly exploited the growing market in the still small British mainland colonies. By the 1690s the company's success produced demands to open the market to competitors, and when the Crown ended the monopoly in 1698 new entrepreneurs plunged into the trade. London, Liverpool, and especially Bristol slave traders soon accounted for the great bulk of eighteenth-century mainland colony slave imports, but colonists also entered the trade. Between 1680 and the 1740s colonial merchants and ship owners began to specialize in slave trading—John Guerard, Richard Hill, Benjamin Savage, and Joseph Wragg in Charleston and Godfrey Malbone, Abraham Redwood, the Wanton family, and Samuel Vernon in Newport, Rhode Island, among others. In addition, the increasing reach of international commerce into all the colonies meant that enslaved Africans were also more easily available from Spanish, French, and especially Dutch traders. By 1710, then, the increasing numbers of colonists who wanted Africans enjoyed considerable choice in both Africans and merchants.[68]

But why slaves? Why not some form of indentured servitude, especially since the English treated at least some Africans as indentured servants before 1650 and since both the English Civil War (1645–1649) and the Glorious Revolution (1688–1689) raised the English commitment to personal freedom? The reasons lodged in slaveholding's attraction. Slavery furnished laborers that European immigration could not stock. Slavery ameliorated the uncertainties that indentured servitude engendered. Slavery imposed a formal legal silence upon laborers denied the rights that indentured servants claimed for shelter, clothing, and even education. And slavery offered lifetime service while indentured servants completed their labor in three or four years. Even if masters breached indenture contracts without fearing lawsuits and even if few servants actually pursued complaints, the comparative point was obvious: slaves offered more attractive, longer-term investments even as they also conveyed new kinds of status to their owners.[69]

But why not Indians rather than Africans? Indian slavery existed in the American colonies from the mid-seventeenth century past the American Revolution. But Indian slavery never prospered. Too many Indians remained free, too many resisted slavery, and too many escaped too easily into a countryside they knew intimately, in striking contrast to captured Africans, who found the countryside even more unfamiliar than did the Europeans in America. Indian slavery existed in colonial America, but it remained an oddity.[70]

The focus on Africans had two causes. Again, one involved convenience. In the sixteenth and seventeenth centuries Europeans discovered in Africa a ready and rapidly expanding supply of slaves. Europeans could purchase captives in African wars that they could then sell as laborers in the New World colonies. A fateful Benin agreement with a Portuguese trader in 1472 to allow the trade of precious metals and "slaves" began a trade that devastated Old World Africa. A rapidly accelerating New World demand for slaves escalated wars among African nations. Previously incidental captives became prime booty to be sold to multiplying numbers of European traders hurrying back to Africa to acquire fresh captives for eager New World markets.[71]

Second, Western perceptions of African culture induced Europeans to ask few, if any, questions about the legal and moral basis of their own behavior. Europeans had long labeled Africans as foreign, heathen, and differently colored, regardless of African national and cultural differences and without help from pseudo-scientific nineteenth-century concepts of "race." African "government" seemed chaotic and incapable. Africans were "savage" and libidinous. And they were not white, or not what passed for "white" in a Europe actually overflowing with considerable varieties of skin color among its peoples. In short, Africans might be human, but Europeans also perceived them as different, disagreeable, and dispensable, ideal candidates for an enslavement that very quickly became indelibly American.[72]

In turning to slavery so widely after 1680, English and other European colonists in America joined a slave trade that became the largest forced human migration in history. Anomalies typified this transformation. Even at its height slave imports to Britain's mainland colonies remained a minor part of the much larger New World slave trade. Ninety-five percent of the captured Africans brought to the New World between 1700 and 1760 went to places other than the British mainland colonies: 400,000 arrived in the Dutch Caribbean, 400,000 in Spanish America, 1,000,000 in the British Caribbean, 1,000,000 in the French Caribbean, and 1,300,000 in Portuguese Brazil. By contrast, only about 250,000 captured Africans came to the British mainland colonies.[73]

The dramatic rise in slave imports after 1680 nonetheless held immense implications for the development of Britain's eighteenth-century mainland colonies. Before 1680 English immigrants constituted the single largest group arriving in the mainland colonies and made up nearly 90 percent of all foreign arrivals in the colonies. But after 1700 and down to the American Revolution, Africans constituted the largest group of arrivals in the colonies and outstripped all European immigrants combined. Africans failed to outnumber European immigrants only between 1750 and 1759 and between 1770 and 1775, although even in those years they still outnumbered any single group of European immigrants. The number of imported Africans climbed from 9,000 between 1700 and 1709 to 40,000 in the 1730s, then doubling to 80,000 in the 1760s, with a dip to 50,000 in the 1750s. Between 1770 and 1775, African imports dropped to less than 20,000, largely because prerevolutionary political tension reduced the demand for slaves among anxious farmers and planters.[74]

Slaveholding became especially prominent in the southern colonies but also prospered in the north. Through the 1670s indentured servants outnumbered slaves in Maryland estate inventories almost four to one. But by the 1690s slaves outnumbered indentured servants four to one. Africans constituted 13 percent of the Maryland population by 1704 and 30 percent of it by 1764. Africans constituted 6 percent of Virginia's population in 1680, 20 percent by 1720, and almost 40 percent by 1760. In South Carolina, this rate grew both higher and faster. The West Indies planters who settled the colony in the 1680s overwhelmingly rejected indentured servitude and turned to slaveholding for imported agricultural labor, just as they had done in the West Indies. Enslaved Africans outnumbered Europeans there by 1710 and constituted two-thirds of the colony's population by 1720.[75]

Population changes in the middle and northern colonies were impressive but not so dramatic. By 1770 Pennsylvania contained more than 4,000 slaves, although the proportion of slaves seldom exceeded 3 percent between 1690 and 1770. As early as 1698 New York contained about 2,000 slaves, or about 12 percent of the population, a legacy, in part, of long-standing Dutch slave trading. But Africans climbed to about 15 percent of the colony's population at mid-century, and in 1771 the colony still contained 20,000 Africans amid 150,000 Europeans.[76]

Even New England knew slavery. Rhode Island always contained the largest percentage of slaves in the region, a by-product of the extensive slave trading pursued by its merchants and shippers. Perhaps reflecting this fact, Rhode Island's enslaved population also fluctuated considerably, 6 percent in 1708, almost 12 percent in 1755, then back to 6 percent in 1771. In Connecticut, enslaved Africans never topped 3.2 percent of the population (in 1762), although this low ratio still placed more than 4,500 slaves in the colony. In Massachusetts, the most "English" of all the colonies, enslaved Africans made up only 2.1 percent of the population in 1764. Yet by the Revolution, more than 5,000 Africans lived in this northern colony where captured Africans had been present since the 1630s and where their antiquity in the land was scarcely younger than the settlement of their Puritan owners.[77]

Death, agony, and bittersweet resilience characterized the African experience in the mainland colonies. Death not only came unusually early, at least by comparison to the experience of European colonists, but in circumstances Europeans never knew. The experience of slavery for Africans began with the deaths of compatriots and kin in local wars. Then more of it came in the infamous "middle passage" from Africa to America, where 10 percent of slaves packed aboard a vessel died regularly and where entrapment on a ship fraught with disease or commanded by an incompetent captain sometimes brought the death rate higher. Then death stalked Africans in America. Typically, they survived less than five years. Sometimes they did not make it through even one year in America: eight of the thirty-two slaves John Mercer bought in Virginia between 1733 and 1742 died in their first year of service, for example. The causes were not difficult to locate: lack of resistance to European and American diseases, unfamiliar foods, poor housing, and depression and anomie, which produced sufficient suicides to prompt owners to complain about the problem. Unlike inanimate property, Africans could and did destroy themselves, a prospect owners feared and resented.[78]

The agony centered on slaveholding itself, and after 1680 European colonists in the mainland settlements constructed a slaveholding of intense control and manipulativeness, a distinctly modern institution that laid the foundation for the even more powerful slaveholding of the postrevolutionary antebellum era. Everywhere in the eighteenth-century mainland colonies, European slaveholders produced an increasingly authoritarian institution ever more concerned with owners' power, slave discipline, and what they regarded as African "misbehavior." Seventeenth-century legislation was often brief in the extreme. But after 1680 assemblies from the Carolinas to New England continuously expanded "slave law" to tighten owners' control and better control slave behavior. Sometimes this happened fitfully, as after "incidents" like the 1712 New York City slave revolt, the 1739 Stono Rebellion in South Carolina, and the rumor of a slave revolt in New York City in 1741. Legislators felt that the rapidly growing enslaved population needed taming, as did those who employed slaves. Thus when New York revised its slave code in 1731 it prohibited Africans from owning or possessing guns and also fined owners for letting slaves wander alone at night.[79]

The eighteenth-century colonial slave laws were not uniform. South Carolina's slave laws were more brutal than those of Virginia and Maryland, though all were harsh enough. South Carolina more readily subjected Africans to death and specified cutting ankle cords, slitting noses, and "gelding" or castration than did Virginia, although everyone sanctioned the whip for almost all offenses. Yet from South Carolina to New York and Rhode Island, legislation everywhere tightened slaveholding. In the process American colonists made modern American slavery primarily between 1680 and 1770. They did not inherit it. Seventeenth-century mainland colony slavery established crucial principles about the ability of one person to own another. Eighteenth-century mainland colony slavery created the modern system of human and legal interrelationships that left a devastating and indelible imprint on America, its society and its conscience.[80]

The increasingly restrictive law measured slavery's coercion only partially. For most captured Africans, the experience of slavery far outstripped any legal description of its parameters. To be captured in wars among African nations, shipped to America on boats where many passengers died from exposure and malnourishment, sold to quizzical Europeans who eagerly purchased a body, labor, and possible offspring—but who had no interest in the person—then to be carted, often in chains, to a farm to perform an unknown labor for a complete stranger who was now one's "owner" but with whom one could not share a single word, much less a sentiment, all led to grudging, difficult labor and sometimes to sickness and worse. Owners might farm with slaves, as did the Huguenot immigrant Elias Horry, whose grandson remembered that Horry "worked many days with a Negro man at the Whip saw" in the early 1700s. But they shared only work, which more often bred contempt than affection.[81]

Slave resistance brought punishment, sometimes gruesome, even when the law prohibited capricious retribution by owners. Whipping occurred routinely and often was accomplished publicly in ritual-like settings as an example to others. But owners went far beyond whipping without fear of punishment, rationalizing their behavior with reference to "necessity" and even self-pity. When an African lost a bundle of rice in 1713, the local Anglican minister described how a South Carolina planter forced a slave "into a hellish Machine . . . [in] the shape of a Coffin where he could not Stirr," there to await death by starvation or heat stroke; the slave's child resolved the affair by slipping a knife inside the coffin so his father could commit suicide. Seventy years later, Crèvecoeur described a depressingly similar episode, the well-known scene in *Letters from an American Farmer* in which an enslaved African awaited death from wild animals, having been locked in a cage hanging from a tree. Birds had "already picked out his eyes; . . . his arms had been attacked in several places; . . . the blood slowly dropped and tinged the ground beneath." The slave begged for a means for suicide: "Tanky you, white man; tanky you; puta some poison and give me." Unlike the slave's son seventy years earlier, Crèvecoeur walked on. A rationalization for the execution came quickly: "Soon [I] reached the house at which I intended to dine. There I heard that the reason for this slave's being thus punished was on account of his having killed the overseer of the plantation. They told me that the laws of self-preservation rendered such executions necessary." Little wonder that retribution for slave misdeeds soon produced its own gruesome material culture—whips, mouthpieces, "iron negro fetters," and "Negro spurs" that appeared in estate inventories catalogued alongside farm implements and household goods as tools of the day.[82]

The enslavement fashioned by European colonists in Britain's mainland colonies devastated traditional culture among captured Africans. Slaves came from increasing numbers of African societies in the eighteenth century, including Ibo, Ashanti, and Yoruba societies on the African west coast, and later from Muslim societies deeper inside the African continent as the century progressed. This growing diversity, combined with European fears and opposition, impeded "ethnic" cultures among mainland colony slaves. African diversity meant that slaves shared relatively little traditional culture, and European fears of assertive individual and group consciousness led slaveholders to prohibit the expression of cultural cohesiveness among Africans they owned. Much of traditional Ibo, Ashanti, and Yoruba secular culture languished in the aftermath even when smaller specific features might survive. Ibo, Ashanti, and Yoruba religious systems likewise failed to reproduce themselves in America. The result was a spiritual and cultural holocaust that shattered the breadth of traditional African culture and religion throughout the mainland colonies. Certain discrete rites persevered, especially those that concerned magic, healing, and burial. But Ashanti, Ibo, or Yoruba religious and cultural systems, among others, never survived in any holistic fashion, and no New World Ashanti, Ibo, or Yoruba ethnicity blossomed in Britain's mainland colonies.[83]

The contrast between the African and European experiences could not have been more startling. The Scots, Scots-Irish, and Germans, among others, replicated Old World cultures in New World society with considerable success. Religiously motivated European immigrants like the Moravians and Mennonites achieved Old World ideals they frequently could not realize at home. Other Europeans, particularly Huguenots but also Scots and Scots-Irish, chose to assimilate within a dominant English culture (and were welcomed in doing so), abandoning their own distinctive cultures and beliefs. But captured and enslaved Africans moved within extraordinarily constricted boundaries. Captivity and slavery prevented them from realizing the goals that Europeans eagerly pursued, especially the freedom and power that arose from improving one's material circumstances.

Yet, with bittersweet persistence, enslaved Africans nonetheless turned an African holocaust into New World culture. Despite incredible difficulties, they reshaped Old World traditions and New World experiences into a new culture and society in the British mainland colonies that proved to be among the most noteworthy of all the New World's creations. Family life underwrote this achievement. This foundation in the family was particularly surprising because the law did not protect slave marriages (nothing prohibited owners from separating couples), and drastically unbalanced sex ratios in the mainland colonies' African population made conjugal relationships difficult. Between 1680 and the 1740s African men outnumbered women by substantial margins, 180 to 250 men for every 100 women in the Chesapeake, and 400 to 100 in South Carolina. Yet a social life rooted in a renewed family structure emerged nonetheless. Most important, captured Africans slowly formed conjugal units and raised children. The law never recognized this reality, but owners embraced it, enjoying social benefits that carried no legal responsibilities or moral obligations. Slave "marriage" fit traditional European social and religious expectations, could be disregarded at will, decreased tensions among the slaves, organized and disciplined the work force, and, conveniently, provided offspring who, as the owners' property, immediately could be bought and sold.[84]

Reconstructed African-American family life merged African past and colonial present. Kinship crisscrossed and reinforced a surrounding culture of visiting and friendship, all of which molded buoyant communities and family life among captured Africans from the Carolinas to New England. Captured Africans traveled to see friends and uncles, lodged with cousins, and fell in love with acquaintances. When owners broke the Africans' extralegal marriages by selling spouses and children, Africans traveled far to see detached spouses and children. They sustained kinship beyond the conjugal family and reconstructed family life when capricious circumstances suddenly brought relatives together years later.[85]

Captured Africans slowly forged a public culture in the colonies. This culture first centered, perhaps not surprisingly, on emerging rituals of family and kinship. The rare contemporary watercolor, *The Old Plantation,* of a late-eighteenth-century African-American celebration in the Chesapeake—perhaps the wedding of the couple to the left—conveys community most obviously in the numerous social groupings—two couples, a cluster of women, and several groups of men—held together with a caring expressed in the joy of the observers, the liveliness of the dancer, and the pleasure in the music. New England, despite its small captive African population, demonstrated the resilience of this thrust; it too produced a public African-American culture after 1730. A develop-

The Old Plantation. Watercolor, c. 1800. Artist unknown, probably South Carolina.

ing folk life took public expression in games (paw paw, a cowrie shell gambling game, for example), music (especially fiddle playing, as in the Chesapeake), dancing, public story-telling, and, in New England, African-American election day celebrations, in which captive Africans elected "kings" and "governors" for one day, a satire that spoofed both European and captive African pretensions yet also symbolized a substantial African-American community.[86]

The advancing realization of community among Africans deepened fear of rebellion among Europeans in America. The two principal rebellions of the colonial era, the 1712 New York City revolt and South Carolina's 1739 Stono Rebellion, never freed captured Africans as their planners hoped. The New York City rebellion lasted only one evening and the Stono Rebellion several days and both cost many African lives. But the two rebellions, plus rumors of revolts in Annapolis, Maryland, in 1740 and in New York City again in 1741, terrorized Europeans. They gave ominous meaning to signs of African-American community and resolve: sustained, persistent labor resistance that ranged from tool breakage, slack work, and running away to assault against Europeans and even homicide.

Running away and work resistance, not revolution, became the most common form of African resistance to slavery and also helped to create community and strengthen individual resolve. Few captured Africans were lucky enough to manage permanent escapes. The wilderness was as strange to them as to Europeans, and slave owners possessed overwhelming powers of chase, detection, and capture. Despite these difficulties, Africans continually resisted owners by running away, even if only for short periods of time, and by resisting work. Runaways produced a peculiar newspaper culture in which runaway advertisements in the *Virginia Gazette* and the *South Carolina Gazette* became a small literary genre. Owners tried to raise alarm among slaveholders almost inured to such departures while attempting to describe the uniqueness of the missing African in ways that would engineer his or her return.[87]

Work resistance could be more subtle. In South Carolina, slaves resisted the arduous labor of pounding rice by hand. Owners recognized the hardship and the cost: one observer described rice pounding as "the severest work the negroes undergo and costs every planter the lives of several slaves annually." Africans sometimes complained about particular jobs, occasionally winning an owner's understanding but most often suffering punishment and a return to work. Some resistance verged on rebellion. Africans sabotaged tools, ruined processed crops, and burned barns. They murdered owners with a wide range of techniques from assault to poisoning. After the 1739 Stono Rebellion, planters in South Carolina and elsewhere feared that such episodes were bringing them closer to an even larger confrontation.[88]

Resistance, flight, and murder reinforced community among Africans. Initiating resistance required cooperation from friends, who made identification of individual culprits difficult, and from relatives, who hid runaway Africans who bolted. Resistance took root in the growing reality of kinship among Africans originally from highly diverse cultures, in a growing sense of place, and in a knowledge that Africans were the backbone of a burgeoning economy and culture whose achievement they guaranteed but whose reward they were denied. Even in the face of retributive Europeans, captured Africans had created community under conditions experienced by no other immigrants to America.

Memories of Africa stood at the center of that community, even if the expression of community remained frustrated and often unfulfilled in America and even if, as we will see, America helped reshape some African traditions. Although difficult to capture, one expression of those memories came from a most unlikely source. Sometime in 1752 or 1753, a white Virginia blacksmith, Charles Hansford, filled a small manuscript notebook with three poems, two on love and religion and a third, "My Country's Worth," on Virginia. Knowledgeable about the 1739 Stono Rebellion and the rumors of revolts in Annapolis and New York City, Hansford compared Virginia to Rome and ancient Egypt, who "bought and bred up slaves as we do now / And yet neglected (or they knew not how) / Those slaves to manage. Sometimes they rebell'd / Which cost much sweat and blood ere they were quell'd."[89]

Yet Hansford's comments on rebellion paled beside his startling observations about the captured Africans' memories of home.

> That most men have a great respect and love
> To their own place of birth I need not prove—
> Experience shows 'tis true; and the black brood
> Of sunburnt Affrick makes the assertion good.
> I oft with pleasure have observ'd how they
> Their sultry country's worth strive to display
> In broken language, how they praise their case
> And happiness when in their native place.
> Such tales and descriptions, when I'd leisure,
> I often have attended to with pleasure,
> And many times with questions would assail
> The sable lad to lengthen out his tale.
> If, then, those wretched people so admire
> Their native place and have so great desire
> To reenjoy and visit it again—
> Which, if by any means they might attain,
> How would they dangers court and pains endure
> If to their country they could get secure!
> But, barr'd of that, some into madness fly,
> Destroy themselves, and wretchedly they die.[90]

ETWEEN 1680 and 1760, the people of America became the American peoples, the multi-hued, multi-voiced men and women who have distinguished American society ever since. Crèvecoeur's 1782 portrait of them in *Letters from an American Farmer* proved perceptive even in its evasions. Crèvecoeur was startling in evoking "blood" as the tie that bound together English, Dutch, French, Scot, Irish, Swede, and German: "that strange mixture of blood, which you will find in no other country." And he understood explicitly and implicitly how thoroughly these Europeans excluded American Indians and captured Africans from their imagined society. In his own way, Crèvecoeur outlined many of the fateful, subtle convergences that would bind the men and women who emerged as the American people after 1680. No other Old or New World society knew such remarkable mixtures of peoples. What they created in America after 1680 proved equally astonishing.[91]

Two

ECONOMY

Here he stands on a larger portion of the globe, not less than its fourth part, and may see the productions of the north, in iron and naval stores; the provisions of Ireland; the grain of Egypt; the indigo, the rice of China.

J. HECTOR ST. JOHN DE CRÈVECOEUR (1782)

BETWEEN 1680 and 1770 the economy of the British mainland colonies in America soared with growth unprecedented by both New and Old World standards. The economy swelled faster than the population expanded. It became more diverse and more complex. It drew from many European immigrants, enslaved Africans, and Indians, women and men alike. It stretched outward, pulling ever larger regions of the North American continent into its lucrative orbit. It brought American goods to expanding international markets and an extraordinary array of world goods to an increasingly affluent colonial American market.

The economy also changed in ways not everyone liked or even understood. Its complexity often frustrated colonists who appreciated the benefits of increasing international exports when prices were high but damned them when prices were low. Competition increased everywhere, from the farm to the city, and families could lose as well as gain across the decades. The gap between the rich and the poor accelerated, probably more rapidly than in any other period in American history, so that poverty became a permanent feature of the American economic landscape. Some poverty represented personal failure and bad luck for European immigrants and their descendants, but far more stemmed from the consignment of Africans to perpetual servitude and enforced destitution through slavery.

After 1680, then, one could become richer or poorer in America in new and quite spectacular ways. Some of these had not been widely experienced in seventeenth-century America. Others were substantially recast in the next eighty years. Many increasingly resonated to regional and local patterns distinctive to the colonies. Taken together, they demonstrated how thoroughly, if quietly, European colonists took command of their own economic life. Even amid a European colonial system they shaped a notably autonomous economy that determined much in colonial life, far beyond the economy itself and well past the American Revolution.

To speak of the economy in prerevolutionary America was to speak of farming, as it had been since the beginning of European colonization and would be through the 1870s. Between 75 and 85 percent of colonial men and women made their living as landholders and tenant farmers, or as servants, seasonal laborers, and slaves who worked on farms. As Crèvecoeur put it, "some few towns excepted, we are all tillers of the earth, from Nova Scotia to West Florida."[1] Despite the rising importance of the merchant and skilled trades and regional differences in farming, the ubiquity of farming meant that most Europeans and Africans in the British mainland colonies shared one common characteristic: they were peoples of the land. What happened to agriculture, therefore, not only determined the fate of the economy generally but determined material rewards for everyone who had ended up in Britain's New World settlements, whether by choice or by force.[2]

Agriculture changed greatly between 1680 and 1760 in complex ways that are not easy to explain. Much colonial farming remained largely "subsistence" in character, so that the entire household raised many crops directed explicitly to household consumption. But farming also became increasingly commercial after 1680, and farmers everywhere paid considerably more attention to "markets" than they had ever done before. Farmers who raised items for their own consumption also very deliberately produced crops to sell not only to neighbors or regional consumers but to "factors," who transported a wide variety of crops—grains, tobacco, rice, indigo, and large timbers—to other markets, mainly European. As a result, by the 1760s farmers were quite commercially oriented, even if their farms also resonated to the rhythms—and work—of subsistence farming for personal consumption.

Agriculture's commercial possibilities transfixed the Chesapeake colonies of Maryland and Virginia from their earliest years. The first settlers found gold, not in the meager metals of the two colonies, but in the "sot weed"—tobacco—that grew luxuriantly in rich American soils and awaited an excited market in Europe. The rush to tobacco was so widespread that the 1616 "Dale's Laws" required every settler to plant two acres of corn to safeguard the food supply as everyone hurried to grow tobacco for export. By the 1620s tobacco was the region's dominant crop, and by the early eighteenth century the influence of tobacco was so immense that one historian has described the region as dominated by a "tobacco culture" that transformed its people and molded its society.[3]

Tobacco farming quickly overwhelmed the early Chesapeake. But after the excitement of the 1610s waned, residents of Virginia and Maryland settled into a substantial subsistence agriculture as well. This subsistence agriculture actually underwrote tobacco's long-term importance because it furnished items for daily living, especially food, whose absence would have necessitated expensive imports and stripped away tobacco's profits.

The interrelationship between early subsistence and commercial agriculture can be seen in the estate of Robert Cole, who emigrated to Maryland in 1652 at about age twenty-five with his wife, four children, and several servants. Cole traveled to Maryland to practice his Catholicism under the protection of Maryland's owner, Cecilius Calvert, Lord Baltimore, and to improve his fortunes. He purchased a 300-acre plot on St. Clement's Manor in Maryland's St. Mary's County (land was as cheap in Maryland as it was in many other colonies) and began clearing the heavily treed plot. But by 1662 he was dead, most likely perishing during a return voyage to England.[4]

Cole had quickly become a tobacco planter, and for a decade after his death, his executor, Luke Gardiner, operated Cole's "plantation" on behalf of Cole's wife and children. Gardiner's unusually meticulous records reveal an intriguing, complex configuration: the Coles' farm was simultaneously subsistence and commercial. Tobacco brought in about 36 percent of its total revenues between Cole's death in 1662 and 1672, including the value of goods produced and consumed on the farm. But 65 percent of the farm's produce came from subsistence farming. The family consumed about two-thirds of this produce themselves, including hogs and cattle used for meat and milk, corn that the Coles ground themselves, and the orchard, whose apples were used to make cider. But they sold between a quarter and a third of their hog, corn, apple, and cider production to neighbors, sales that other Chesapeake farmers matched if they could. For the Coles and other Chesapeake farmers, both tobacco and subsistence agriculture were crucial to their New World prosperity.[5]

Seventeenth-century northern and middle colony settlements lagged behind the Chesapeake in developing a strongly commercial agriculture. New England farmers held substantially less land than did settlers in the Chesapeake, seldom more than twenty or thirty acres between 1630 and 1650, and they only cultivated perhaps ten to twenty acres after trees were cleared. They consumed most of the wheat and corn they planted and the hogs and cattle they butchered. But they sold enough of what remained to allow early New England merchants some overseas sales. In the 1640s and 1650s men like George Story, Samuel Maverick, and Edward Gibbons sold products ranging from grains to clapboard to the Caribbean island colonies and Spain. Subsistence agriculture dominated early farming in the New Netherlands, with most cash sales confined to local markets. Yet farmers worked hard to produce crops for cash sale, and their labor, together with the desire for cash profit, made the farmers incipient capitalists. After the English conquest turned the New Netherlands into New York, farmers there and in newly settled East New Jersey had access to New York City's merchants and ports and sold surpluses there. But the fur trade, not corn, wheat, or other agricultural output, provided New York City's primary exports in the seventeenth century.[6]

The changes that occurred in colonial agriculture after 1680 created an economic climate markedly different from the one seventeenth-century farmers had known. At two important points of great economic expansion, first after 1680 and then again after 1750, colonists who farmed or planted paid substantially more attention to the purely commercial aspects of their operations than their predecessors had done. Only a few ever became wholly commercial farmers or abandoned the subsistence agriculture that fed their households. But especially in the South, farmers of all kinds transformed their labor system and later diversified their crops to maximize profits generated by sales of goods beyond the farm. By 1760 most farmers in most colonies could be considered "commercial farmers" despite the strong presence of subsistence elements that touched colonial agriculture everywhere. And by 1760 as well, most farmers would have wondered at the simplicity of a few generations earlier.

The mixed character of the agricultural economy—production for both use and profit—only increased the production value of every family and household member, especially women. Labor was divided, men doing work that was regarded as the most physically laborious, women doing work associated with the household but also a wide variety of highly specialized tasks. Men generally ploughed and planted, moved rocks and deforested, and slaughtered and butchered large animals. In the household, women cooked and cleaned, preserved food, and made clothing. They also milked, a ubiquitous task from South Carolina to northern Massachusetts. This was a highly detailed activity, not a simple one. For example, it required far greater cleanliness in pails, tubs, pots, and churns for milk and butter-making than was expected or even desired in seventeenth- and eighteenth-century households generally, and it taught highly specialized skills in understanding and executing each detail of complicated processes from managing cows to the final production of milk, cream, and butter. Dairying's centrality for both subsistence and commercial agriculture—producing highly perishable but desirable foods whose surpluses brought good prices or bartering with neighbors—only increased the value of the women's labor that created it.[7]

Women's labor stretched far beyond household duties and dairying. Women usually managed the orchards common on most farms and frequently supervised cider production. Unlike many dairy products, cider's popularity and relatively long shelf life meant that extra production could be sold. Although men slaughtered and butchered large animals, women commonly salted and cured the meat, not only of large animals but of small game like chicken. German women customarily made sausage and liver pudding—*brothswurscht* and *lewerwurscht*—both for consumption and for sale, while colonial women everywhere managed gardens, from which they sold herbs, vegetables, berries, and nuts. They also sold small animals, including chicken and geese, which furnished eggs and meat.[8]

Most important, women's labor inside and outside the household bespoke the utter arduousness of all labor in an emerging modern, materially calculating society. Men and women worked long, difficult, exhausting hours, not always to ends they appreciated. Consider entries in the diary of a Long Island woman, Mary Cooper, then in her fifties, for July 1769:

> 6 Thirsday. Up late makeing wine. 7 Friday. Hot as yesterday. I am dirty and distressed, almost weared to death. Dear Lord, deliver mee . . . 11 Tuesday. Clear and very hot. O, I am very unwell, tiered almost to death cooking for so many peopel. 12 Wednsday. Fine clear weather. Much freting a bout dinner. 13 July the 13, 1769, Thirsday. This day is forty years sinc I left my father's house and come here, and here have I seene little els but harde labour and sorrow, crosses of every kind. I think in every rspect the state of my affairs is more then forty times worse then when I came here first, except that I am nearer the desierered haven. A fine clear'cool day. I am un well.[9]

THE southern colonies led the way in the mainland colonies' complex economic transformation between 1680 and 1760. The immense rise of imports of captured Africans became both effect and cause in this transformation. Especially between 1670 and 1700, the growing scarcity of English indentured servants and the ease of acquiring captive Africans reflected the profitability of the modestly commercial agriculture that had already evolved in the Chesapeake by the 1650s. At the same time, the accelerating growth of slaveholding after 1680 and its spread throughout the European population substantially raised economic stakes in the southern colonies. It made economic competition tougher, even if it also increased the rewards for those who succeeded. To compete, farmers had to acquire more labor, which meant more slaves. After 1710 slaves began to equal the value of all other elements of an estate in the southern colonies, including land, and became the most important determinant of an individual's wealth. In turn, the expenses incurred in acquiring and maintaining slaves increased pressure to pursue commercial farming, something farmers did willingly, eagerly, and for the most part profitably.[10]

Labor on Chesapeake farms shifted dramatically after 1680. In Maryland, the number of slaves rose as farmers' dependence on English indentured servants receded. Between 1660 and 1680 indentured servants in Maryland estates declined from an average of between 1.5 and 2.0 in each estate to barely 0.25 by 1717. In contrast, the average number of Africans rose from about 0.25 in the 1660s and 1670s to more than 2.0 by the 1710s. This growth occurred because Chesapeake farmers turned to enslaved Africans for laborers after 1690. In the 1690s fewer than 5 percent of Maryland households contained slaves, but by 1733, 45 percent of Calvert County households, for example, contained captured Africans. Another measure was even more graphic: servants outnumbered slaves by 4 to 1 in the mid-1670s, but slaves outnumbered servants 3 to 1 as early as 1710.[11]

Slaveholding proved even more ubiquitous in South Carolina. Captured Africans outnumbered Europeans after about 1705, with the great rush toward slaveholding among Europeans occurring in the 1710s. As it occurred, it proved overwhelming. A careful census made by Rev. Francis Varnod in 1726 of St. George's Parish, which itself had only been formed in 1717, revealed the spread of slaveholding there. Eighty-seven of the parish's 108 households contained Africans, and Africans outnumbered Europeans 1,300 to 537. The 7 households with 50 or more slaves accounted for 38 percent of all slaves in the parish, and the largest slaveholders were almost startlingly outnumbered by their slaves. John Williams's farm contained only three whites—himself, his wife, and one child—but 94 enslaved Africans—48 men, 24 women, and 22 children; Walter Izard's farm contained himself, his wife, his four children, and another white man, but 91 enslaved Africans—29 men, 23 women, and 39 children.[12]

Slaveholding was widely distributed in St. George's Parish, not just confined to a few farms. Fifty-four planters owned 1–9 slaves, 31 owned 10–19 slaves, and 6 owned 20–29 slaves. Even on farms with fewer than 10 Africans, there were 2 Africans for every 5 whites, and on farms with 10–19 Africans, Africans typically outnumbered whites by 8 to 5. By 1726, farms without slaves in St. George's Parish were rare (Reverend Varnod counted only 21 in 1726). Nor was St. George's unique in South Carolina. In the 1720s, 78 percent of low-country estates contained slaves; in 1743–1745, 81 percent; and in 1764, 88 percent. By the 1720s, then, slaveholding in South Carolina had become a way of life for Europeans, and even poorer planters at the very bottom of the South Carolina economy would own Africans in the next decades.[13]

As the slave population climbed and expanded into so many households throughout the southern colonies, planters also began rationalizing their slaves' labor in ways they had seldom done before 1700, at least not in the mainland colonies. Most notably, and especially but not exclusively in the lowcountry, a "task system" emerged. It competed with the gang labor system that also became increasingly regularized, especially where slaves were numerous. When captured Africans worked in gangs or groups, owners and overseers tended to emphasize speed and sacrifice results. The task system, which became common in the 1730s and 1740s, emphasized the responsibility of a single slave or small group of slaves for given tasks like planting, harvesting assigned acreage, or managing acreage through the growing season. The task system allowed for a peculiar combination of independence and supervision by Africans themselves in a society where it was also increasingly difficult to recruit and retain white managers.

Both systems reflected farmers' perceived need to regularize labor as they increased their investment in slave numbers, foodstuffs, and housing. Both systems also fostered community, although this was an African achievement, not a desired result of the labor system. The gang system quickly became infamous for its harshness, a symbol of slavery's evil long past the Civil War. By contrast, most captured Africans viewed the task system as preferable because it decreased immediate supervision and allowed greater individual initiative for the slave.[14]

The southern colonies led the diversification of colonial agriculture in unexpected ways. South Carolina developed the most unique economy. Subsistence agriculture had been bountifully described in early pamphlets distributed among potential British and continental European settlers. A 1683 letter from a Huguenot immigrant ardently described a land ready-made for self-sufficient farms—"fine rivers full of fish," "bountiful crops of peas, wheat, and garden-melons," cherries "as red as wine inside." The letter described success for skilled tradesmen as well, like Jacques Varein of Rouen, France, who was "making lots of money at his trade," which was linen weaving.[15] But it was rice and later indigo, not subsistence agriculture or the skilled trades, that dominated South Carolina's economy from the 1690s to the Revolution.

The South Carolina economy was complex, as were so many provincial economies. From the 1680s forward, farmers often planted peas, wheat, and cherries, raised hogs and cattle, and harvested fish just as the promotion literature suggested they could. But they also quickly exported foodstuffs, deerskins, timbers for ship construction, and naval stores, such as pitch and tar, to provide cash income. Pitch and tar exports reached 6,500 barrels by 1712 and 60,000 barrels by 1725, and the colony exported substantial amounts of corn (95,000 bushels in 1735) and increasing amounts of leather, meat, and barrel staves at least through the 1730s.[16]

But it was rice that became South Carolina's dominant crop and turned the Carolina lowcountry into a profit-drenched entrepôt with a unique configuration of agriculture, population, and exports. This did not happen until Britain substantially reduced its naval stores bounty in 1729, which had subsidized the boom in pitch and tar production for two decades. Rice production began to escalate as farmers looked elsewhere for profits. The commercial character of South Carolina's rice production was vividly evident in one simple fact: rice was not a traditional English crop, and English farmers knew almost nothing about it. South Carolina farmers planted it for export to Europe and to the West Indies, where it was consumed by slaves as a diet staple. In fact, Africans provided critical crop knowledge and technology to European farmers with no experience in rice production. Advertisements for newly arrived Africans sometimes pointedly described their experience in "rice culture" and broadcast the arrival of Africans from "the Windward & Rice Coast" who would be knowledgeable in rice cultivation.[17]

South Carolina farmers also pursued rice even as prices fell, a pattern reminiscent not only of Chesapeake tobacco production in the eighteenth century but of much nineteenth- and twentieth-century commercial agriculture in America. In doing so, South Carolinians pursued a "micro" answer to a "macro" problem: they bet they could increase production faster than prices fell and thus create a gap that would guarantee their profit, all the while trying to reduce costs. The strategy worked fitfully for almost a half century. Although currency fluctuations make it difficult to determine actual rice prices in the early eighteenth century, the price of rice per pound appears to have fallen rather steadily after 1710. In response, and in demonstration of both their will and their commitment to commercial farming, South Carolina farmers and planters ratcheted rice production voluminously upward in just a few years. Rice exports grew from 10,000 pounds in 1698 to 6.5 million pounds in 1720, then to 43 million pounds by 1740. Even though the price declined precipitously in the face of this wildly increasing supply, the South Carolina planters' strategy worked for many but not all planters. Despite the drop in the price of rice per pound, the value of the colony's rice crop climbed from £20,000 sterling in 1720 to around £100,000 sterling in 1740. Most important, the gain financed the purchase and clearing of ever more land, the acquisition, feeding, and housing of ever more Africans, and often lavish consumer consumption.[18]

Planters began to lose their race with declining prices in the 1740s, however, and did so rather dramatically. Although rice production declined from 40 million pounds in the late 1730s to 30 million pounds in the late 1740s, prices fell even faster, and a crop worth over £100,000 sterling in 1740 plummeted to less than £30,000 sterling five years later. The effects were devastating. One historian summarizes: "Since rice was 'king' in the lowcountry, its troubles affected everything. The land boom of the 1730s came to a halt, planters stopped importing Africans, . . . European goods became scarce and expensive, the local credit market tightened, and overextended planters were forced into bankruptcy."[19]

As the rice bubble burst, South Carolina planters and farmers diversified, strengthening a powerful if injured economy and using British trade policy to support further agricultural commercialization. They turned to indigo, a shrub or herb of the pea family used in dyeing cloth. Indigo imports from the French Caribbean to England had been curtailed by King George's War (1744–1748) and by the Seven Years' War (1756–1763). To stimulate production, the British government offered a bounty to support a turn to indigo growth, not unlike federal government "price supports" for farmers in the twentieth century. South Carolinians responded, and the value of their indigo crops grew dramatically from about £10,000 sterling around 1750 to about £150,000 sterling before the American Revolution. By the time of the Revolution, the indigo crop was worth fully a third as much as the colony's rice crop and provided a hedge against overdependence on rice, along with the continuing export of naval stores, meat, and corn from the colony. The results were staggering exports from South Carolina and, later, Georgia by the eve of the American Revolution—over £500,000 yearly in all, £325,000 in rice, £110,000 in indigo, £28,000 in deerskins, £10,000 each in grains, wood products, and miscellaneous items, and £7,000 each in livestock and naval stores. Many low-country farmers still produced much of what they and their slaves consumed, especially in food. But they had long since turned to commercial agriculture and cash profits through their vigorous pursuit of export-only commercial crops.[20]

A different diversification occurred earlier in the Chesapeake in two stages. The first stretched from about 1700 to 1720, as tobacco prices slowly bottomed out and farmers diversified to supplement or expand their income, especially in locales where tobacco was difficult to grow and poorer in quality. Increasingly they emphasized livestock, grains, wood products, and naval stores. A second and more powerful wave of diversification came after about 1740. Planters responded to the extreme fluctuations that typified tobacco prices between 1740 and 1770, when prices rose or fell as much as 50 percent in two- or three-year groups. To cushion these blows, planters abruptly but decisively added wheat grown in open fields to the tobacco grown in hills, a change that again demonstrated their agricultural versatility.[21]

This post-1740 "wheat boom" was also fueled by an increasing import demand from southern Europe as well as from the middle and northern colonies, important signs that farmers responded positively to both international markets and the growing strength of "internal" markets across the mainland colonies themselves. By the eve of the Revolution, Maryland, Virginia, and North Carolina farmers exported more than £1,100,000 sterling in crops each year. They disgorged the largest regional exports anywhere in the mainland colonies—£760,000 in tobacco, £200,000 in grains (mainly the wheat grown after 1740), £35,000 each in naval stores and wood products, and even £30,000 in iron, which was exported almost exclusively to Great Britain and was emblematic of the infant manufacturing that could be supported in the upper South's increasingly sophisticated economy.[22]

Middle colony and northern colony farming also experienced substantial change in the eighteenth century, some but not all predicted by seventeenth-century patterns. On the one hand, middle and northern colony farmers continued to produce crops and goods for cash sale and did so increasingly after 1680. On the other hand, this commercial farming consumed relatively little of their planted acreage and farming operations and never equaled the commercial production found in the southern colonies. Middle and northern colony farms concentrated on wheat and corn as grain crops, on fruit trees (largely apples) for cider, and on animal husbandry, mainly the production of cows for milk and of steers and hogs for butchering. Like farms in the southern colonies, middle and northern colony households consumed a good deal of this production, and much of their agriculture should be termed "subsistence." But middle and northern colony farmers sold excesses, and there is every reason to believe that they saw themselves as engaged in commercial agriculture, however modest it might have been by the standards of the southern colonies.[23]

The use of indentured servants and short-term laborers underlined the commercial aims of much middle and northern colony farming. Immigrants from Scotland and Germany could use the indenture and redemption systems to pay their passage overseas because they could find work in the middle colonies. Overwhelmingly, this meant working for farmers who came to Philadelphia to negotiate labor contracts that would "redeem" the costs of the immigrants' passage to America or fulfill the indenture contracts they had signed before departing.[24]

Pennsylvania, New Jersey, and New York farmers also hired temporary laborers. The farm accounts of Samuel Swayne, a small farmer in Chester County, Pennsylvania, reveal a reasonably typical pattern of an extremely modest farmer. Swayne earned a third of his income from his business as a maker of "saddletrees"—frames for leather saddles. Another 20 percent came from the sale of grains, mostly wheat but also rye, oats, hay, corn, and barley. Thirteen percent derived from the butter and cheese made by his wife, Hannah, and another 20 percent from a wide variety of goods, including peaches and apples and the cider they made. In the 1760s, before his children became accomplished workers, Swayne hired landless neighbors—Chester County residents called them "cottagers"—to "draw dirt" and "dig dung," to plow, hoe, reap, and thresh, and to make cider. Elsewhere in Chester County and to the west and north, farmers signed contracts with indentured servants or redemptioners to perform similar labor. Like Swayne, they were taking a calculated risk to expand production and increase their potential income, not merely to solidify their "subsistence" farming.[25]

This relatively small-scale middle colony commercial farming probably achieved modestly increased efficiency between the 1690s and the 1770s, and it produced substantially rising agricultural exports after 1730 when combined with the large-scale population explosion that added thousands of new European settlers and thousands of newly cultivated acres each year. Between 1768 and 1772 average yearly exports from the middle colonies—valued at roughly £525,000—only came to about half of those for Virginia, Maryland, and North Carolina but equaled those of South Carolina and coastal Georgia. Grains sent mainly to southern Europe in open violation of the 1753 Navigation Acts and to the West Indies to feed slaves constituted 75 percent of those exports. The rest was a mix ranging from flaxseed, livestock, potash, and wood products to the iron production that glimpsed at early "industrial" production in the middle colonies just as it did in the southern colonies.[26]

New England's labor system reflected its farming peculiarities. Indentured servants seem to have been less common there in the eighteenth century than earlier, and slaveholding never became more than a curiosity. Slaves were occasionally found on farms in western Massachusetts and in Connecticut, especially along the Long Island Sound, and some worked primarily as household servants, as with the theologian Jonathan Edwards; Rhode Island knew more extensive slaveholding, in part because of the involvement of Newport merchants in the slave trade. Yet both slaves and indentured servants were costly in a region where the growing season was short; they needed to be fed, clothed, and housed even when their labor and productivity might be minimal or nonexistent. As a result, most eighteenth-century New England farmers more commonly turned to and depended upon a familiar source for labor, their own children. This was true elsewhere, of course, but never so emphatically as in New England. Farmers sometimes "hired out" work to male and female laborers and consistently paid women laborers less. But in the main, their large families allowed them to be parsimonious. They worked their children, especially their young boys and men, who commonly labored steadily for their fathers from their prepubescent years forward.[27]

New England labor patterns, landholding, and geography dictated a different kind of farming than the agriculture found in the middle and southern colonies. Landholdings averaged about 75 acres in the late seventeenth century and declined to around 50 acres by the mid-eighteenth century. The New England soil well deserved its infamous reputation as unforgiving and rocky. This was not true everywhere, especially in the Connecticut River valley, but it was sufficiently true to encourage farmers to "pasture" as much or more land for roaming cattle as they planted.

As a consequence, New England farmers relied on both animal husbandry and grains. They emphasized cattle and hogs, planted corn and rye, and could harvest hay effectively only in July and August. Horses were common in Rhode Island but not elsewhere, and many farmers rented horses only when they were needed. They produced relatively meager harvests on smaller, less fertile farms, which they tried to improve by spreading stored dung on the soil every spring. They tried to farm more acres and cut ever more trees to make new fields even as they also planted trees and sometimes conserved wood lots for continual use as firewood. They only occasionally rotated crops to prevent soil exhaustion on old, worn-out farms, and sometimes they simply abandoned poor farms for newer ones. Under these circumstances, it is not surprising that between 1768 and 1772 New England exports of potash (£22,000), wood products (£65,000), and livestock, beef, and pork (£90,000) greatly outstripped their grain exports (£20,000). Still, anomalies flourished. By the 1750s flaxseed became Connecticut's second largest export, facilitated by a rapidly assembled chain of farmers, local merchants, and exporters from Newport, New York, and Philadelphia. Much of the seed was sent to Ireland.[28]

Fish constituted New England's largest export and British America's closest tie to a traditional sixteenth- and seventeenth-century Old World economic activity. The famous Newfoundland Banks, which were international waters, were exploited first by the Basques and the French, then the British, and the story of fishing (and later, whaling) in the eighteenth century largely centered on expansion rather than on substantial changes in the nature or style of the trade. As early as the

1620s, observers counted hundreds of ships, most coming directly from England, mining the rich harvest of the Grand Banks fisheries off Newfoundland. The New England fishing industry developed in the 1640s and 1650s, when the English command of cod fishing off the Grand Banks receded for reasons that are not clear. Although this early New England fishing industry supplied local demand, from the 1630s forward both English officials and colonists deemed exports to England important and desirable.[29]

By the 1690s whaling played an even larger role in the refinement and expansion of maritime industry in New England. Here seaborne success helped develop "extractive" industries as the harvested whales were "mined" for a range of products far beyond the simple drying and consumption of fish in the cod trade. Whale oil was used for lamps; white, waxy spermaceti taken from the whale's head was used for candles; the elastic yet stiff whalebones were used for stiffeners and stays; ambergris, a waxy, grayish material found in whale intestines, was used to retard evaporation in perfumes. Most of these demanded processing, which in turn employed others, women as well as men, sometimes members of the household and sometimes hired laborers, all of them expanding the trade and the economy.[30]

Little wonder, then, that the fishing and whaling industries employed fully 10 percent of New Englanders throughout the eighteenth century. The rate of growth in these industries slowed after 1700, a consequence of the fact that expansion had been so high between 1650 and 1690. But the industries expanded substantially nonetheless, and the maritime trades produced fully half of New England's eighteenth-century exports; they accounted for negligible exports in other regions. Between 1768 and 1772, a third of New England's total exports came from fish alone, which were worth £150,000 per year, and whale exports added another £60,000 per year.[31]

Mainland colony agriculture thus was never uniform. Between 1680 and 1770 regional differences expanded, new patterns blossomed, and anomalies accelerated. Total cultivated acreage boomed due to steady European immigration, accelerating slaveholding, and natural population expansion, yet average acres per free person probably shrank modestly in all the colonies. Everywhere farmers took advantage of British imperial trade policies, especially in the southern colonies with their massively commercial agriculture. Yet everywhere, including the southern colonies, "subsistence" production for farm consumption and sale to neighbors proved crucial to most farmers' success. Women and men alike labored to produce these crops, sometimes as members of households, sometimes as indentured servants, sometimes as temporary seasonal workers, and sometimes as enslaved laborers, all of them bringing long-developed skills and astute judgments to their work.

Farming in these years did not modernize with the drama that transformed nineteenth- and twentieth-century American agriculture. Beyond the introduction of new crops like rice and indigo, major technological advances proved uncommon between 1680 and 1770, and persistent, systematic exploitation of new machinery, planting, fertilizing, and cultivating techniques interested only a few. Jared Eliot of New England experimented with new plows developed in Britain, and his *Essays upon Field-Husbandry* (1761) briefly raised consciousness about agricultural improvements and reforms. But Eliot's work won little attention beyond an elite circle that included Benjamin Franklin. Unlike British and European farmers, who had to entice crops from land frequently cultivated for centuries already, eighteenth-century American colonists seemed convinced that their newly tilled lands did not require such methods of intensive farming, even when this view was slowly becoming unhelpful.[32]

Amid these complexities, most farmers prospered in America. The substantial recognition of this success brought over two hundred thousand European immigrants into the colonies between 1680 and 1770 and fueled the importation of another quarter-million Africans into the southern colonies. The one group provided enthusiastic and the other grim testaments to the remarkable opportunities that colonists created through their deliberate management of eighteenth-century America's agricultural possibilities.

INDIAN economies throughout the post-1680 British mainland settlements and frontiers accommodated to one simple fact: a shift from episodic European presence along the eastern seaboard before 1650 to an overwhelming European presence and insistent westward push after 1680. The now inexorable European presence dramatically restructured the Indians' internal economies, not necessarily making them wholly dependent on Europeans but certainly making Indians and Europeans fatally interdependent.

After 1680, Indian economies moved ever closer to European market systems while retaining some important traditional characteristics, yet with incredible variation from group to group. Mahicans of the Connecticut River valley near Stockbridge, where Congregationalists proselytized among them, farmed in largely European or Anglicized fashion while those at Shekomeko, under Moravian missionary instruction, used more traditional farming techniques. Mahicans traded in both places, moving from go-betweens among the English and New England Indian groups before 1700 to trading with the English and Algonquians to the west in the eighteenth century, and other Mahicans worked as day laborers for Dutch settlers living east of the Hudson River. Indians in Natick, one of the so-called Indian praying towns created under John Eliot's supervision in the seventeenth century, were ultimately "dispossessed by degrees," as their historian describes it. In 1719 Natick's Indians established Indian "proprietors" to control their land. English residents bought up property the proprietors sold, and by the 1760s, the town contained fewer than forty Indians.[33]

For the Iroquois to the west and north, the fur trade remained important despite severe price swings in the eighteenth century. Prices fell sharply in the late seventeenth century, fell again in the 1730s, rose somewhat in the 1740s, then fell again into the 1760s, ricocheting across the Iroquois confederation and leaving substantial internal difficulties in their wake. Yet as with the Mahicans, Iroquois men also worked as day laborers for English and Dutch merchants at the far western trading posts in Oswego and Niagara. After about 1700 Choctaws in the lower Mississippi River valley left their traditional towns and moved to land previously used for hunting, where they successfully pursued the cattle trade with colonists and then Americans well into the nineteenth century. In South Carolina, Catawbas provided substantial deerskins in a trade valued at £35,000 sterling in the 1740s, or almost 15 percent of the colony's exports, and £55,000 sterling in the 1770s, when it had fallen to about 10 percent of South Carolina exports. Yet agriculture remained central to Catawba life throughout the eighteenth century, so much so that when Indians at Christanna in Virginia failed to plant corn in the spring of 1729, Virginia governor

William Gooch rightly guessed that their change in habits signaled their imminent departure.[34]

Trade created a series of dependency relationships with the Europeans in America—never complete but increasingly powerful—that shaped far more than economics. The range of European goods consumed in Indian societies varied greatly and, to a significant extent, hinged on proximity. From the early seventeenth century to the Revolution, Indians living near Europeans consumed substantial amounts of European goods, from utensils and cloth to firearms and ammunition. Yet the spread of these goods was neither even nor universal. The far interior regions near the Great Lakes depended on native utensils throughout much of the seventeenth century and saw only a slow rise in European goods as late as the 1680s and 1690s. But in the next century the steady press of English settlement from the west and the success of French traders from the east and north brought Indians even there within the European trade orbit. It was for a reason—increased commerce—that French traders shifted from the small canoes of the first *voyageurs* to large *canots de maître* because the latter could carry so much more cargo both east and west, all to be traded far from European settlement. New York's Iroquois became dependent on land sales to the New York government to keep their economy going, even though each sale further circumscribed the Iroquois. Mohawk leaders wrote in 1730, for example, that "our hearts grieves us when we Consider what small parcel of Lands is remaining to us." They urged "that for the future all Christians may be strictly forbid to intice any of our Indians to purchase any of our Lands."[35]

The almost dizzying multiplicity of these economic changes among Indians usually bore one consistent result: everywhere Indians along the eastern seaboard became enmeshed in complex and powerful economic interrelationships with Europeans. Many groups, such as the Catawbas and Choctaws, persevered through considerable ingenuity and independence, shaping economies subject to continental and international market forces beyond their control, yet not often more so than their European neighbors. Others, including the societies that composed the Iroquois Confederacy of western New York and Pennsylvania, found the relationship often difficult and frequently bloody.

The economic tangle intertwined with international politics, particularly in the Seven Years' War from 1756 to 1763 between Britain and France, where most if not all Indians supported the French. But a formal peace did not end persistent frontier tensions between Indians and European settlers for territorial control. In western Pennsylvania the contest for settlement stimulated local attacks on Indians in the spring and summer of 1763 despite the end of international hostilities. In October of that year Indians attacked and killed nine settlers recently arrived in Pennsylvania from Connecticut, all of them "most cruelly butchered; the Woman was roasted . . . and several of the men had Awls thrust in their Eyes." In mid-December colonists from Paxton raided an Indian village at Conestoga, killing its inhabitants, and on December 27 they murdered more than a dozen Indian men, women, and children detained in the workhouse at Lancaster; a Moravian observer described how the Indian "men, women and children [were] spread about . . . shot—scalped—hacked—and cut to pieces."[36]

The reciprocal attacks bespoke the visceral struggle between Indians and Europeans for the most valuable economic resource the New World ironically possessed in abundance—land—and what Indians and Europeans knew to be control of their economic destinies. For many Indians, the grinding competitiveness of an encroaching modern economic life produced not merely change in agriculture and modes of livelihood but a relentless bloodshed that cruelly predicted Indian-American economic and political relations long past 1776.

EUROPEAN merchants and traders were present in America from the beginning of colonization. At Jamestown they marketed the earliest tobacco grown in the 1610s and 1620s, and in Massachusetts they arranged the colony's earliest agricultural exports in the 1630s and 1640s. Their very importance stimulated suspicions in both places, and early Massachusetts leaders demanded that the merchants corral personal profits for the community good; in one of early Boston's most famous incidents, the Boston church disciplined the merchant Robert Keayne for "extortion" because he sold goods above a "just price." It is too strong to say that in eighteenth-century America, personal profit substituted for community good. But it is not too strong to note how steadily eighteenth-century colonial merchants won wealth and status throughout the colonies in ways that went far beyond what anyone might have predicted for mere "colonial" tradesmen.[37]

Between 1680 and 1770 three things changed the merchant trades in the British mainland colonies: expansion, extension, and specialization. Expansion and extension constituted the most obvious changes. Merchants grew enormously in number in all the colonies after 1680, possibly even faster than the rapidly swelling population, and their presence may have stimulated trade beyond increases that would have been encouraged by population growth alone. By the 1760s merchants were found not merely in the colonial cities but everywhere throughout the mainland colonies. When Governor James Glen estimated inhabitants in South Carolina at mid-century, he counted "traders" as "1 1/2 of 12 Parts," or about 13 percent. This translated to a commercial domination of Charleston by 1750, obviously encouraged by the colony's burgeoning commercial agriculture. Fifty-nine of one hundred "houses and lotts fronting the river on the Bay of Charlestown" belonged to merchants, Glen wrote. This was not surprising, given the importance of trade to the colony. Glen also counted more than two hundred vessels loading an extensive range of exports in Charleston each year from 1735 to 1745. They carried "Corn and Grain, Roots and Fruits [including 296,000 oranges], Cattle, Beef, and Pork, Naval Stores, and Vegetable Produce of other Sorts," ranging from indigo to sassafras and boards.[38]

South Carolina was not unique. Other seaports experienced similarly dramatic increases in merchants between 1680 and 1770. Philadelphia, only settled since 1682, contained about 50 merchants in 1700, about 230 merchants in 1756, and more than 300 in 1774 as the Continental Congress debated American independence. New York had at least 150 merchants by 1730 and probably 300 by the Revolution.[39]

But merchants also plied the rural countryside. Agents or factors of Charleston, Annapolis, Philadelphia, New York, and Boston merchants visited farmers to purchase crops and sell standard merchandise. Many other areas had their own resident merchants. A traveler's description of Mingo Bottom in Ohio in 1789 echoed many rural settlements at their foundation earlier in the century: "a settlement of five log huts, or cabins, and not more than fifty acres of land cleared, . . . yet, small as the settlement is, here is a store, with a very good assortment of goods, to the value, as I suppose, of £1,000." The broad range of goods even in the rural stores only expanded in the cities. Governor James Glen reported a wide variety of goods among Charleston merchants. This included "British Woolen Manufactures"; "Cloths, broad and narrow, of all Sorts, from the finest broad Cloth down to Negroe Cloth," long since a disparaging term meaning cloth of poor quality; linen, cotton, silk, and laces; "Metallic Manufactures" including "Tin-wares, Pewter, in Household Utensils"; and "Miscellaneous Manufactures" that ranged from books, chairs, beds, glassware, gloves, and "paper of all types," to tiles, coal, gunpowder, quills and snuff.[40]

The extension in goods reflected the widening range of merchant activities across the colonies and across the Atlantic. Former Old World merchants customarily used European connections to fight for business in the New. When André Faneuil set up in Boston in the 1680s after fleeing Catholic persecution in Rochelle, France, he tapped into what one historian has called the "Protestant international," a vast network of French, Dutch, and English Protestant merchants whose connections he exploited from America. Jewish merchants emigrating to America plied similar connections developed in Portuguese Brazil, the Netherlands, and the Caribbean, and like the early Huguenots, they corresponded with religious compatriots as trading partners. Later, Scots traded with other Scots, following Old World connections to New World markets. In the early modern milieu, friendship created trade, and ethnicity and religion provided the touchstone of personal relationships and, often, business arrangements.[41]

As in Europe, successful colonial merchants thus worked hard to make profitable acquaintances, and they accomplished this task through wide ranges of correspondence. Robert Pringle offers one example. He was a Charleston merchant who started as an apprentice to a West Indian merchant in London, moved to Charleston in 1725 to work as a "factor" for London and West Indies merchants, and struck out on his own after he married Jane Allen, the daughter of a prominent Charleston merchant, Andrew Allen. Pringle kept up a correspondence that would have tired even the most faithful seventeenth-century Puritan diarist. Between 1738 and 1744, he wrote over seven hundred letters, over one hundred a year, virtually all of them concerning business, interspersed with personal observations.[42]

Like other merchants, Pringle specialized first in relationships, then in places and goods. Those whom Pringle knew, or came to know, led him to pursue certain lines of trade and, most likely, to eschew others. His first correspondence with Boston's Peter Faneuil, son of André Faneuil, demonstrates the way in which he cultivated a possible connection. Through a friend, Faneuil had sent Pringle some goods on the ship *Rochelle*, and Pringle's response was a model of simultaneous courtship and evasion. He promised to "dispose of" the goods "to your best advantage," but noted that "the New England goods happen to come to but an Indifferent Markett here at present, especially the fish which is too late for the Season." Following Faneuil's directions, Pringle loaded the *Rochelle* with rice and expected it to sail for Bristol "in a few days," taking care to "Encourage you to a further Correspondance this way as I shall . . . always very much Esteem your Command." Faneuil never became one of Pringle's major trading clients, but Pringle worked to sustain the relationship, using Faneuil as one of the several hundred clients who constituted his business.[43]

Pringle's broad intercolonial letter writing contrasts sharply with his centralized Old World correspondence. In 1743, for example, more of his letters—almost fifty—went to London than anywhere else, not surprising given London's importance in British colonial trade. Another ten letters went to merchants elsewhere in England, two went to Lisbon, and one each went to Rotterdam and Gibraltar. Yet Pringle's New World correspondence already outnumbered his Old World letters and was spread across many colonies. In 1743, for example, Pringle sent twenty-seven letters to South Carolina correspondents, most of them to other merchants in Charleston, nineteen letters to West Indies merchants, eleven to merchants in Boston, six to Pennsylvania, five to North Carolina, two to Georgia, and one each to New York, Maryland, and Virginia.[44]

Philadelphia demonstrated how complex the post-1680 colonial merchant world became and how vigorously colonial merchants of all kinds worked to carve out niches of friendly trade. Philadelphia's extremely rapid growth throughout the eighteenth century created a highly competitive merchant community. Smaller firms specialized as a way of managing that competition, turning their necessarily narrower range of goods to a competitive advantage if they read the markets correctly. Larger firms traded in more places and more goods. Yet often they too specialized in one of two trades. One was imported dry goods that came from England and included cloth and sewing goods. The other was exported foodstuffs, such as bread, flour, meat, and grains. These came to Philadelphia from rural Pennsylvania, the Chesapeake, and even South Carolina. It was this extensive trade in colonial food-stuffs that encouraged Philadelphia merchants to reach out to traders far from Philadelphia and that produced the expansive trading connections that typified colonial merchants from Boston to Charleston.[45]

Some merchants did specialize in one notable trade as it escalated after 1680: Africans. The specialization was not unusual among rural merchants in the Chesapeake or Charleston's urban merchants, but it ranged far across the colonies. Importing hundreds of Africans yearly was a big and profitable business that mainland colony merchants found little reason to leave to British, French, or Spanish traders. They moved into it aggressively. In Charleston, over four hundred men paid duties on importing captured Africans between 1735 and 1775, most doing so casually in one or two shipments to supplement other business. Yet some Charleston merchants concentrated on the trade. The firm of Austin and Laurans and its successor, Austin, Laurans, and Appleby brought in more than sixty cargoes of slaves in the decade between 1751 and 1761, probably accounting for more than five thousand Africans alone. In Newport, African trading became a mainstay of the port's business, not only because Rhode Island was the most vigorous importer of captured Africans in the North but because its traders so deliberately pursued the trade as a part of their commercial enterprise. Even in Philadelphia a merchant might pursue slave trading as a lucrative sideline. Philadelphia's Robert Ellis bought and sold widely in the Indies, in Europe, and in mainland colonies with substantial slave populations, namely Rhode Island, New York, Virginia, South Carolina, and Georgia. Partly through these connections, and partly through his experience in shepherding German redemptioners to Pennsylvania, Ellis developed a dependable trade in Africans in a colony where slaveholding remained uncommon.[46]

Creation of a powerful merchant elite constituted the merchants' most visible transformation after 1680. The wealth and influence of eighteenth-century colonial merchants dwarfed that of their seventeenth-century predecessors. Boston's Faneuil Hall, given to the town by Peter Faneuil in 1742, symbolized the achievement of Boston's post-1680 merchant elite. Faneuil amassed a fortune in the 1720s and 1730s and left an estate worth £7,500 sterling when he died unexpectedly in 1743. He exemplified a group of Boston merchants who created immensely successful businesses in Boston between 1700 and 1730. Jonathan Waldo died a decade earlier in 1731 with an estate valued at £9,600 sterling, and several other merchants who also died in the 1730s left estates worth £3,000 to £5,000 sterling.[47]

Philadelphia's merchant elite claimed less power over the city's highly competitive trade, but its members exercised significant influence nonetheless. Philadelphia's "merchant community" was divided by ethnicity (largely among English, Scottish, and German merchants), religion (Quakers, Anglicans, Presbyterians, Jews), and generation (immigrant merchants arrived in Philadelphia continuously up to the Revolution; others were second and third generation). By 1750 the city's top fifty merchants managed fully half of the city's shipping tonnage; the other four hundred city merchants scrambled for the rest of Philadelphia's trade. Boston, New York, and Charleston witnessed even greater merchant stratification after 1680. By the 1740s Boston's trade was heavily dominated by the Faneuils, Hancocks, Hutchinsons, and Lloyds, New York's by the Philipses, Van Cortlandts, DeLanceys, and Schuylers, and Charleston's by the Wraggs and the Manigaults.[48]

Resentment against the great merchants' power and wealth sometimes exploded into popular discontent. New York's prominent merchant families sought to channel this general resentment against specific competitors in both trade and politics. More than in other colonial cities, New York's several great merchant families managed political "parties," each of which claimed to serve common people better than the other, although they all doubtless served themselves best. After 1750 Boston found itself riven by political disputes often centered on complaints against the "merchant elite," some of which fed into the discontent of the American Revolution. It was no accident that some of Boston's most prestigious merchants, including the Faneuils, fled to England at the Revolution, never to return.[49]

Yet the steady growth of the colonial population, the expansion of cultivated acreage, and mounting imports and exports between 1680 and 1770 kept merchant stratification from exploding into real and deep conflict in Boston or New York or even Philadelphia. Many of the wealthiest found themselves hard-pressed to keep up with the expanding colonial economy, much less control it, though they certainly tried. The economy's expansion, fueled by population growth rather than greater efficiency, lured new merchants into the trade and helped others improve their lot, at least if they were calculating or lucky. As this happened, the numbers of merchants grew at least as fast as the population. A few of the newcomers broke into the powerful merchant elite; many more joined the ranks of middling and small merchants whose expansion between 1680 and 1760 created the first real merchant class in America. Nowhere could these colonial merchants compete for power and influence with those in London. But America was not London, nor was London the world. In their own places and times the eighteenth-century colonial merchants were carving out their own empires, smaller though not necessarily tidier, over which they exercised real direction and, even, independence.[50]

THE rise of artisans and skilled craftsmen reshaped the colonial economy in different and important ways after 1680 because it provided obscure, out-of-the way colonies with producers of finished products at a range and depth that at least equaled the British provinces at home and surpassed some. This judgment is not easily made. On the one hand, it is difficult to demonstrate the importance of artisans and skilled craftsmen in the burgeoning colonial economy, because colonial authorities generally kept records only of exports. This complicates efforts to calculate the trade that artisans generated or the value of the work they produced. On the other hand, their numbers, surviving account books, and products suggest that after 1680 they began to assume an increasing, if not overweening, importance that, together with subsistence and local-market agriculture, helped make the colonial economy more autonomous than it would otherwise have been.

Between 1680 and 1770 artisans and craftsmen became commonplace in an economy where they had been scarce. This happened most obviously in the colonial cities. Like merchants, artisans had been present at the founding of the colonies. But they remained fewer in number than the merchants into the 1670s. Between 1680 and 1720, however, artisans appeared in all the colonial towns—Boston, Newport, New Haven, New York, Philadelphia, Annapolis, Williamsburg, and Charleston—and proliferated in most of these places between 1720 and 1770. As the towns grew, residents found themselves much more easily able to purchase locally produced goods from local craftsmen. Wig-makers, silversmiths, and goldsmiths benefited from the colonists' in-creasing desire for status. Tailors, seamstresses, weavers, hatters, and shoemakers sold goods more widely, at least through the 1730s or 1740s. Gradually, as the population expanded and wealth increased, some artisans began to produce fine goods only for wealthy customers, others producing more common goods for more common people. Metalworkers sold finished goods to businessmen for ships and for construction, as did sailmakers and mastmakers. Early furniture mak-ers made sturdy but not refined furniture. But like other craftsmen, some also began to produce largely for wealthier clients, who formed an increasingly identifiable market after 1730.[51]

The refinement of apprenticeship marked another sign of artisanal maturity after 1680. Seventeenth-century apprentices usually served in families and then more often in New England than elsewhere. The growth of artisanal trades after 1680 stimulated the development of an apprenticeship system in most colonial cities. Here, too, family and connections as much dictated the choice of master and servant as did sheer need and professional skill. Most important, the growing appren-ticeship system provided trained workers and, ultimately, masters of new shops trained in America. Benjamin Franklin's experience in work-ing for the eccentric Samuel Keimer after Franklin's flight from Boston at age sixteen may not have represented the worst apprentice experi-ence, since Keimer was merely cranky and mystical where some masters were openly cruel and vindictive. But the ubiquity and persistence of craft apprenticeship through the whole of the eighteenth century sug-gests that enough apprentices, once on their own, were satisfied with their experience to perpetuate it with younger, still eager applicants.[52]

The proliferation of artisan and craft trades throughout the rural countryside perhaps best symbolized their growing importance in eigh-teenth-century colonial society. This is a recent discovery of historians, who had earlier assumed that artisans and craftsmen were limited to the colonial cities. Two examples from Connecticut and Maryland suggest how thoroughly craftsmen spread across rural areas. Rural Connecticut possessed an unusual number of furniture craftsmen. Newtown and Woodbury, located eighteen miles apart in southwestern Connecticut and more than thirty miles from New Haven, claimed more than forty joiners between 1760 and 1780 who specialized in furniture making in the two towns. Two-thirds of the joiners were born in Newtown and Woodbury, and most probably were apprenticed and trained locally, which suggests that the skills extended back into the earlier eighteenth century.[53]

In Talbot County, Maryland, over eight hundred men plied a wide variety of artisan and craft trades between 1690 and 1760. Not surprising in a rural, agricultural society, half were woodworkers—carpenters, coopers, and sawyers. The remaining four hundred practiced a wide spectrum of skilled occupations: cloth workers (tailors, weavers, hatters, and "fullers," who cleansed and thickened cloth to make it "full"); leather workers (shoemakers, tanners, saddlers, and glovers); metalworkers (blacksmiths, silversmiths, and brass workers); shipbuilders (ship carpenters, caulkers, sailmakers, and blockmakers); nonwood builders (bricklayers, plasterers, brickmakers, and glaziers); and barbers, butchers, and bakers. Carpenters greatly outnumbered fine artisans. Still, by the 1740s many rural areas in Connecticut, Maryland, and elsewhere enjoyed ranges of skilled trades far beyond those that might be expected in still young New World colonies.[54]

The Connecticut and Maryland examples raise two critical issues. First, how did the proliferation of artisan and craft trades there compare with provincial Britain? Certainly not all colonies possessed the rich diversity of artisan and craft trades found in Connecticut and Maryland. Rural South Carolina, for example, especially the lowcountry, was notably deficient in these rural trades throughout the eighteenth century. Unfortunately, direct comparisons with Britain are difficult to make because the early modern British regional economy, unlike the imperial economy, has received relatively little sustained historical study. Still, even the most rudimentary comparison might easily establish one principal point: that artisan and craft trades in both urban and rural America compared favorably in breadth and possibly in depth with those found in Britain. As late as 1760 artisan and skilled craft trades were as weakly developed in some areas of rural Britain as in rural South Carolina, especially northern Scotland, Wales, and the west of England. It would be difficult to say that any British city or town outside London or any area in rural Britain substantially outpaced the British mainland colonies in artisan and craft trades, a striking comment on the breadth of eighteenth-century colonial American economic achievement and, for Britain, perhaps a quietly ominous one as well.

Second, how did proliferating artisan and skilled crafts affect the gender division of work in eighteenth-century America? Women practiced a few of the major and minor artisan and skilled trades increasingly found throughout eighteenth-century America, working as milliners, seamstresses, and spinners. On the one hand, an advancing household economy meant more housekeeping and, thereby, gave busy consumers reason to seek out practitioners of specialized crafts. On the other hand, dressmaking and its allied crafts seem to have increased in the colonial cities, especially after 1740. Certain trades—those of silversmiths, goldsmiths, coopers, carpenters, ironworkers—remained exclusively male even as they expanded. The pattern exemplified one found in the industrial order of later decades: trade specialization increased the separation of men and women in work. It is difficult to determine whether this labor segregation exaggerated old agricultural patterns or represented a fundamentally new pattern. The exclusion of women in skilled trades and crafts was not always universal in colonial America. In Pennsylvania, for example, immigrant men dominated the weaving trades. But women played important roles in the same trade in eighteenth-century New England. Yet this difference within a single craft was probably exceptional. By the Revolution, then, women stood outside most of the skilled crafts while they created important inroads in others, especially those involving weaving, spinning, and dressmaking, all the while finding their roles in the household economies ever more important as farms and merchant businesses expanded.[55]

D ID men and women succeed as the British colonies expanded between 1680 and 1770? This question, hotly debated by historians in recent years, is not a modern invention. It stood at the heart of the promotional literature that pulled Europeans to America, and it was implicit in Crèvecoeur's observation about the newcomers' behavior in America. After a European's arrival, Crèvecoeur wrote, he "no sooner breathes our air than he forms schemes, and embarks in designs he never would have thought of in his own country." These schemes might center on many things, including new theologies and political intrigue. But they often centered on material reward. What did immigrants' labor win them in America, whether they were European or African?

The answer is that the result proved mixed, generally positive for Europeans with important disparities that emerged with special effect between 1680 and 1770, but overwhelmingly negative for Africans, whose denial of material reward compounded the agony of enslavement. In short, the years from 1680 to 1760 created America's incipient "two cultures"—one white and often prosperous, and one black, bereft both of freedom and material reward.[56]

Regrettably, measuring prosperity in a people is far more complex than enjoying it. First, relatively few records about profit and loss exist for the colonial era. When they do, they usually are unique and not helpful in determining broad trends throughout often disparate colonies. Second, a truism about wealth makes the task even harder: wealth generally increases with age. To know that someone died poor at age twenty-five is really only to know that he or she died. This is because in the eighteenth as much as in the twentieth century, financial success generally increased with time. Put tritely, old people had far more assets than young people did. Thus systematic measures of changes in wealth across the eighteenth century really should center on people who died at about the same age. Third, even when documents do exist, differences in measuring estates and taxes in different places and alterations in assessing estates and taxes from decade to decade (such as changes in the law concerning what was to be taxed) make it extremely difficult to compare different places at different times.

Although the results are therefore tentative, several crucial economic patterns can be said to have distinguished the colonies between 1680 and 1770. The first pattern was borne out in the persistence of European emigration to America across the entire eighteenth century. Most Europeans experienced satisfying success in America, especially in rural America, an experience confirmed by nine decades of increasing immigration. Thomas Pownall, colonial administrator and several times a

Thomas Pownall, *A Design to Represent the Beginning and Completion of an American Settlement or Farm.* Engraving, 1763.

governor, portrayed this success in a 1768 illustration entitled *A Design to Represent the Beginning and Completion of an American Settlement or Farm*. Pownall had warned British officials about underestimating America in his 1764 book *The Administration of the Colonies*, and four years later he sought to illustrate the point. Pownall portrayed a rising progression from an early log cabin farm to more refined and prosperous farmsteads in the center and right, with cattle and children enjoying an easy harmony with nature. (Pownall's use of the log cabin to represent an early farm was an interesting anomaly. Log cabins were more common in the mid- and late eighteenth century, since earlier settlers had little or no experience building them. By the nineteenth century, the log cabin had come to symbolize American democracy, as in the Whig Party's "Log Cabin Campaign" of 1840.)[57]

Pownall's illustration idealized many aspects of colonial agriculture. It avoided slavery, hid the work of clearing land (Pownall showed little cultivated land at all), missed the eclectic commercialism of colonial agriculture, and, above all, bypassed individual failure. Yet abundant evidence suggests that Pownall conveyed a common European adventure well. For many Europeans, Britain's mainland colonies were indeed the "best poor man's country." True, no historian has compared the achievements of European immigrants in America with those who went to Prussia, the Netherlands, Poland, and the area of the modern Czech Republic, Slovakia, and Hungary. Perhaps it is sufficient to say that the massive European immigration to America is evidence enough. Enormous numbers of British and continental European immigrants and their descendants farmed with considerable independence in Britain's mainland colonies (historians have never tried to count their numbers, either). Many owned their own land, and others leased land as tenant farmers, especially in New York and Maryland. The rising exports from America, the push to clear additional land, the escalating purchases of Africans in the southern colonies, and the continuing demand to buy more land from neighbors, speculators, or directly from the colonial governments all suggest substantial general prosperity, including at least the perception of Europeans themselves that they made the right decision in coming to America. Only convicts returned to Europe in any substantial numbers, but then perhaps it could be said that only they possessed the lucrative Old World business networks that might readily cause them to return home.

Estate inventories revealed similar success. Even modest farmers, merchants, and artisans possessed ample furniture, clothing, homes, and the accoutrements of the agricultural, artisanal, or merchant trades, far more so than was true of seventeenth-century colonial estates. Books illustrate the process well. In the seventeenth-century Chesapeake and New England executors often listed each book owned by the deceased when they inventoried estates; executors for the late-seventeenth-century Virginia minister, Thomas Teackle, carefully inscribed the titles of all but a dozen of his 333 books, even opening some books to provide publishers' names. But almost all eighteenth-century estate inventories merely estimated the number of books. By the 1720s people owned too many books to count, and too many other objects were more valuable. The spate of books symbolized Crèvecoeur's deft observation about European material success in eighteenth-century America: "A pleasing uniformity of decent competence appears throughout our habitations."[58]

Two issues tempered but did not negate this portrait. First, between 1680 and 1760, economic inequality probably increased in the colonial cities and in many if not all older settled areas along the eastern seaboard. Historians have debated this issue vigorously. In the 1960s and 1970s, historians discovered important increases in the percentage of wealth held by the richest members of society between the 1690s and the 1770s, while in the late 1970s and 1980s, critics argued that inconsistent measures and dubious tracking of changes through the decades made these assessments unreliable.[59]

More recent studies suggest that different patterns characterized different regions and places, although the issue is still contested. Wealth disparities clearly solidified between 1680 and 1770, especially in the cities. But this also occurred in long-settled rural areas, such as South Carolina's lowcountry, eastern Virginia and Maryland, and even eastern Pennsylvania. The wealthy owned more of each region's assets at the end of the period than at the beginning. For example, in Boston, the top 10 percent of the city's taxpayers owned 46 percent of its wealth in 1687 but 63 percent in 1771. This meant that as the decades passed, wealth was more firmly held by a few, not more widely distributed among the many. As the decades passed it became somewhat harder, rather than easier, for beginners in the economy to succeed, prosper, or become wealthy.

Yet developing regions—the western Carolinas, Virginia and Pennsylvania, northern New York, plus New Hampshire and Maine—perhaps not the "frontier" but nearby—witnessed quick, substantial economic development between 1680 and 1770. In them, the wealthy were few, and where they were present they were less rich and controlled less of the economy than their counterparts in the cities or in older rural areas. The combination presented contradictory results. Newly settled areas softened the impact of the tightening social structure in the cities for the colonies generally.[60]

Regional differences in wealth escalated between 1680 and 1770 and stemmed largely from a single cause: the dramatic expansion of slaveholding in the colonial South and its creation of substantial wealth unknown elsewhere. By the 1760s slaveholding made southern farmers substantially wealthier than their middle or northern colony counterparts. Even if wealth was measured without regard to captured Africans, the southern colonies still emerged as wealthier. In 1774 per capita wealth among European colonists without slaves stood at £38 for the northern colonies, £44.1 for the middle colonies, and £61.6 for the southern colonies. But the southern colonies zoomed even farther ahead when slaves were counted. Total per capita wealth (meaning enslaved Africans, land, and other property) amounted to £38.2 in the northern colonies, £45.8 in the middle colonies, but £92.7 in the southern colonies (which, in turn, did not come close to Jamaica, where the enormous slave population pushed European wealth to £1,200 per capita). Slaveholding and southern export crops enjoyed a devastatingly symbiotic relationship that increased the South's regional distinctiveness: slaveholding stimulated the region's highly profitable cash export crops, and the highly profitable exports dramatically increased the slaves' value.[61]

The decades between 1680 and 1770 witnessed the emergence among Europeans of major reservoirs of wealth and poverty. Americans possessed only minor wealth by British standards. Not even the most ostentatiously wealthy colonists, such as the Faneuils, Livingstons, or Manigaults, approached the display or wealth known to Britain's titled nobility. Yet after 1680 America's wealthy colonists claimed substantial possessions, both in comparison with neighbors and by the standards of middling British society. When Peter Manigault of Goose Creek and Charleston, South Carolina, died in 1774, his estate came to £32,700 sterling. It was twice the value of the second wealthiest colonial decedent of the year (based on a massive study of estates probated in 1774), and it almost equaled the combined estates of the next five richest colonists who died in 1774, all of whom also were from South Carolina.[62]

Slaves thus made an enormous difference in regional wealth. Manigault's estate contained more than 270 slaves, who made up about 45 percent of his physical wealth. Although he owned far more slaves than others did, he was reasonably representative of South Carolina planters, who essentially doubled their wealth by holding Africans in slavery. In short, slaveholding's proliferation in the southern colonies after 1680 almost single-handedly accounted for the region's substantial advantage in wealth over the middle and northern colonies at the American Revolution.[63]

One characteristic of wealth did not change in this period, however: its gender associations. Wealth belonged to men, not women. "Wealthy" women owned far less than wealthy men, and this pattern did not change between 1680 and 1770. The wealthiest woman dying in 1774 was worth £3,412 sterling, and the average wealth of the top ten women dying in 1774 (£1,552 sterling) paled beside that of the ten richest men (£11,931 sterling, or 7.7 times more than the women). Yet women's wealth also followed regional patterns within this gender-diminished world. Southern women proved wealthier than their middle and northern colony counterparts, largely because they inherited slaves from their husbands' estates. Although the single wealthiest woman to die in 1774 was a rural Pennsylvania widow named Margaret Williams, worth £3,412 sterling, all the other wealthiest women were from the southern colonies. The estates of the wealthiest five women from the southern colonies averaged £1,779 sterling, compared with £734 sterling for estates of middle colony women (excluding Margaret Williams's exceptional estate), and £235 sterling for "wealthy" women from the northern colonies (the average estate for men was £372 in the southern colonies, £211 in the middle colonies, and £138 in New England).[64]

Wealth also bred wealth in America, as it did in Europe. The years after 1680 witnessed the development of a colonial aristocracy, often built on inheritances, with tight family connections among the wealthy. Contemporaries used the term "aristocracy" loosely, as have historians.

None of this new colonial "aristocracy" ever possessed either the wealth or the royal titles of Britain's nobility. But from the 1680s forward, and especially from 1720 to 1750, leading families grouped together in each colony to display a formidable combination of wealth, material consumption, and (usually) political and social power.

The unity of this emerging provincial elite can be exaggerated. As in Philadelphia's merchant community, tension and discord emerged from the competition for business, political power, and social prestige, and religion and ethnicity sometimes undermined political, social, and economic strategies for authority. But the expanding ranks of the elite allowed for the creation of friendships and alliances that could transcend the penchant for division. Merchants formed partnerships, usually informal rather than formal; this was why Charleston's Robert Pringle wrote so many letters to other local and regional merchants. Their families extended business relationships. Pringle arrived in Charleston as the agent of London merchants, but his "independent" career only began after he married a Charleston merchant's daughter. And status sometimes upended religious loyalties. When the Jewish woman Phila Franks secretly married the Anglican Oliver DeLancey in 1743, she as much chose class over religion or ethnicity as she married for love. Even her mother described DeLancey as "a man of worth and Charector" despite her grief at Phila Franks's apostasy.[65]

Poverty also expanded in the colonies after 1680. In part, poverty grew only in relative terms. Poverty had been present in the seventeenth-century colonies, and the daily life of impoverished men, women, and children changed little across the two centuries. After 1680 the numbers of the poor escalated as the European population rose in America. As this happened, rural and urban areas alike increasingly treated poverty as a persistent feature of colonial life that required systematic public intervention, not merely private pity. Yet the "rise" of poverty in the colonies never approached the starvation and rampant disease that typified London and Paris, for example, and that provided grist for novelists for more than two centuries.[66]

Still, the poor were poor, and after 1680 they became especially obvious in the colonial towns and cities. This happened in America for the same reason it happened in Europe: the poor more readily found shelter and perhaps even companionable solace in cities than in small towns or rural areas. War produced substantial increases in poverty, especially among women and children. In Boston poverty emerged in the 1690s among widows and children left by soldiers killed in the disastrously unsuccessful attack on Quebec in the same year. The fitful Queen Anne's War that dragged on erratically between 1702 and 1713 widowed more women, all of whom became dependent on charity in a society that made it difficult for women to be independent. In the 1740s and 1750s, war created still more widows while shortages boosted prices for goods even as an oversupply of settled colonists and newly arrived European immigrants depressed wages. In these circumstances, the European poor in the colonies crossed all boundaries: men, women, children, old as well as young, and in all nationalities. And they were indeed poor. Among decedents in 1774, some possessed property, but debts left their estates bankrupt. Many others literally died with neither debts nor possessions, bearing nothing more than their own clothing.[67]

Colonial authorities became almost desperate in trying schemes to alleviate, if not eliminate, poverty as it escalated. Some of these efforts mainly relieved governments from their responsibilities. Boston, like the much smaller towns that surrounded it, "warned out" men and women who might require welfare. The city did this so it could refuse to give them public aid if they asked for it. Boston also bound out poor children as apprentices, and in 1735 it established a workhouse for the poor in which fifty-five people lived by 1741. Despite these efforts, the costs of the poor for the workhouse, for "out-relief" programs that placed the poor in working families, and for simple aid mounted precipitously from £800 in 1727 to over £4,000 by 1742. New York's vestrymen and churchwardens distributed aid to the poor on an ad hoc basis through the 1730s, and New York also built an almshouse in 1736, believing (probably rightly) that centralization reduced aid costs. In Philadelphia, the relatively strong regional economy briefly uplifted employment. Public aid went largely to the disabled, who were cared for in Philadelphia families and through a small almshouse built in 1729.[68]

War again increased poverty at mid-century, this time during and after the Seven Years' War. In 1757 Boston reported more than one thousand people on poor relief, and "warnings-out" increased to over two hundred per year. In 1764 the town spent £2,000 sterling on poor relief. New York City's churchwardens ran out of money for poor relief in January 1765, and although the city's wealthy businessmen organized a linen manufacturing business to employ three hundred of the town's poor, the business proved risky and employed only a few of the city's poor men.[69]

In 1751 the Pennsylvania legislature gave £2,000 toward establishing the Pennsylvania Hospital for the Sick Poor, a favorite project of Benjamin Franklin's. Franklin believed it would reduce the cost of care in the city's almshouse and out-relief program. But the war meant that unemployment expanded the ranks of the poor substantially beyond the sick. Although the *Pennsylvania Gazette* reported fewer than 50 foreclosures per year in Philadelphia before 1762, it counted 81 in 1763 and 111 in 1765. The old almshouse constructed in 1729 housed more than 150 people during the winter of 1764–65. An additional 150 secured "out relief," and as in New York, prominent Philadelphia merchants established a linen manufacturing business to employ the poor, though to no better effect than its neighbor's effort. In sum, by the time of the American Revolution, poverty had become such a perpetual feature among Europeans in America that it required institutional responses, even if it paled by comparison with Europe.[70]

Yet poverty created by slaveholding after 1680 left far greater scars on eighteenth-century colonial culture and society. Slaveholding stole more than the freedom of captured Africans. As it evolved in America, including the British mainland colonies, it created an imposed poverty that denied virtually all the fruits of labor to men and women captured and forced to work against their will. In a society where so many had come to prosper, and in a society where so many prospered regardless of their reasons for coming, the poverty enforced among Africans by chattel slavery made American slaveholding all the more grotesque.

Slaveholders indeed allowed Africans the long-term use of objects, though enslaved Africans could not legally own anything. Chesapeake planters ended the occasional practice of "self-purchase," which before 1680 had been achieved by allowing Africans to sell small crops, as planters rushed toward massive slaveholding after 1680. As the eighteenth century advanced, though self-purchase was rarely allowed anywhere, Africans still often grew small crops on their own, gardened, and raised chickens and occasionally hogs. They traded among themselves and sometimes with masters. Occasionally masters bought from slaves, and sometimes they allowed slaves to sell garden crops, baskets, bowls, and even leather products they made. It was what one scholar has called a "peculiam," an "investment by the master of a partial, and temporary, capacity in his slave to possess and enjoy a given range of goods."[71]

Africans used pots and pans, customarily handed down from slave-holders, and traded for utensils, furniture, bowls, and clothing among themselves. The 1714 South Carolina assembly passed legislation deny-ing slave claims on "any stock of hogs, cattle or horses," and eight years later it allowed seizures of animals or boats "belonging" to slaves. In fact, owners seem to have allowed slaves the use of such property, including horses, at sufficient length for it to constitute effective "own-ership" by slaves, although one legally indefensible. And slaves stole property, as owners occasionally discovered when they accidentally or deliberately searched slave quarters. There they found a vast range of objects taken from owners—clothes, dishes, silverware, utensils, sheets, jewelry, and money.[72]

But few Africans possessed the wide range of goods commonly owned by even poorer European farmers—beds, chairs, tables, a few "nice" pieces of silverware, decorative china, decorated chests, and books. The expansion of the eighteenth-century economy and the con-siderable gain in material goods after 1680 made it easier for slaves to acquire goods by the time of the Revolution than earlier. But slaves were the last stop for most of these items. Any doubt about this is cured by examining estate inventories. Appraisers often valued servants' beds at £1.5, but "old bedding" for slaves at only 15 pence, and they often failed to value slave "goods" at all.[73]

The illustration of African wedding festivity in South Carolina in the watercolor *The Old Plantation* subtly reveals the anomalies of slave impoverishment in eighteenth-century America. The Africans depicted were ornately, even impeccably dressed. Yet the picture subtly discloses the sparseness of economic reward and material life among Africans brought to America. Even after a century of slaveholding in South Carolina, these Africans displayed only a few physical possessions—a banjo, a small drum, bottle gourds most likely used as musical instru-ments, and benches for the players. The lack of other physical objects and the plainness of the slave quarters, with their unfinished plank doors and lack of windows, revealed all too well a life bereft not only of freedom but also of things. Such a portrait well fits slaveholder estate inventories that usually bypassed slave quarters. Many Africans lived their whole lives in America with no beds, chairs, or tables, and precious few other physical objects, whether they were newly arrived from Africa or had been in America generations longer than recent European immigrants. The contrast with Europeans was remarkable. Time allowed Europeans to calculate ample material rewards in America, but for Africans time calibrated a cruel, perpetually enforced poverty.[74]

Thus as Europeans enlarged their freedom and amassed satisfying, if not always overwhelming, material possessions in America, Africans lost both their freedom and virtually everything their enslaved labor produced. These patterns of accumulation and denial, firmly established between 1680 and 1770 as slaveholding expanded in America, long outlasted slavery as one of America's most enduring patterns. In provinces of plenty, they demonstrated how the experience of wealth and impoverishment descended not from the land, but from human invention.

Three

POLITICS

> Whence proceed these laws? From our government. Whence that government? It is derived from the original genius and strong desire of the people ratified and confirmed by the Crown. This is the great chain which links us all, this is the picture which every province exhibits.
>
> J. HECTOR ST. JOHN DE CRÈVECOEUR (1782)

CRÈVECOEUR, famed for his early elucidation of the American "character," proved remarkably obtuse when he wrote about colonial politics. Crèvecoeur, a Loyalist, saw colonial politics originating in royal edicts, not evolving from historical developments or the crucial and creative shifts that produced such a vital political culture in America. Hence his perfunctory homily summarizing colonial law and government. They derived, he wrote, "from the original genius and strong desire of the people ratified and confirmed by the Crown." Despite six years of British failure to bring colonists to heel, Crèvecoeur still proclaimed that colonial government, "confirmed by the Crown," was "the great chain which links us all."[1]

In fact, Crèvecoeur wrote almost nothing about politics in his *Letters from an American Farmer.* He traced Americans' peculiarities and distinctions, yet only in the strangely allusive final chapter entitled "The Distresses of a Frontier Man" did Crèvecoeur discuss the revolutionary struggle even obliquely, closing with dark ruminations on America's fateful choice:

> You certainly cannot avoid feeling for my distresses; you cannot avoid mourning with me over that load of physical and moral evil with which we are all oppressed. My own share of it I often overlook when I minutely contemplate all that hath befallen our native country.[2]

Crèvecoeur's failure could be dismissed as the disappointment of a Loyalist writing from England. But it reflected an important reality: colonial politics were so complex that they often baffled observers, whether participants or recently arrived commentators. It was one thing to describe fascinating features of colonial social life, as Crèvecoeur did brilliantly. But it was another to translate the often confused political configurations of so many individual colonies into a common colonial politics or appreciate the tumble-down history that created those differences and made politics in the American colonies so different from politics in the British provinces at home.

Prerevolutionary American politics stemmed directly from its participants' willful and disciplined engagement between 1680 and 1770. Colonial politics was not democratic. Yet it was often strangely "popular," sometimes ugly, frequently exciting, and increasingly centered on important principles that would bear both short- and long-term significance. In this regard, the colonies' eighteenth-century politics proved uncannily American in its disappointments as well as in its glories. Its partisanship, partiality, incessant personal intrigue, and institutional creativity turned otherwise placid New World backwaters into laboratories for exceptional yet unplanned political experiments. The roots of this experiment ran deep into both American and European soil, but the plant that flowered predicted America's political future in all its complexity and wonder.

WHEN Tip O'Neill, speaker of the House of Representatives, wryly observed in the 1970s that all politics was local, he meant that national politics and international ideologies were no more powerful than local perceptions allowed them to be. But in the eighteenth century vigorous politics were more likely provincial than local. Provincial, colonywide politics mattered considerably more, in part because outside New England local offices were as often appointed as elected and because everywhere, including New England, provincial rather than local politics saw the greatest degree of public involvement.

This abatement of local politics in the eighteenth-century colonies stemmed from colonial institutional development and actual political practice. Colonial political institutions, which stretched well back into the seventeenth century, evolved two important patterns by the early eighteenth century. First, only in New England and a few of the middle colonies did voters select most or even some local officials. New England towns governed themselves through town meetings where all freemen (usually all land-owning men) were eligible to vote. "Selectmen" elected by the freemen administered town affairs between meetings, and their short terms gave them no statutory claim to longevity or privilege.[3]

Outside New England, many local governmental institutions were appointed, not elected, although great variation existed from colony to colony. New York's local government was especially confusing. Long Island had a town system like New England's because its early residents came from Connecticut. Other New York towns elected local officials, but governors appointed sheriffs, clerks, justices of the peace, and militia officers. The great manor lords like Robert Livingston and Adolph Philipse were authorized to hold "courts leet and baron" that enforced manorial regulations and settled land tenure claims and disputes among tenants. But most administered justice through the county judicial system. Finally, after 1686 New York City's freemen elected the town's aldermen and councillors, but the governor appointed the mayor, sheriff, and other local officials, as he did in rural areas of the colony.[4]

Local political arrangements in other colonies could be almost equally confusing. Freemen elected New Jersey town officials and township boards of supervisors, but governors appointed local justices. Pennsylvania voters elected county commissioners and assessors, cast ballots for a sheriff and coroner appointed by the governor from the top two candidates, and never developed a vigorous county meeting system. Maryland and Virginia centered local government in vestries and county courts whose members were appointed by the governor; North Carolina's governors appointed all local officials from justices of the peace, clerks, and coroners to sheriffs, a system that continued through the Revolution. In South Carolina elected parish vestries managed Church of England affairs and poor relief, but elections drew few voters and the vestries usually met only once or twice a year. Local politics there centered on the legislature, which even directly managed local road construction until it established road districts in 1721, whose commissioners it also named. Local justices heard cases individually and never established the collective identity that characterized Virginia's eighteenth-century county courts.[5]

Second, local governments functioned quite similarly in the colonies whether they were elected or appointed. For example, in most places relatively prosperous local families tended to hold local office. John Adams observed in his *Defense of the Constitutions of Government of the United States of America* that New England officeholders "generally descended from generation to generation, in three or four families at most." This was especially true in New England's moderate and larger towns, where most New Englanders lived. Their voters constantly elected members of a few families to public office in the eighteenth century, and these men were regularly substantial property holders, not tenants or laborers. In Andover, Massachusetts, for example, fathers, sons, and grandsons from eleven families accounted for 76 percent of the town's leaders between 1720 and 1760, and this pattern typified town politics throughout eighteenth-century New England.[6]

Local officeholding in New England typically became the foundation for future political appointments. The rise of appointed office in New England strengthened the pattern of selectivity in local officeholding. Governors in both Massachusetts and Connecticut usually named county justices from lists prepared by advisers that confirmed local patterns of town leadership. Ninety percent of county judicial appointments went to men who had already served as town selectmen. Only in the larger towns of Boston, Cambridge, and Salem did the figure dip to 60 percent, and then because some nominees, also from families with other members who had furnished town leadership, apparently believed they were too prominent to bother with town office.[7]

Local politics were often stormy, whether elected or appointed. Here the seventeenth century offered a good preview. In Sudbury, Massachusetts, laymen rebuked the town minister, Edmund Brown, for "meddling" in a 1656 land dispute; Brown was "a dishonor to God . . . a prejudice to his ministry . . . a scandal to his name." A century later, town meetings in Kent, Connecticut, constantly wrangled over land policy and rebuffed losers' appeals to the Massachusetts General Assembly for redress of grievances. Overwhelmingly, New England town disputes involved land, and for obvious reasons. The towns controlled large ungranted acreage whose value only increased as parents lived into their sixties and seventies, as children multiplied and aged, and as new settlers from other towns and from England sought land in settled towns rather than risk settlement on the still dangerous Indian frontier.[8]

In the middle and southern colonies, where many officials were appointed by the Crown, land ownership also determined officeholding. In Middlesex County, Virginia, one's wealth determined much of one's political career between 1650 and 1750. Men named by the county court to minor local posts, such as estate appraisers, tobacco counters, and processioners of land (they measured boundaries) typically owned 180 acres of land and had estates valued at £85 sterling. But vestrymen and justices, plus the sheriff, coroner, and clerk of court, who were appointed by the governor, possessed far more—over 800 acres of land and estates valued at more than £600 sterling. Moreover, unless these men moved on to higher office—election to the Virginia Burgesses or appointment to the colony council—they served a long time, often for life. The case of a failure in the late 1670s demonstrates the importance of wealth and landholding in Virginia politics. By age twenty-three, Richard Perrott had already joined the Middlesex County vestry and county court, then was named sheriff, the result of having inherited well (more than 800 acres at age nine) and having married well (a widow with land). But Perrot disappeared from county politics when his farming enterprises collapsed. He quietly relinquished his sheriff's post, left the county court (though formally he remained a member), avoided vestry meetings, and never again figured in Middlesex County politics.[9]

Still, the complexity of some settlements produced interesting variations. Local officeholding in St. Mary's County, Maryland, dipped far lower down the social scale than was true elsewhere, because Maryland prohibited Catholics from holding office after 1649 and because almost half of the colony's European population was Catholic, including a large proportion of its wealthier residents. The result rankled Catholics, who sometimes protested their exclusion. In 1743 one Catholic felt bold enough to complain that he could not get a fair trial because "a great many freeholders in the said County . . . are Roman Cathlicks and by being so [are] disqualified . . . to be jury men." The protest had no effect.[10]

Courts and the professionalization of the law changed colonists' experience with local politics after 1680. These changes occurred everywhere. In New England, a new layer of appointed judicial positions made at the county rather than the town level provided a new venue for achieving local status. Courts offered new places for conducting local politics through lawsuits, and they not so subtly challenged the local sovereignty of the towns. New Englanders increasingly settled town disputes as well as personal contests through lawsuits heard by justices appointed by governors who used the appointments to curry favor or reward supporters. In the middle and southern colonies, courts became the principal arena of local politics. This tradition started in the seventeenth century in Virginia and Maryland but was perfected in the eighteenth century. By the 1710s "court day" in the Chesapeake had become a major site for local politics. It drew large public attendance, became a focus for regional markets, and for at least a day or two established on a regular basis an almost urban feel to rural areas of scattered farms.[11]

A dramatic increase in lawsuits, mostly to collect debts, typified the growth of the courts after 1700. Everywhere, aggressive, willful colonists sought to collect bad debts. Lawsuits in Richmond County, Virginia, and Gloucester County, New Jersey, ran substantially ahead of population growth in the 1710s, 1720s, and 1730s. In New York, the population grew by six times between 1690 and 1750 but cases before the colony's Supreme Court grew by twelve times. Lawsuits rose by more than 225 percent in the Massachusetts Superior Court of Judicature between 1710 and 1730. Fully 10 of every 100 adults in Hartford County, Connecticut, filed a lawsuit to recover debts in 1740—more than 1,500 such suits—and in Plymouth, Massachusetts, 8 of every 100 adults filed a suit in the 1730s. In Plymouth, the caseload in the court of common pleas zoomed from 16 cases in 1703 to 385 cases in 1730, then declined but never dropped below 200.[12]

Professionally trained lawyers increasingly displaced part-time practitioners as lawsuits multiplied. Amateurs had handled most legal work in the seventeenth century, but in the eighteenth century aspiring lawyers who "read" the law with a practicing lawyer (himself usually but not always trained in England) displaced the old amateur lawyers. In New England, Yale and Harvard graduates turned increasingly to the law after 1720, with a real rush occurring after 1740. By 1770 New England contained about one hundred practicing lawyers, roughly one for every five clergymen. The comparison was more than casual. Now men openly rejected the ministry for the law. Against his father's wishes, John Adams eschewed the ministry to read for the law after graduating from Harvard in 1755. The combination of Coke and Descartes, whom he read with his mentor, the lawyer James Putnam, transformed Adams's Puritan heritage from a religion of faith grounded in a personal conversion experience to a religion of civic morality especially suited to the practice of both law and politics.[13]

In Virginia, there was less to reject but much to affirm, then criticize. About 150 men practiced law in Virginia between 1716 and 1770, although lawyers had been rare in seventeenth-century Virginia. In the old tidewater counties, the 35 lawyers of the 1740s almost doubled by 1760. Two-thirds were American-born, and most studied locally. The other third were English-born and usually attended the Inns of Court in London, as did wealthy Virginians such as Peyton Randolph, William Byrd III, and Robert Beverley. The rise of lawsuits and lawyers stimulated criticism, especially after 1750. The *Virginia Almanac* regularly lampooned lawyers and courts. "We in the Country know no difference between a Lawyer and a Lyar" it observed in 1764, repeating a popular aphorism.[14]

Urban politics added a prominent class dimension to local politics. Mid-eighteenth-century New York City was famous for its disputes between the DeLanceys and the Livingstons, and similar contests sometimes characterized Boston and Philadelphia politics as well. But urban politics also introduced additional polarizing issues, particularly merchant efforts to control the economy. Bostonians fought over public markets in the 1730s. Established merchants supported a regulated public market where competition would be reduced, while the smaller, more numerous entrepreneurial merchants backed open, unregulated markets. The contest brought a mob to destroy several market houses in 1737, but Peter Faneuil finally tipped the issue with his gift of Faneuil Hall to the city in 1742, which was a calculated effort to win victory for the larger merchants and a regulated market, not merely an act of disinterested generosity.[15]

In Philadelphia, Governor Sir William Keith appealed for popular support against factions surrounding the Penn family and the city's most prosperous merchants. Keith advocated paper money that devalued debts owed to city merchants, sought easier naturalization for immigrants (opponents feared immigrants were an "Army of Mirmydons"), and organized artisans into a political group called the "Leather Apron Club." The faction that supported Governor Lewis Morris in New York City in the 1730s appealed for support from economically hard-pressed voters in the city's 1733 and 1734 municipal elections. Faction members promised to create a new almshouse and poorhouse and to support the issuance of £12,000 in paper currency to construct fortifications.[16]

Yet both rural and urban politics in the colonies paled by comparison with provincial politics that involved the governors, councils, and especially the elected assemblies. It was at the provincial level that the most powerful and most important political institutions and processes arose in the British mainland colonies after 1680 and transformed colonial political life.

COLONYWIDE politics—provincial politics—greatly overshadowed local politics in both immediate and long-term impact as the colonies developed after 1680. The political contests were sharper and more momentous. The franchise was more important because all colonies elected lower assemblies, while only some colonies elected local governments. Provincial elections prompted widespread public discussions of political issues and the formation of political groups that sometimes assumed almost modern, partylike appearances. Assemblies became sophisticated, complex political institutions far beyond anything seventeenth-century legislators could have imagined. In contrast, the colonial councils lagged in institutional development, never maturing like the assemblies despite, or perhaps because of, the wealth and personal prestige of their appointed members. Finally, despite the odious reputation they acquired in the revolutionary struggle, governors often successfully contested the assemblies before 1760 and frequently demonstrated substantial executive leadership that maintained and even strengthened royal authority down to the contest with Britain.

The franchise determined who participated in electoral politics, and carried two notable traits between 1680 and 1770—malleable property qualifications and low voter turnout. The property qualification in the colonies reflected the dominant early modern view that voting was a privilege held by orthodox Christian men with property, not a right enjoyed by all. By modern standards, the colonial franchise was narrow, although by eighteenth-century European standards it was generous. The law denied the vote to whole classes of people: women, servants, slaves, religious minorities, Indians, and many without property.

This meant that women's roles in colonial "politics" hinged not on their power with the franchise, where they had none, but often on their potential roles in other areas of government and law. Colonial maturation after 1680 increased legal marginalization for women. For example, as Connecticut's economy matured, as religious diversity increased even among old Puritans, and as the law and its practice increasingly emulated formal British patterns, Connecticut courts increasingly invoked a double standard—leniency for men, strictness for women—that had indeed pertained in witchcraft cases in the previous century but had not widely characterized earlier prosecutions for moral offenses. In the eighteenth century down to the Revolution, men routinely won almost all cases centering on sex and marriage, including child custody and property cases when men had committed adultery or deserted their wives. Men litigated virtually all debt cases, and women seldom appeared even as defendants.[17]

Yet in property law, women increased their independence in colonies that developed separate courts of chancery—New York, Maryland, Virginia, and South Carolina. These courts of chancery tended to give "femes coverts"—married women—greater independence in owning property separate from their husbands or in managing property they owned before marriage. But colonies without separate chancery courts held to traditional British restrictions. Similarly, the colonies that adhered to primogeniture—the right of the eldest son to all or most of an estate—compromised the rights of daughters. As estates gained in value in the eighteenth century, the enforcement of primogeniture in New York, Maryland, Virginia, and South Carolina placed women at considerable disadvantage. Fathers could avoid these consequences through their wills in New York but not necessarily in Virginia. For European women, the exercise of the law and justice after 1680 through colonial courts—a principal way politics involved colonial women—thus brought no necessary improvement, and in some cases proved as barren a political arena for them as electoral politics.[18]

For European men in the colonies, the law opened the franchise to thousands of possible voters through low property qualifications or alternatives to outright property ownership. For example, Virginia required only twenty-five acres of settled land or one hundred acres of unsettled land, Rhode Island required only £400 of property measured in inflated local paper currency, and New York qualified voters who held lifetime leases but did not own land outright. Half of the colonies offered similarly variable routes to the property qualification, including tax payments and ownership of goods, not just land. Yet it was the cheap availability of land that qualified many men to vote. Although historians have argued about the exact numbers, it is likely that between 50 and 60 percent of white men could vote in the colonies, a rate far greater than in Britain or on the Continent.[19]

Yet even as the franchise expanded after 1680, colonial election turnouts were low, not high. Virginians voted more frequently than others; about 40 percent of eligible men voted there from the 1740s to the 1770s. Pennsylvania and New York elections drew only between 20 and 40 percent of the eligible voters. In New England, between 10 and 25 percent of eligible men voted, a surprising result given historians' frequent emphasis on the region's role in creating American democracy. Only South Carolina fared worse. Charleston voters showed up most frequently, with 30 percent of the town's eligible men voting in the mid-eighteenth century, similar to the patterns in Pennsylvania and New York. But rural elections in South Carolina often drew less than 10 percent of eligible voters. Very tiny numbers of voters showed up for assembly elections in some parishes, and observers claimed that in some cases only the election judges actually voted.[20]

In contrast, far smaller percentages of adults voted in eighteenth-century Britain, and far fewer elections were contested. The number of contested parliamentary seats declined precipitously in the eighteenth century until 1761, when fewer than 20 percent of the seats were contested, 10 percent in rural areas and 20 percent in urban ones. In Britain most seats were controlled by patronage, something uncommon in the mainland colonies. A markedly different pattern characterized colonial Virginia politics through most of the eighteenth century. Less than a third of Virginia's Burgess districts were noncompetitive, and these ranged geographically from old settled counties like the Isle of Wight to far western districts like Pittsylvania and Hampshire. Elsewhere, candidates competed vigorously in at least a third of the Burgess districts, also spread throughout the colony, and competed modestly in another third. Certainly political competition in Virginia was episodic, if not necessarily cyclical, and rose and fell without explanation. But Virginia politics never settled into the pattern of stasis and overweening patronage common in eighteenth-century British parliamentary elections.[21]

Vigorous election contests did not necessarily increase colonial turnout, however. One contest in North Providence, Rhode Island, drew 82.8 percent of eligible men, and some of New York's bitter and partisan elections sent the ratio of eligible men voting up over 50 percent. But hard-fought contests could draw surprisingly few voters. For example, sharp gubernatorial contests in Rhode Island between 1758 and 1767 drew only 45–48 percent of eligible men, then fell to 32–34 percent of eligible men in 1768 and 1770, figures substantially lower than election turnouts in either Jacksonian society or late-twentieth-century America. In Connecticut, 23 percent of eligible voters turned out when Jonathan Law ran unopposed for governor in 1748, but when Thomas Fitch opposed Roger Wolcott in 1755, turnout declined to 20.5 percent. However widely available, voting was an innovation that many eligible men used reluctantly, an anomaly in a society so otherwise aggressive and demanding.[22]

Peculiarities in seeking office and voter solicitation suggest that the period between 1680 and 1770 represented a transition from an early modern hierarchical and quasi-deferential society to a more open, ultimately democratic nation. Sometimes, even officeholders found politics awkward. In 1754 Maryland governor Horatio Sharpe complained that he could not win friends in the assembly because "few Gentlemen will submit so frequently to the inconveniences that such a canvass for Seats in that House must necessarily subject themselves to." In Connecticut, which elected its governors, Gurdon Saltonstall and Jonathan Law ran unopposed in 1723 and 1748, although from two to five candidates contested the seat in other years. "Campaigning" in such a relatively intimate, face-to-face society usually was intensely personal, if it occurred at all. Few candidates gave speeches or made public appearances. Most talked to voters individually and asked for support personally and sometimes only indirectly. As a result, "electioneering" implicitly stressed a candidate's personal standing and prestige and only sometimes bore on issues or ideology. The *New York Gazette* summarized the process in 1761: "A Squeeze of the Hand of a great man, a few well timed compliments . . . a little facetious Chat in a strain of Freedom and Equality, have been sufficient to win the Heart of many a voter."[23]

One election practice, "treating," became increasingly common as the colonies expanded after 1700 and stood awkwardly between traditional and modern politics. Treating was a minor potlatch that evidenced gracious humility before voters. The object was not so much to purchase votes as to seal relationships. It allowed well-off candidates a pleasant way to approach modest voters in a face-to-face society. Called "swilling the planters with bumbo" in Virginia, treating involving buying wine, beer, and food for voters on election day. In 1758 George Washington spent £39 during his first election on 160 gallons of liquor, "28 gallons of rum, 50 gallons of rum punch, 34 gallons of wine, 46 gallons of beer, and 2 gallons of cider royal." Nor was treating merely a southern custom. Candidates in a 1728 assembly contest in Philadelphia provided 4,500 gallons of beer for voters. Colonial "treating" strongly paralleled English practices, likely won few votes, yet also reinforced participation.[24]

Open bribery appears to have been rare in America and probably not as common as in eighteenth-century England, where its frequency was exaggerated. When Peter DeLancey defeated Lewis Morris for a New York assembly seat in Westchester County in 1752, Morris complained that DeLancey used "threatenings & bribery . . . barefacedly." Yet Morris quickly entered another race rather than pursuing his claim, and little evidence suggests that bribery regularly compromised colonial elections. In Britain, bribery was much more publicized but most likely localized rather than widespread. In Hull, voters expected and got 2 guineas when they voted, and in Bristol candidates often spent £10,000 on elections, some of it on bribery. Yet bribery affected only a few eighteenth-century British elections and was not nearly as common as some claimed, then or later.[25]

Strongly argued issues sometimes drove provincial-level politics in the eighteenth-century colonies and produced party-like interest groups active in colonial elections. Economic discord stimulated the most obvious examples. Financial difficulties among small merchants and farmers often influenced local and provincial elections in eighteenth-century

Massachusetts. Debates over paper money and the development of a "land bank" created powerful interest groups and in Boston gave rise to a "popular" party that contested and won many local and provincial elections in the 1720s and 1730s. New York factions sometimes appealed openly for votes to artisans, small merchants, and laborers based on occupational and economic issues in municipal and assembly elections.[26]

Religion sometimes affected colonial elections and provides interesting comparisons to British election patterns. In the mainland colonies, religion carried episodic importance in eighteenth-century contests. It appeared most commonly in anti-Anglican sentiment. Fears about Church of England legal establishments and alleged Anglican efforts to abridge religious freedom brought out voters in both New York and Virginia in the 1750s and 1760s. In Pennsylvania, proprietary leaders exploited Presbyterian and German resentment against dominant Quaker merchants and politicians to challenge the latter's grip on the colony's assembly, though to little avail. Yet these episodic instances of religious influence in colonial elections paled by comparison with the situation in Britain. There, sentiment for and against high-church Anglicanism and the Tory party as well as strong party identification by dissenting Quakers, Baptists, and later, Methodists (they constituted less than 10 percent of the British population but local concentrations increased their political clout) consistently affected elections throughout mid- and late-eighteenth-century Britain. The reason was simple. The Church of England was far more powerfully established in Britain than in America, and its sheer power there won it both intense support and intense opposition. In America, however, religious questions shifted from colony to colony and from decade to decade; few consistent religious themes in politics appeared, and in many places and decades—but not all—religious beliefs were not important in colonial elections.[27]

What distinguished colonial politics after 1680, however, was the organization of loosely gathered, reasonably persistent political interest groups in several colonies. These groups were provincial, not "national" or transatlantic. Sometimes they took ideological leads from British groups, particularly Britain's Whigs, who opposed Anglican supremacy and held high political office throughout most of the eighteenth century until the reign of George III. Yet even as late as the 1760s colonial political groups remained provincial in character and operation and seldom cultivated relationships with similar groups in other colonies. As anti-British rhetoric, sentiment, and action accelerated after 1763, other interests, not the putative colonial "parties," took the lead in coordinating antiparliamentary resistance.[28]

The idiosyncratic political histories of Pennsylvania and New York demonstrated how different circumstances nonetheless produced political "systems" closer to modern politics than might have seemed possible. Through the 1730s, provincial politics in Pennsylvania flourished largely through personal connections and relationships. After bitter divisions between William Penn and major Quaker merchants and a tumultuous Quaker schism in the 1690s, David Lloyd increased the assembly's effective power in the late 1690s and early 1700s by manipulating his personal power as assembly speaker. In the next decades, mild-mannered governors, an often incapacitated Penn (he died in 1718), and arguments among Penn's heirs allowed the assembly its way on much legislation well into the 1730s and slowly increased the assembly's power beyond anything specified in the colony's charter.[29]

Pennsylvania's famous "Quaker party" emerged in the provincial election of 1739 when a group of "stiff Quakers," wanting to choose "none but people of that perswasion," arranged a slate of assembly candidates for seats vacated by the antiproprietary speaker, Andrew Hamilton, who led forces opposed to the Penns, and several other supportive Quaker and non-Quaker assemblymen. Quakers and their supporters dominated the assembly for the next twenty years, holding 70 to 90 percent of assembly seats through the mid-1750s. Supporters of the Penns won only a few seats, although proprietary supporters also assembled "tickets" of favored candidates.[30] The Quaker party transformed Pennsylvania politics. It brought a substantial discipline to the assembly, fielding candidates, securing votes on important issues, and providing leadership in both partisan and policy matters. It identified antiproprietary sentiment with the "Quaker interest," a perhaps unexpected outcome since, as the colony's dominant religious group and social elite, Quakers might have been expected to align themselves with the Penn family. The Quaker party's partisanship aroused a sharp-tongued and often witty political literature in the colony's newspapers.

And like modern parties, the party recruited allies in other groups, especially among immigrant Germans. German-language pamphlets and broadsides urged immigrants to believe that their freedom and liberty of conscience in Pennsylvania stemmed from Quaker party vigilance, and at least one envious proprietary supporter claimed that German voting increased tenfold under Quaker party tutelage after 1740.[31]

Double crises in the 1750s demonstrated the Quaker party's resilience. Western settlers demanded that the Pennsylvania government take a more aggressive military stance against Indians as London authorities demanded troops and money for what would become the Seven Years' War with France. In addition, a spiritual and disciplinary crisis in the Quaker meetings induced Friends to tighten Quaker meeting discipline after 1750 and make a famous "withdrawal" from Pennsylvania politics in 1756, seemingly imploding the Quaker party and threatening to end more than twenty years of relative political stability. But at the last minute, less circumspect Quakers resurrected the party, made new alliances with Germans and Scottish Presbyterians, and compromised on the issue of "defensive warfare," much as their predecessors had done. They received substantial support from an opportunistic Benjamin Franklin, who backed military reinforcements on the Pennsylvania frontier, and they waged crafty campaigns in 1754 and 1756 to retain their majority in the assembly, one that the party, now perhaps more "secular" than before, retained into the revolutionary contest.[32]

The Quaker party's achievement was singular, however. Its competitor, the "Proprietary party," was a party in name only. It never achieved a real political identity, developed little internal cohesion, seldom succeeded with voters, especially among Pennsylvania's immigrants, and never won a majority in the Pennsylvania assembly. Still, however dependent on only one party, Pennsylvania's emerging eighteenth-century political system produced a cohesive politics in a potentially tumultuous colony and looked forward to the nineteenth century far more readily than it looked back to the seventeenth.

New York also developed a political "system," but of a different kind and in substantially different circumstances. Tension filled New York politics from the 1665 Dutch conquest forward. A short-lived government headed by Jacob Leisler, a disaffected anti-Catholic Protestant, came to power in 1689, then was overthrown with Leisler executed.

The governorships of Benjamin Fletcher (1692–1698) and Edward Hyde, Lord Cornbury (1702–1708), brought further turmoil to the colony. The antagonisms of New York politics could be seen in the charge made by Cornbury's enemies, possibly true but most likely false, that he wore women's clothes on his balcony on Sundays to irritate worshipers in the Dutch Reformed congregation.[33]

The accusation belied far more serious problems of corruption throughout New York politics. Governors like Fletcher and Cornbury diverted huge sums of revenue raised for the military to personal and political uses. A host of political appointees or "placemen," from the weighmaster of New York harbor to the colony's attorney general, inflated charges and took kickbacks. New York governors rewarded political cronies with large tracts of land into the 1730s, and members of the New York elite openly solicited land grants in exchange for political favors, the land sometimes granted outright and sometimes purchased at absurdly low prices. In the 1690s the Reverend Godfrey Dellius, Dutch missionary to Indians living in Albany, attempted to secure the entire Mohawk Valley as a personal possession even though he had already been granted a thousand square miles east and south of Lake Champlain. The land grants retarded immigration. New York's many manors and estates, whose lands were leased to tenants farming small plots, encouraged immigrants to settle elsewhere. As Richard Coote, Earl of Bellomont and New York governor between 1699 and 1701, put it, "What man will be such a fool as to become a base tenant to Mr. Delius, Colonel Schuyler, [and] Mr. Livingston . . . when for crossing Hudson's river that man can for a song purchase a good freehold in the Jersies."[34]

New York's great families competed intensely from the 1710s into the 1760s through hotly debated elections that might seem to have frustrated orderly politics. Family alliances among the Philipses, Morrises, Smiths, Alexanders, and DeLanceys shifted from decade to decade. In turn, the frequency of elections reinforced rancorous vote seeking and partisanship. Although the New York assembly won a Septennial Act in 1743 that required assembly elections every seven years, elections actually were held far more frequently down to the Revolution—in 1743, 1745, 1747, 1750, 1752, 1759, 1761, 1768, 1769 and 1775. And New York elections were usually tumultuous. Oliver DeLancey, the man who married Phila Franks in 1743, was well known for his attempts at voter intimidation and all but trumpeted the use of violence to win elections. Governor George Clinton remarked in 1752 that DeLancey won "his Elections by the Numbers . . . [he] horsewhipped."[35]

Yet the hostility of New York's many factions did not preclude some striking ideological and political alliances. In the 1720s and 1730s one faction that circled around Adolph Philipse and another that circled around Lewis Morris and James Alexander dominated assembly elections. In the 1750s and 1760s a faction dominated by James DeLancey and David Jones and another dominated by William Livingston and William Smith, Jr., won the loyalties of most voters. Both were accurately described as "Whig" factions, meaning that generally they adopted political strategies and rhetoric associated with the Whig opposition to England's eighteenth-century Tory party. This included attacks on cronyism, venality, and conspiracy within the reigning Tory government in England and the sitting governors in New York, a stress on opposition to tyranny, and criticism of divine right theories of government. These notions, summed up in the term "liberty," propelled a vague but explosive term into New York politics, with immense implications when both local and transatlantic British politics changed substantially after 1763. But long before that, and despite the seeming tumult and factionalism of New York politics, New Yorkers had come to find a certain order in the disciplined factionalism that characterized New York politics, groups united by their loyalties to various clusters of families and reflecting the persistent importance of personal connections in the advancing modern world.[36]

A few other colonies also produced political regimes that bore at least imperfect similarities to modern party systems. Factionalism and election skullduggery in South Carolina between 1690 and 1710 gave way to a period of rather unusual political harmony from the 1730s into the 1750s. Part of it derived from the European need for unity in a colony where after 1710 captured African slaves generally outnumbered whites 2 to 1 and in some rural counties outnumbered them 5 and 10 to 1. But part of it also stemmed from the sheer power of South Carolina's unusually wealthy planters, low voter turnout despite mild property qualifications for white men, broad commitment to general Whig values among planters, and striking personal harmony among planters whose resources could have taken politics in different directions, as New Yorkers' did.[37]

Massachusetts politics differed markedly from city to town. In Boston, "parties" more often represented discontented artisans and tradesmen. This was especially true as anger rose among the artisan and laboring classes when living costs outstripped wage increases, and war and unsteady markets pushed the economy into erratic ups and downs. Artisans joined and advanced antiparliamentary protest from 1760 forward, and several leaders, from James Otis to Samuel Adams, stressed the right of popular participation in politics and the importance of persistent pressure in town meetings and assembly elections.[38]

But in the towns, political leadership came largely from experienced members of the assembly. These men were not loyal to an election mechanism, as in New York or Pennsylvania. Rather, they were merchants and farmers who frequently resisted governors' demands for permanent revenues and prerogative powers and who upheld Whig principles yet could also shift their positions depending on the particular issue. These leaders may have behaved rather similarly to those in New York and Pennsylvania, but they never developed a "party" mechanism to draw them together. After 1763 disastrous British policies would do that effectively enough.[39]

THE lower assemblies became the most significant political institutions of the colonial era. The process began in Virginia, where the Virginia charter created an assembly that first met in 1619, the first representative body in the English New World experience. The early Virginia assemblies were far from what they would become after 1680. The representatives did not meet regularly until the 1630s. The House of Burgesses, the lower assembly of representatives elected from the burghs and hundreds, did not meet separately until the 1630s. Instead, it met with the Virginia Council, which was appointed by the governor, advised on policy, and heard appeals from lower court decisions. The Burgesses was not authorized as a separate institution by the Crown until either 1639 or 1641, the date not being clear. This process was not unique to Virginia. Most mainland colony legislatures did not divide into bicameral bodies until after 1680, Connecticut not until 1698.[40]

After 1680 the assemblies of the old seventeenth-century colonies—Virginia, Massachusetts, Maryland, Connecticut, and Rhode Island—and the newer colonies conquered or established after the 1660 Restoration—New York, North and South Carolina, Pennsylvania, and New Jersey—rapidly matured and expanded. Three developments accounted for the development of the assemblies as especially powerful political institutions. One was autocratic and involved the rise of the assembly speaker as a powerful post. Another was oligarchic and stemmed from the development of powerful coteries of assemblymen to dominate much assembly business. A third seems modern but was only modestly linked to the rise of modern democracy—seemingly irrepressible antagonisms with governors that generated heat, popular following, and broad discussions of political principle.

The quickly developing power of many colonial assembly speakers brought cohesion to the assemblies at the cost of raising the stature of a single individual, an exchange assemblymen seem to have made eagerly. The election of a speaker gave credence to the fear (from London, at least) that assemblies pretended to Parliament-like authority, or viewed themselves as "little parliaments." This occurred because disputes in England about the speaker of Parliament, especially the Crown's right to approve the speaker (a battle the Crown finally lost in 1679), stood at the center of England's bloody seventeenth-century politics and symbolized Parliament's independence. But in the 1680s and 1690s electing a speaker for a nascent colonial assembly did not so much dramatize the assembly's independence (it did so thirty years later), as it organized and focused infant institutions lacking substantial chartered authority and even the most rudimentary "tradition."[41]

If the office of speaker in a colonial assembly became an honor by mid-century, this was because early occupants of the position transformed it from a curiosity into a powerful post. Between 1680 and 1720 New York, Pennsylvania, Massachusetts, Virginia, and South Carolina assembly speakers not only represented the assemblies to governors but increasingly set assembly agendas and appointed assembly committees to develop bills. After 1680 a relatively small number of individuals—David Lloyd and Isaac Norris, Jr., of Pennsylvania, Adolph Philipse and David Jones of New York, Robert "King" Carter and John Robinson of Virginia, and William Bull II and Peter Manigault of South Carolina—managed assembly proceedings for more than a decade each. Most exercised an autocratic leadership that as often benefited them personally as it strengthened their assemblies' powers. Nonetheless, they dramatically increased the authority of the assemblies beyond anything that had ever before existed in the colonies and in the process transformed the institutions they headed.[42]

The oligarchical development occurred when assemblies used committee systems to manage specialized legislative concerns and placed relevant policy issues in the hands of a few assemblymen. Not all assemblies used these committees; New Jersey did not develop standing committees until 1771, for example. The committees produced specialized leadership and expertise about important legislative matters among long-serving members. The South Carolina assembly's standing committee on Indian affairs perfected superior intelligence about Indians and the Indian trade that shaped government policy for decades. The revenue committees of the New York and Massachusetts assemblies craftily resisted demands for permanent revenues for the governor while developing revenue schemes that usually, if not always, met colony expenses without aggravating voters. The Virginia Burgesses appointed its first committee in 1658 but greatly developed the system after 1680, when three committees met regularly: public claims, privileges and elections, and propositions and grievances. The Burgesses added committees on trade and courts after 1700, and a committee on religion in 1769, which handled problems with the Anglican establishment, clerical salaries, vestry prerogatives, and dissenter rights just as anti-British antagonism was expanding.[43]

In turn, leadership in the committees tended to come from the prestigious, wealthy men who were most frequently reelected. In South Carolina, assembly leadership lodged in the hands of men like Henry Laurens, Joseph Allston, Charles Pinckney, and John and Andrew Rutledge, all of whom acquired substantial wealth in the colony through adroit marriages, crafty speculation in land and goods, and, most important, slaveholding. In Massachusetts, assembly leaders like James Bowdoin came from gentry families of substantial but not always overwhelming wealth, had frequently graduated from Harvard, had often served as magistrates, and whose personal stature catapulted them to assembly leadership. Leaders in the Virginia Burgesses were usually far wealthier than their Massachusetts counterparts. Nonetheless, they worked their way up a seniority ladder within the Burgesses that required both substantial service as well as frequent reelection. Thus, if the path to leadership differed in the various assemblies, the compilation and display of wealth, education, and social prestige clearly brought political profits to those who succeeded in these acquisitive societies.[44]

One episode in Virginia illustrates the achievement of the eighteenth-century assemblies compared with their seventeenth-century predecessors, albeit in dubious fashion. The episode is the infamous financial scandal involving John Robinson, the powerful speaker of the Virginia Burgesses and colony treasurer. Robinson died in 1766 after serving for twenty-eight years as assembly speaker. Shortly after his death, auditors discovered that Robinson had surreptitiously lent thousands of pounds sterling of public money to some of Virginia's most prestigious politicians, presumably to win votes and favor among men who often acquired substantial personal debts in the eighteenth century. Robinson's bribery has never been proved, but the "Robinson affair" demonstrated just how far the Burgesses and its speaker had come since the late seventeenth century. In several contests with the Virginia governors in the 1690s, the Burgesses wrested the power to appoint the colony treasurer. Then, from the 1710s until John Robinson's death, the Burgesses regularly gave the treasurer's position to its speaker, who worked assiduously to increase the Burgesses' power, in part because it increased his own. The Robinson scandal broke that fusion of the speaker and colony treasurer. But it did not break the Burgesses' claim to name the treasurer, which it retained down to the Revolution.[45]

The weak development of the colonial councils demonstrated the growing power of the colonial assemblies. The councils aged but never matured. Unlike the assemblies, most councils became less powerful rather than more powerful between 1680 and 1760. Most but not all councils were appointed by the governors and contained about a dozen members, but despite their different origins and size, they all performed similar functions. They advised governors, usually served as each colony's appeals court, and functioned as the upper house in most legislative systems. Under the tutelage of able governors, some councils exercised substantial influence in colony affairs. Their members were among the wealthiest men in the colony, although others were often "placemen," political appointees who were personal favorites of the governor, less wealthy, and perhaps more easily won to a governor's side in a political milieu where friendship was a crucial political tool.[46]

But the councils did not always serve powerfully as upper houses of the legislature. In New York, Virginia, and South Carolina, assemblies wrested substantial power from the councils, particularly in money matters. The councils never developed effective committee systems, perhaps, in part, because they were so small. And they never developed effective individual leaders to compare or even compete with the assemblies' speakers. As a result, the councils' legislative authority stagnated while the assemblies increased their authority.

Ironically, perhaps, the councils' failure to mature may have stemmed from their membership. A colony's wealthiest and most prestigious men exercised so much power personally that they did not see the institution of a council as necessary to extending it, although they enjoyed the access to the governor it provided. In addition, the councils' size and ties to governors hindered their institutional development. Only after the Revolution and, in fact, largely after 1800, did the successors of the colonial councils, the U.S. Senate and the various state senates, come to possess the authority and power that the colonial councils might have wielded in the prerevolutionary period when, by many measures, they should have been unusually influential, if not triumphant.[47]

FINALLY, provincial politics also created a broad, vital avenue of discussion for public issues—a "public space" with distinct modern overtones quite different from the private, aristocratic politics that typified politics previously in both Europe and America—that was unusual for such otherwise modest New World colonies. In America, this stemmed from the presence of numerous printers, presses, and newspapers, the achievement of widespread literacy in the European population, and the presence of taverns throughout the colonies where political issues were hotly debated. At least one newspaper was available in Boston by 1704, Philadelphia by 1719, New York by 1725, and Charleston by 1732. By 1760 Philadelphia and New York had two newspapers, Boston had four, and Christopher Sauer had been publishing his German-language newspaper from Germantown in Pennsylvania since 1739. All printed political news, especially if it was combustible, which it frequently was in the overheated political climate many colonies developed.[48]

And colonists could read. Literacy in New England approached 70 percent among men and 45 percent among women by 1750, figures unparalleled in Europe. In the southern colonies literacy approached 50 to 60 percent among European men and 40 percent among European women. This literacy, together with the flourishing economy, accounted for the exceptional proliferation of newspapers in the British mainland colonies, more than there were in England. After all, the literacy rate for European men and women in America outdistanced Britain's, despite some important regional variations.[49]

The literature generated about taxes, religion, political dissent, and public policy turned eighteenth-century America into a raucous political hothouse. Many assemblies boosted the colonial economy through economic strategies that generated heated partisan debate. The New York assembly, for example, often approved monopolies and import tariffs to bolster local artisans such as coopers, sugar refiners, and lampblack makers. But the plans drew charges of favoritism and mismanagement, and by the 1720s printers furiously issued pamphlets and broadsides with titles like *The Interest of the Country in Laying Duties* and *The Interest of the City and Country to Lay No Duties,* followed by yet another optimistically entitled *The Two Interests Reconciled.*[50]

Virginia roiled through two boisterous controversies about money in the 1750s alone. The "pistole fee" controversy of 1752–1754 centered on the governor's right to collect a fee in the value of the Spanish pistole on all land grants when the Burgesses believed it had the right to set all fees. The Two-Penny Act of 1758 raised hackles because it set the rate of Anglican clergymen's salaries at 2 pence per pound of tobacco, although the shifting value of tobacco gave the ministers unjustified pay raises and cost taxpayers dearly. The disputes sparked scathing debates in the Virginia Burgesses, in pamphlets, and in the *Virginia Gazette.* Pamphlets entitled *The Colonel Dismounted or the Rector Vindicted, The Rector Detected,* and *A Review of the Rector Detected: or the Colonel Reconnoitred* employed wit and vitriol to attack and defend

Virginia's Anglican clergymen. And the vitriol extended beyond familiar political bounds. When the Anglican clergyman in Fredericksville, James Maury, sued to collect his salary in traditional tobacco rather than devalued cash, Patrick Henry defended the parish and lashed out in ways that would become strikingly familiar a decade later. Henry declared that any monarch who would so rebuff the Virginia assembly and force colonists to pay inflated clerical salaries surely "degenerates into a Tyrant, and forfeits all Right to his Subjects' Obedience." The sharp images Henry projected and the controversy they caused, including claims that Henry later exaggerated his criticism of the Crown, reflected a unique political style that easily mixed moralizing with bluntness. One eighteenth-century observer remarked that Henry succeeded in Virginia politics because

> his style . . . was vehement, without transporting him beyond the power of self-command . . . His figures of speech . . . were often borrowed from the Scriptures. The prototypes of others were the sublime scenes and objects of nature. . . . His lightning consisted in quick successive flashes, which rested only to alarm the more.[51]

Satire shared the colonial stage with vitriol and usually complemented it, a valuable commodity in face-to-face societies that enjoyed the exposure of individual foibles. The satire common to European and British politics quickly extended to the colonies. Governor Robert Hunter's *Androboros*, the first play published in British America, fitted its cast of fools, villains, and New York politicians with language and scenes so scatological, lewd, and rapacious that it has long embarrassed even modern readers. The "Dinwiddinæ" poems, written between 1754 and 1757, probably by a Stafford County attorney named John Mercer, humorously ridiculed Robert Dinwiddie, Virginia's lieutenant governor and originator of the "pistole fee," as a pretentious crook:

> You promis'd to relieve our woes,
> and with great kindness treat us.
> but whoof, Awaw! each Infant knows
> your whole design's to cheat us.[52]

Newspapers played crucial roles in advancing this biting political dialogue. By the 1730s political commentary regularly appeared in the colonial newspapers from Charleston to Boston next to the standard commercial notices and news cribbed from London papers. Most of this commentary followed Whig lines. Authors left little to the imagination, and criticism matched wit, usually at officeholders' expense. New York's *Independent Reflector,* published in 1752 and 1753 by William Livingston, John Morin Scott, and William Smith, Jr., advocated reforms ranging from medicine to religion. It took British Whig papers like the *Tatler* and the *Spectator* and especially Thomas Gordon's and John Trenchard's *The Independent Whig* as models. But politics, not medicine, was the lifeblood of the *Independent Reflector.* Issue after issue excoriated the sale of offices, corruption, and the public and private immorality of New York's venal public officials.[53]

This New World cacophony sometimes produced efforts at suppression, most often from colonial assemblies. Assemblies, sensitive to their rising power and authority, sought to protect public order and decorum, even if individual members and whole blocs benefited from the political agitation that the newspapers and pamphlets promoted. Quaker magistrates jailed the Philadelphia printer William Bradford in 1693 when he published work by the Quaker schismatic George Keith, and through the early 1720s the Massachusetts assembly attempted to control newspaper opinion by threatening editors. The assembly jailed James Franklin in 1723 to stifle his *New England Courant.* But when James gave control of the paper to his brother, Benjamin, and when the Boston grand jury refused to indict James for failing to publish under the supervision of the colony's secretary, the colonial government abandoned efforts at prior restraint in newspaper publishing. Yet in Massachusetts and elsewhere, colonial governments continued prosecuting printers for seditious libel down to the Revolution.[54]

The famous Zenger case, involving the prosecution of the New York printer Peter Zenger for seditious libel in August 1735, demonstrated the complexity of the mid-eighteenth-century debate about politics and press freedom. Like other editors, Zenger vigorously attacked the sitting colonial government and supported outsiders both out of commitment to Whig principles and in a desire to reap the profits of notoriety. Sick of the attacks, Lieutenant Governor James DeLancey oversaw Zenger's arraignment on seditious libel charges and disbarred Zenger's attorney, only to face the Pennsylvania assembly leader, Andrew Hamilton, as Zenger's defender.

Hamilton, knowing that the jury contained Zenger supporters, challenged it to defy the law. He argued that the truth could not be libelous even though colonial and English law said otherwise: "Moses, meek as he was, libeled Cain; and who is it that has not libeled the Devil?" Hamilton also raised the importance of Zenger's prosecution: "It may in its Consequence, affect every Freeman that lives under a British Government on the main of America." The jury thoroughly rebuked the government. As Zenger described it, "They answered . . . Not Guilty, Upon which there were three Huzzas in the Hall, which was crowded with People and the next Day I was discharged from my Imprisonment."[55]

Yet the victory had only momentary significance. Even Whiggish politicians did not support modern freedom of the press. When William Smith wrote on "the Use, Abuse, and Liberty of the Press" for New York's *Independent Reflector* in 1753, he backed printers in publishing the truth and "what is conducive of general Utility, . . . be the Author a Christian, Jew, Turk, or Infidel." But Smith also called "the Publication of any Thing injurious to his Country" a "criminal" act and "high Treason against the State." He cautioned, "The usual Alarm rung in such cases, the common cry of an Attack upon the LIBERTY OF THE PRESS, is groundless and trifling. The Press neither has, nor can have such a Liberty, and whenever it is assumed, the Printer should be punished."[56]

T HE *Independent Reflector's* protective Whiggish view of the public reflected a special colonial application of distinctive British Whig political thought. These notions took root in a collective view of society. Whig political ideology on both sides of the Atlantic asserted that the public welfare properly derived from a people viewed as homogeneous whose best interests were rightly treated as one. That such a view could be maintained in mid-eighteenth-century Britain was not surprising, even if Britain itself was a complex nation incorporating not merely England but Wales and Scotland.

But advocating Whig political ideology, with its emphasis on a collective homogeneous public good, in the eighteenth-century British mainland colonies bordered on the self-contradictory. New York itself exhibited an ethnic and religious heterogeneity that was not unusual in eighteenth-century America and that defied any common social analysis. In this regard, the circumstances in which colonial American writers applied Whig thought constituted its major political creativity. Through the 1760s, their thought remained quite conventional and derived largely from British sources, especially the writings of Thomas Gordon and John Trenchard. To insist on finding a common public good in a society so diverse, with so many immigrants, so many regional differences, so many differences even within a single colony, at least outside New England, became a major, if short-lived, achievement.[57]

Whig rhetoric applied in America had important religious and secular origins. Certainly it reflected adherence to a kind of generic Protestantism and even to a Protestant ethos in which life's occurrences were weighed against an absolute standard, as when Luther and Calvin weighed Catholic teaching against a "true" interpretation of the Bible. But Whig rhetoric also stressed freedom and liberty. English Whigs bitterly attacked Anglican authoritarianism and ecclesiastical tyranny in eighteenth-century England. They pointed out that the Anglican slogan "No Bishop, No King" had "formerly filled our Prisons with Dissenters, and chased many of them to America."[58]

Yet much Whig rhetoric also lodged in decidedly secular views about virtue, disinterestedness, and freedom that existed quite independently of specifically religious or theological doctrine. Many authors, including those who wrote for New York's *Independent Reflector,* did not emphasize distinctly Christian or Protestant views but appealed openly to historical example, reason, and ethical standards applicable to humanity generally that were characteristic of the secular eighteenth-century Enlightenment. These writers were not antireligious, as some of the more extreme European Enlightenment thinkers would be. But their vantage point meant that the mid-eighteenth-century colonial discussion of the public good extended far beyond organized religion.[59]

EVERY modern discussion of Britain's eighteenth-century empire is fatefully tagged by the British loss of the American war for independence. This inflection is not unwarranted. Poor planning and incompetence played a leading role in losing the American struggle. The British politicians who underestimated American military strength after 1776 similarly underestimated colonial anger and resentment for a dozen years earlier as London planners attempted to restructure the empire after the Seven Years' War ended in 1763. It is not a record that casts a noble light back over the previous ninety years.

Yet examining the history of the empire and the place of imperial politics in the mainland colonies before 1770 might also suggest a different perspective. Little or nothing in imperial politics before 1763 necessitated the dismal British performance in the political struggles over parliamentary sovereignty between 1763 and 1774 or the loss of the Revolutionary War. This did not mean that the British empire was not troubled before 1763 or that its troubles were minor. The empire had emerged without substantial planning in the seventeenth century, and its commercial success after 1680 demanded fine tuning at the least and, more likely, major overhaul. Most important, the empire exhibited no signs of imminent collapse between 1680 and at least 1760, whatever the complaints directed against it.[60]

Sometimes the empire almost begged criticism. In the 1760s many American colonists were upset because they resented the purposes, conduct, and even results of all the imperial wars, most recently the Seven Years' War, whose victory meant incorporating Catholic French Canadians inside the empire. But these complaints represented routine objections in a political milieu where internal tensions were customary, not unusual. In a nation where King Charles I had been beheaded in 1649 and James II had been exiled in 1688, far more drastic plans for political change could have been put forward between 1680 and 1760 than American colonists ever suggested.

Of course, in theory an empire had existed since the early seventeenth century. The first Act of Trade and Navigation of 1660 reflected late-sixteenth-century convictions that the colonies should provide agricultural produce and raw materials to reduce England's dependence on foreign goods. In turn, the colonies would exercise enough government to manage local affairs but not enough to become masters of their own fates, certainly not at Britain's expense. Not until 1675 did a board exist to advise on colonial affairs—the Lords of Trade—and it was a subcommittee of the king's Privy Council whose secretaries compiled information on the colonies but possessed no enforcement mechanisms or officers. This meant that through the 1680s the empire was best described as an idea honored casually rather than as an institution distinguished by carefully drawn policies, impressive institutions, and powerful officials.[61]

The apparatus of the modern British empire first emerged in the 1690s, in response to the obvious expansion of the mainland colonies begun in the 1680s with the settlement of Pennsylvania and the Carolinas and the earlier acquisition of Dutch New Netherlands. In 1696 the British created the Board of Trade to replace the old Lords of Trade. The board retained the secretariat of the old Lords of Trade. But the new board was a specialized body no longer connected to the prestigious Privy Council, where colonial affairs had been lost amid a stress on domestic politics and European affairs. The board concentrated entirely on the American colonies, investigated what it wanted to investigate, and down to the Revolution made specific recommendations for changes in law and colonial administration to tighten and refine the empire. Parliament also passed a new Act of Trade in 1696 that regularized the colonial customs service headquartered in London and created colonial admiralty courts in the colonies to enforce the navigation laws. These, in turn, initiated a long, often episodic series of administrative appointments ranging from customs inspectors to admiralty court judges and navigation law inspectors, whose presence made the empire far more visible in the mainland colonies after 1700 than had ever been the case before.[62]

To most colonists, the eighteenth-century empire meant four things: wars and governors, plus placemen in the colonies and colonial agents in London. The wars came in two forms: imperial and Indian. Between 1680 and 1763 the British fought four major wars growing out of European politics, each involving the American mainland colonies. King William's War between England and France (1689–1697), also called the War of the League of Augsburg, led to British attacks on Newfoundland and the French destruction of Schenectady. Under Sir William Phips, Massachusetts militia captured Port Royal but failed to capture Quebec. Queen Anne's War between England and France (1702–1713) led to the Indian destruction of Deerfield, Massachusetts, another English victory at Port Royal (given back to France after King

William's War), and failed British attacks against Quebec in Canada and St. Augustine in Florida.

In King George's War with Spain and France (1744–1748), the British met defeat at Cartagena in the Caribbean (from which the Spanish treasure fleet sailed) but defeated the French at the heavily defended fortress at Louisbourg in Canada in 1745 (although the British returned Louisbourg to the French when the war ended). The Seven Years' War between Britain and France from 1756 to 1763, also known as the French and Indian War, produced early British defeats. At Fort Duquesne in western Pennsylvania the French killed Major General Edward Braddock and shot two horses from under George Washington, and in New York the British lost both Fort Oswego and Fort William Henry (famously described in James Fenimore Cooper's novel of 1826, *The Last of the Mohicans*). But in 1758 the French lost Fort Duquesne and Louisbourg (again), and in 1760 the British general James Wolfe finally captured Quebec for the British. The great British siege at Quebec cost the lives of Wolfe, the French commander, the Marquis de Montcalm, and hundreds of colonial soldiers but won for Britain most of France's North American territory, excluding St. Pierre and Miquelon, which remained and still are French possessions.[63]

Colonists found much terror and frustration in Britain's imperial wars. The British and colonial victories were notable, particularly the capture of Louisbourg in 1745, which was accomplished with 4,000 New England troops and widely celebrated in the colonies. Hence the colonists' bitterness when Britain returned Louisbourg to the French at the end of the war, just as it had earlier returned Port Royal after Queen Anne's War. For what had colonists sacrificed their lives? The colonial losses were major. Of the 3,000 colonial troops who fought Spain in the battle at Cartagena in the Caribbean, 2,400 were killed or died from disease and malnutrition. Braddock's defeat in 1755 at Fort Duquesne in 1758 killed and wounded 900 colonial soldiers. More than 5,000 colonial soldiers were wounded or killed in the Seven Years' War. Tragic under any circumstances, the deaths, injuries, and disruptions upended colonial life. The death and injury of so many young men meant less labor for farm families. Widows were forced to search for new husbands, to depend on extended families for support, or to manage for themselves on farms or in small shops. Exports and imports declined, often drastically, and sometimes produced both food shortages and rampant unemployment in the colonial cities.[64]

Colonists also customarily traced Indian attacks to failed British imperial policy. Some difficulties with Indians surely bore local causes. The Yamasee War in South Carolina in 1715 likely stemmed more from tensions between local settlers and Indians than from imperial policies. Especially after 1740, moreover, British colonial authorities often tried to corral colonists' push into western territory occupied by Indians. Yet the very existence of the colonies, the massive population growth after 1680, the drive for greater exports, including the fur trade that depended on Indians, and the continual British-French hostility, in which Indians were used as pawns, all indelibly linked Indian tensions to the empire.[65]

The loss of life at Indian hands engendered a fateful anger and belligerence in colonists. The 1704 Indian attack on Deerfield, Massachusetts, during Queen Anne's War cost 44 settlers their lives—9 men, 10 women, and 25 children—and sent 109 settlers into Canada as captives. These included seven-year-old Eunice Williams, daughter of Rev. John Williams, who remained with her captives and married an Indian, a fate that terrified colonists. Colonists died in Indian attacks in the other imperial wars, especially the Seven Years' War, and in local encounters like the Tuscarora and the Yamasee wars in North and South Carolina between 1712 and 1715. New Indian attacks in western Pennsylvania in May 1763 stemming from continuing Indian-European antagonism and further western settlement encouraged local settlers, forming the group called the "Paxton Boys," to retaliate, killing Indians at the village of Conestoga and murdering and scalping those in the jail in Lancaster. But they then marched on Philadelphia, meeting Benjamin Franklin and the Quakers who controlled the Pennsylvania assembly, to demand greater "protection" from the western Pennsylvania Indians. In short, both the Indian wars and their imperial cousins produced highly ambivalent views of the empire's benefits and costs among colonists.[66]

The governors were the most visible and most important colonial officials. They also drew the worst reputations. These reputations derived in part from their roles in opposing anti-British colonial protest after 1763. Unlike most governors, who came from Britain, revolutionary-era Massachusetts governor Thomas Hutchinson was a fourth-

generation Puritan who graduated from Harvard and made a distinguished name for himself in provincial politics before being named governor in 1771. But Hutchinson ruined his reputation forever, and that
of other governors, by publicly supporting British policy with a passion
and completeness that seemed to belie his colonial origins—not merely
a Tory but an apostate. That he lobbied privately against the Stamp Act,
for example, never redeemed him.[67]

Hutchinson was neither mediocre nor incompetent, yet many colonial governors were. New York's experience may have been worse than
others, but not much worse. The colony endured thoroughly uneven or
lackluster governors with Lord Bellomont (1698–1702), John
Montgomerie (1728–1731), William Cosby (1732–1736), George
Clark (1736–1743), and George Clinton (1743–1753). Several New
York governors proved thoroughly venal. Benjamin Fletcher (1692–
1697) and Edward Hyde, Lord Cornbury (1702–1708), took bribes
from almost anyone who would give them and sold or gave thousands
of acres to cronies. What the eighteenth-century New York historian,
William Smith, Jr., wrote of Cornbury sufficed for both men: "His
excessive avarice, his embezzlement of the publick money, and his sor-
did refusal to pay his private debts, bore so heavily upon his reputation,
that it was impossible for his adherents, either to support him, or themselves, against the general opposition."[68]

Yet after 1700 the colony also knew thoroughly competent, even
imaginative governors who pursued reasonably amicable relations with
the New York assembly, administered fairly, and bolstered New York's
place in the empire. Robert Hunter (1709–1719) stressed defense
against Indians and worked assiduously to better relations with the
assembly, especially on issues of the governor's power. William Burnet
(1720–1728), son of England's famous Anglican bishop Gilbert Burnet,
also concentrated on Indian affairs, and although his contests with the
colony's great merchants produced substantial tension, even contemporaries regarded him as a successful and able governor. And if Cadwal-
lader Colden, lieutenant governor from 1741 until his death in 1776 as
well as surveyor-general from 1720 forward, was vain and difficult, he
also was regarded as a brilliant intellectual whose vision of New York
included an extraordinary knowledge of Indians and Indian affairs,
about which he wrote at considerable length. Differences between cen-

turies aside, it is not at all clear that the record of New York's appointed eighteenth-century governors was substantially different from the record of governors elected in the nineteenth century.[69]

Eighteenth-century colonial governors found their personal strengths and weaknesses fully tested by institutional difficulties. On the one hand, governors arriving in America after 1700 appeared to hold immense power. Unlike the English Crown after 1707, legislation passed by the assemblies and councils could be vetoed by the governors or, usually following the governors' private recommendations, could be disallowed by the Privy Council in England. Governors could prorogue or dismiss the assemblies virtually at will, which the Crown could not do with Parliament. Governors could dismiss judges and magistrates in America, although British judges enjoyed lifetime tenure after 1701. Governors could also create courts, such as chancery courts that heard land cases without juries and were especially resented. In a few colonies governors could appoint Anglican ministers where the Church of England was established, and could set a wide range of government fees. Finally, governors possessed substantial patronage power that included naming magistrates, justices of the peace, military officers, and members of the prestigious colonial councils, a power that was as important in the eighteenth-century colonies as it would be in nineteenth- and twentieth-century American cities and states.[70]

As the eighteenth century wore on, governors retained much of their legal authority. They did not surrender their right to create new courts, even though many governors approved assembly legislation authorizing other courts. In some colonies, they prorogued the assemblies regularly, so that elections ran on the governors' timetables. They also kept the right to dismiss judges and justices of the peace. Most important, most governors retained substantial patronage power. Men they appointed to paid offices all too often constituted the principal cadre of the king's defenders in the 1760s and 1770s, a pattern of dubious value as other colonists became increasingly aggressive about the evils of king and Parliament, then about independence.[71]

Yet even eighteenth-century observers noted that after 1700 many governors lost substantial authority and power. One postrevolutionary British writer, Anthony Stokes, argued without qualification that the patronage system all but died in eighteenth-century America. As a result, he believed, the Crown was doomed to failure: "The King and government of Great Britain held no patronage in the country, which could create attachment and influence sufficient to counteract that restless, arrogating spirit . . . [of] popular assemblies." If the writer wrongly—yet tellingly—assumed that loyalty gravitated exclusively around financial ties, ample evidence suggests that the governors' patronage eroded substantially, even if it never disappeared. The New Jersey and Maryland assemblies demanded that local officials reside in the counties they served, thus limiting their governors' flexibility in making appointments. Some colonies limited offices to strict terms, such as four years for a sheriff. New York paid judges year by year to keep them in tow. The South Carolina governor lost the power to name Anglican clergymen by 1708, and Virginia's governor lost the same power by 1718, each after confrontations with their assemblies. South Carolina prohibited colonists holding offices of profit from sitting in the assembly. And most assemblies, like Virginia's, effectively won the right to name the colony treasurer. Governor James Glen of South Carolina summarized a broad process when he listed the numerous powers grabbed by his own assembly over the years: "besides the Treasurer, they appoint the Comissary, the Indian Comissioner, the Comptroller, of the dutys imposed by Law upon Goods imported, the Powder Received, (etc.)."[72]

Not only did eighteenth-century governors gain little in return, they found themselves increasingly constricted by imperial demands, planning, and regulations. Certainly, the governors seldom gained the one item they and imperial officials in London most desperately wanted and were frequently instructed to obtain—a permanent salary for themselves and permanent funds for colony operation that did not have to be negotiated with the colonial assemblies in each assembly session. If an increasing number of administrative positions authorized by London, such as customs inspectors and tax collectors, added to the governors' patronage, the posts never compensated for patronage lost. Moreover, instructions from London sounded imposing when read on the way to America but proved hollow and hopelessly inflexible after arrival. Detailed instructions often crippled governors because they could lose their jobs when they violated them, something their colonial antagonists well knew.[73]

The fate of Sir Danvers Osborne, named New York governor in

1753, tragically revealed the gap between formal authority and political reality. Osborne, only recently widowed and seriously depressed, arrived in New York in October 1753 to considerable gaiety—"a splendid dinner," nighttime illumination of the city, cannons, "and two bonfires lighted up on the common." But Osborne quickly received a rude introduction to assembly power. When he informed assembly leaders that his instructions enjoined "permanent indefinite support of government," meaning a permanent salary for the governor and budget for the colony government, he met a wall of opposition. "With a distressed countenance, and in a plaintive voice, he addressed Mr. [William] Smith," a prominent lawyer and member of the New York Council. Smith "had not yet spoke a word—'What, sir, is your opinion?'—and when [Osborne] heard a similar answer, he sighed, turned about, reclined against the window frame, and exclaimed, 'then what am I come here for?'" Osborne's housekeepers found him the next morning, "hanging dead against the fence at the lower end of the garden."[74]

Placemen included the increasing number of appointed judges and inspectors named after 1690 to administer imperial regulations in the colonies. These officials clearly served the empire, not individual colonies. They included Navigation Act officials, port inspectors, tree inspectors (the Navigation Acts demanded that large timbers be saved for ship construction), admiralty court judges, and surveyors. Governors also appointed justices of the peace, sheriffs, and militia commanders, as well as the infamous stamp collectors of the 1760s, who imagined that their commissions were yet more plums to be picked from the growing tree of colonial preferments.[75]

Colonists often frustrated these royal appointees. Navigation law inspectors frequently found themselves overwhelmed and undermanned. The colonial ports contained too many ships to inspect, and intrigue among captains and crews made the inspectors' jobs difficult to perform. Local residents outfoxed naval stores inspectors. Timbers reserved for large masts were sometimes sawed into shorter lengths for quicker profit, the evidence thus neatly disappearing. Local magistrates sympathetic to local millmen shifted trial venues to distant locations to frustrate their prosecution. One magistrate demanded "ocular" evidence—testimony from witnesses who had seen the alleged timber cutting—before he would convict anyone prosecuted by Crown officials; illegal timbers found on the accused's property did not constitute proof of the cutting. From the 1690s into the 1770s, colonists used conflicting provincial and English case law and artful delaying tactics to frustrate the admiralty courts to escape convictions.[76]

Yet patronage and the growing imperial bureaucracy also produced results. Skillful governors like Massachusetts's Jonathan Belcher used patronage to influence provincial politics in the 1730s. If the colony's political system was too extensive to control fully with a governor's patronage—too many offices and too many officeholders—patronage gave governors crucial influence they otherwise lacked. Belcher, for example, sometimes offered two positions to a single person to strengthen imperial ties. He placed the leader of the so-called popular party, Elisha Cooke, on the Suffolk County Court of Common Pleas to dent Cooke's antiproprietary instincts. Governors in most other colonies did likewise if the law allowed and if they were as clever as Belcher. Although colonists sometimes complained, many were eager to accept preferments when they came their way. And come their way they did in a world where day-to-day politics usually hinged on personal connections as well as parties and ideology, connections endemic in nineteenth- and twentieth-century politics as well.[77]

The growing numbers of imperial officials exercised a reasonable authority throughout the colonies from the 1690s into the 1760s, much postrevolutionary rhetoric to the contrary. The work of customs inspectors proceeded apace even if colonial merchants and visiting ship captains sought to avoid them. Naval stores inspectors regularly marked goods for the naval stores trade and helped stimulate that trade through their efforts. For sixty years the admiralty courts exercised jurisdiction over naval and imperial affairs. Most cases proceeded without controversy, and between 1702 and 1763 a third were "prize cases" involving the disposition of enemy ships and goods seized during the many eighteenth-century wars. From the 1690s well into the 1760s many merchants preferred to have cases tried in admiralty courts because their relatively simple procedures were especially suited to maritime affairs; proceedings in colonial common law courts could be protracted and hence costly.[78]

Finally, after 1680 colonial assemblies, merchants, and religious groups used agents to represent their own interests in London. Colonial assemblies regularly hired agents to lobby with Parliament or the Board of Trade on general issues or specific interests or to speed legal disputes. Quakers, Presbyterians, Baptists, and Huguenots all used London contacts to represent their American interests in the seat of the empire. Farmers, especially southern planters, hired agents or worked through British merchants to represent their interests, often doing their business in London coffee houses. The resort to agents revealed how widely colonists believed they had a place in the empire, a valuable place that needed asserting and protecting. The agents revealed the empire's utter centrality in colonial life and served as a principal avenue for articulating colonial sentiment at its hub.[79]

YET despite the remarkable success of Britain's eighteenth-century empire, feelings of unease typified almost everyone's thoughts about the imperial transatlantic relationship between 1680 and 1760, even before the great contests of the 1760s and 1770s emerged full force. This was true of both British officials and European colonists in America. "Metropolitans" in London associated with the Board of Trade long worried about the empire as a smoothly functioning contrivance. The discomfort began in the 1690s. Figures like Edward Randolph, collector of customs for New England, William Blathwayt, a canny administrator with the Board of Trade in London, and Francis Nicholson, sometime governor of Virginia and Maryland, all represented the "new" empire created in the 1690s. They called for making governors and imperial officials more powerful and restricting the assemblies, even when the assemblies were still relatively weak and governors were still quite powerful. In 1701 the Board of Trade unsuccessfully proposed abolishing the private colonies of Massachusetts, New Hampshire, Rhode Island, Connecticut, East and West New Jersey, Pennsylvania, Maryland, and North and South Carolina, largely to streamline the empire. And after considerable frustration, the Board of Trade began implementing serious reform in the late 1740s, restricting the iron industry because it competed with the industry in Britain, curtailing colonial currency that often depreciated in value, and further tightening the Navigation Acts.[80]

Complaints about deficiencies in the empire and connections to Britain also moved colonists. French threats to the colonies in the early

1750s prompted the Board of Trade to ask the mainland colonies to "enter into articles of union and confederation with each other for the mutual defence of His Majesty's subjects and interests in North America, as well in time of peace as war," and to call a conference in Albany in 1754. Benjamin Franklin, ever tinkering, printed a cartoon in the *Pennsylvania Gazette,* "Join, or Die," whose sectioned snake bespoke the empire's fractures and the colonies' piecemeal responses to French challenges on the western frontiers. More important, in 1751 Franklin had proposed creating a council of representatives, one from each colony, to manage Indian affairs and colonial defense and whose meetings would rotate from colony to colony so "they might thereby become better acquainted with the circumstances, interests, strength, or weaknesses, &c., of all." Passed by the colonial representatives in Albany in 1754, the proposal failed to win approval in a single assembly. All that lingered from Franklin's proposal was his famous cartoon, which colonists resuscitated after 1774 to serve as a warning about their own need for unity, now against Britain.[81]

Some British officials understood the complexity and tension rampant throughout the eighteenth-century empire. Thomas Pownall, former governor of Massachusetts, was one. Pownall's *Administration of the Colonies,* published in 1764, went through five editions in the next two decades and later was widely regarded as an almost prophetic analysis. Pownall believed that a new, more forceful, administrative structure should be created in London, a secretariat of colonial affairs to handle all colonial matters, including defense, Indians, trade, and government. He proposed curtailing assembly power and strengthening the power and authority of governors. He proposed creating appeals courts to correct provincial judges and juries. He proposed tightening the use of paper money, which the 1751 Currency Act had not sufficiently curtailed. And he proposed broadening foreign trade by establishing "British markets even in other countries" to which colonists could ship goods without violating the Navigation Acts.[82]

Pownall also pressed metropolitan planners in London to understand the remarkable strength of the eighteenth-century empire, especially the British mainland colonies. His circuit court judges, for example, were not merely to be imported from Britain but men "learned in the law, not only of the mother country, but of the several governments in its said district," meaning the colonies. Colonists were not unskilled, unsophisticated, unlearned, or unpatriotic. They were, rather, "our own people, our brethren, faithful, good and beneficial subjects, and free-born Englishmen, or by adoption, possessing all the right of freedom."[83]

Y ET it was war and the ubiquitous experience of war, not elaborate schemes hatched by observant, well-meaning former governors, that decided much about both the fate of the empire and the future of American politics. Colonists' experiences of the colonial wars, but especially the Seven Years' War with France between 1756 and 1763, produced a quiet but decidedly negative view of the empire and the nation that managed it. In the Seven Years' War colonists from South Carolina to New Hampshire found themselves involved in military action against the French and their Indian allies. All the colonies were asked to provide troops, which they did unevenly and with more than a little bitterness. Some colonists demanded more support from Britain itself, arguing that American colonists lacked the resources that the empire possessed to fight such a major action. Other colonists, especially in Virginia, Pennsylvania, New York, and New England, volunteered to fight, and several thousand lost their lives, with many others wounded and permanently affected by their experience of the war.

Colonists agonized in the early defeats of the war—the defeat and death of Major General Edward Braddock at Fort Duquesne in July 1755, the failures of Massachusetts governor William Shirley at Fort Niagara, the defeat of New York governor William Johnson at Crown Point, and the loss of Fort Oswego in 1756. They rejoiced in the victories in Nova Scotia in 1755 and especially in the great and stunning victory at Montreal in 1760 that suddenly ended French rule in Canada and doubled the size of Britain's North American possessions. Soldiers created mementos of the war. One carved an elaborate powder horn, inscribing onto it the major sites of battles in New York, a sign that fighting in the Seven Years' War demanded commemoration.[84]

Yet the Seven Years' War and its aftermath also introduced substantial tensions into colonial views about empire and about the colonists' relationship to Britain. Colonists questioned British motives more vigorously and wondered if something more than the Atlantic did not

Powder horn depicting New York battle sites in the Seven Years' War, made by Samuel Davison for Samuel Hubbs, May 27, 1765.

separate Britons and Americans. This happened in part because the Seven Years' War brought such a large contingent of British troops into intimate contact with colonists. Almost 25,000 British troops descended upon the colonies, and many colonists found them not only different but disagreeable. British troops and Massachusetts militia members discovered that they kept different holidays. The British did not celebrate election day or Pope's Day, and the colonists did not celebrate the king's birthday or Saint George's Day. Colonists admired the courage of the British troops in battle but were shocked by their mercilessness. British officers regularly used physical coercion, including whipping, to enforce discipline in their own ranks, a practice colonial militia officers largely forswore. British troops often ridiculed militia members and seemed eager to pursue physical confrontations with the colonial militia. Finally, the New England militia members frequently expressed shock at the obscenity and ignorance of religion among British troops. Rev. John Cleaveland thought that "profain swearing seems to be the naturalized language of the regulars," who also seemed addicted to "Gaming, Robbery, Thieft, Whoring, [and] bad-company-keeping." Neither regular British troops nor even officers observed the Sabbath.[85]

The Seven Years' War brought a subtle shock of recognition to many colonists. On the one hand, the war quietly bound many colonists together in modest but telling ways. Militias from several provinces joined the British campaigns at Fort Duquesne, the New York frontier, and the great victory at Montreal. These soldiers shared a common experience of one another. The war did not unite them. But the experience of soldiering with other colonists did suggest that in the mainland colonies European settlers might be more alike than different despite regional contrasts and mismatched backgrounds. On the other hand, colonists also shared common experiences of the British, or at least of British soldiers, and far too many of these experiences cast the British and their soldiers in a poor light. It was only ironic, then, that achieving an imperial victory in the Seven Years' War quietly undermined the very relationship that the war had been designed to preserve.

It was unfortunate, certainly for the British, that colonists entered major political contests with Parliament and Crown in the mid-1760s with such a dualistic view of empire and politics. The experience of the Seven Years' War summarized all too well, and all too negatively, long-standing difficulties about war and peace that colonists regularly, if not always fairly, laid to the failures of British policy and even to the British character by the 1760s. Yet the possession of so many political tools aggressively honed in seven to nine decades of exceptional political development created remarkably autonomous provincial political environments in America. Certainly, all the colonies moved within the empire, economically and politically. Yet the political rhythms of each mainland province differed greatly from any of Britain's provinces, however much the American colonies might differ politically from one another. For many decades, these growing contrasts did not matter. Colonists complained about the empire and its officials for years without thinking of independence. They pursued provincial and local politics in America without turning incessantly, much less anxiously, to Britain for approval or disapproval. But as British planners and politicians made abrupt changes in the empire after 1763, the divergence between political perceptions and practices in Britain and the mainland colonies became fateful in ways late-seventeenth-century colonists and Britons never imagined. For ninety years after 1680, colonists driving for authority and power built political institutions and processes whose significance extended far beyond their provincial and often partisan origins, achievements and consequences British politicians comprehended even less fully than did colonists.

Four

THINGS MATERIAL

I often visit them and carefully examine their houses, their
modes of ingenuity, their different ways.

J. HECTOR ST. JOHN DE CRÈVECOEUR (1782)

JONATHAN EDWARDS needed a desk. Edwards, who became the most
important British theologian of the eighteenth century and one of the
world's great exponents of Calvinist thought, wrote prodigiously. In his
relatively short lifetime—1703 to 1758—he composed many acclaimed
books, including *The History of Redemption; The Freedom of the Will;
The Religious Affections; Charity and Its Fruits; Two Dissertations,
Concerning the End for Which God Created the World, and The Nature of True Virtue; Original Sin; The Life of David Brainerd; A History
of the Work of Redemption; Notes on the Apocalypse; An Humble
Attempt to Promote Explicit Agreement and Visible Union of God's
People in Extraordinary Prayer; Images of Divine Things and Types;*
more than one thousand sermons; many publications on revivalism;
scientific and philosophical writings; three volumes of interleaved anno-
tations in his King James Bible; hundreds of letters from a voluminous
correspondence; and nine manuscript volumes of "Miscellaneous Observations" into which Edwards poured an ongoing dialogue with
everything he read and thought.[1]

Edwards indeed needed storage space for his many manuscripts, plus
his pens, inks, blank paper, and books. Sometime between a stint as a
Yale tutor in 1724 and his move to Northampton, Massachusetts, in
1726, Edwards acquired a handsome, if modest, desk, most likely made
by a joiner in either New Haven or the upper Connecticut River valley.

Jonathan Edwards's "scrutore," or writing desk, with side cabinets and sliding-door box shelves. Makers unknown, probably between 1720 and 1750.

It was not long before Edwards or a woodworker constructed drawer dividers to fit precisely the duodecimo-, small octavo-, and quarto-sized papers that Edwards carefully trimmed from Flemish, Dutch, and English paper quires he proudly imported from Europe. As he wrote, Edwards slowly scraped a small hole in his desktop, no doubt with the pen knife he used to sharpen his quill points. The scar bespoke the quiet tension that came to someone who spent up to thirteen hours a day writing and who berated himself as a man hampered by "disagreeable dullness and stiffness, much unfitting me for conversation."[2]

Edwards also expanded his desk. At some unknown point he attached two cupboards for his mounting piles of manuscripts, one to each side. Perhaps after his arrival in Stockbridge, Massachusetts, in August 1751, where he ministered to Indians on a still dangerous frontier, he stacked three long, sliding-door bookcases above the desk and cupboards; these could double as book boxes if he had to move quickly. By now Edwards and his woodworkers had turned a small, handsome desk into a tinkerer's contraption that might have delighted Benjamin Franklin, if not a Philadelphia cabinetmaker. Yet whatever the loss in elegance, the desk, cupboards, and bookcases well served Edwards's pressing demand to shelter the extensive materials necessary to an intellectual life on the Massachusetts frontier.[3]

Jonathan Edwards's "scrutore" symbolized the modern complication of secular life in the British mainland colonies between 1680 and 1770. The increasingly diverse population, broadening and deepening economy, and vigorous, inventive politics affected secular life throughout the colonies, although never uniformly and with considerable regional, ethnic, and gender variation. Europeans who descended upon America searching for material prosperity, Africans forced to work for profits they seldom reaped, and American Indians who reshaped traditional cultures while moving farther west all found their secular and material worlds markedly changed between 1680 and 1770.

Some changes after 1680 seem contradictory. European colonists reached back across the Atlantic to import a rising tide of Old World objects—a process sometimes called "Europeanization" that brought British and European cloth, dishes, utensils, silverware, and furniture to America in record quantities—even as provincial American industries and crafts flourished at record rates, their goods obviously going to local American consumers. As slavery tightened, becoming more brittle and ever more authoritarian, Africans created a reasonably autonomous secular and material culture within its brutal confines. And American Indians reshaped their secular and material life in ways that predicted an apprehensive future. The results, unevenly realized, created subtle, complex new patterns of living that reshaped the material and secular meaning of "America" before political independence arrived.

THE colonists' material world began with what they ate, and for Europeans the principal transformation in food occurred in the seventeenth, not the eighteenth, century. From the 1610s forward and perhaps well into the twentieth century, diet improved when Europeans moved to America. The primary cause—a not uncontested matter among historians—probably centered on the availability of land in America, the relative ease with which Europeans obtained and worked it, and the bountiful crops it produced. In Europe, meat was relatively scarce, and nutrition came largely from "gruel," meaning grains cooked in liquids that were often thin and only modestly nutritious. By modern standards, the European diet between 1500 and 1800 lacked the proteins and vitamins essential to improved height, weight, and longevity.

In early America, new soils tilled by new property owners produced more nutritious, varied crops and diets. From Virginia to New England, settlers from the 1620s forward consumed meat far more regularly than did their compatriots at home and, because high yields meant that grains did not have to be stretched so far, ate more nutritious gruel. The result was dramatic and obvious by the time of the American Revolution: American soldiers were fully 3 to 3.5 inches taller than British Royal Marines and only a half-inch shorter than northern recruits in the Civil War a half century later. This American "exceptionalism" stemmed directly from dietary improvements that began at colonization and, for Europeans, continued throughout the colonial period.[4]

Some important exceptions aside, this seventeenth-century dietary improvement for Europeans continued in the eighteenth century. Maintaining the initial colonial pattern was not easy. The vast population increase in the mainland colonies after 1680 pressed domestic colonial agricultural production, and growing poverty among laborers and indentured servants, to say nothing of the persistent poverty among slaves, introduced thousands of workers with little ability to acquire the better colonial foodstuffs. Still, after 1680 most Europeans continued to eat better in New England, New York and Pennsylvania, the Chesapeake, and the Carolinas than most had been able to do in Europe. The diet also remained highly varied, with cattle, pigs, and wild animals providing meat, a wide variety of grains providing additional protein, and a truly astonishing variety of locally grown fruits, which added vitamins uncommon to many European diets. Apple orchards, for example, constituted one of the most common features of eighteenth-century agricultural estate inventories.[5]

Diets also changed for Europeans after 1680 in ways that did not necessarily affect the nutritional level. One change centered on the kind and source of meats. Perhaps first in the Chesapeake, then in the middle colonies, New England, and the Carolinas, the proportion of meat from domestic animal production increased while the proportion coming from hunted animals declined. After 1660, farmers everywhere aggressively pursued domestic livestock production and depended less and less on hunting as a source of meat. The eighteenth-century colonial farm was as often studded with animals being fattened for slaughter as it was laden with grains and other crops to be harvested and sold. Farmers kept animals in every possible way. Hogs and cattle frequently ran wild, hence the quick importance of "marking" or "branding." Some farmers penned animals for easier control, although pens spread disease more rapidly. The importance of domestic animal production stimulated surprising explanations for disaster. In 1745 all the horses and cattle owned by the Virginia Scottish Presbyterian minister, John Craig, sickened and died in pens where other neighbors' animals remained healthy. Half a century after the Salem witch trials, Craig worried that his neighbors' witchcraft caused the sickness, even if he consoled himself that perhaps the "Divel had higher Designe than to kill Brutes."[6]

Regional dietary variations created by women's inventiveness in the kitchens increased after 1680, and the resulting cuisines sometimes bore strong associations with religious or ethnic groups. New Englanders became well known for baking and for dishes such as beans and brown bread. Pennsylvania Quaker women boiled meats and developed a taste for creamed cheese and dry beef. Southerners more often roasted and fried meats, in part a result of their substantial domestic animal production, and showed a preference for fricassees. German women introduced sausage-making and cottage cheese.[7]

Slave diets resembled the diets of many poorer whites, but with less meat. In the lower South especially, slaves developed more unique cuisines as their numbers increased and as owners slowly allowed slaves to do their own cooking. Africans increasingly ate apart from their owners, and African women mixed African customs and African and American crops to produce distinctive dishes. Corn formed a staple almost everywhere in the slave diet, but Africans in South Carolina especially favored vegetables and African roots like the "tania" as well as African crops like millet and sorghum. In contrast, a recent archaeological excavation at Jefferson's Monticello of garbage from the postrevolutionary period suggests a higher rate of meat consumption among slaves than historians had previously encountered. Still, evidence of considerable irregularity in the slave diet abounds, and whatever the regional differences, by the Revolution the consequence of separate eating, different foods, and erratic supplies meant that the colonial slave diet, by comparison with the diet of Europeans in America, remained not merely different but also less nutritious.[8]

Indian diets apparently remained relatively consistent in the seventeenth and eighteenth centuries, although with more extensive archaeological study, this verdict may change. Most Indian groups consumed a starchy diet of corn, squash, and beans grown in gardens often but not exclusively tended by women, plus gathered nuts and berries. Men hunted and fished, but red meat and even fish made up relatively small portions of most Indian diets. For example, among the Iroquois soups cooked with corn and beans in large pots managed by both men and women typified the diet, supplemented by cornbreads. Meat and fish filled out the diet, but only occasionally. Catawbas in the Carolinas enjoyed a similar diet obtained through similar labor. Women managed much but not all agriculture throughout the spring, summer, and fall, men were responsible for hunting through the winter, and both cooperated throughout the year in collecting, processing, and cooking food.[9]

If Indians had healthy diets by modern standards, their principal eighteenth-century threat stemmed not from dietary change but from food shortages. Bad weather could severely restrict the diet, as was also true for Europeans. Droughts in the 1750s forced the Catawbas to seek corn from colonists, and the South Carolina government provided Catawbas 700 bushels of corn during the winter of 1755–56 and 900 bushels in the next year. The sicknesses that raged through Indian communities throughout the seventeenth and eighteenth centuries reduced care for crops and agricultural productivity at the very time when nourishment was most important, and alcohol abuse that also continued into the eighteenth century and beyond reduced labor that might have gone into agricultural production. The westward movement of many Indian groups, escalating land competition with Europeans as well as with other Indians, and diminished plantings restricted Indian agricultural productivity in the very times that growing economic interdependence with Europeans made life difficult and sometimes disastrous for Indians.[10]

The squeeze caused immense pain, and the pressure came from many directions. New York's Iroquois suffered numerous severe food shortages in the eighteenth century. They sometimes sold corn even when they were short of food, not only because they desired supplies, guns, and ammunition but also because they wanted rum. English and Dutch traders were only too eager to encourage Indian drinking before the exchanges were completed, because they could manipulate drunken Indians more easily than sober Indians. But even without the immense complication introduced by Indian drinking, the Iroquois had found that the question of nourishment and starvation hinged not merely on nature and tradition but on economic relationships that placed them and other Indians at increasing disadvantage.[11]

Economic standing also affected European diets in America after 1680. Eighteenth-century colonial laborers ate better than did European laborers despite some decline in the colonial diet between 1680 and 1770. This decline occurred for two reasons. Laborers tended to eat separately, not with employers or masters, as rural seasonal labor and skilled and unskilled labor increased in towns and cities after 1680, and wage dependence strained their food budgets. In addition, the numbers of the abject poor expanded, including the thoroughly unemployed and unemployable. As a result, the gap between the diet of most laborers and that of their employers most likely rose, while the diet for the poorest laborers probably worsened considerably.[12]

Yet most colonial laborers still ate better than European laborers after 1680 in good part because food costs remained relatively low, at least by European standards. In Philadelphia, for example, laborers typically consumed meat, but did so more infrequently and used cheaper cuts, ranging from fresh and salted pork to turkey and rabbit. They also ate locally caught fish and seafood as well as vegetables, breads made from wheat, bran, and oats, plus butter, cheese, and eggs and a wide variety of fruits, from apples to lemons and currants. Workers cut back when food costs soared, as they did during the wars of the 1740s and 1750s. They reduced meat consumption and increased their consumption of bread, cooked grains and greens, and fruit, and these items continued to be cheaper than in Europe.[13]

THE history of clothing manufacture in the eighteenth-century colonies reveals the importance of the mainland colonies' growing economic complexity. Most clothing used by seventeenth-century colonists was imported from England because textile production and clothing manufacture were far more labor-intensive and technically demanding than infant colonial societies could manage, at least on a large scale. Little wonder that seventeenth-century estate inventories from the Chesapeake to New England often describe clothing carefully and place high values on it, especially if it was "fancy." Yet all clothing was valuable. Maryland estate evaluators priced scarce locally produced "countrymade" cloth almost as highly as imported cloth because "countrymade" took so much time to produce, even if it was rough and inferior.[14]

The advancing colonial economy and rising population after 1680 increased cloth imports and colonial domestic production almost simultaneously. Imports rose steadily from the 1680s to the 1740s, then steeply from the 1740s to the 1770s. Increased British cloth production and the expansion of shippers and retail merchants in the colonies made more clothing available at cheaper prices, and colonists bought all they could. By the 1740s merchants sometimes specialized in cloth and finished clothing, although this was rare in the seventeenth and early eighteenth centuries. They drew on well-established British accounts to secure wide arrays of material and finished goods from undergarments and shirts to shoes and hats. By 1768 and most likely for several decades earlier, woolens and linens accounted for more than 35 percent of Britain's vastly expanded exports to the British mainland colonies.[15]

Domestic cloth production increased in the colonies as imports rose, and the increase outran the eighteenth-century population explosion in the mainland colonies. Enhanced prosperity, rising population, and the desire for additional income offered important reasons for this expanding domestic production. Farmers advanced their estates by purchasing more tools, including spinning wheels and even looms, which in turn added to their possible incomes. In the 1660s and 1670s only 1 percent of Virginia estates recorded spinning wheels. But between the 1690s and the 1720s spinning wheels increased in Maryland from less than 10 percent to about 35 percent of all estates, including an impressive 27 percent of poor estates. By the 1750s, 56 percent of estates probated in Plymouth County, Massachusetts, had spinning wheels and 33 percent had looms. In some cases, including Plymouth, farmers turned to spinning to supplement lagging income.[16]

The rise of spinning wheels and especially looms signaled fascinating regional differences in the gender division of labor in a highly specialized craft. In both Europe and America, women overwhelmingly did the spinning in the seventeenth century, while men traditionally wove cloth. Eighteenth-century Pennsylvania added an ethnic dimension, since weaving there remained an overwhelmingly male pursuit of largely immigrant German and Scottish weavers. But eighteenth-century New England developed a markedly different pattern. By the 1750s New England women often assumed the weaving crafts, giving weaving there a female identification it lacked elsewhere and increasing, rather than decreasing, the self-sufficiency of the household through cloth production. Yet whether through male weavers elsewhere or women in New England, eighteenth-century colonists developed multiple ways of obtaining clothes that simultaneously lowered prices and increased variety, style, and quality.[17]

Freedom, class, and wealth determined what one wore even more than what one ate. This was most obvious among enslaved Africans. In the late seventeenth and early eighteenth centuries, newly imported Africans were rather quickly dressed in European clothes, African clothing being undesired by slaveholders and largely unobtainable by Africans in any case. A regimen of poor clothing for slaves quickly emerged. In 1672 the Surry County, Virginia, court heard complaints about the "apparrell commonly worne by negroes" and ordered that "Noe Negro shall be allowed to weare anywhite Linninge, but shall weare blew shirts and shifts." Not to worry. At best, Maryland slaves wore very much what poor whites wore: castoffs, rough-cut cloth, and relatively little of it. Indentured servants might expect to get a new item of clothing each year, making do with worn and used items for years, sometimes until the breeches or shirts were literally threadbare. But Africans could expect less, for they very quickly emerged at the bottom of the clothing chain. In the mid-eighteenth century, many Africans possessed "fine" clothes for weddings and funerals, like the ceremony depicted in the watercolor *The Old Plantation* (see Chapter 1). But the metaphor effortlessly plied by a white Maryland apprentice demonstrated how well Europeans knew the truth about slave clothing. His master, he complained, "doth not use him as a son but a servant or rather a white Negro[,] clothing him in such things as Negroes are usually clothed."[18]

Yet Africans placed their own stamp on the clothing they did wear. If they lacked spinning wheels and looms to make yarn and cloth, they could dye and decorate the cloth they obtained as castoffs or as imports obtained specifically for slave clothing by owners. Like both European colonists and Africans, slaves liked bright, vivid colors. Owners variously reported slaves in purple, blue, orange, and yellow jackets, shirts, and pants. Slaves patched clothing and seldom refrained from doing so in decorative ways. One African wore a brown coat with "two patches on the left Side of the Back sewed in with white Thread."[19]

For the European colonists, the expansion of imports and domestic production after 1680 significantly broadened the choice of clothing, made multiple wardrobes possible, and, especially for the rich, turned clothing into an artful display. Here again, regional, ethnic, and even religiously defined variations emerged. Clothing in New England exemplified middle-range eighteenth-century British models, with silk stockings and satin-trimmed coats highly desirable on formal occasions. Pennsylvania Quakers adopted the "plain style" but turned it into a higher style. Their fine cloth and superb craftsmanship became a model for others, ranging from immigrant German Mennonites to Benjamin Franklin, Benjamin Rush, and even Thomas Paine. Upper-class Virginians emulated British aristocratic clothing with vivid colors and fine, well-tailored coats and dresses.[20]

The "Four Indian Kings" episode that occurred in London in 1710, certainly a peculiar event, nonetheless reveals much about clothing and the material world of American Indians in the eighteenth-century Brit-

Bernard Lens the Elder, *The Four Indian Kings*. Engraving, c. 1710.

ish mainland colonies. In 1710 British officials secured the London passage of four "Sachims" of the Five Nations in order to impress the Iroquois with British power at home. The ceremonial occasions held for the Indians in London said much about what the British imagined them to be, and nothing said it so well as the portraits drawn and painted during their visit. The set of engravings by Bernard Lens the Elder conveyed British notions. Lens dressed several in silk shirts and formal wool coats. But even the most Europeanized, Tee Yee Neen Ho Ga Row, the "Emperor of the Five Nations," maintained seemingly traditional hair and feathered ear decorations, while Sa Ga Yean Qua Rah Tow, the "King of the Maquas," or Mahicans, revealed substantial body painting on his face and under a broadly opened shirt. Lens made them "kings" but displayed their Indian heritage under their clothing.[21]

Lens's portraits revealed important syncretic dimensions of prerevolutionary Indian life, perhaps more than even the artist understood. Indian clothing increasingly reflected the highly mobile, eclectic, and international world in which Indians lived in British America. In the old Southeast as well as in the Northeast, surviving Indian men especially wore European shirts and, sometimes, pants, although generally they preferred leggings. They sometimes donned ruffled shirts and acquired European shoes. Over these, they often placed blankets worn as capes. Indian women frequently retained more traditional dress yet also used blankets as capes. Some Indians, especially in areas with large European populations, wore complete European clothes regularly. The Scottish colonist and traveler, Alexander Hamilton of Annapolis, reported that the wife of Ninigret, the Niantic chief, wore European clothing, and another traveler reported that in 1759 Virginia Indians "commonly dress[ed] like the Virginians," meaning in European fashion. A 1736 drawing of the Yuchi Indian commander Kipahalgwa by the Salzberger refugee, Philip Georg Friedrich von Reck, depicted Kipahalgwa with a European-style white shift but also in leather breeches, traditional body decoration, and "soft feathers drawn through the ear, from which a pearl is hanging."[22]

THE development of housing and furnishings in the colonies after 1680 magnified emerging patterns in food and clothing. The variety of housing reflected and extended all the proliferating distinctions of wealth and poverty, race, ethnicity, and urban and rural residence that occurred in the colonies between 1680 and 1770. Indeed, the colonists' material culture exemplified their aggressive drive to shape their own material world. Whether in the choices available or unavailable, the source of materials, imported or domestic, or the simple care, quality, and sophistication of work, residents of the mainland colonies created an increasingly distinctive secular material culture. This was not surprising in peoples for whom America was the reality as well as the hope of strong material dreams, regardless of the reasons that kept them in the New World or brought them there.

Eighteenth-century European colonists were sufficiently dissatisfied with their seventeenth-century housing that almost no unmodified seventeenth-century dwellings survived past the eighteenth century. Almost every home touted as "built in 1640" or "built in 1660" in contemporary tour guides has undergone so much modification since 1680 that it is difficult to discern its original character. Colonists simply demolished most unmodified seventeenth-century houses. Only reconstructed buildings, such as those at Plimoth Plantation or Jamestown, readily approximate pre-1680 colonial architecture.[23]

The colonists' earliest housing emerged in two stages. In both the Chesapeake and New England, colonists constructed or located temporary housing that served them until they had the time and resources to build "permanent" housing. These ranged from huts and tents to caves and dugouts, and colonists moved as quickly as possible to construct more adequate traditional housing. One early Marylander described the next structures built as "generally after the manner of . . . farme houses in England." These first colonists were not innovative when they built permanently. They seldom if ever followed American Indian housing, for example, or constructed buildings that experimented with new American conditions and circumstances. They built what they knew and generally emulated what they had long seen at home.[24]

Colonists' first permanent houses of the seventeenth century were small and crude. Early homes often had earthen floors and only later acquired raised wooden flooring. Some were not framed buildings but "puncheon" structures, named for posts "punched" into the ground on which outside boards were nailed to create crude walls. Windows were few, usually of paper, and doors and fireplaces were simple. Above all, the early seventeenth-century homes were very small, often no more than 12 feet by 12 feet or perhaps 20 feet by 30 feet at the largest. Many seventeenth-century houses contained only a single room, and most had half-story attics, not full second floors, usually used for sleeping. In short, these buildings did not create modern privacy.[25]

After 1680 European housing expanded dramatically in size, scope, and sophistication to create what survives in modern times as "early American architecture." This expansion occurred in two different ways. Most commonly, settlers expanded their original housing. "Seventeenth-century" buildings customarily reveal numerous additions and changes occurring after 1680. Samuel Harrison's substantial if not elegant plantation home in Anne Arundel County, Maryland, underwent several kinds of expansion across thirty years. Harrison built his original home in 1698, a one-story wood house with two window bays. He first expanded the house in 1713 by adding a room, a loft, and a brick chimney. A second addition in the 1720s added a parlor, a dining room with a built-in china case, a large stairway, and larger second floor rooms. Now exterior columns supported an overhanging room. A courtyard, perhaps absurdly small by European standards, gave the house stature. Brickwork covered the entire structure, and Harrison painted the decorative wood trim in reds, greens, and creams, colors likely repeated inside the house. Proud of his hard-won accomplishment, Harrison then had the home depicted in an oil on wood painting that is possibly the oldest surviving painting of a European house in British America.[26]

The famous House of Seven Gables in Salem, Massachusetts, immortalized by Nathaniel Hawthorne's novel, reflected not the haunting dourness of early Puritanism but the advancing material splendor evident in the colonies after 1680. John Turner began a small house containing one central chimney in 1668. About 1680 he added his first two-and-a-half-story addition to the front and side of the original house. Then, probably in the 1690s, Turner built another addition at the rear containing a new kitchen and larger rooms on the second floor.[27]

New construction also expanded in size, scope, and sophistication after 1680. Recent settlers often repeated the process of early-seventeenth-century immigration and built small, serviceable buildings first,

Samuel Harrison's Land near Herring Bay, Anne Arundel County, Maryland. Oil on wood, c. 1730. Signed "A.S." Courtesy Brice M. Clagett. Photograph courtesy Colonial Williamsburg Foundation.

Turner House. Photograph, c. 1910–1920.

then constructed more elaborate and pleasing homes later. The wealthy Quaker merchant James Claypoole built a rather large temporary house, 20' by 40', with a small cellar beneath it to house him upon his arrival in Pennsylvania in 1683. But almost immediately he started construction on a larger brick house, contracting a bricklayer as an indentured servant and looking for "one or 2 good stout negroes" in Barbados to use as construction laborers.[28]

Houses expanded in size almost everywhere after 1680. Small and poorer farmers used locally tutored craftsmen and builders to draw on expanding traditions in vernacular architecture that could gain them larger homes as materials became easier to acquire and labor costs declined. Between 1680 and the Revolution, rooms got slightly larger, with a few more windows, and houses regularly had finished walls and wood rather than earth floors. In addition, the increasing population made it easier to raise frames for houses and barns and, in turn, furnished additional laborers who might be paid by the day or week for intensive construction tasks.[29]

Hired laborers, the underemployed, and the poor constituted an important exception to improved housing in post-1680 America. The colonial cities from Boston to Charleston all featured substantial rented housing, much of it of poor quality even when first constructed. Building owners made more money by renting smaller spaces to more people, and they acquired and constructed buildings that would serve this purpose. Philadelphia's better rental housing of the 1750s customarily measured 12' by 18' or 11' by 14', while other rental housing off alleys sometimes had even less space. Families often shared these small spaces, such as a Philadelphia shoemaker, Christian Fight, who lived with his wife and four children in a tiny dwelling they shared with the family of Christian Nail. Even by the 1710s hired laborers, the unemployed, and the poor jammed buildings whose physical condition declined as new immigrants made the spaces even tighter and the housing shortage persistently worsened.[30]

Slaveholders provided minimal housing for Africans and seldom improved it. Between the 1690s and the 1740s slave quarters shifted from dormitory-style group or communal quarters to separate quarters for the growing number of conjugal families. This change produced little substantial increase either in space or in housing quality. One of the few surviving eighteenth-century slave quarters, a 12'-by-16' building in Mecklenburg County, Virginia, probably housed six to ten people. Clapboard covered its thin frame. It had exposed beams, no inside walls, and a wooden floor, which was rare since most owners used earth floors in slave quarters. Its eighteen-inch doorways and diminutive windows saved building costs; larger doors and windows were more expensive. Owners seldom enlarged buildings or installed boards or plaster to cover interior beams once slave quarters had been constructed. Some slave quarters may have been constructed by Africans working under the supervision of owners, with the buildings designed as construction proceeded in a process common to home construction for Europeans in America as well. The pointed thatched roofs of the slave quarters depicted at the Mulberry plantation in South Carolina about 1800 suggest African influences more strongly than other slave quarters for which architectural documentation has survived. Yet the Mulberry plantation slave quarters were crudely constructed, were smaller than the cramped laborers' housing of Philadelphia, and contained only one tiny window and one door. Owners refused to invest in more substantial housing for slaves when they perceived that cruder, cheaper housing sufficed and reduced their costs.[31]

This pattern of sparse, cheap housing changed little throughout the eighteenth century. One slaveholder ordered that newly constructed African quarters be "tight and warm," but this was not the rule in most places. Slave cabins had few furnishings. One African described Maryland beds as "collections of straw, and old rags thrown down in the corners and boxed in with boards; a single blanket the only covering." Africans sometimes added interior planking at the roof line to increase sleeping space.[32]

Yet old patterns persisted, and in prominent places. A European visitor to George Washington's Mount Vernon in 1798 noted that "G[en-

Wood-framed houses of laboring people, Philadelphia, c. 1750.

Thomas Coram, *View of Mulberry.* Oil on paper, c. 1800.

era]l Washington treats his slaves far more humanely than do most of his fellow citizens." Still, he wrote, the "huts of the Blacks . . . are more miserable than the most miserable of the cottages of our peasants. The husband and wife sleep on a mean pallet, the children on the ground." As late as the 1810s Thomas Jefferson described the slave quarters at Monticello as "20 1/2 f. by 12 f. of wood, with a wooden chimney, & earth floor." We have no record of any valuation of the Monticello slave quarters, but a visitor knowledgeable about plantation life graphically described the contrast in 1809:

> We passed the outhouses of the slaves and workmen [at Monticello]. They are all much better than I have seen on any other plantation, but to an eye unaccustomed to such sights they appear poor and their cabins form a most unpleasant contrast with the palace that rises so near them.[33]

Indian housing underwent subtle changes between 1680 and the American Revolution, although as with the question of diet, limited study makes conclusions tentative. Indians adopted some technological innovations in the eighteenth century based on European precedents. Eighteenth-century Iroquois longhouses, the long narrow buildings 20 feet wide and up to 200 feet long that traditionally housed entire Iroquois matrilineal clans, sometimes used hewn joists, not bent saplings, and even employed sawn boards, not bark, to make partitions. In the Carolinas, mid-eighteenth-century Catawba houses used logs and rafters rather than bent saplings but still employed bark to cover the buildings, and the houses usually went without windows and furniture. In short, many Indians often incorporated some European elements in housing while largely retaining a considerable traditional appearance, a mixture not always achieved elsewhere.[34]

Still, an important change among the Iroquois demonstrates powerful links between housing and broader cultural change. Eighteenth-century Iroquois longhouses were distinctly smaller than their seventeenth-century predecessors and put to different uses. They were narrower, shorter, and built for ceremonial functions, such as Iroquois council meetings. The change was noticeable to English officials: New York lieutenant governor George Clark wrote in 1742 that "most of the 6 Nations have of late years lived dispersed forgetting their Antient Custom of dwelling together in Castles." After the 1740s Onadagas lived in "cabins" that one observer described as "made of bark, bound fast to poles set in the ground, and bent round on the top" and housing one or two families, not entire clans. Eighteenth-century Senecas built European-style cabins, also holding only one or two families, although they used a smoke hole rather than a European chimney. Only the Cayugas seem to have retained some traditional longhouses. Yet among the Cayugas, Onadagas, and Senecas alike the change in function produced at least symbolic change, and their principal historian notes that in all three societies the eighteenth-century buildings lacked "the elaborate carvings of clan animals or other figures that adorned the entrances to dwellings a century earlier." For the Iroquois as for Europeans and Africans, housing said much about culture and power, not just taste and refinement.[35]

Affluent Europeans in America experienced dramatically improved housing between the late seventeenth century and the Revolution. The large mansions constructed by the British nobility in the eighteenth century had no parallels in America, even among the wealthiest colonists. But eighteenth-century colonial homes built for affluent and even middling colonists dramatically distanced themselves from any seventeenth-century predecessors. They opened the way not only for estates far larger than those even imagined in the seventeenth century but for an explosion of allied crafts that brought unprecedented artisanry to the mainland colonies' lifestyle.[36]

The most significant expansion in colonial home size after 1680 occurred among the middling Europeans so critical to the colonial economy, politics, and society. When William Hancock built his large two-and-a-half-story house in New Jersey in 1734, for example, he used a complex interior plan with different-sized rooms and highly visible zig-zag brickwork bearing his own initials and the date of the house construction. In contrast, the Rochester House in Westmoreland County, Virginia, thought to have been constructed at mid-century, appears small at first glance and perhaps not larger than some slave quarters. But it employed solidly built frame construction with a substantial brick fireplace and a raised wood floor, quite unlike any slave housing, and contained numerous windows and a high roof that turned what could have been a cramped loft into a full second story, which itself had windows at each end. In both cases, the homes represented a refinement of "vernacular" styles, designs created by local craftsmen and artisans—not architects—who converted an owner's general desires into a building.[37]

After 1680 the most affluent colonists constructed homes beyond anything achieved in the seventeenth century. In William Burgiss's 1722 engraving *A North East View of the Great Town of Boston,* church spires punctuated the skyline, rising perhaps higher in the engraving than in fact. More important was the first appearance of private homes in a New World city engraving, including the home of the Huguenot refugee merchant André Faneuil. Faneuil's house, constructed in 1710, dwarfed anything yet built in the town. Set back on an unusually large lot, it stood opposite King's Chapel, the place of worship for the town's Anglican congregation, and served as an elegant mansion into the mid-nineteenth century. Quaker Philadelphia knew similar structures. The Scottish merchant Edward Stiles constructed a massive Palladian-style home he named "Mount Pleasant" in 1761, whose spectacular front stairway and entrance served it well as a distinguished mansion into the twentieth century.[38]

The slaveholding wealth of the southern colonies produced even more spectacular residences. Washington's Mount Vernon, constructed between the 1730s and 1787, exemplified the process of addition and expansion seen in Samuel Harrison's plantation on a very large scale. The original house, constructed by Washington's father in the 1730s, was a one-and-a-half-story farmhouse, large but not massive or elegant. Washington expanded the house in 1759, enlarging the second floor and adding a half-story attic, before his marriage to the widow Martha Dandridge Custis. Then Washington lengthened the house between 1776 and 1779 (as the Revolutionary War was beginning), later adding the pediment and cupola in 1778 and 1787 that established Mount Vernon's final appearance.[39]

Westover, built by Virginia's William Byrd II about 1750, represented the achievement of massive slaveholding wealth, a desire to replicate English elite styles, and the presence of subtle but important provincial features in colonial American design and taste. Westover's massive size—it was a true mansion of 2,500 square feet with three tall stories, seven windows across the front and four deep, with four fireplaces—conveyed Byrd's sheer wealth. The style, early Georgian, replicated smaller mid-eighteenth-century English mansions for affluent minor local figures. Yet in America the home also quietly accommodated regional tastes and skills. The local craftsmen and artisans who "designed" the house used English models but imposed regional patterns and styles that gave Westover a distinctive, if not unique, appearance. Westover's lack of corner quoins, which ornamented English Georgian-style homes, gave it a plainer appearance than its British counterparts. Its interior space allocation followed local vernacular patterns as much as English models, especially in its approach to room openings and the importance of hallways. Almost all the materials used to construct the house were local, including the brick that dominated its exterior appearance. In short, Westover was an essentially European design overtaken with local detailing, space arrangements, and materials.[40]

In Charleston, architecture on the eve of the American Revolution followed local rather than British style. Affluent home owners developed a taste for long and tall homes whose narrow end faced the street, a design that was believed to maximize breezes and control temperatures in the hot, humid Charleston summers. Their façades looked toward other houses on the block rather than toward the street, and many of the houses served as business headquarters as well as residences, with

Westover, James City County, Virginia, c. 1750. Photograph about 1909.

rooms on both the first and the second floors serving as formal reception rooms segregated away from more private rooms located toward the rear of the buildings. For the wealthy, the effect was spectacular. In 1773 a Boston visitor described the second floor of Miles Brewton's Charleston home as "the grandest hall I ever beheld, azure blue satin window curtains, rich blue paper with gilt, mashee [papier-mâché] borders, most elegant pictures, excessive grand and costly looking glasses etc." Brewton also ate well: "A most elegant table, three courses."[41]

Miles Brewton's home never typified colonial residences, however. Many colonists lived crudely in small if solid houses with relatively few possessions down to and past the Revolution. Even among Europeans, goods were unevenly distributed in the same region and from region to region. The rise in the number and proportion of poor colonists among European settlers meant increases in the range of poor housing. If slaveholders seldom improved slave quarters by finishing the walls or replacing wood floors with dirt floors, dirt-floor cabins became increasingly common for poor whites as the eighteenth century progressed and lasted well into the nineteenth century.[42]

THE goods found inside the wide variety of colonial homes raise fascinating questions not only about the expanse of material objects across the colonies but about the origins of these products and, hence, about "Europeanization," "Anglicization," or "Americanization" in the eighteenth-century British mainland colonies. In fact, all these processes occurred. Colonists in America participated in what historians now call a "consumer revolution" in eighteenth-century Western society. In eighteenth-century Britain, France, and the Netherlands especially, material goods appeared with increasing frequency at cheaper prices among far more consumers than ever before. Items that in the sixteenth and seventeenth centuries were deemed luxuries—more furniture, more elaborate and greater amounts of clothing, increased quantities of dishes, silverware, and household goods—became far more widely available, if not yet common. European production facilities increased, and economic development stressed the crafts and trades that produced these goods as well as their means of distribution and sale. From Wedgwood pottery to suits, dresses, and men's shaving equipment, commercial products became a means of economic expansion and a major symbol of social prestige.[43]

Colonists imported enormous quantities of European goods. They demonstrated an "Anglicizing" desire to achieve British-style display and consumption in the colonies. But the imported European goods and the self-conscious Anglicizing desires emerged in a society significantly different from either Britain or continental Europe. In eighteenth-century America neither the goods nor the desires ever produced an imitation Europe that some may have dreamed about, but others could not achieve, did not appreciate, and may have rejected. Whether in New York or Williamsburg, rural Massachusetts or aristocratic Virginia, those who might have sought to reproduce Europe in America simply never succeeded.

Nor did the imported European goods and self-conscious Anglicizing desires preclude the simultaneous and widespread patronage of colonial artisans and craftsmen by mainland colony residents. Not only were the colonial craftsmen as common in America as they were in provincial Britain, but they challenged and often surpassed their British provincial counterparts in the quality of the objects they made. Thus, if Americans were increasingly known by their "things," these included a wide variety of objects made both overseas and in the colonies, objects whose acquisition and even production stemmed from a vigorous colonial economy in an increasingly distinctive society.

Initially after 1680, then with even more rapidity after 1740, colonists imported enormous quantities of European goods in a flurry of purchasing that demonstrated how broadly the eighteenth-century consumer revolution affected Europeans on both sides of the Atlantic. Consumption increased everywhere, not least in Britain's expanding American colonies. An extremely wide range of goods found their way from Britain and Europe to America. This included clothing of all kinds, from fine clothing made from English-made cloth and fashioned in London to modest and rough clothing made cheaply for quick sale at home or overseas. It also included furniture. Here, too, wealthy colonists bought fancy English furniture in an effort to affect English taste in reception rooms, dining rooms, hallways, and bedrooms. A Charleston merchant, Richard Baker, advertised London-made furniture in 1735, including a "Variety of mahaganny tables, chests of drawers, burroes, desks, cloath chests, cupboards, [and] back-gammon tables." But imports of far more modest furniture from tables to chests to chairs accounted for even more objects and a greater volume. American colonists were hungry to consume fine but not necessarily ornate English furniture and eager to display it in their ever-enlarging homes.[44]

Colonists also imported paintings, prints, and drawings. They brought in clocks and silver, not only silverware but teapots, mugs, serving platters, and a host of decorative and even ceremonial objects. They especially imported ceramics, sometimes from Staffordshire. They acquired carpets from England and "Turkey," meaning the Middle East. Above all, they imported tea and its accoutrements—tables, pots, cups, tongs, and side dishes. One New Yorker reported in the 1730s that "tea and china ware cost the province, yearly, near the sum of £10,000." The rage for tea transcended class. When poorer colonists imbibed, they too used imported pots and cups, although of lower price and quality. Colonists also imported skilled craftsmen, including carvers for the cabinetmaking shops of Newport, Philadelphia, Williamsburg, and Charleston.[45]

But equally intriguing, and in the long run at least equally significant, colonists also supported a vast array of colonial craftsmen and artisans whose work emerged as increasingly refined and, in some cases, even spectacular. The most subtle and permanently visible occurred among joiners and woodworkers, whose labors decorated colonial dwellings. They created, sometimes from plan books and sometimes through memory and their own invention, the large fireplace mantels that typified the finest colonial homes, and the wood paneling so common in eighteenth-century houses. Typically, their work represented a fusion of Old and New Worlds or, often, a variety of each. Like their British and European counterparts, colonial carpenters, craftsmen, and joiners used a wide variety of local woods plus imported woods, such as mahogany from Spanish America. They finished these woods with ever more sophisticated techniques into finely crafted mantels, wallboards, and spectacular stair casings. The practice was so common that by 1764 Henry Laurens of Charleston easily advised a Liverpool merchant about the beauties and economies of mahogany staircases: "Mahogany is the thing by all means for your Stair case. (I believe you would agree in opinion with me if you saw mine.)."[46]

Silver offered another example of fine colonial craftsmanship. Crude silversmithing was available in the colonies almost from the earliest days of settlement and certainly after 1650. But the decades after 1680 brought the first significant silver production in the mainland colonies, and the 1710s witnessed the beginnings of substantial and sustained sophisticated silver work. The New York Huguenot immigrant Simeon Soumaine, very likely trained in London in the 1680s or 1690s, produced a wide range of excellent work, including a silver bowl modeled on a Chinese porcelain bowl regarded as one of the finest examples of the early eighteenth-century colonial silversmith's art. Soumaine's work presents an interesting contrast with Huguenot silversmiths in London. Through much of the eighteenth century, refugee Huguenots dominated London's silver trade, producing baroque pieces whose heavy ornamentation and ornate fussiness complemented their high-quality craftsmanship. But Soumaine's work, like that of other colonial Huguenot silversmiths, exhibited far simpler characteristics, a cleanness of line and simplicity of content that set it far from the work of London's Huguenot silversmiths. Soumaine's style, rather than prefiguring the "American simplicity" of nineteenth-century American Shaker furniture, more likely represented a regional difference within the transatlantic British empire.[47]

Part of this regional difference may have stemmed from an increasingly autonomous apprenticeship system employed by silversmiths throughout the colonies. Certainly, immigrant silversmiths continued to arrive in America from Europe, especially from London. Not surprisingly, London's Huguenot silversmiths sent their own apprentices to America, such as Lewis Janviere and James Courteonne, who arrived in Charleston at mid-century. They were joined by non-Huguenots trained in London and elsewhere who greatly increased the simple numbers of silversmiths in the colonies. But colonial silversmiths regularly trained their own apprentices as both shop workers and successors. So common was this practice that by mid-century, a substantial number of colonial silver shops had gone into their third generation with colonial apprentices. Boston's most famous colonial silversmith, Paul Revere, was himself a product of this native apprenticeship system. His father, the French immigrant Apollos Revere, learned his silver crafts from the Boston silversmith John Coney, and Paul Revere apprenticed to his own father. Yet regional differences affected the results of apprenticeship. Greater continuity appeared in Boston than in Virginia or Charleston, where craftsmen came and went, drawn away by fluid opportunities elsewhere.[48]

By mid-century, colonists who could afford to purchase silver had innumerable choices. The wealthiest could import silver from London, Rotterdam, and even Paris. Silver imports appear to have risen substantially in the eighteenth century. More wealth had been created in the colonies, and the concern for status drove colonists who could afford these purchases to make them from European silversmiths.[49]

But colonial silversmiths were producing work of exceptional merit even by the 1710s and 1720s, and their skill only increased by mid-century. One intriguing example is found in the work of the New York silversmith Myer Myers. Myers developed both a Jewish and a Gentile clientele. He produced sacred as well as secular silver objects of exquisite beauty and fine craftsmanship for Jews in New York and Philadelphia, many of whom were also his relatives. But Myers also regularly sold objects to English and Dutch residents, including the Livingstons, one of New York's powerful Presbyterian families.[50]

Finally, there was Revere himself, widely acknowledged both in his own time and since as the single finest silversmith of the colonial era. Revere's output was prodigious, and his surviving silver pieces number several thousand. More important, Revere produced an extraordinary number of exquisite pieces that found a special place in the lavish homes of Boston's elite long before and after the American Revolution. Little wonder that John Singleton Copley painted Revere in 1770 in enthusiastically secular enjoyment of his craft, lovingly admiring a teapot of his own making, the kind that he had produced for innumerable Boston clients who displayed them with equal pride in their homes and mansions.[51]

FURNITURE represented the supreme artistic accomplishment of the post-1680 period. By mid-century, colonial furniture makers produced pieces of such quality, sometimes equaling the best of those in London, that wealthy colonists often preferred American furniture to its British competition. Philadelphia, true to its reputation among modern collectors of early American antiques, produced the most highly ornamented furniture in the colonies. The city became famous for its high chests of drawers that bore elaborate rococo scrolling plus claw feet, shell drawers, and other carving. This added decorative work, accomplished with unsurpassed skill, increased the price of the basic chest from £8 to £13 sterling in the mid-eighteenth century, furniture that can bring prices above one million dollars in the modern market. Yet many colonial customers appear to have preferred plainer, simpler styles, equally sophisticated and beautifully constructed, for which colonial furniture makers achieved considerable local renown in the 1740s, 1750s, and 1760s. Simplicity was sought even when colonists ordered from London. When Charleston's wealthy Peter Manigault ordered some "plate and furniture" for his newly constructed home in 1771, he noted that he would "be glad to have them out as soon as possible & the plainer the better so that they are fashionable."[52]

John Singleton Copley, *Paul Revere*. Oil on canvas, 1768.
Courtesy Museum of Fine Arts, Boston; gift of Joseph W. Revere,
William B. Revere, and Edward H. R. Revere.

Virtually all the colonies supported joiners and craftsmen who produced fine, expensive furniture. A chest produced in Marblehead, Massachusetts, sometime after 1760 might have been more squat and less
ornate than a Philadelphia chest of drawers, but it exhibited superb
workmanship and style, especially in its undulated lower drawers. And
an unknown craftsman produced a magnificent library bookcase in
Charleston between 1765 and 1775, nine feet high by seven feet wide,
to fit the tall ceilings in Charleston mansions. With four glassed-in

{159}

Library bookcase. Design of Thomas Chippendale,
maker unknown, Charleston, c. 1765–1775.

doors on the top and four wooden doors on the bottom in what builders called a "Chinese style," the bookcase may not have exhibited the finesse that typified Philadelphia or Newport furniture. But it surely would have impressed Jonathan Edwards, even if he might have been more interested in its storage capacity than its refined appearance.[53]

Comparisons of provincial furniture in the mainland colonies with similar furniture in Britain, though difficult, suggests several important differences and crucially important trends. The study of regional furniture is not as advanced for Britain as for colonial America; the high prices long paid for early American furniture have stimulated a scholarship that far exceeds studies of comparable English pieces. Yet several interesting contrasts detail important differences between Old and New World furniture making. Colonial America never produced the extraordinarily ornate furniture produced for the wealthiest British subjects and nobility—high canopied beds with elaborately carved scrolls holding florid textile draping, marble-topped tables with exquisitely carved legs in the shape of animals, gilded tables with legs carved as human figures, and desks with highly ornate brass ornaments—rococo patterns that typified the silver trade as well.[54]

Colonial American originality consisted in perfecting simpler British styles, whose essential forms colonial craftsmen followed. Sometimes this originality stemmed from work with material resources more plentiful in America, such as wider boards (from older trees) in vernacular furniture, and sometimes it stemmed from a near perfection in form, as in Newport, Rhode Island, block-and-shell desks, dressers, and highboys. Following mid-range English styles, colonial craftsmanship easily equaled and sometimes surpassed English regional furniture after 1700 and especially after 1740, and the best colonial silver matched all but the finest pieces available in London.[55]

More modest productions from other joiners and craftsmen proved even more significant, because these builders filled the colonies with a wide range of furniture available to European colonists of more average means. Some of this furniture suggests modest differences in vernacular furniture in rural New England, Virginia, and rural Britain. For example, a cupboard with a raised display shelf made in southeastern Virginia between about 1660 and 1680, and a chest made in Wethersfield, Connecticut, between 1680 and 1700, display only minor differences in style, the Virginia cupboard lacking decorative carving. They also demonstrate remarkable similarities in spindles darkened to imitate ebony, in the black decorative motifs added to the front panels, and in their general construction and quality, though the anonymous Connecticut joiner used oak while the Virginia builder largely employed pine. By comparison, British chests from the late seventeenth and early eighteenth centuries bear more decorative carving but less in the way of artificial ebony spindles, with little if any substantial difference in the quality of finishing.[56]

The colonies' increasing heterogeneity produced its own distinctiveness. German furniture from mid-eighteenth-century Pennsylvania and the rural backcountry of the Carolinas usually embodied folk themes in its decoration and was by no means crudely made, with dovetailed joints and mitred drawers. Chests built for German consumers to display objects on top with storage underneath carried traditional German arts in vivid colors and graphic designs that might have reminded owners of home. But German builders also incorporated English elements in their designs. A large wardrobe made in Pennsylvania's Berks County about 1781 contained elements common to German furniture—scrolling, seashell sculpture, large paneled doors—but also included English-style drawers in the center of the wardrobe (German wardrobes did not include drawers) that reflected the influence of English customers and examples in Pennsylvania.[57]

Chairs offer especially fascinating examples of the dramatic blossoming of wood crafts in America after 1680. Everywhere there were chairs, both because colonists demanded them and because many craftsmen were available to make them. This proliferation of chairs stemmed from the unusual combination of artisan immigration, strong colonial apprenticeship, a broadly expanding economy, and a demand from settlers to consume commercially made products such as chairs at many levels and prices. Unfortunately, this variety is not known to us in its fullness. Colonists and their nineteenth-century descendants often discarded the crude furniture owners made themselves or purchased cheaply from rough woodworkers. But many modest and good chairs have survived that show the wide distribution of both craftsmen and their products.[58]

In Newtown and Woodbury in western Connecticut, for example, far from both New York and New Haven, a coterie of joiners and wood-

German *schrank* (wardrobe), Berks County, Pennsylvania, c. 1781.

workers, who also made drawers, chests, and desks, fashioned an extensive variety of chairs—round-top chairs, fiddleback chairs (in several different forms), fiddleback rocking chairs, crookedback chairs, and crookedback armchairs (called "great crookedbacks"). Southern joiners matched their northern counterparts. By the 1730s Virginia and North Carolina joiners produced chairs of all kinds, including finely made armchairs of mahogany and heavy yet impressive mahogany corner chairs. And like northern makers, southern chair makers tried out their own intriguing if peculiar styles, such as an armchair that mixed post-and-round and Windsor styles with a caned seat, which, of course, required imported cane and demonstrated the way in which the joiners exemplified both a vigorous internationalism and the development of local patterns and traditions.[59]

Colonial chair makers, like other colonial furniture craftsmen, usually equaled their British counterparts. No clear "American" style yet characterized this furniture. Regional differences in construction details, such as the handling of joints, best differentiated chairs of one colonial region from those of another, just as was true of Britain. Yet the technical capacity to create or pursue a distinctive style clearly existed, awaiting only an impetus, the kind that sprang forth in the 1790s and later when independence produced nationalism as strongly in crafts as in politics.[60]

THE transformation of public space matched the transformation of private space after 1680. Virtually all early seventeenth-century public buildings, like houses, disappeared in the eighteenth century when they were replaced by far larger, more elaborate facilities. The seventeenth-century New England "meeting house," which served both political and spiritual needs, fell victim to its very importance. Colonists who saw town and church as central to their purpose erected buildings that measured the authority of these crucial institutions, and after 1680 they increasingly demolished the meager to make way for the impressive. Sudbury, Massachusetts, built a 20′ by 30′ meeting house in 1643 and a larger one in 1653, but both had thatched roofs and were relatively crude. In 1688, with its population and tax base greatly increased, Sudbury tore down the 1653 meeting house to construct a third with a wood roof and obviously larger than either of its predecessors. Hingham followed closely behind. Hingham's Old Ship meeting house, constructed between 1681 and 1684 and named for the exposed beam interior that resembled the inside of a ship, is one of the few seventeenth-century New England meeting houses to survive into modern times. Its exposed beam construction and two-story height represents the sometimes dramatic turn to larger, more substantial buildings in late-seventeenth-century New England. Unlike earlier buildings too small to expand, this one was also widened in the mid-eighteenth century when a raised pulpit with a sounding board and finely finished pews were added to the interior, features that typified the large, more elaborate town meeting houses common throughout eighteenth-century New England.[61]

In the southern colonies, especially in Virginia, the courthouse emerged as a major focus of secular culture. Before 1680 Maryland and Virginia held court in the homes of prominent justices, in cheap public buildings that had used crude puncheon or post-hole construction, or in parish churches if the parish had a church. After 1680 Virginia counties regularly erected thoroughly secular courthouses whose size, substance, and style aggressively conveyed the authority increasingly pursued by its rising county courts. The arcaded courthouses constructed in Hanover and King William counties in the 1730s and early 1740s and in Isle of Wight County about 1752, for example, were more elaborate than most other eighteenth-century Virginia courthouses and possibly drew their inspiration from arcades constructed earlier at the College of William and Mary. Virginia's investment in public buildings, however variable from county to county, also demonstrated its planter prosperity and the popularity of "court days," where markets, crowds, and political intrigue absorbed the Virginia social experience. The only scene in Robert Munford's 1770 political satire *The Candidates; or, the Humours of a Virginia Election* not set in a home or an open field offered a view of three secular scenes familiar to all Virginians—taverns, courthouses, and roads: "a porch of a tavern: a Court-house on one side, and an high road behind."[62]

Eighteenth-century colonial officials also commissioned ceremonial objects that reinforced the authority they sought in their offices, institutions, and public buildings. The New York City silversmith Charles Le Roux executed many commissions for the New York Common Council in the 1720s and 1730s, including a silver mace to symbolize the authority of the New York City Vice Admiralty Court. Boston's Admiralty Court magistrates commissioned Jacob Hurd to make a two-foot mace in the shape of a silver oar to represent their authority, probably in the 1730s. North Carolina magistrates ordered construction of raised platforms that conveyed the power of judicial authority by elevating magistrates above the attending sheriff, clerk, constables, jury, and general public. The Chowan County, North Carolina, courthouse, constructed about 1750, included a superbly crafted thronelike seat for the chief magistrate that honored hierarchical authority and monarchical government at the very edge of Britain's New World possessions.[63]

Public buildings in the colonial cities outstripped their rural counterparts in size but not in purpose and, sometimes, not in splendor either. After 1680 colonists everywhere replaced older, inadequate government buildings and erected new ones that measured the growing wealth of the societies they led and the advancing power of the governments they commanded. After a fire in 1711 leveled Boston's wooden 1657 Town House, a new brick and stone structure emerged to house the expanding town and provincial governments, the courts, and the old

Courthouse, Hanover County, Virginia, c. 1735–1743.

Chief Magistrate's chair, Chowan County Courthouse,
North Carolina, c. 1767–1775.

merchant's exchange. This was, in turn, partially superseded by the magnificent hall that Peter Faneuil gave to the city in 1742 to house a new, more centralized market. Even at its original size (nine bays in length and three wide), Faneuil Hall was a major building (the modern Faneuil Hall is twice as wide and has three stories rather than the original two, a remodeling accomplished by Charles Bulfinch in 1805). New York City constructed a new city hall in 1703 to replace a tiny structure built in the Dutch period. This was, in turn, demolished after a much larger two-story city hall was constructed between 1745 and 1747 to house city and provincial governments, including the colony's Supreme Court, a building that was itself remodeled by Pierre L'Enfant in 1789 to serve as the first United States Capitol. By 1739 Charleston had a combined council chamber, guardhouse and courthouse, a custom house and workhouse, and several large public markets and batteries, and in 1756 the colony constructed a new state house, 120 feet by 40 feet and in brick with a four-column front. It was destroyed by fire in 1788.[64]

Williamsburg, Virginia, evidenced the most spectacular attempt to translate the expanding wealth of Britain's colonies into a self-consciously impressive public architecture. Between 1700 and 1730 Virginia deliberately moved its government from a low-lying Jamestown to a more promising inland site named after William of Orange, the successor to the deposed Catholic, James II. At Williamsburg, political function followed architectural form. The rapidly expanding colonial government invested heavily in magnificent college and government buildings that seemed to spur on the very institutions they served. The college buildings represented this process least well, since the president's home and the magnificent building possibly but not assuredly designed by the great British architect Christopher Wren, Brafferton Hall, leaped far ahead of its faculty, curriculum, and students throughout the eighteenth century. But the capitol and governor's mansion well expressed the expanding power and authority of eighteenth-century Virginia government. By the 1750s, Virginia's colonial political institutions in both Williamsburg and the colony's rural counties easily fit the spacious buildings, from capitol to county courthouses, that might have seemed at least slightly grandiose when first constructed. In Virginia as in other colonies, architecture and material culture reflected

New York's Old City Hall, plan and elevation, c. 1745, formerly standing on
Wall Street. Drawing by David Grim, 1818.

and led colonists' steady drive to command their society and government.[65]

SECULAR group life complemented and reinforced the increasingly autonomous material culture of the eighteenth-century British mainland colonies. Secular associations deepened interpersonal relationships at the same time that they reinforced hierarchical differences among colonists, separating as they joined, whether men from women, rich from poor, whites from blacks, or New World from Old. Even when colonists created associations that emulated European models, they frequently gave their groups a reasonably if not wholly distinctive colonial character. As a result, these associations, clubs, informal groupings, and societies produced centrifugal and centripetal effects simultaneously. They turned their members' attention inward as much as outward. In the process, they created crucial materials for making a modestly distinctive colonial identity, or, at least, a colonial frame of reference.

Corporate associational life flourished among European men almost everywhere in the mainland colonies after 1680. Clubs, groups, and societies all emerged to challenge the social sparseness, if not individualism, of the seventeenth century. Before 1680 it had been difficult to "belong" to secular associations in the colonies, because few existed. But in eighteenth-century America, joining the corporate association came to be a way of life for European men that turned them toward one another as it also separated them from others—from "outsiders."

Informal tavern life involved the largest numbers of colonial men and, because it contained important elements of class, previewed more formal corporate associational life. Like so much else in eighteenth-century America, the tavern was not unique to the century or to the place, having been a ubiquitous feature of seventeenth-century European life in England, Scotland, and the Continent. But two characteristics attenuated its growth in the seventeenth-century colonies: Puritan moralism to the north and population scarcity everywhere else. In New England, Puritan moralism did not demand abstinence. But it strongly encouraged temperance, to the point that Massachusetts and Connecticut provincial and town governments vigorously restricted the number of taverns and watched them carefully to control public drinking. Into the 1710s the Massachusetts General Court and the Boston Town Council limited tavern licenses and suspended licenses of owners who tolerated bad behavior. At the same time, the sparse rural population often made taverns economically unfeasible, so that their numbers remained relatively small, not only in New England but apparently in other colonies as well. Rural drinking before 1680 emerged most commonly at planned and impromptu social occasions—marriages, harvests, and deaths—rather than in convivial taverns patronized by solitary individuals.[66]

The restrictive seventeenth-century patterns changed after 1680 as colonial society expanded and altered. Changes began in New England in the 1710s in two different ways. Puritan campaigning against drinking and restrictive licensing failed. Although clergymen fulminated frequently against drinking and the Massachusetts assembly passed its most restrictive licensing act in 1712, these measures faced waning public support. One minister lamented in 1728, "unless you are carefull and conscientious in [observing the law], all our laws for the reforming of the manners and morals of a corrupt people are insufficient and our lawmakers labored in vain." Such laments might have increased because local governments licensed many more taverns and retail shops after 1710, almost doubling the number previously available and retreating from seventeenth-century restrictiveness. In Boston, for example, licensed shops and taverns increased by 81 percent, from 74 to 134, between 1719 and 1722, approximately one retail outlet for every one hundred adults in Boston, a ratio that remained relatively steady into the 1760s. Rural taverns also increased after 1710, both because public demand rose and because the increasingly dense rural population made taverns more profitable. In general, the expansion of taverns strongly paralleled the expansion of craft shops, small-scale commercial agriculture, and weaving, which were driven by population growth, consumption, and the need for part-time employment.[67]

Taverns provided a culture of belonging broader than clubs and without the trappings of organization. Rural taverns became important sites of political legitimization, where candidates came to meet constituents and, most important, where constituents measured candidates. Here men drank, socialized, critiqued, and schemed, sometimes to promote individual interests, often to create and expand neighborhood and town interests. Sometimes town members quarreled over "their" tavern or used the tavern as a platform in town disputes; some tavern owners complained that they lost their licenses because authorities manifested "party spirit" in the renewal process. Thus John Adams griped that "you will find the house full of people, drinking drams, phlip, [and] toddy," all while "plotting with the landlord to get him, at the next town meeting and election, either for selectman or representative."[68]

Urban taverns, like those in Boston, drew specialized clienteles that helped create and reinforce emerging social and economic distinctions. Some taverns appealed to the wealthy through well-appointed rooms, diverse and expensive liquors, coffee, and sometimes libraries, where customers might peruse pamphlets on contemporary issues such as the currency disputes that disrupted many colonies. Other taverns and retail shops offered exotic fare, such as caged bears and lions and even a camel and a black moose. But most were small retail shops located in poorer neighborhoods. These retailers sold liquor by the drink and offered little in the way of furniture or food, much less selection in liquor. In these neighborhoods women also were more likely to own taverns, though the clientele remained exclusively male. In Boston, for example, women held the licenses for 30 to 40 percent of Boston's taverns after 1710. Most were for taverns and retail shops with middling and poor clienteles, although the increasingly open and competitive market made women retailers more vulnerable to the vicissitudes of economic fluctuation, including the rise and fall of their customers' wages and jobs, even as it increased their chances to obtain licenses.[69]

Finally, urban taverns often became associated with politics, political intrigue, parties, and ideology. Urban taverns promoted political argument and distributed political literature in ways unmatched by any other mainland colony institution beyond government institutions themselves. New York assembly committees often met in D'Honneur's Tavern in the 1730s. Boston taverns gave birth to a "popular party" under Elisha Cooke's leadership in the 1730s and then to antiparliamentary protest in the 1760s and 1770s. Boston's old Puritans could not control simple drinking in the late seventeenth century, since beer was a staple of household consumption and breweries proliferated. How could Crown appointees check the deep political and social camaraderie that taverns created in the next half century, much less curb both the taverns and their politics in the 1760s and 1770s?[70]

Clubs and associations further enriched and complicated colonial social life in the cities after 1680. Between 1700 and 1710 urban coffee-houses and taverns often spawned eating clubs identified by national sentiment—the Irish Club and the French Club in New York, for example. Some clubs claimed civic functions, their members gathering together to promote civic virtue and town improvement. Benjamin Franklin's Union Fire Company, formed in 1736 in Philadelphia, promoted its members' prestige by advancing the technology of fire fighting and importing an English-made engine that actually improved fire fighting in the city. Franklin's printing competitor, William Bradford, formed a competing company in 1738, the Fellowship Fire Company, and Franklin and Bradford were in turn joined by a third company, the Hand-in-Hand Fire Company, in 1742, whose members also came from the ranks of prominent Philadelphians.[71]

Benjamin Franklin's penchant for clubs and organizations mirrored patterns common in many towns and cities after 1700. Franklin's formation in 1727 of the Junto, a "Club for mutual improvement," represented the fusion of social status and civic virtue that produced crucial new institutions in the colonial cities. The dozen members of Franklin's Junto collected books and proposed the formation of the Philadelphia Library Company in 1730. The Library Company, even with its subscription format, reached out to only a few in the city. Yet it created an institution whose importance rose as more open, democratic forces reshaped Philadelphia, and America, in the next century. On the basis of his correspondence with European scientific figures, in 1743 Franklin suggested the formation of an American Philosophical Society, clearly derived from European models but with a New World membership which was inevitably drawn to American artifacts and to the intellectual puzzles they created. Finally, Franklin's fascination for learning led him to propose a college for Philadelphia in 1743, an idea that finally took shape in 1755.[72]

Franklin's boosterism reflected organizational attainments typical of the colonial cities after 1710. Charleston demonstrated the scale and organizational dynamic of this penchant for organizations. Between 1729 and 1750 Charleston residents organized some fifteen men's civic groups, and between 1750 and 1775 they added twenty-six new groups. Some were ethnic. The St. Andrews Society celebrated Scots.

Huguenot descendants organized the Two-Bitt Club, and Welsh, Irish, and German clubs also emerged. Still, ethnicity took a back seat to the members' affluence, and all the clubs remained social, not political, organizations through the 1760s. Clubs that lacked ethnic significance best conveyed the purely social character of those in Charleston: the Beef-Steak Club, the Smoking Club, the Candlestick Club, and the Segoon-Pop Club.[73]

Clubs in Charleston and other cities pursued seemingly civic-minded goals through elite, private-membership organizations. Twenty men formed a Fire Society in Boston in 1717, nineteen years before Franklin founded Philadelphia's Union Fire Company in 1736. Newport residents formed a Fire Club in 1726, although the town assumed responsibility for its operation by 1729, and the New York assembly authorized a fire brigade in 1737. Prominent residents of Newport, Charleston, and New York all organized private libraries between 1747 and 1751, with the Newport and New York libraries modeled directly on Franklin's Philadelphia Library Company. Peter Harrison's lovely Palladian-style building designed for Newport's Redwood Library in 1750 offered an elegant example of the stature to which colonial libraries might aspire.[74]

A fascinating literature penned by both men and women emerged out of the vigorous pub and coffeehouse life of post-1680 America. Women's involvement in making this private elite literature, especially in the several decades prior to the Revolution, reveals the growing complexity of colonial society. The social status, education, and assertiveness of women from prosperous, well-educated families fit the elite tea and coffeehouse culture not only of eighteenth-century London and Paris, but of New York, Philadelphia, Charleston, and even Boston.

Women attended public functions at the "Court Room" of Gignilliat's Tavern in Charleston (named because the Court of Common Pleas also met there before the construction of Charleston's State House in 1756), where they mixed with men in polite company at plays and lectures, not unlike the custom at European spas and salons. Women in Philadelphia's elite families gathered in country and town houses to engage in philosophical and romantic discussions and sometimes exchange literary productions.[75]

Milcah Martha Moore, daughter of a prosperous Pennsylvania

Quaker couple, grew to adolescence in this elite literary culture and participated in it her entire life. She wrote her first letter at age eight, asking her sister for "some verses." She maintained an elaborate correspondence throughout her life (she died in 1829 at age eighty-nine), and in 1787 she published her successful *Miscellanies, Moral and Instructive,* a collection of largely English poetry for use in schools. But beginning in the 1760s Moore kept far more interesting and important manuscript copybooks in which she entered a wide variety of poems, letters, and prose. Moore's manuscripts demonstrated the extraordinary correspondence that circulated among the prominent Philadelphia-area women she knew, including Elizabeth Graeme, the prolific Hanna Griffitts, and Susanna Wright. Indeed, Griffitts's "Essay on Friendship," the first piece in Moore's earliest surviving manuscript book, argued that writing stood at the heart of the women's friendships. Writing bound women conscious both of their restricted place in colonial society and of their talents, achievements, and concerns:

> The Friend requires, & friendship does demand
> At least th' attempt from my inferior Hand.
> The Heart shall dictate & the Pen rehearse
> And keep the Subject flowing with the Verse[.][76]

Other women kept up extensive correspondences that probed colonial intellectual, political, and social affairs. Esther Edwards Burr, one of the daughters of the Northampton minister and theologian Jonathan Edwards, maintained a substantial correspondence with Sarah Prince throughout the 1750s that reveals Burr's extensive reading patterns, her views on family and life, her spirituality, and her simple distress at the frequent vicissitudes of daily life: "I feel but very indifferently to day, what with [be]ing disturbed for several Nights past, and what with Drums, [G]uns, Trumpets, and [F]iddles, I have a very bad Head-ach—tis Training-day h[er]e. I wish I was out of the noise of it." Eliza Pinckney of South Carolina maintained an extensive correspondence that ranged from household and family life to business affairs, including her interest in indigo production as a potential ingredient in improving the South Carolina economy. Phillis Wheatley, the African-American poet of Boston who had arrived in America as an enslaved child in 1761, demonstrated how a determined woman facing immense obstacles might win not only recognition but respect. She was best known for her poem on the death of the revivalist George Whitefield in 1770, and her book, *Poems on Various Subjects, Religious and Moral,* appeared in London in 1773.[77]

Literature by both women and men also concerned love. The Philadelphia literary and friendship group to which Milcah Moore belonged included men as well as women, some of whom used their literary avocations to pursue romantic interests. William Franklin, Benjamin Franklin's illegitimate son who was regarded as one of Philadelphia's most eligible bachelors, wrote "A Song" at age twenty-two meant for a circle of young Philadelphia women. It found its way into the copybook of the young Elizabeth Graeme:

> Sometimes to kill a tedious hour,
> We venture at piquet
> Yet even there we feel your pow'r
> And know not how to Bett
> For Cupid laughs at our mistakes
> We love our money for your sakes.

The Philadelphia poet, Princeton graduate, and provincial army officer Joseph Shippen penned "Lines Written in an Assembly Room" in the 1760s, describing eight Philadelphia women:

> In Sally Coxe's form and face,
> True index of her mind,
> The most exact of human race
> Not one defect can find.
>
> Thy beauty every breast alarms,
> And many a swain can prove
> That he who views your conquering charms,
> Must soon submit to love.[78]

Other eighteenth-century colonial literature focused on politics, international relations, the empire, and agriculture, including tobacco and indigo, and has only recently been uncovered as historians have turned away from a long-standing focus on religious literature. This colonial literature frequently originated in coffeehouses, taverns, clubs, and social occasions, including dances. Much of it was satirical and witty, like the period's political literature, and it often appeared anonymously in newspapers or circulated privately along with the more personal, introspective literature common to Philadelphia's men's and women's literary groups, which led historians to ignore it for years.

This secular literature was stylistically derivative, emulating the standard fare of eighteenth-century British and continental European literature, especially in its emphasis on satire and wit. Its topics, however, were colonial and focused on events and features of the British mainland colonies. An intense focus on politics was often closely intertwined with the personal. Authors celebrated or ridiculed balls, state occasions, and other public and political "entertainments." One very early New York expression of the genre well represented the rambunctious public literature of subsequent decades. New York governor Robert Hunter's play *Androboros,* published in 1714, dissected Hunter's Tory opponents with mercilessly applied scatological dialogues (*Androboros* meant "man eater" and referred to the Tory Crown official and sometime colonial governor, Colonel Francis Nicholson). In February 1714 Rev. William Vesey, a Tory supporter and Anglican commissary for New York, charged that Hunter and other Whigs had desecrated Anglican vestments and prayer books at Trinity Church. In the play, Hunter laid the desecration to Vesey himself, whom he portrayed in the character "Fizle," and began with a scatological prologue:

> And it was a most Masterly stroke of Art
> To give Fizle Room to Act his part;
> For a Fizle restrain'd will bounce like a F—t,
> Which no Body can Deny, Deny
> Which no Body can Deny.
> But when it Escapes from Canonical Hose
> And fly's in your Face, as it's odds it does,
> That a Man should be hang'd for stopping his Nose,
> That I flatly and boldly Deny, Deny,
> That I flatly and boldly Deny.
> Long kept under Hatches, 'twill force a Vent
> In the Shape of a Turd, with its Size and Scent
> And perhaps in it way may beshit a Vestement,
> Which no body can Deny, Deny
> Which no body can Deny.

But However 'tis Dignify'd or Disguis'd,
That it should be for that the higher Priz'd
And either Don Commis'd or Canoniz'd,
That I flatly and boldly Deny, Deny
That I flatly and boldly Deny.[79]

Colleges formed in the post-1680 period represented a different kind of organization that also served private, corporate ends. The founding of Yale in 1701 occurred because conservative New England clerics regarded Harvard, established in 1636, as too secular and perhaps too liberal. Connecticut's provincial government chartered the college and listed the Connecticut governor and lieutenant governor as members of its governing corporate body, as it still does. But the college was intended to train Calvinist clergymen, and it served the public interest only indirectly. Even when Yale graduates became more interested in secular professions, such as law, the college, like Harvard, solidified its private corporate character and never emerged as a public institution. All the colleges established in America between 1680 and 1770—William and Mary (1693), Yale (1701), the College of New Jersey, later Princeton (1746), the College of Rhode Island, later Brown (1764), Queen's College, later Rutgers (1766), and Dartmouth (1769)—remained private institutions through the nineteenth century, with William and Mary and Rutgers becoming public institutions only in the twentieth century.[80]

European men also formed ritualistic, restrictive societies in the colonial cities after 1720, some local and some with transatlantic ties. Members came from the same prestigious clientele that formed library companies and private clubs and that patronized expensive taverns and coffeehouses. But where the library societies advertised for subscribers, the semisecret societies openly touted their restricted membership and hidden liturgies. They deliberately revealed just enough about both to stir public envy, and they exhibited the pattern of emulation and distinctiveness that so often characterized the colonial elite.[81]

Freemasonry, the international semisecret "Free and Accepted Masons" who established a Grand Lodge in London in 1717, offers a glimpse at the sometimes peculiar fascinations of wealthy, educated men in colonial cities. Freemasonry constituted a "speculative" fraternity whose secrets revealed a deep interest in learning and philosophical discourse. Freemasons emphasized mystical as well as rational sources of human knowledge and an ethics that transcended traditional Christianity. They mixed stories about Druidic secrets with "Hermetic" philosophy derived from the writings of the alleged sixth century B.C. Egyptian magus, Hermes Trismegistus. They put forward a deep faith in scientific rationalism, especially in geometry, which they regarded as a universal language unbounded by national borders and religious doctrine.[82]

The surface egalitarianism of Freemason ritual, with its stress on brotherhood, fellowship, and courtesy, belied its initiates' desire for authority and status. A series of "degrees"—Entered Apprentice, Fellow Craft, Master Mason—introduced new handshakes, whispered secrets, and occult knowledge that carried initiates toward greater social standing and authority—metaphors for their own rise inside the upper echelons of colonial society.[83]

A complex material culture accompanied colonial Masonic rituals. Masons paraded before the public to advertise their status, wealth, and semisecret knowledge. The *Pennsylvania Gazette* described Philadelphia Masons who opened a new Masonic hall with a parade as "all new cloathed with Aprons, white Gloves and Stockings, and the officers in the proper Cloathing and Jewels of their respective Lodges, with their other Badges of Dignity." And Masons knew dignity when they sat. The Masonic Master's chair, made by Benjamin Bucktrout of the Anthony Hay shop in Williamsburg, Virginia, about 1770, replete with all of Freemasonry's major symbols, is the single finest chair known to be made in colonial America.[84]

Colonial Masonic lodges demonstrated strongly local urges inside both the colonial and British Masonic worlds. They used British guides to Masonic ritual and acknowledged the supremacy of London's Grand Lodge. But once established, they operated with a strong native flavor, and rituals differed substantially from lodge to lodge in the colonies, just as was true in Britain as well. The result was a series of British-inspired secret societies that flourished among colonial elites prepared to promote universal principles of human understanding in colonial lodges that were themselves different from place to place.[85]

Annapolis's Tuesday Club, a local elite society active between 1745 and 1756, exhibited a particularly fascinating celebration of the vigor-

Masonic Master's chair. Benjamin Bucktrout,
Williamsburg, Virginia, c. 1766–1777.

ous, skilled, and even uniquely material secular culture of Britain's eighteenth-century American colonies. The manuscript minutes and history of the club by its secretary, the Edinburgh-trained physician Alexander Hamilton, described the extraordinary literary and club culture that energized urban elite life in eighteenth-century America.[86]

The Tuesday Club reveled in literary and artistic creativity, satire, satires within satires, scatological wit, political mimicry, music, and private and public ritual, all simultaneously serious and self-mocking. Like other mid-eighteenth-century clubs and literary societies, its members came from Maryland's intellectual and social elite, and their pseudonyms satirized themselves and their social roles. These included Dr. Hamilton (Loquacious Scribble, Secretary and Orator); Thomas Bacon, Maryland Anglican minister and pro-slavery writer (Signior Lardini); the Reverend John Gordon, a Scot and sometime Mason (Serious Social); John Beale Bordley, member of the Maryland Council (Quirpum Comic, Master of Ceremonies); and Jonas Green, publisher and printer of the *Maryland Gazette* (Jonathan Grog, Poet Laureate and Master of Ceremonies). Benjamin Franklin visited the club in 1754, joined its revelry, and found himself tabbed "Mr. Electro Vitrifrice."[87]

The Tuesday Club epitomized the artisanal, political, and literary creativity that could pour out from the colonies by the 1740s. The club banned humorless discussions of "party matters" and observed a "gelastic law" requiring satire and laughter. Should a member discuss politics and philosophy without humor, "the Society shall laugh at the member offending, in order to divert the discourse." Skits lampooned the control of tax funds and ridiculed debates about government by divine right or civil contract. The club satirized Maryland elections and unctuous Whig pronouncements on civic virtue, while mock "revolutions" led to stolen property and disappearing club records, all in imitation of Maryland politics and private scandals. The club derided Masonic mysticism by relating how the "Genius of the Club" appeared to members in a vision when the Tuesday Club president was absent.[88]

The Tuesday Club simultaneously ridiculed Marylanders' search for status and authority. A portrait of the club's fictitious founder, "Congallus de Rutheren," lampooned the Maryland gentility's penchant for Old World respectability and ancient secrets. A mock battle with the "royalist club" sent chairs, glasses, pipes, and scientific instruments

"Second Grand Anniversary Procession." *History of the Tuesday Club,* 1750.

flying through the air. A variety of presidential "badges," seals, and shields parodied the pretensions of governors, assemblymen, and magistrates.[89]

The Tuesday Club's "grand anniversary processions" revealed the emphasis on the public display of private gain that typified the eighteenth-century colonies. In its first "grand anniversary procession," the club marched from the president's home, "ornamented with their badges and Ribbans" to another member's home for the anniversary feast. As they returned, and "keeping their Ranks, they were Sufficiently stared at, as they passed, by persons of all Ranks and degrees, who seemed to be as much astonished, as the mob is at a coronation procession, or any such like Idle pageantry."[90]

The Tuesday Club expired in 1756 when Hamilton, its secretary and "historian," died at the relatively young age of forty-four. Hamilton's history was far more than mere description or chronicle. His narration of expanding social status, material plenty, and the quest for authority targeted the very core of elite Maryland society. And however much the Tuesday Club both emulated and mocked secret societies in the colonies and in Britain, Maryland society and its pretensions remained the center of its rituals, ceremonies, and satire. Its satires and ceremonies made sense precisely because they derived from and reflected colonial American experience and aims, not because they mechanically emulated British culture.

Hamilton's history of Annapolis's Tuesday Club bespoke the power of things to communicate the meaning of secular life in the eighteenth-century colonies. Desks, portraits, houses, clubs, literature, and ceremonies all bore consequences beyond their material form. They signified an extraordinary capacity to produce as well as to consume, sometimes in imitation, but sometimes not, and often with plenteous vigor, imagination, and a protean independence. Just two years before his death and a full decade before the eruption of controversy about the Stamp Act, Hamilton described a "revolution" and its origins in the Tuesday Club. One can only wonder if anyone went back to Hamilton's history in the 1790s, then still in manuscript, as it would remain for two hundred years, to marvel at Hamilton's sagacity. Here was an almost eerie prediction of the coming and causes of the American Revolution. As Hamilton put it, "the Tuesday Club had nothing but Rhapsodies concerning Liberty and property sounded in their ears for those 4 years past, . . . it was no wonder, that they had now become mere Enthusiasts on these points, and, being such Enthusiasts, the Secretary found them ready Tools for his purposes, vizt: to raise a disturbance, unhinge the Constitution, and set all things into the utmost confusion, that there might be a necessity for modelling the Club anew."[91]

Five

THINGS SPIRITUAL

As I have endeavored to show you how Europeans become Americans, it may not be disagreeable to show you likewise how various Christian sects introduced wear out and how religious indifference becomes prevalent.

J. HECTOR ST. JOHN DE CRÈVECOEUR (1782)

BRITISH colonists of 1770 would have found themselves spiritually unidentifiable if, after 1680, they had merely expanded religious patterns laid down in the earlier seventeenth century. New England would have remained almost exclusively Congregational, its internal tensions perhaps shifting from intense theological debate or witchcraft accusation to more prosaic ecclesiastical disputes. Southern colonies might have claimed formal Church of England establishments, but with lethargic leadership, an indifferent parish life, and a still overwhelmingly secular culture. Only New York might have looked "modern." Its early diversity of faiths—Dutch Reformed, Walloons, French Protestants, British Anglicans, Presbyterians, Quakers, and a few Jews—was accompanied by considerable religious "indifference" in many more residents. As Governor Thomas Dongan, himself Catholic, described the colony in 1687, "Here bee not many of the Church of England; few Roman Catholicks; abundance of Quakers preachers . . . Women especially; Singing Quakers, Ranting Quakers; Sabbatarians; Antisabbatarians; Some Anabaptists[;] some Independents; some Jews; in short[,] of all sorts of opinions there are some, and the most part [are] of none at all."[1]

Colonial American religion became far more varied and rich between 1680 and the American Revolution than even Thomas Dongan might have imagined. By 1770 an unprecedented array of European denominations and sects peopled the eighteenth-century colonies from New England to the Carolinas. Religious groups mastered this potential chaos through powerful new denominational institutions that effectively made Philadelphia, not Boston, the capital of American Protestantism. In turn, these religious groups figuratively and literally sacralized the landscape. They constructed far more church and synagogue buildings to serve more newly organized congregations than ever before, and the increase outpaced the colonies' population growth.

The denominations ushered in—or fell victim to—an evangelical revivalism that divided many of them and, in some cases, established patterns of proselytizing that characterized American culture for two centuries. American Indians underwent their own awakenings, some turning to Christianity, some turning against it with violence. Africans endured a spiritual holocaust that undermined traditional African religious systems. But some traditional African practices survived, and an extensive Christianization took root that would in the next century reshape both African-American society and American Christianity itself. In short, between 1680 and 1770 colonists transformed the religious patterns laid down in the seventeenth century, creating the religious pluralism and vitality long since identified as the very soul of modern American culture.[2]

B EFORE 1680 little public religious life existed in the colonies outside government-supported Christianity. This simple fact created a remarkably monochromatic religious landscape in early America. Roughly 90 percent of all congregations formed in the British mainland colonies before 1680 were either Anglican or Congregational, that is, congregations of the Church of England or of its "Puritan" critics who demanded "further reformation" in England's state church. This orthodoxy—Anglicanism in Virginia and Congregationalism in New England—never guaranteed order or success. In Virginia, the Church of England establishment proved unusually weak. An early empathy between Puritan merchants and the Virginia Company waned. Many Virginia counties never constructed church buildings. In other counties, crudely built churches decayed after their ministers departed. Ministers who served Virginia seldom enjoyed good reputations. A 1656 description called Virginia's Anglican ministers drunkards who "babble in a Pulpet, roare in a Tavern, . . . [and] by their dissoluteness destroy rather than feed their Flocks." New England Puritans fell out over doctrinal and gender issues in the Antinomian controversy that banished the dissident Anne Hutchinson from Massachusetts in 1638. After 1660 many Puritan congregations stagnated, taking in few new members and watching the children of old members ignore the churches, even if they did not reject them outright.[3]

Seventeenth-century Maryland demonstrated what happened when no religious establishment existed at all. Catholic congregations dotted early Maryland because the first settlers, including Maryland's founder, Lord Baltimore, were Catholic. But non-Catholic English immigrants soon outnumbered their Catholic neighbors, and tension rose over religion. The English Civil War of the 1640s and the Glorious Revolution of 1688 produced sharp anti-Catholic rioting that desecrated Maryland's Catholic chapels and drove Catholic worshipers into private homes. Still, the demise of public Catholicism produced no Protestant renaissance. Only three or four Protestant congregations existed in Maryland before 1680, all of them small and of little influence, and by the 1680s many Marylanders had seldom witnessed the public performance of elemental Christian ritual. At death, Marylanders were best known for their elaborate funeral banquets, characterized by heavy drinking, rowdiness, even riots.[4]

After 1680 striking alterations recast religion's public appearance in Britain's mainland colonies. Denominational expansion occurring in two waves, between 1680 and 1710 and between 1740 and 1770, thoroughly upended the old Congregational and Anglican hegemony in seventeenth-century colonial religion. The first wave enlarged, renewed, and strengthened the colonies' state church tradition and also brought forth major growth within dissenting denominations.

Puritan New England's state church establishments underwent a subtle but powerful expansion from the 1690s into the 1720s. New England governments adapted statutes and traditions established in the 1630s and 1640s to new settlement patterns. Massachusetts and Connecticut, for example, restructured their system of town churches to create a new, more supple "parish" organization that was legally separate from the town and better able to supervise religious activity in a larger, more diverse society. New Hampshire adopted a local establishment law that allowed each town to name its own Protestant tax-supported congregation, most being Congregational, as were all the established congregations in Massachusetts and Connecticut.[5]

Outside New England, the Church of England strengthened its establishment in Virginia and won important new legal powers in South Carolina, North Carolina, Maryland, and New York. More than half of Virginia's thirty-five parishes lacked ministers in 1680, and many were without church buildings. But in the 1690s a campaign led by James Blair, the commissary of the Anglican bishop of London (who also effectively created the College of William and Mary), utterly transformed the old moribund establishment. Under Blair's guidance, the Virginia Burgesses strengthened the laws regarding church administration, laid out new parish boundaries, authorized new vestries, levied new taxes, and backed new church construction in a program of Anglican renewal that lasted into the 1720s.[6]

The Church of England also prospered dramatically outside Virginia. A Ministry Act approved in New York in 1693 provided tax support to any Protestant church, but effective Anglican political manipulation secured establishments for Church of England congregations in most of the colony. A 1692 Anglican establishment in Maryland was vetoed in London, but new parishes operated in an informal establishment until the Maryland assembly passed a new Anglican establishment act in 1702. South Carolina Anglicans won establishment after a bitter battle in 1706, and Anglicans won legal establishment in North Carolina in 1715 after previous acts were vetoed in 1701, 1704, and 1711.[7]

Anglicans bolstered the Church of England in other ways as well. In 1699 Anglican reformers in London created the Society for Promoting Christian Knowledge (SPCK) to publish and distribute popular tracts on personal morality and Christian faithfulness. Then in 1701 they formed the Society for the Propagation of the Gospel in Foreign Parts (SPG) to advance Christianity and the Church of England among English settlers in the New World. Explicitly modeled on Quaker institutions in London, the SPCK and the SPG were intended to provide Anglican tracts for American settlers, salary support for Anglican clergymen, and financial support for new church buildings in the American wilderness.[8]

Mainland colony governments, including the four colonies that never adopted a legal establishment of one denomination—Rhode Island, Pennsylvania, New Jersey, and Delaware—also used the law to support Christianity and Protestantism generally. The law in colonies with church establishments may have tolerated dissenting religious activity in some instances, but it did not always do so and at times made dissent difficult. In colonies without establishments, the law customarily penalized a wide variety of settlers who did not observe Protestant Christianity in at least some perfunctory fashion. It openly discriminated against Catholics and Jews and punished blasphemers who spoke ill of Protestant Christianity. Long after the Salem witch trials of 1692 the law criminalized magic and witchcraft. Quaker Pennsylvania, a mecca for European immigrants seeking religious toleration, illustrated the general trend. Throughout the eighteenth century, Pennsylvania law forced officeholders to affirm their belief in Christ's divinity, banned blasphemy, forbade Sunday labor, and urged settlers to attend church so "looseness, irreligion, and Atheism may not creep in under pretense of conscience."[9]

After 1680, dissenting Protestants—British Quakers, Presbyterians, Baptists, and German Lutherans and Reformed—strengthened denominational authority even more dramatically, especially in and around Philadelphia. Between 1685 and 1710 Philadelphia witnessed the formation of America's first major Protestant denominational institutions. Quakers formed the Philadelphia Yearly Meeting in 1685, and it quickly assumed authority over Quaker meetings in Maryland, Delaware, Pennsylvania, and New York. English and Scottish Presbyterians organized the Presbytery of Philadelphia in 1706, then created the even more powerful Synod of Philadelphia in 1716 with presbyteries to exercise authority in smaller local districts. Baptists organized the Philadelphia Baptist Association in 1707. Then in the 1740s German immigrants organized the first "Coetus" of the Reformed or German Calvinist Church, while Lutherans organized the Lutheran Ministerium of Pennsylvania a year later in 1748.[10]

Similar denominational institutions even came to New England and the southern colonies. An association of Congregationalist ministers first met in Cambridge, Massachusetts, in 1690, modeling their activity on a group from Essex, England. Other clerical associations emerged elsewhere in Massachusetts and Connecticut after 1710, and by the 1730s several small presbyteries had appeared there as well. By the 1760s Presbyterian presbyteries and Baptist associations had also been organized in the southern colonies following significant proselytizing there in the 1750s, some of it sponsored by the Synod of Philadelphia and the Philadelphia Baptist Association. Ironically, among Protestants only the Church of England failed to transplant its traditional ecclesiastical structure to the New World. No bishop was ever appointed for the American colonies anywhere, largely because of political problems in Parliament. Anglicans had to depend on church establishments in individual colonies, the SPCK and SPG, and occasional commissaries, or deputies of the bishop of London. But although commissaries were sometimes appointed to manage church affairs in various colonies, their powers were questionable and easily disputed by local clergymen and parish vestries.[11]

These new colonial denominational institutions achieved importance because, like colonial assemblies, they reached for and attained authority. Power in them flowed down from the top, not up from the bottom. An essentially oligarchic coterie of men in the ministry held power in most of the colonial denominational institutions. Men designed as "Public Friends" and authorized to preach publicly dominated the Quakers' hierarchical monthly, quarterly, and yearly meetings, although both British and colonial Quakers were unusual in creating women's meetings to manage women's affairs, charity, and marriage problems. Ministers dominated the Synod of Philadelphia and its constituent regional presbyteries, and lay elders from congregations attended solely when their ministers were present, usually only occasionally. A variety of men deemed to be "in the ministry," ranging from ordained clergymen to elders, led the Philadelphia Baptist Association, while ordained clergymen managed affairs in the German Reformed Coetus and the Lutheran Ministerium of Pennsylvania. The denominational meetings grew in power because they successfully settled disputes, provided and often tested preaching, established doctrinal standards, and served as the principal conduit to Old World denominations, leaders, and congregations.[12]

The new and renewed state church establishments in New England and the southern colonies and the dissenting Protestant denominations ushered in a near frenzy of congregational expansion after 1680. Two measures graphically display the result. Fully 85 percent of the colonial congregations that existed at the beginning of the American Revolution had been formed after 1700 and no less than 60 percent of these congregations had been formed after 1740. Essentially, congregational growth outpaced population expansion in the eighteenth-century colonies. Tracing the numbers is dizzying but illuminating. About 110 Protestant congregations had been established in New England by the first Puritans before 1680. But 80 more congregations were organized there between 1680 and 1710 alone, 300 were added between 1710 and 1740, and another 400 organized between 1740 and 1770. The middle and southern colonies exhibited similar patterns. About 150 congregations existed in the middle colonies by 1710, but about 350 were organized between 1710 and 1740, and more than 550 were organized between 1740 and 1770. In the southern colonies, fewer than 100 congregations had been organized before 1680. Another 200 were organized between 1680 and 1740, then more than 350 between 1740 and 1770. Perhaps a third or more of these congregations failed. Still, those that survived far outnumbered their seventeenth-century predecessors.[13]

The post-1680 explosion of organized religious activity moved the mainland colonies far beyond Anglicanism and Congregationalism. Even New England, the least diverse region, exemplified the pattern. On the one hand, Congregationalists accounted for 75 percent of all Christian congregations in the 1770s. Yet the region also knew Presbyterians, Baptists, Quakers, Seventh-Day Baptists, Rogerenes, and Sandemanians, and in the 1740s Congregationalists and Presbyterians themselves split bitterly between revivalists and nonrevivalists.

In sharp contrast, the middle and southern colonies exhibited such religious and ethnic pluralism that no group could claim a majority of congregations or adherents in any of them. In the middle colonies German-speaking congregations accounted for nearly a third of all churches and were divided into six major groups—Lutheran, Reformed (Calvinists), Amish, Mennonite, Moravian, and Baptist. English settlers, who also accounted for about a third of all churches, were divided among four major groups—Anglican, Baptist, Presbyterian, and Quaker. The largest of the middle colony denominations, the Presbyte-

rians, accounted for no more than 21 percent of the region's congregations. In the southern colonies, though they exhibited less heterogeneity,
Anglicans, Baptists, and Presbyterians counted roughly equal numbers
of congregations by the 1770s. Anglicans could count only 30 percent
of all congregations in the southern colonies by 1770 despite their legal
establishment there.

The presence of Catholics and Jews symbolized not only the growing
spiritual heterogeneity of colonial America but the eighteenth century's
importance in making it. Catholics and Jews had been present in the
mainland colonies in the seventeenth century, Catholics in Maryland
and Jews in New Netherlands. But the renewal and enlargement of that
presence after 1680 made them noticed and even important by the
1770s. German Catholic immigration to the colonies after 1740 returned public Catholic worship to Maryland, and Jesuits officiated
there and in southern and western Pennsylvania until the Church itself
suppressed the order in 1773. Continuing Jewish immigration to the
mainland colonies brought the first synagogue to New York by the
1690s and led to the formation of congregations in Newport, Rhode
Island, Philadelphia, Charleston, and Savannah by the American Revolution. The result was a religious pluralism far more extensive than any
found in Europe. As Crèvecoeur wrote in the 1780s, in America "all
sects are mixed as well as all nations."[14]

The rapid formation of congregations in America after 1680 transformed the placement and appearance of religion in the colonial landscape. Settlements that had never seen the presence of Christian buildings increasingly found such buildings in striking profusion. The
sacralization of the landscape in Maryland was especially notable. Notorious for its public irreligion, Maryland contained only four or five
religious structures at the time of the first Church of England establishment act in 1692. Old Trinity Church in Dorchester County, built
about 1692, typified the buildings constructed in the next decade, small,
remarkably neat, surrounded by a consecrated burial ground that might
encourage proper Christian funerals rather than the drunken feasts that
had prevailed earlier.[15]

Anglican churches appeared everywhere. Between 1690 and 1715
Anglican church structures went up in New York City, Staten Island,
Westchester, Eastchester, New Rochelle (where the SPG helped turn
French Protestants, or Huguenots, into Anglican conformists), and

Queens. They remained the only free-standing English church buildings in the colony until the 1710s, when small Baptist and Presbyterian buildings were erected. In North Carolina, three Anglican buildings went up after passage of the 1701 establishment act that was, in fact, vetoed by the proprietors, and a dozen more buildings were erected after passage of the successful 1715 establishment act, all serving newly laid out, tax-supported parishes. As in New York, and aside from several small Quaker meetings, these buildings remained the principal visible evidence of Christian worship in the colony until the rise of Baptist and Presbyterian evangelizing in the 1740s.[16]

The Anglican renaissance brought the scale and sometimes the style of rural English church architecture to the newly sacralized American wilderness. Especially outside Virginia, the church buildings were usually small and reflected modest establishment acts and smaller, less well developed communities. South Carolina's small, rural Anglican churches, such as St. Andrews (built in 1706), St. James Goose Creek (1708), and Strawberry Chapel (1725), possessed stucco exteriors. The building interiors proclaimed the sovereignty of Britain's monarchs and Christ together. In the 1750s St. James Goose Creek parish in South Carolina installed an especially handsome royal coat of arms, in reds, blues, and golds, and a cantilevered mahogany pulpit that suspended its clerical occupants over the congregation when preaching and reading the Scriptures.[17]

Meeting house design throughout the colonies reflected both Old and New World elements, the latter often coming in details inevitably imposed by the local craftsmen who constructed the buildings. Designs for the largest colonial churches emulated British styles most closely, whether in Boston, New York, or Charleston, and sometimes followed design books, such as James Gibbs's *Book of Architecture* (London, 1728), which provided exterior and interior designs and details. The smaller rural churches exhibited greater local influence. In part, this stemmed from their customary wood construction, which contrasted with the more frequent use of stone in British church construction, even in small rural British buildings. Exterior design and details might follow general British practice but accommodated local styles. In New England, for example, church entrances sometimes followed designs already present in home construction.[18]

The colonial carpenters and craftsmen who put up the buildings imposed local construction styles, from the use of beams and design of joists to interior furnishings—pew designs, finials, and pulpit design. A master woodworker carved an especially imaginative flame finial for the fourth meeting house constructed in Concord, Massachusetts, in 1744, and the massive, finely detailed pulpit at the Ipswich, Massachusetts, meeting house constructed in 1749 typified the pulpits produced for eighteenth-century New England meeting houses. Colonists also painted their meeting houses and churches throughout the colonies in vibrant colors—orange, yellow, red, green, pea green, "peachblow," and blue, to emulate the sky—not always the white that became ubiquitous in the nineteenth century. In 1762 authorities in Pomfret, Massachusetts, ordered church colors that belied even the slightest reticence about a vivid decor: "The new meeting-house should be colored on the outside of an orange color—the doors and bottom boards of a chocolate color—the windows, jets, corner boards and weather boards, colored white."[19]

The aural landscape changed too. The first church bells heard in many colonies appeared after 1680, though not always in steeples. Few rural congregations could afford bell towers, which were added later in the century. Instead, most bells hung from platforms at the front or side of the church buildings. The bells were widely noticed and were sometimes missed when they did not exist. They cut through the thickened forests to call the half-interested to ritual, and in the cities, where they usually hung in steeples, they spread their sound out across the steadily enlarging urban population. Gottlieb Mittelberger noted that rural central Pennsylvania remained largely bereft of bells in the 1750s, even though it was filling up with German settlers and German Lutheran and Reformed congregations: "The whole year long one hears neither ringing nor striking of bells." When Ebenezer Parkman of Westborough visited Boston in 1742, he wrote that he "gratifyed my Curiosity at the chiming of the Ring of Bells at Dr. Cutler's Church—viewed the bells—the Organ, Vestry, etc." The bells could be problematic. The town officers of Guilford, Connecticut, ordered the town's 120-foot steeple turned "so as to have the Bell Swing east and West; the better to prevent the rocking of the Meeting House." Still, bells went up everywhere in Boston, New York, Philadelphia, and Charleston, after 1700, then in rural areas, and became a regular feature of colonial American church life.[20]

The sacralization of the colonial landscape markedly transformed the emerging cityscapes of eighteenth-century America. As late as 1695 New York still possessed the skyline of the old Dutch period with low buildings and no church steeples. By 1730 new immigrants viewed a cityscape thoroughly changed, with the spires of Trinity Church, a Lutheran congregation, the new Dutch Church, French Church, city hall, Secretary's office, and the Anglican church in Fort George at the tip of Manhattan making a particularly striking "modern" view. By the eve of the Revolution even modestly sized towns, such as New Haven, could claim several large church buildings that dwarfed anything constructed in the seventeenth century.

Boston and Charleston underwent similar transformations. In Boston, the Anglican King's Chapel challenged Congregational competitors with its massive stone construction. Over the next thirty years, Congregationalists responded with buildings for Boston's old and expanding Puritan congregations, nearly all with bell towers and ever more elaborate interiors. Charleston underwent a similar change. In 1700 the city knew only small meeting houses for Anglicans and French Protestants. In 1722, comparatively late, Anglicans constructed the most impressive church building yet erected in the mainland colonies—St. Philip's—which still dominated the Charleston skyline down to 1752, when the construction of St. Michael's Church, still standing, gave Charleston two major and massive Anglican churches.[21]

The urban churches and synagogues brought a new aesthetic of faith to colonial America that complemented the rise of artisan crafts in colonial secular life. Here, amid sacred settings, hand-carved wooden pews, massive pulpits, velvet seat cushions, hanging lamps, two-ton bells, and silver communion chalices and plates, colonial worshipers witnessed Christianity's material glory in the New World wilderness. In the early eighteenth century neither budgets nor available skills could produce all these objects in America. Many congregations purchased communion silver in London through the 1720s, while immigrants from Germany, Scotland, and elsewhere brought communion silver with them or ordered it from home. But by mid-century, many colonists received communion wine and bread in colonial chalices and plates, just as New York and Philadelphia Jews purchased silver Torah scroll ornaments and ceremonial circumcision instruments from New York's Jewish silversmith, Myer Myers. Much as in secular life, religious colonists

William Giles Munson, *View of the New Haven Green in 1800.*
Oil on canvas, c. 1830. Gift of the Botwinik Foundation, Inc., 1952.
Courtesy New Haven Colony Historical Society.

from Anglicans and Protestant dissenters to Catholics and Jews enlarged, refined, and transformed the institutional and material expression of their faith. Slowly, quietly, and perhaps even imperceptibly they
swung crucial points of spiritual reference toward a colonial frame,
ranging from increasingly authoritative denominational institutions to
traditional liturgical accoutrements created by American craftsmen.[22]

BETWEEN the 1680s and the mid-eighteenth century, Western society
witnessed numerous "revivals," or efforts to renew piety among
laymen and laywomen. Modern revivals were not invented in America,
although historians sometimes write as though they were. They originated in Prussia, where Lutheran reformers stressed a pietism directed
toward inner spiritual vitality. A renewed commitment to Christ, a
"new birth," would transform the life of every believer.

Torah ornaments by Myer Myers, c. 1770.

The pietistic revivals spread across Protestant and Catholic Europe to different ends. Prussian revivalism stressed personal introspection and transformation. Its institutional headquarters in Halle in eastern Germany developed links to a wide array of Protestants—Huguenot refugees from the Cevennes mountain warfare in France in the early 1700s, Count Nikolaus Ludwig von Zinzendorf and the Moravians, Swiss and Dutch religious reformers, and a formidable number of British reformers. These included Anglicans in the SPCK, John and Charles Wesley and their "Methodists," the Anglican George Whitefield, and the Welshman Howel Harris, whose preaching produced influential, ecstatic revivals in Cambuslang, Scotland, in 1742.[23]

Revivals in America proved equally diverse in character, doctrine, and dynamics. Several different revivals appeared briefly in New England between the 1680s and the 1730s, but the major periods of revival occurred in the early 1740s in the middle and northern colonies, then in the 1760s in the southern colonies, especially Virginia. Middle colony religious renewal began tumultuously with the rise of "singing Quakers" on Long Island in the 1680s, sometimes led by women, then continued with Dutch revivals in New Jersey in the 1720s and Presbyterian and German revivals in Pennsylvania in the 1740s. In the southern colonies efforts at religious renewal appeared for short periods in both South Carolina and Virginia in the 1740s, stimulated by the preaching of the Anglican itinerant George Whitefield, but drew more sustained support in the 1760s when Presbyterians and Baptists pressed their preaching in Virginia and North and South Carolina.[24]

The eighteenth-century colonial revivals promoted substantial discord, notoriety, and claims of political radicalism, most of which were substantially exaggerated. The Anglican commissary of South Carolina, Alexander Garden, and the Boston Congregationalist Charles Chauncy both charged that the religious enthusiasts in the 1740s were descended from London's infamous French Prophets of the 1710s, who reputedly raised followers from the dead, prophesied Christ's imminent return to earth, and used female preachers. Jonathan Edwards apparently permitted some emotional outbursts in his early revivals in Northampton, Massachusetts, and James Davenport took them much further in his New London, Connecticut, revivals, where his followers burned books in the 1740s to demonstrate their rejection of old ways. Yet such incidents were rare, as was any political radicalism linked to the revivals. Jonathan Edwards held back when he saw his own and nearby revivals heading toward too much emotion, and he steered clear of politics. The 1720 revivals in New Jersey's Dutch churches led by Bernardus Freeman and Theodore Frelinghuysen emphasized personal discipline rather than emotion as evidence for true conversion. Baptist revivals in both Virginia and New England in the 1760s defined success in terms of the listeners' sober reception of new doctrine rather than emotionalism.[25]

Doctrinal diversity matched the colonies' growing ethnic and national differences, although it took root in neither. Calvinism clearly dominated New England revivalism. But it had been preceded in the 1710s by a major interest in German Pietist doctrines, circulated through the writings of the Halle reformer August Herman Francke. In the 1750s much colonial revivalism incorporated the British Wesleyan Arminian slogan and question, "What must I do to be saved?" Calvinism dominated Scottish Presbyterian revivalism in the middle colonies. Dutch Reformed revivalism took root in the Netherlands' renewal traditions linked to German Pietism. Revivalism with somewhat different emphases found favor among German Lutherans and German Calvinists or Reformed. To further complicate matters, the immigrant German printer Christopher Sauer variously supported Lutheran sacramentalism, Hermetic Rosicrucianism, and universalist Freemasonry. Finally, Baptists in Virginia and North Carolina favored Arminian doctrines that stressed free choice and rejected the Calvinist theology of predestination.[26]

The lack of clear, unified theological principles opened colonial revivalism to strong regional and local influences. New England revivals flourished amid religious, social, and economic tensions stemming from growing cultural diversity, disparities in wealth, and social stratification. Middle colony revivalism was more narrowly circumscribed and customarily articulated Scottish and German ethnic sensibilities and religious sentiments. Virginia's Baptist revivalism of the 1760s, coming almost twenty years after the principal revival movements in the middle colonies and New England, bore fruit from the inability and even refusal of the established Anglican churches to comprehend broadening religious needs, particularly among growing numbers of poorer farmers.[27]

The actual tenor of colonial revivalism, in all its varieties, fed on the seemingly contradictory mix of provincialism, regionalism, and internationalism. In 1739 George Whitefield, a devout Calvinist in a highly latitudinarian church who had stunned listeners in England and Scotland with his highly dramatic preaching, used this success to build an audience in America that was already familiar with newspaper reports of his preaching at home. Revival ministers established elaborate letter-writing networks and created what they termed a "concert of prayer" that brought forth revival on both sides of the Atlantic. Moreover, Thomas Prince's Boston and Edinburgh newspaper, *The Christian History*, brought as much news of America to Europe as of Europe to America. And Whitefield paid obeisance to early colonial "revivalists" when, in visiting Jonathan Edwards in Northampton, Massachusetts, in 1740, he wrote that he also came to honor Edwards's grandfather Solomon Stoddard, who had led revivals there four decades earlier and whose books "I would recommend to all."[28]

Most colonial revivals of the tumultuous 1740s embraced relatively conservative rather than egalitarian or radical theologies. They encouraged personal introspection of one's spiritual and moral life, yet demanded a doctrinal conformity—among New England Congregationalists and Pennsylvania and New Jersey Scottish Presbyterians to a conservative Calvinism—that kept an enthused laity within religious and social bounds. Clergy and laity who moved in different directions did not do so for long. James Davenport, the controversial, even troubled, Connecticut revival preacher took dangerous egalitarian steps in his denunciations of traditional New England Christianity. Davenport was arrested in both Hartford and Boston and charged with making a public disturbance. Recognizing his background and credentials (he was a descendant of the Puritan founder John Davenport and a Yale graduate), they declared him *non compos mentis*, "out of mind," and even pro-revivalists deserted him. In South Carolina, an Anglican layman, Hugh Bryan, fascinated by the preaching of George Whitefield and imbibing both millennialist and apocalyptic views, criticized slavery and predicted a violent apocalyptic contest in 1742 that would destroy "Charleston and the country as far as Ponpon Bridge . . . by fire and sword . . . by the negroes before the first day of the next month." But after South Carolina authorities brought him before the colony's assembly, Bryan withdrew his predictions and confessed that he had been "guided by a spirit of delusion."[29]

Revivals conducted by the Tennent brothers of Pennsylvania and New Jersey and by Whitefield demonstrate the complexities and significance of eighteenth-century religious renewal in the British mainland colonies. The four sons of William Tennent, Sr., who left northern Ireland in 1718 for Pennsylvania—Gilbert, John, William, Jr., and Charles—constituted the best-known ministerial family in the middle colonies, and their revivalism plumbed local loyalties among largely Scottish immigrants and, more broadly, the wide, controversial boundaries of early modern supernatural belief. The Tennents' revivals occurred in congregations they had served for years. John and William, Jr., consecutively monopolized Presbyterian preaching among Scots for forty years in Freehold, New Jersey. Gilbert Tennent served only two congregations in New Brunswick, New Jersey, and Philadelphia in thirty-eight years, and Charles Tennent served his entire career at White Clay Creek, Delaware, the only Tennent to serve an English rather than a Scottish congregation. They catechized extensively in these congregations, and Gilbert described John Tennent as a "keen disputant" and "expert Casuist." They stressed personal regeneration—spiritual rebirth that came through a conversion experience, a "born-again" experience in modern parlance. They believed that Christian adherence would reshape the life of the individual and, ultimately, of the community.[30]

The Tennents also tapped popular conceptions of supernatural intervention that strayed far from the intellectually probing Calvinism of New England revivals. Three of the Tennent sons—Gilbert, John, and William, Jr.—became living exemplars of supernatural, even miraculous, intervention. Gilbert Tennent compared his recovery from a sickness to the biblical raising of Lazarus. John Tennent was given to ecstatic weeping and sighing. "In his private Studies," Gilbert later wrote, John "often took the *Bible* in his hand, and walked up and down the room, *Weeping,* and *moaning* over it," and John displayed this weeping and moaning "to almost all that came near him." William, Jr., bore signs of even more direct divine favor. A couple who dreamed he was in legal trouble traveled on their own to a New Jersey court to corroborate Tennent's testimony in a stolen horse case, seemingly a case of divine intervention. William, Jr., also died and then was raised from the dead after being "laid out on a board," as Gilbert Tennent later proclaimed. In yet another incident, he awoke one morning to discover that the toes of one foot were missing, an event he variously laid to either the Devil or God but not to natural causes.[31]

The Tennents' critics lambasted the family's apparent solicitude for superstition, even magic. David Evans, a conservative, nonrevivalistic Presbyterian openly compared Gilbert Tennent to an astrologer and fortune-teller. Could Tennent really ascertain "Men's *inward feelings*"? If so, "Must not Mr. T have some cuning Art, beyond what is common to Man[?]." These critics aside, the Tennents nonetheless exemplified a vital supernaturalist tradition in American evangelical revivalism that would extend into the nineteenth century, from early Methodist revivalists who used dreams and visions in their preaching, to the Shakers and the Mormon prophet Joseph Smith, to the twentieth century's Father Divine, A. A. Allen, and Oral Roberts.[32]

George Whitefield looked forward to modern times but in a different way. He was, it could be said, one of the first modern celebrities. Whitefield never accepted a settled ministry and traveled all his life, making his reputation among people he impressed but seldom knew. In thirty-two years, between 1738 and his death in Newburyport, Massachusetts, in 1770, Whitefield made seven tours of English America, the shortest lasting seven months (1738), the longest lasting three and a half years (1744–1748).[33]

Whitefield's sermons stressed original sin rather than regeneration, asking a famous question in almost every sermon, "Are you saved?" Unable to say yes, listeners took home an overwhelming sense of guilt, failure, and fear that Whitefield believed, and many listeners could confirm, would result in the surrender of their lives to Christ. Listeners attached significance to bodily characteristics even when he did not. Portraitists and cartoonists emphasized an apparent facial tic that made Whitefield appear cross-eyed and which listeners associated with divine blessing. A 1760 satirical cartoon disparaged his listeners' fascination with Whitefield's crossed eyes—"His poor Eye Sparkles with Holy Zeal," says one—and ridiculed their sexual attraction to Whitefield, one listener saying, "I wish his Spirit was in my Flesh."[34]

Yet Whitefield was not the Tennents. Increasingly, he was famous simply because he was famous. Notices in colonial newspapers prompted colonists to swoon at news of his coming. Nathan Cole, a farmer, described Whitefield's appearance in Middletown, Connecticut, in 1740: "When I see Mr. Whitefield come upon the Scaffold [at Middletown], he looked almost angellical—a young, slim, slender youth before some thousands of people, and with a bold, undaunted countenance. And my hearing how God was with him everywhere as he came along, it . . . put me in a trembling fear before he began to preach, for he looked as if he was Cloathed with authority with the great God."[35]

Whitefield, in short, was the first modern revivalist. An Anglican who never abandoned the Church of England, he worked outside traditional denominational channels, preaching in open squares and many different kinds of churches, quite unlike the Tennents. Ironically, perhaps, his legacy was personal, not institutional. Although followers in Salem, Boston, and Philadelphia established "nondenominational" congregations to promulgate Whitefield's message, they disbanded not long after his death. Whitefield's nondenominational, media-conscious revival thus prefigured another strain in American revivalism, the rise of the great individualistic evangelical preachers, exemplified in the careers of Charles Grandison Finney in the nineteenth century and in Billy Sunday, Billy Graham, and Robert Schuller in the twentieth century.[36]

What was the effect of revivalism on listeners and potential church members? Exhilarating for many. Revivals in the form of Whitefield's popular preaching and the proselytizing of local clergymen brought Christianity notice and visible form in a society where it was far from dominant in the settlers' daily affairs. Many men as well as women became "born again," joined congregations, and lived out the remainder of their lives as committed Christians. Indeed, men often outnumbered women as converts in local revivals, just as men also flocked to hear Whitefield, Benjamin Franklin not least among them. When Whitefield appeared in Philadelphia in 1739 and 1740, even the often skeptical Franklin could express amazement at the result: "It seem'd as if all the World were growing Religious; so that one could not walk thro' the Town in an Evening without Hearing Psalms sung in different families of every Street."[37]

But revivalism combined with pluralism also proved at least momentarily debilitating. The Anglican itinerant Charles Woodmason, who worked the backcountry of North Carolina in the 1760s, often belittled the men and women he sought to convert: "The people are of all Sects and Denominations—A mix'd Medly from all Countries and the Off Scouring of America." Only a handful took communion, and most, he believed, behaved licentiously: "Many hundreds live in Concubinage—swopping their Wives as Cattel, and living in a State of Nature, more irregularly and unchastely than the Indians." And their spiritual ignorance was amazing: "All of them [are] totally ignorant of the first Principles of things—So I cannot baptize them . . . not a Bible among them . . . Not the least Rudiments of Religion."[38]

Competing Presbyterian and Baptist revivalists only worsened matters. To Woodmason, however, the revivalists' greatest sin lay not in their doctrinal errors but in the confusion they spawned, confusion that turned settlers away from Christianity of any kind: "They complain'd of being eaten up by Itinerant Teachers, Preachers, and Imposters from New England and Pennsylvania—Baptists, New Lights, Presbyterians, Independants, and an hundred other Sects—So that one day You might hear this System of Doctrine—the next day another—next day another, retrograde to both." Woodmason described the effect: "By the Variety of Taylors who would pretend to know the best fashion in which Christ[']s Coat is to be worn[,] none will put it on."[39]

Woodmason offered a different, richer way of understanding the nagging confusion of spiritual variety in America that Crèvecoeur also described twenty years later in *Letters from an American Farmer.* Crèvecoeur felt obliged to tell readers "how various Christian sects introduced wear out and how religious indifference becomes prevalent" in the colonies, and he saw America's expanse as their cause: "Zeal in Europe is confined; here it evaporates in the great distance it has to travel . . . it burns away in the open air and consumes without effect." But Woodmason saw colonial religious indifference as the product of human invention, not nature, a consequence of the often spectacularly open society Europeans were making for themselves in America. Although Woodmason misunderstood the long-term consequences of religious pluralism and revivalism in America because he disliked and mistrusted each, he was far more prescient than Crèvecoeur, who almost wholly bypassed both and thereby elided two of the most central features of American culture before and after 1776.[40]

WOMEN'S roles in prerevolutionary colonial religious groups changed in subtle ways from their roles in the seventeenth century. The changes were important but not dramatic, and they better predicted transformations in the nineteenth century than they changed religion for colonial women before the American Revolution.

The changes in women's religious roles occurred against a backdrop of overwhelming male authority and power in colonial churches. In both the seventeenth and the eighteenth centuries women could not be ordained as ministers in any colonial religious group, and in all groups except the Quakers women could hold no formal meetings or offices in colonial congregations and denominations. This meant that it was extremely difficult for women to exercise direct influence in colonial congregation life. Such conditions were not unexpected, since they paralleled women's status in secular life. In the eighteenth century women could not vote, lost most property rights when they married, and often had property managed for them even when they inherited it or purchased it themselves.

Understanding women's roles in colonial congregations after 1680 must be set against an important anomalous fact: that after about 1680—earlier in some parts of New England—women constituted between 55 and 70 percent of the membership in most colonial congregations. This pattern, which continued into the nineteenth century, held true throughout most of the colonies, with the possible exception of German Lutheran and Reformed congregations. The cause of this pattern was probably social. For reasons still not clear, women joined congregations earlier than men, usually in their early twenties, while men often waited until their thirties and forties, sometimes long after they had married. As a result, women outnumbered men two to one in many colonial congregations.[41]

Female predominance in church membership was especially important because membership carried implicit, and sometimes explicit, opportunities to affect policy, from discipline to hiring ministers. Women who could not be magistrates, assemblymen, or constables or who could not belong to colonial eating and social clubs could be church members. Moreover, New England Puritan women had been accorded a clear standing of respect in church matters from the early seventeenth century. Clergymen preached on women's special spiritual responsibilities, especially in the quiet religious training of children, and congregations listened respectfully to their confessions of faith and disciplined women seriously and not necessarily with prejudice. The record was less equitable in the seventeenth-century Chesapeake. Courts and congregations in early Maryland and Virginia punished women for moral offenses frequently and severely. Virginia congregations—at least the few that continued functioning in the early- and mid-seventeenth century—often made women disciplined for fornication stand on stools in white gowns holding wands during church services but shamed men less often and with less humiliation.[42]

The changing roles of European women in colonial religion after 1680 contributed to the sometimes conflicting changes that typified their shifting positions in eighteenth-century colonial society. The emergence of female majorities within most congregations tested the theory and practice of male domination in church governance but did not shatter it. Women occasionally spoke out on church discipline and on the hiring of new ministers in New England Congregational churches. Women in the Congregational church in Essex, Connecticut, signed new "Articles of Faith and Discipline" in 1746, although men clearly wrote it. Women, perhaps more than men, pressed for construction of new, more convenient meeting houses in New England and appear to have voted in congregational matters in some New England congregations.[43]

Yet men filled all offices in Congregational, Presbyterian, Lutheran, and Reformed churches from ordained clergymen to elders, and in these denominations female voting remained a curiosity if it existed at all. The pattern was well demonstrated in a Boston episode at the very end of the seventeenth century. Benjamin Colman challenged the town's old Congregational churches in a "manifesto" that proposed to give congregational votes to "every Baptized Adult Person who contributes to the [congregation's] Maintenance." Opponents immediately castigated Colman for the obvious gender implications. "Then many women must have that Priviledge," Increase Mather responded. Although Colman upheld the principle, it is not clear whether female contributors ever voted regularly in Colman's own Brattle Street Church, much less in other New England Congregational churches.[44]

Baptists and Quakers, however, gave women more direct roles in denominational affairs, though within considerable limits. "New Light" congregations formed in New England during Baptist revivals of the 1730s and 1740s and at least several Baptist congregations in Pennsylvania gave women considerable voice in congregational affairs. Women publicly addressed issues important to congregational life, ranging from the discipline of sinful members for sexual misconduct to "pridefulness," theft, and improper preaching. Women apparently voted in the selection of certain ministers and in admitting members and choosing deacons. In some New England and Pennsylvania congregations women participated in the "washing of feet," a ritual that symbolized the equality of all believers. These practices, especially female voting, seem to have been a largely eighteenth-century colonial American practice, since British Baptists appear to have discarded some moves toward female voting that emerged in the 1640s and 1650s during the religious radicalism that flowered within the English Commonwealth.[45]

These practices did not go unchallenged. The Philadelphia Baptist Association's answer to a question about female voting in 1746 demonstrated an important middle ground. The association reasoned that "absolute silence in all respects cannot be intended" by biblical texts, because women could not then confess their faith or answer charges brought against them. Women should not "open the floodgate of speech in an imperious, tumultuous, masterly manner." But there must be "times and ways in and by which women, as members of the body, may discharge their conscience and duty towards God and man." Women should be excluded "from all degrees of teaching, ruling, governing, dictating, and leading in the church of God . . . But if a woman's vote be singular, her reasons ought to be called for, heard, and maturely considered, without contempt."[46]

A dispute in the Philadelphia Baptist congregation in 1764 demonstrated that women still voted there on congregational matters for two decades after the 1746 advice. But the practice obviously rankled some men, who were encouraged by a new minister, Morgan Edwards, who criticized it. Although the complicated dispute is difficult to assess, the vigor of both sides is not. One member, Joanna Anthony, challenged men, including Morgan Edwards, who sought to avoid female voting. In a letter to the church in 1764, Anthony castigated Edwards for failing to consult the women in choosing elders, "the first instance this we

ever knew of sisters being treated with such contempt in that church."
As Anthony wrote, "We know our former rights and we beg to know
who had a right to deprive us of them." Had the women "thought their
privilege or their practices contrary to the word of God," Anthony
wrote, "they would or ought to have kept themselves separate from
them."[47]

Although the Philadelphia congregation continued female voting, the
long-term pattern proved decidedly less positive. After the American
Revolution, most Baptist congregations stopped female voting and restricted women's participation in formal church affairs. The causes for
this decline probably rested in the growing Baptist identity as a "main-
stream" denomination in a society that restricted women's rights, liberties, and powers. As Baptists became merely one denomination among
many, they acted more like everyone else around them. Yet between the
early eighteenth century and the Revolution itself, the limited Baptist
practice of female suffrage suggested a spiritual assertiveness, determination, and willfulness that augured well for the distant, if not the
immediate, future.[48]

Quakers offered the most important exception to Christian restrictions on colonial women's religious leadership and officeholding.
Official Quaker recognition of women's spiritual authority flourished
on both sides of the Atlantic, not merely in America, as with Baptist
female voting. Quaker theology made women's religious leadership
possible. George Fox, founder of the Quaker movement in the 1650s,
acknowledged in 1672 that after the fall of Adam "man was to rule
over his wife." But he also argued that God had inspired Quakers to
lead a restoration in which men and women were to be "help-
meets . . . as they were before the fall." Quaker emphasis on the family
underscored the cooperation required of men and women and explicitly
emphasized women's capabilities in managing affairs in the family and
elsewhere.[49]

The English Quakers' meeting system established in the 1670s provided for separate men's and women's meetings that quickly were carried to the colonies. Ultimately, the men's meetings were more powerful.
Men dominated the principal disciplinary meetings, especially the London Yearly Meeting and the Philadelphia Yearly Meeting that estab-

lished basic principles for the movement. Yet these men expected important leadership from women in two special areas, charity and marriage. In both Pennsylvania and Britain, Quaker women's meetings made arrangements for the elderly poor of both sexes, for widows, and for orphaned children. They gave cash to the destitute and found homes for orphans. They disciplined women and men who violated Quaker marriage regulations, especially marriage to non-Quakers, or marrying "out of unity with Friends." When these marriages reached epidemic proportions in Pennsylvania in the early 1750s, the women's meetings initiated the disownments of offenders and the men's meetings regularly upheld them. Most of the women who exercised this leadership were married, lived in wealthier families, and as a consequence sometimes owned slaves, even though slaveholding was not widespread in Pennsylvania.[50]

Thus if Quaker women's meetings were not independent of the men's meetings, they were recognized as powerful by them. Together, the working relationship between the men's and women's meetings reinforced and upheld male authority in society generally and even within Quakerism. But no other Christian denomination went so far in granting women such crucial institutional authority. While Quaker women used their long-standing institutional experience and power to pursue broad-scaled work in humanitarian, educational, and temperance reform in the nineteenth century, women in other denominations achieved similar results only by forming voluntary societies outside regular denominational channels or by asserting leadership in new religious movements, such as Spiritualism.[51]

Yet it was women's surprising and modestly increasing appearance as religious speakers between 1680 and 1770 that constituted the most intriguing and potentially significant development for women's role in American religion. Colonists first witnessed this development in the late 1650s, when several Quaker women preached in Boston and were banished on pain of death. When the Rhode Island Quaker Mary Dyer returned, she was executed in May 1660. In fact, women served regularly as "Public Friends" authorized to preach to non-Friends. English women frequently preached in America, and after 1710 colonial Quaker women engaged in preaching tours of Britain.[52]

Women's appearances in the episodic revivals of the 1730s and 1740s brought them more attention, occasional notoriety, and some serious notice as expositors of the Christian experience. The notoriety stemmed from emotional outbursts in colonial revivals that played into eighteenth-century prejudices about women's penchant for instability. When George Whitefield preached in New York City in 1740 "upon the miracle of the woman healed of the bloody [flux]," the Massachusetts minister, Daniel Rogers, noted that "one or two women cryd out loud." It was the kind of outburst that Boston's Charles Chauncy, an opponent of revivalism, criticized in 1742 when he claimed that revivalists' "frightful language . . . has its intended effect upon one or two weak women," whose "shrieks catch from one to another, till a great part of the congregation is affected."[53]

Amid this cant women nonetheless spoke up in religious affairs from the 1730s forward. Jonathan Edwards used the spiritual transformation of his wife, Sarah, as a model for others in *Some Thoughts concerning the Revival of Religion in New England* (1742). Edwards found no pathology in Sarah's spiritual experience and transformation, although his deletion of all reference to her identity and sex demonstrated the caution with which he wrote. The Durham, New Hampshire, minister Nicholas Gilman "added a word of Exhortation to the People" when Mary Reed "declared in Publick the close of Her last Vision" in 1742. Gilman later spent four days at Reed's home "Singing praises to God in Extempore Verse" and instructing her. As one historian describes the scene, "Gilman neither counseled nor tried to 'cure' Mary Reed. He marveled at her receptivity to the spirit, and when she spoke, he listened. All boundaries—of sex, of wealth, or of education—dissolved in a common rapture."[54]

Female spiritual authority emerged in places far from New England as well. At the death of Mary Hutson of Charleston, her husband, the local Presbyterian clergyman, published her diaries in London in 1760 to promote Christian piety in all readers, not women alone. Yet criticism always lurked nearby. Several women took such leading roles in a ministerial dispute at New York's Presbyterian congregation in the early 1750s that one prominent male Presbyterian felt free to complain that "they have four *Popes* in Newyork, *women popes*."[55]

Some women organized groups to promote spiritual renewal. Esther Edwards Burr alluded in her diary to several gatherings of women who discussed religious issues between 1754 and 1757, and ministers sometimes casually reported the existence of similar groups throughout the eighteenth-century colonies. Sarah Osborne, of Newport, Rhode Island, verged on a formal ministry when she promoted spiritual renewal. She started a women's prayer society in the 1760s. During revivals in 1766 and 1767 as many as five hundred people, men as well as women, flocked to her home to hear her speak, a scene reminiscent of Anne Hutchinson's semipublic commentaries on Boston's clergymen in the 1630s. When a clergyman questioned Osborne on the ground that she was, essentially, assuming a clerical role, she defended herself. The proof of her legitimacy rested in the souls she had awakened, and she would not "shut up my Mouth and doors and creep into obscurity."[56]

For European women in America, then, conflicting patterns emerged in religion between 1680 and 1770. Quakers transferred a meeting system from England that recognized women's authority through separate women's meetings with important and expanding functions in eighteenth-century colonial Quakerism. Baptists allowed women to vote in some congregations in New England and Pennsylvania, and women defended this voice when challenged. Individual women promoted spiritual renewal publicly as well as privately, sometimes with surprising vigor.

Yet these activities did not overturn strong male dominance of religious leadership and authority in Britain's American colonies. Women's leadership within the Society of Friends was not so much autonomous as parallel and took energy from a vigorous partnership with men and the Quakers' men's meetings. Female voting among Baptists never established itself firmly within the movement and eroded as Baptists followed other denominations in rejecting the practice after the Revolution. Although public religious activity by women probably increased in the eighteenth-century colonies and spread across several denominations, critics frequently challenged its most vigorous expressions outside Quakerism and even supporters understood it as a supplement to male ministry and authority. However filled with potency for the future, eighteenth-century colonial women's religious activity still largely reflected the constraints of a secular culture that valued women's work and sentiments yet awarded women little independent, autonomous authority.[57]

R ELIGIOUS patterns among American Indians settled into three models of great importance in the eighteenth century. All carried seventeenth- and even sixteenth-century origins but their solidification after 1680 firmly established crucial patterns that typified Indian religious life for the next several centuries. One was a pattern of both episodic and continuous spiritual creativity by which Indians merged tribal practice, traditional practices of other Indian nations, and European practice into unique spiritual configurations. The second involved the use of native religious prophecy to resist acculturation and Indian decline. The third brought Christianization, often of high unevenness and attended with considerable conflict.

Most eighteenth-century Indians experienced substantial change in their religious world. This process began with English contact in the sixteenth century. The alterations in nature and ecology produced by European colonization threatened many native religions. The extraordinary slaughter of animals questioned beliefs that assigned crucial supernatural roles to animals, for example. The four hundred tons of deerskin exports shipped from the Southeast to Europe in 1764, a reasonably typical year, changed the deer from an animal with sacred standing, though still hunted, to a commodity with little ritual or spiritual meaning. The Micmacs of far eastern Canada found their special relationship with the beaver imperiled by the unchecked harvest of beaver skins, a trade in which the Micmacs themselves indulged. The spirits residing in nature no longer spoke, or when they did they sometimes lashed back at the Micmacs, who were now attacking them.[58]

Other Indian groups demonstrated a remarkable resilience in the face of the multiple threats to their political, cultural, and spiritual universe. They incorporated the material goods that Europeans brought into their existing religious milieu. This syncretism, or fusing of different beliefs and practices, helped shifting native cultures survive and demonstrated the Indians' creative adaptability. A Micmac medicine woman used Catholic rosary beads as the centerpiece of her Micmac healing practice. An unhappy Jesuit priest described it: "These she carefully preserved, and gave them only to those who were her friends, protesting . . . that the gift which she gave them had come originally from heaven." Indians sometimes plied their spiritual knowledge among both Europeans and Indians. On Long Island in 1769 Mary Cooper reported "an old Indian come here to day that lets fortans [fortunes] and ueses charmes to cure tooth ach and drive away rats."[59]

New cultures and new religious systems emerged among Indians as European expansion continued. The Catawba nation that emerged in the Carolinas between 1700 and 1740 gave birth to new religious expressions as well as secular ones. The religious expressions mixed traditional Indian beliefs with Christianity learned through missionaries. One Catawba, a former Saponi Indian named Ned Bearskin, described the Catawba belief in a single supreme being who punished goodness and badness. This was not, however, the Christian God in a Christian world. Bearskin described a sacred world where deer and turkey meat could not be mixed, where the "regions of bliss" after death contained beautiful women and men, abundant game, and plentiful crops, and where "regions of misery" brought cold, hunger, and constant sexual aggressiveness. New ceremonies bound Catawbas together in life and death. Catawba rituals commemorated harvests and honored the dead.[60]

Other Indians turned to prophecy to fuel resistance to Europeans, especially to the British. British travelers and missionaries reported "seers" or "prophets" in the 1740s. A Shawnee or Onondaga "seer" claimed in 1737 that Indians who had traded game for alcohol had "driven the wild animals out of the country," and another reported by the Presbyterian missionary David Brainerd blamed the Indians' "degenerate and corrupt" society on alcohol. In 1751 an Indian woman in Wyoming in western Pennsylvania described visions of the "Great Power" that challenged the Delaware Indians' old male leadership and attacked the "poison" in their midst, presumably both alcohol and the British. Papoonan, a Munsee Delaware, also criticized alcohol as well as Indian greed that made them "proud & Covetous, which causes God to be Angry & to send dry & hot Summers & hard Winters, & also Sickness among the People." Wangomend, sometimes called the Assinsink Prophet, also experienced visions in the early 1750s, denounced rum, and reintroduced old rituals where Indians related "Dreams and Revelations everyone had from his Infancy."[61]

This new eighteenth-century religious prophecy increasingly crossed tribal identity through three means. It frequently identified alcohol as the major cause of the Indians' demise. It identified Europeans, and especially the British, as the principal sources of alcohol and agents of that demise. And it offered a restorationist nativism as a solution to the Indians' problems, urging Indians to return to "traditional" Indian values, through pan-Indian values that could draw together numerous Indian groups rather than narrower efforts to restore merely one group. The prophecies of Neolin, the so-called Delaware prophet who began working in western Pennsylvania and Ohio in the early 1760s, exemplified this potent strategy. He explained that "White people" blocked the Indians' path to heaven, fulminated against rum and alcohol, and urged Indians to avoid British trade and reject British goods. Neolin introduced rituals that symbolized the restorationist impulse, namely ritual drinks that induced Indians to vomit, a ritual practiced so thoroughly among his followers that one Shawnee settlement was called "vomit town."[62]

More denominations became involved in missions to Indians in the eighteenth-century British colonies, though not always with great success. The Church of England sponsored a mere handful of missions among Indians and succeeded with even fewer. Officials at the College of William and Mary in Virginia set aside a residence for Indian students, but efforts to secure "Indian Scholars" were soon forgotten. The Congregationalist minister Eleazer Wheelock trained Indians at a special school in Lebanon, Connecticut, and later, at what would become Dartmouth College, in New Hampshire. He separated Indian students from their native communities so he could train and discipline them without interference. Samson Occom, a Mohegan, became Wheelock's greatest success and ministered to Indians on Long Island, elsewhere in New York, and in New England. But both Wheelock and Occom won relatively few converts, and Wheelock's school was generally considered a failure.[63]

Moravian missionaries in New York and Pennsylvania experienced greater success. Like the Jesuits, the Moravians learned much about native cultures and exhibited considerable patience in awaiting conversions. They also distanced themselves from aggressive government policies on English settlement and warfare. But most important, Moravian theology fit both the realities of the conversion process and many important themes in traditional native belief. Moravians stressed piety and the love of Christ, both of which could be learned by example. Unlike Puritans, they did not stress doctrine. Moravians lived among the Indians and used native language in day-to-day conversation, not merely in translated books. Like Indians, they discussed the ways in which dreams could communicate religious truths and moral lessons. A Presbyterian observer in Pennsylvania commented enviously, "the Moravians appear to have adopted the best mode of Christianizing the Indians. They go among them without noise or parade, and by their friendly behavior conciliate their good will."

By 1770 Indians in Britain's colonies had evolved a religious pluralism that paralleled the escalating religious diversity found among Europeans in America. Yet this was a largely forced pluralism and a stark contrast to the spiritual variety that had emerged so freely among European settlers. The pan-Indian spiritual themes introduced by Neolin and other late-eighteenth-century Indian prophets simultaneously bridged that pluralism and extended it. Yet wherever these prophets found listeners, they succeeded because the evils they identified—Indian drinking, decline in traditional Indian religious sensibility, threats to tribal identity and cohesion, all collapsed into more than a century of frequent Indian hatred of Europeans—so clearly touched the very soul of Indian existence.

THE history of religion among Africans in the mainland colonies contrasted sharply with the religious history of European settlers in America. Europeans explored an increasing variety of religious expressions in America after 1680 and established a wide array of denominational institutions and congregations, creating an unprecedented religious pluralism among Europeans in Britain's American colonies. By contrast, Africans underwent a spiritual holocaust of major dimensions that prevented traditional African religious systems from prospering in Britain's mainland colonies, revived some traditional African beliefs and practices, especially those surrounding burials, and adopted and changed a Christianity to which small yet increasing numbers of Africans converted after 1750. No other peoples in New World society experienced such wrenching spiritual change under such difficult conditions. No other people underwent change so thoroughly dictated by external circumstances. And few exhibited the spiritual creativity by which Africans responded to the difficulties they faced.

The fate of traditional African religious practice among Africans brought to the mainland colonies between 1619 and 1680 remains unknown. Before 1680 the British mainland colonies held only small numbers of slaves, and neither they, their owners, nor the Africans who won freedom in the 1650s, 1660s, and 1670s left substantial evidence about their religious practice. Moreover, what happened to African religion in the crucial century after 1680 when some 250,000 Africans arrived in the British mainland colonies has provoked considerable debate among historians. Some have insisted that African "survivals" made African-American culture and religion possible and that these can be traced from Africa to nineteenth-century African-American society, especially in the South. Others have argued that the question of survivals is not really provable given vagaries of evidence, while noting that the "spiritual experience of the slaves took place as part of a tradition emanating from Africa." Still others argue that historians have exaggerated the survivals and that the real story of African-American religion and culture should center on the vibrant new culture shaped from the hardscrabble materials offered by American culture and religion generally.[64]

The story of an emerging African-American religious tradition is indeed complex and focuses on three crucially important features. First, between 1680 and 1770 African slaves in the British mainland colonies experienced the substantial destruction of traditional African religious systems, although some important discrete rituals and customs survived nonetheless. Second, outlines of new religious practices using both Christian and African elements emerged as family and kinship systems began to appear among captured Africans, especially in the Chesapeake, between the 1720s and the 1770s. Third, through the 1770s, the emerging public religious life among slaves probably bore more fully European elements than might have been the case in the nineteenth century, when more independent African-American congregational life could draw more freely on previously suppressed and redis-covered African traditions, especially in music and ritual.

This model did not appear everywhere. In New England, which had relatively few slaves throughout the colonial era, the very tiny numbers of Africans and their thorough dispersion throughout society created a significantly different dynamic of cultural and religious development among captured Africans. Pulled into different households, separated by long distances, usually owned by affluent church members and not infrequently by clergymen (like Jonathan Edwards, for example), many slaves converted to Christianity and were allowed to join Christian congregations. Although Africans in New England celebrated their own festival days, these were secular, not religious, and many slaves, cer-tainly a higher percentage than elsewhere in the colonies, had become attached to Christian congregations.[65]

Where captured Africans were more numerous, however, important evidence suggests that certain traditional religious practices persisted as slaveholding evolved after 1680. This occurred despite the difficulties of cultural transfer and European suppression of group life among the enslaved. Captured Africans planning New York City's slave revolt of 1712 supposedly received powder from a free African sorcerer that they spread on their clothing to make them invulnerable to their owners' weapons. The conspirators also allegedly sucked blood from one an-other's arms to forge a ritual bond among themselves. South Carolina planters complained of "rites and revels" among recently imported slaves who had come directly from Africa, and throughout the eigh-teenth century southern planters often referred to their slaves as "hea-thens" and "pagans" as they sought to Christianize them.[66]

Yet it is remarkable how little evidence exists that documents tradi-tional African religious practice in Britain's mainland colonies, espe-cially of the public practice that strongly characterized religious rites in the Old World. Gossipy European planters, such as William Byrd II and Landon Carter of Virginia, chattered endlessly in letters and diaries about nearly all aspects of their slaves' lives but said little or nothing about religion. When they did comment on religion, they were vague, formulaic, and uninformative. They customarily castigated slaves as "heathens" and "pagans" but failed in any significant way to specify the nature and substance of the Africans' offending religions. Colonists seem to have known far more about religion among American Indians. Both Robert Beverley in the 1710s and Thomas Jefferson in the 1780s offered extensive comments on religion among American Indians without in any way thinking to comment on religion among Africans. Beverley never mentioned the Africans' religion, and Jefferson's chapter on "The Different Religions Received into That State" ignored African religion altogether, though it did not ignore Indian religion.[67]

Traditional African religion appears to have fueled few colonial slave revolts, and converted Christians led the few nineteenth-century revolts. Except for the 1712 New York City revolt, religion, either African or Christian, figured little in colonial slave rebellions. South Carolinians traced the 1739 Stono Rebellion to secular discontent among slaves, not to religion, and New Yorkers laid the alleged 1741 slave plot to Catholic agitators sent from French Canada, not to African sorcerers practicing in the city. This pattern contrasts sharply with nineteenth-century developments. Gabriel Prosser might have succeeded in the Virginia revolt of 1800 had he accepted the support of traditional African occultists working in slave quarters, which he rejected. In 1822 Denmark Vesey and the plotters of revolt in Charleston all belonged to the city's African Methodist congregation. And in 1831 Nat Turner, leader of the bloody Southampton, Virginia, slave revolt, was a Baptist preacher who saw freedom in the Scriptures.[68]

Significant evidence points up a spiritual holocaust that all but destroyed any substantial collective or public practice of African religion in the mainland colonies between 1680 and 1770 and may have suppressed traditional private or personal religious practice as well. Slave capture, the rigors of the experience of slavery, and Anglican and evangelical suppression of African religious practice decimated African religious systems in the mainland colonies. This African spiritual holocaust differed significantly from the Jewish holocaust of the twentieth century. The African spiritual holocaust occurred as a by-product of slaveholding rather than as the result of efforts to destroy a people. It did not stem from a carefully planned program, and it was not a step in the promotion of a master race. Still, it induced violence and repression and flourished amid an open contempt for non-Christian beliefs. Moreover, it produced extraordinary religious destruction among the quarter-million Africans brought to the mainland colonies between 1680 and 1770. No other religious event of the entire colonial period, including the evolution of seventeenth-century Puritanism or the emergence of pluralism and diversity among European colonists in the eighteenth century, so profoundly reshaped a people's experience of religion in the New World.

The slave trade initiated this African spiritual holocaust in the British mainland colonies. It was, quite profoundly, spiritually "deselective." Unlike Europeans emigrating to the New World, Africans could not choose to bring men and women who fulfilled unique spiritual functions and exercised important religious leadership. Africans who might have had special religious knowledge arrived in America only because they may have been captured, the unlucky victims of a massive slave trade. Even when an African possessed of special knowledge in religion arrived in America, the tensions and bitterness of slavery could undermine inclinations to fulfill important spiritual roles. The nineteenth-century slave Charles Ball recalled in his narrative, *Fifty Years in Chains,* that in the 1740s his eighty-year-old grandfather "retained his native traditions respecting the Deity and hereafter" but kept these traditions to himself because "he was an African of rank in his native land" who only "expressed contempt for his fellow slaves."[69]

Colonial slaveholding further exacerbated the religious consequences of Old World capture because its social and demographic patterns reinforced the suppression of traditional public religious practice among captured Africans. Mainland slave settlements were far more dispersed than the far larger, more dense slave settlements in Brazil or Hispaniola, and this dispersion greatly constrained the social conditions under which public religious practice could be maintained. In addition, Africans enslaved in America came from as many different cultures as did European colonists, few of whom necessarily shared common spiritual sensibilities. Moreover, slave mortality was high, especially before 1740. These deaths, plus frequent suicides and the suppression of traditional African religious practices by slaveholders, placed Africans in a setting of exceptional spiritual constraint.[70]

Coercion and labor discipline further limited collective public African religious practice in the colonies. As slaveholding expanded after

1680, planters worried constantly about collective activity among slaves of all kinds, including religion. In 1709 the South Carolina Anglican Francis Le Jau worried that he had not yet fully suppressed African "feasts, dances, and merry Meetings upon the Lord's day," which he reported were "pretty well over in this parish, but not absolutely." To remedy these spiritual excursions among already baptized slaves, Le Jau threatened to bar converted Africans from communion. A year later he happily reported that "the Lord's day is no more profaned by their dancings, at least about me."[71]

The most obvious result of these mainland colony conditions was the destruction of the traditional African religious systems as systems. The comparison with the experience of European settlers is telling. Puritans, Scottish Presbyterians, German Lutherans, Dutch Reformed, Quakers, and Jews not only survived in America but eventually prospered, both individually and spiritually, despite the difficulties and anomalies of colonization. But Akan, Ashanti, Dahoman, Ibo, and Yoruba religious systems collapsed in the shattering cultural destructiveness of British mainland colony slaveholding. These religious systems bore breathtakingly expansive worldviews, theories of causality, systems of moral obligation, and supernatural vitality. All were distinctive, certainly as distinctive as the English, German, or French views of Christianity, Protestant or Catholic. Like Christianity, they took public activity as a major measure of their vitality, and none appears to have regarded private, secretive practice as the measure of its force. By 1770, however, none of them survived as religious systems in the British mainland colonies.

Yet discrete religious practices reflecting partial survivals from the larger religious systems of African societies did survive. One form centered on healing. As early as 1710 Thomas Walduck described the work of an "Obeah man" in Barbados who used diabolical magic to injure other slaves, as well as another man, later called a "Myal man," who cured diseases. Walduck compared them directly to English witches and cunning persons: "Their manner of bewitching is the same we read of in Books." Walduck also argued that their skills were found not among Barbados's few American-born slaves but only among newly imported Africans, "chiefly the Calamale Negroes." Virginia freed an African named James Papaw because of his "many wonderful cures," and African words employed in South Carolina carried substantial magical significance, such as *ndzoso* (spirit or magic), *juju* (evil spirit), and *wudu* (sorcery).[72]

Recent archaeological excavations in the Chesapeake underscore perhaps reasonably regular, if secret, private, and small-scaled traditional African ritual practice. Several discoveries of beads, buttons, rock crystals, disks with pierce holes, glass, and bone, sometimes hidden in walls and sometimes found under floorboards in the northeast corners of eighteenth-century homes, suggest regularized African rituals to heal, to call upon ancestor spirits, to divine the future, and to protect. Africans appear to have practiced these rituals secretly, hence the location of the objects inside walls and under floors.[73]

Rituals surrounding death and burial constituted an important exception to the European resistance to traditional African ritual practice among American slaves. The earliest and most extensive evidence of these practices comes again from the Caribbean. According to Richard Ligon's *True and Exact History of the Island of Barbados* (1657), the colony's first slaves, believing they would be resurrected and returned to Africa, practiced traditional burials, while Griffith Hughes recorded traditional slave burial rites in his *Natural History of Barbados* (1750). Modern archaeological studies detect signs of creolization, or important New World patterns among enslaved Africans. Burials of apparently African-born slaves before 1750 placed the deceased's head to the east, while burials of New World–born slaves after 1750 placed the head to the west. Africans laid bodies out in fully articulated form in common burial grounds with objects of clear, if often unknown, ritual significance.[74]

Eighteenth-century British mainland colony planters allowed slaves to bury their dead with at least some African customs. Even though they suppressed other African religious practice, they felt reluctant to intrude directly upon slave burial rites. Baptized slaves appear to have received a Christian burial, though not necessarily in the same ground with Europeans. The reluctance to interfere with African burials and the segregation of Christian slaves in separate burial plots helps account for the elaboration of distinctive African-American burial customs after the American Revolution and in the nineteenth century. These included decorating the grave with a wide variety of objects, including personal items belonging to the deceased, and seashells, cups, and bottles, some of which were broken deliberately so the spirits inside them were free to roam with the spirit of the deceased.[75]

Christianization occurred among Africans in the southern colonies very slowly and generally followed in the wake of an advancing secular life, particularly the development of family and kinship systems. Anglicans led the initial efforts toward substantial slave Christianization in both southern and northern colonies, true to their prominence in state church societies. Before 1730 only the Church of England created sustained, persistent parish life across the southern colonies, and it was in these parishes that enslaved Africans first learned Christianity, however small their numbers. The first Anglican minister at St. James Goose Creek parish in South Carolina, Francis Le Jau, attempted to teach Christian doctrine, the meaning of baptism and communion, and Christianity's promise of life in the aftermath of death to Africans in his parish. Le Jau worked hard at this task. To counter planter resistance—they feared slaves would become "uppity" if owners and slaves shared the same religion—Le Jau required Africans to repeat an oath he created for them at their baptism: "that you do not ask for the holy baptism out of any design to free your self from the Duty and Obedience you owe to your Master while you live."[76]

Anglicans took the initial lead in Christianizing slaves elsewhere as well. A former French Protestant, Elie Neau, developed the first school for slaves in New York City in 1704. From London, the SPG pressed Anglican ministers in America to Christianize slaves, though this had not been a major aim when the society was founded in 1701. Another Anglican organization, the Associates of Dr. Bray, named for the SPG founder and organized in 1731, sought to establish schools for slaves throughout the colonies, slave Christianization being one of the group's purposes. When the SPG inherited the massive Codrington plantation in Barbados in 1710, it moved quickly to establish the plantation as a "model" for both the humane treatment of slaves and large-scale slave Christianization, but it freed no Africans and used agents to manage the plantation, not wanting to risk profits.[77]

Evangelical dissenting Protestants only began serious efforts at Christianizing Africans in the 1740s and 1750s, and then with caution. Presbyterian efforts remained relatively modest. Samuel Davies, John Todd, and John Wright preached to Africans in Virginia and at one point gathered "40 of them around the table of the Lord," later estimating that perhaps a thousand Africans had once heard their sermons. But in a society where captured Africans constituted 45 percent of the population, these numbers were small, particularly if we remember that only a handful ever joined Presbyterian congregations.[78]

Baptist proselytizing among Africans began even later, a consequence of the late Baptist entry into southern society generally; Baptists did not become a powerful force there until the 1760s. As this happened, however, Baptists proselytized among Africans, and although their numbers remained small, by the 1770s Africans could be found in many southern Baptist congregations. There they regularly recited their own spiritual conversion narratives, received a public baptism, and, though still in small numbers, became formal members of a congregation. Methodists experienced more success very late in the colonial period. Joseph Pilmore, a Methodist itinerant, and Devereaux Jarratt, an Anglican Methodist sympathizer, reported that Africans frequently attended Methodist revivals in the 1770s "with tears streaming down their faces." Formal Methodist opposition to the American Revolution, however, cut this early success short, although after the Revolution, Methodists resumed and expanded their proselytizing among slaves with much success.[79]

Before 1770 early slave Christianity in the mainland colonies was tied far more closely to white sponsorship and isolated from African influences than would ever be the case again. Before 1770 Christian slaves worshiped almost exclusively with white planters, whether Anglican, Baptist, or Presbyterian. These congregations were merely mixed, not integrated, so that Africans sat with owners or in segregated balconies and back benches and enjoyed no role in governance. The number of converted Africans remained small. Among Anglicans and Presbyterians, only whites preached. Baptists only rarely allowed some slaves to preach before 1770. Africans did not vote in congregational affairs, exercised no disciplinary authority, and were not allowed to lead. Occasional exceptions only reinforced the general pattern in which white Baptists, Anglicans, and Methodists taught Africans a Christianity in which the converts were expected to play only a very passive congregational role.[80]

Before 1770, then, slave Christianity retained largely English characteristics even among Africans worshiping in the evangelical tradition. In the British mainland colonies, slave Christianity never developed the richly syncretistic patterns that emerged in other New World slave societies, as in the eighteenth-century Caribbean or Brazil. That this did not happen is a dramatic measure of the degree to which in religion as in secular life, the African experience of slavery in eighteenth-century America all too frequently hinged on the vicissitudes of planter coercion and suppression, combined with relatively small and isolated rural slave concentrations and neighborhoods.[81]

The contrast between the constrictions placed on African religious practice and the extraordinary freedom allowed to Europeans in Britain's mainland colonies demonstrated how differently human contrivance shaped and enabled religion and secular life in prerevolutionary America. Under dramatically different circumstances, the many peoples of America recast the colonial American spiritual milieu. The resuscitation of state-church Anglicanism and Congregationalism, the rise of evangelical revivalism, the thinned flowering of women's religious activity, and the growth of pluralism dramatically altered European religious life. The reshaping of traditional American Indian religious practice, deriving in part from the merger and disappearance of many groups, the Christianization of some Indian groups, and the first calls to pan-Indian religious commitments, produced important shifts in American Indian religion. The suppression of whole African religious systems, the survival of discrete African rites and customs, especially concerning death, and the emergence of a Christianization that later became endemic in nineteenth-century America remade African-American religious practice. Individually and collectively these distinctive religious patterns emerged as special, sometimes unique, American choices of the years between 1680 and 1770 and the bedrock for exceptional spiritual metamorphoses in a new nation.

Six

1776

We are not the little people now, which we were sixty years ago.
THOMAS PAINE (1776)

THOMAS PAINE saw an America radiantly destined for independence when he published *Common Sense* in January 1776.
"The *time hath found us*," Paine exulted. America owed little to England because "Europe, and not England, is the parent country of America." Indeed, Britain had only harmed America. "America would have
flourished as much, and probably much more had no European power
had any thing to do with her." America was "the asylum for the persecuted lovers of civil and religious liberty from *every part* of Europe."
Soon, America would "be too weighty, and intricate, to be managed
with any tolerable degree of convenience, by a power, so distant from
us, and so very ignorant of us." American independence was destiny,
not choice. "We are not the little people now, which we were sixty years
ago," Paine proclaimed, and it was "repugnant to reason, to the universal order of things, to all examples from the former ages, to suppose,
that this continent can longer remain subject to any external power."[1]

Paine was wrong about many things. The Revolution was not the
logical culmination of eighteenth-century European emigration to
America. It was not the inevitable consequence of the changes that
transformed Britain's mainland colonies after 1680. Not everyone
agreed that Britain tyrannized America before 1776, and not even everyone who did thought American independence answered the affront.
Paine's stress on the broadly European character of the American peo-

ple largely ignored the colonies' engagement with African and Indian populations. Nor did "the times" find independence in America on their own. American freedom from Britain required immense, painful labor, a cause to which *Common Sense* contributed mightily.

Yet Paine's *Common Sense* indelibly penetrated critical elements of the American and modern transformations that preceded the struggle with Britain. Paine proved especially prescient about one very important fact. The America of 1776 was not the America of 1716 or of 1680. Americans were indeed "not the little people now, that we were sixty years ago." In 1770 America had become a society strikingly different from what it had been only decades earlier. Emigration, forced and voluntary, as well as conquest reshaped the colonial population, creating a diverse and uneasy mix of peoples unknown anywhere else. Economic development had produced an extraordinarily vital domestic as well as export economy without forceful central planning and, certainly, without always understanding important subtle and direct consequences of this achievement. Politics emerged as assertive, provincially driven, institutionally sophisticated, and cohesive, not only within most colonies but from region to region. A vibrant secular life capped by explosive, broadly available arrays of material goods turned European colonists into powerful consumers. A vigorous and unprecedented religious pluralism proved simultaneously astonishing and distressing for Europeans, added new and not always welcome choices to American Indian religious life, and turned Africans toward an engagement with Christianity that would ultimately transform African-American culture, though not before 1770. As a result, Paine indeed wrote *Common Sense* at the precipice of something so utterly remarkable that it is not clear even he understood what it was—the first modern revolution in the first modern society.

The conjunction is easily misunderstood. Contrary even to Paine's intimations and desires, the fiercely antimonarchical revolt Paine sought was neither necessary nor inevitable in 1776. However different America was becoming from Britain or from Europe generally, the process of differentiation had been occurring for decades, and colonists had long since learned to maneuver the contradictions. After all, the art of politics in all the colonies often centered on negotiating those contradictions, a constant feature of colonial politics since the 1710s. Independence from Britain would have occurred at some point, very likely before 1867, when it occurred for Canada. Yet even after a dozen years of bitter, hostile protest, American independence was not a reasonable wager until April 1775, after fighting erupted between British troops and the Massachusetts militia in Lexington and Concord, Massachusetts.

What, then, was the relationship between the American Revolution and the society created in Britain's mainland colonies between 1680 and 1770? Their most important shared characteristic was their modernity—relative, of course, but modernity nonetheless. The political revolution of 1776—a long process that stretched from the eruption of colonial protest against the sugar tax and Stamp Act in 1763 to the ratification of the Federal Constitution in 1789—was indeed the first modern revolution. It was not without elements that looked back, of course. The Revolution drank from British political experience, early-eighteenth-century Whig political ideology, historical British means of protest and riot, and "traditional" modes of military conduct and tactics. The Revolution also lacked dominant elements commonly found in revolutions since. Although "class" tensions appeared in the colonial cities and in the demand for freedom by enslaved Africans, class differences did not drive the Revolution, as happened so dramatically in the French, Russian, and Chinese revolutions. Nor could it be said that a single, cohesive ideology comparable to modern Marxism, for example, propelled the Revolution despite the obvious influence of eighteenth-century Whig political ideology on patriotic American thinking in the 1760s and 1770s.[2]

Still, the American Revolution of 1763–1789 can rightly be called the first modern revolution, *the* model for the French Revolution of 1789 and subsequently for so many nineteenth- and twentieth-century revolutions. The American Revolution emphasized rights, not conditional "liberties" granted or removed by a monarch. It located these rights, at least in theory, in each individual's humanity, not in his or her status in society. It insisted that "citizens," not subjects, justly formed governments, notions embodied in the Declaration of Independence, the state constitutions, and the federal Constitution in 1787. It created the broad-scale popular mobilization that typified the French, Russian, and Chinese revolutions. Between 1760 and 1790 it reinforced and enlarged concepts of popular sovereignty only partially articulated in England's earlier upheavals, such as the English Civil War and Commonwealth in the 1640s and 1650s or in the Glorious Revolution. It built tension that incorporated political competition for authority and power in the very structure of government, creating now classic divisions between executive, legislative, and judicial powers that previously had been the object of largely theoretical speculation. And the Revolution guaranteed freedom of religion broadly, not merely freedom for Protestants, Catholics, or Christians, and rejected a national church, achievements that were unprecedented in Western societies. In the American Revolution, citizens shaped a nation by claiming the capacity to manage human nature and recast human institutions while acknowledging human limitations expressed in history. It was not surprising that the American Revolution could claim to initiate a "new order of the ages." Despite weaknesses of both theory and practice, the claim fit.[3]

Perhaps anticlimactically, the modernity that had emerged in America between 1680 and 1770 influenced but did not determine the Revolution. Eighteenth-century America was far from wholly new. Hierarchy remained important within its European population. Men and women paid close attention to social status, carefully measured their neighbors' attainments against their own, and judged suitability for politics as much by wealth and class as by intellect and personal rectitude. The economy bore close relationships with European influences, depended heavily upon colonial exports, and thrived on British and European credit. The mainland colonies imported more, not fewer, European goods per person in the early 1760s than in 1700.

Yet the first modern society that emerged in prerevolutionary America bore immense consequences for all the men and women who lived there and ultimately affected the process and outcome of American political independence in powerful ways. Prerevolutionary America exhibited the broad ethnic and religious heterogeneity that would typify America and so many modern societies throughout the nineteenth and twentieth centuries. Its provincial politics exemplified the stress on recruitment, public debate, a public sphere occupied by modest yet persistent sorts, and electioneering that have long distinguished modern politics and, ultimately, modern democracy. Its popular materialism continuously attracted European immigrants and drove the widely dispersed technological advances that propelled nineteenth-century America. Its stress on authority as well as liberty in politics, economics, and social relationships typified modernity's confidence in its mastery of the world and of individual and collective lives. It upheld glaring inequities with law, most obviously in its treatment of Africans and Indians. Its moral blindness reflected the hubris born of modernity's material and technological fertility and wide-reaching political authority.

Colonial America's aggressive self-referentialism turned colonists to their own business as often as it turned them to the business of the empire or of domestic Britain. It kindled a combative provincialism that ultimately fueled the revolutionary crisis and buoyed revolutionary and postrevolutionary American nationalism. Whether in material life, economics, politics, or seemingly innocuous clubs and fraternal societies, colonists employed strong colonial lenses to filter their views of British, European, and colonial societies that gave to America different colors and hues seldom found anywhere else.

In short, amid so many elements that appeared so traditional, the New World shores had produced not merely colonies in an ever larger transatlantic British empire but aggressive, willful, modern societies far more self-sufficient and self-directing than anyone ever imagined they could be or would be—dangerous societies capable of remarkable resistance to overweening, foolish, ill-considered political provocations and ultimately capable of utterly surprising acts of national creation.

How did the first modern society shape the first modern revolution? The relationship was complex, not simple or automatic. The transformation of Britain's mainland colonies between 1680 and 1770 did not cause or necessitate the Revolution. Instead, the Revolution was fomented by specific, frequently disastrous events of the 1760s and 1770s. It hinged on colonists' reactions to major changes that British politicians and administrators hoped to impose on the empire in America. British success in the Seven Years' War ironically required changes, or so British administrators and politicians believed, because military success worsened the empire's long-standing fiscal problems and administrative discord. The acquisition of French Canada brought a sprawling new territory to administer. The government needed money. The

Sugar Act passed in 1764 reduced molasses duties but raised other duties, including sugar levies, to produce a revenue of £45,000. The Stamp Act passed in 1765 required stamps for court documents, deeds, liquor licenses, apprenticeship contracts, calendars, and newspapers. Violations would be heard in vice-admiralty courts staffed largely by "placemen," fines were payable in sterling, not colonial paper currency, and revenues would pay salaries for colonial officials and costs for British troops, robbing colonial legislatures of their now traditional financial leverage over governors and London officials.[4]

Colonists' reaction to British plans to rationalize and finance the expanded empire produced a series of confrontations that finally triggered independence. The Stamp Act brought unprecedented formal protests from assemblies in Virginia, New York, Connecticut, Rhode Island, and Massachusetts and a "Stamp Act Congress" in New York in October 1765 to guide nonimportation agreements. Parliament withdrew the stamp tax in March 1766 but passed a Declaratory Act justifying parliamentary taxation of the colonies. In 1767 a new government led by Charles Townsend proposed new duties, the Townsend duties, on tea, paint, paper, lead, and glass, again to raise revenue. Again, colonists denied both the taxes and the right to levy them. By 1768 more nonimportation agreements had been made, better coordinated among the colonies, and British troops arrived in Boston. When the Virginia assembly claimed an exclusive right to tax its residents, Governor Norbonne Berkeley, baron de Botetourt, dismissed it, but the assembly ratified nonimportation extralegally.[5]

The repeal of all Townsend duties except those on tea withered nonimportation but not the political tension. Colonists organized "committees of correspondence" in November 1772, first in Boston. A new act imposing tea taxes brought the Boston Tea Party in December 1773. Now the spiral was out of hand, fed by rising British nationalism at home and colonists' anger in America. "Coercive Acts" shutting the Boston port, suspending provincial and local government, assuming control of courts, and providing for quartering troops in vacant public buildings passed Parliament between March and June 1774. The first Continental Congress met in September and October 1774 and set in motion a nonimportation and nonconsumption campaign against British products. It approved a resolution authored by John Adams that the colonies were not currently represented in Parliament and "cannot properly be represented"; therefore they "are entitled to a free and exclusive power of legislation in their several provincial legislatures," though they acquiesced to acts "as are bona fide restrained to the regulation of our external commerce."[6]

On April 19, 1775, Paul Revere made his famous ride to signal the approach of British troops seeking illegal arms in Lexington and Concord and initiating the towns' fateful combat. An "Olive Branch" petition to the king went out from the Second Continental Congress in July 1775, but by May 1776 the Congress had urged colonies to form new governments, and towns, counties, grand juries, and assemblies began instructing delegates to secure independence. By July 1776 the Continental Congress, affirming Jefferson's wording "that all men are created equal" and are "endowed by their Creator with certain inalienable rights," among them "life, liberty, and the pursuit of happiness," proclaimed that "these united colonies are and of right ought to be free and independent states."[7]

The transformation of the British mainland colonies between 1680 and 1770 dictated much of the character of the American Revolution even if the political events of 1763–1776 brought the Revolution itself into being. A comparison helps make the point. Protests surely would have followed Parliament's imposition of colonial taxes in the 1670s or 1680s. But the infant colonial assemblies would have been ill equipped to lead the sustained, vigorous protests that led the colonies to independence between 1763 and 1776. Except possibly in Virginia, the seventeenth-century assemblies lacked the institutional experience, resolve, and depth to sustain the increasingly bitter contest with Britain that characterized transatlantic imperial politics after 1763.

Colonial assemblies from South Carolina to Massachusetts spoke to surprisingly common effect in the colonial protests despite different institutional histories. "We look upon those Duties as a tax, and which we humbly apprehend ought not to be laid without the Representatives of the People affected by them," claimed the Massachusetts assembly in 1765, a view echoed by the Virginia Burgesses: "The taxation of the people by themselves, or by persons chosen by themselves to represent them . . . is the only security against a burdensome taxation, and the distinguishing characteristic of British freedom."[8]

British actions from 1763 forward—not merely those of 1774 and 1775—challenged the very existence of provincial government as colonists had come to know it. As early as July 1767 Parliament passed a Restraining Act that would have suspended the New York legislature until it raised money for British troops in the colony. Although both sides backed away, the threat set a precedent ominously fulfilled in the Coercive or Intolerable Acts of 1774. These acts shut the Boston port, returned British officials accused of crimes to England for trial, forced local authorities to house British troops in unoccupied public buildings, replaced the elected Massachusetts council with one appointed by the Crown, empowered the governor to remove all sheriffs, justices of the peace, and lower court judges in the colonies, and allowed towns to hold only one town meeting per year without the governor's permission. By 1774 these acts not only epitomized what men and women had previously only imagined as tyranny but denied the century-long historical experience of politics in the mainland colonies.[9]

The leadership of colonial protest and independence flowed with remarkable directness out of the developing complexities of eighteenth-century colonial American political life. Much principal political leadership of the 1760s and 1770s descended directly from the increasingly modern electoral politics of colonial America between 1680 and 1770. The men who ran for and occupied public office in the American provinces made and legitimated protest against British policy between 1763 and 1776. Disputes and differences among protesters reflected the frequently chaotic politics of prerevolutionary America, not merely in New York, with its highly personalized politics, but in Virginia, Massachusetts, and the Carolinas as well.[10]

One group stood apart, almost as if to prove the overwhelming power of elected officeholding in the eighteenth-century colonies—the placemen, like Massachusetts's Peter Oliver, who had made their livings through connections to royal governors, appointed councils, and London merchants and even politicians. This eighteenth-century dependency and cronyism cut a wide swath and involved men who found it difficult to surrender its perquisites. It took a Connecticut mob three hours to convince Jared Ingersol to resign his stamp distributor's post in 1765, but when he finally gave in the mob shouted "liberty and property," in part a tribute to its participants' own power. Other placemen proved more resilient. Merchants, magistrates, Anglican clergymen, members of colonial councils, even farmers and writers like Crèvecoeur streamed out of the colonies, perhaps fifty thousand in all, bitter that neighbors and friends had betrayed the king in America.[11]

Anti-British leadership also emerged from the tradition of popular protest in colonial provincial and urban politics. Especially in Boston and New York, but also in the countryside, artisans, laborers, and farmers had agitated in colonial politics from the 1720s into the 1760s in contests over paper money, land allocation and taxes, and aggressive anti-Indian demands, actions that paralleled mob behavior in eighteenth-century Britain. Artisans like George Robert Twelves Hewes, an unsuccessful Boston shoemaker and sometime resident of debtor's prison, provided leadership and muscle for mobs, tarring and feathering, and effigy hangings. Seamen led protests in Philadelphia. In New York, perhaps more than elsewhere, artisans and laborers joined complaints about low wages, high rents, and erratic employment with the protests against parliamentary taxation. The mob behavior often was highly controlled, almost ritualized, and customarily resulted in little actual violence. The scandal of the Boston Massacre of March 5, 1770, for example, hinged in part on long-developed expectations about riotous engagement and the British violation of them. Five colonists were killed; the deaths helped corrupt the king's sovereignty in America. Yet colonial anti-British rioting also sometimes went beyond traditional mob action in early modern Britain. Its sustained, increasingly purposeful action shot past the redress of particular grievances and sullied, then openly attacked, both Parliament and monarchy. The mobs, often of poorer men as well as women, did not bring down the colonial aristocracy, as would happen shortly in France. But they substantially eroded British monarchical sovereignty in America, and it is impossible to imagine the Revolution without them.[12]

Colonial protest and the Revolution reemphasized the British foundations of the mainland colonies and for some time reduced the potential impact of ethnic and national pluralism in America. The objects of protest in Parliament and king, the British charters of the colonial governments, the British ethnicity of almost all colonial officeholders, and the importance of Whig political ideology in eighteenth-century colonial political rhetoric and antiparliamentary protests solidified the colonies' British political identity even when Britons composed only a third of all residents by 1770.[13]

In addition, non-English political agitation was repressed or proved only obliquely related to colonial political turmoil. Colonists segregated Africans, the greatest exemplars of American cultural pluralism, from political agitation through slaveholding. Non-English European suspicions about colonial protest generally stemmed more from the accidents of geography, namely western settlement, than from uniquely ethnic causes. Colonial assemblies, especially in Pennsylvania and the Carolinas, often gave scant attention to problems in their far western settlements; the neglect rankled the German, Scot, and Scots-Irish settlers who constituted many of the Europeans there. These difficulties produced the Regulator movement in North Carolina between 1768 and 1771, when western settlers were defeated in a military battle and several leaders of the movement were hung, developments that gave new immigrants a jaundiced view of colonial protests against British "tyranny."[14]

The retreat of ethnic influence during the Revolution proved short-lived. Over the next half century ethnicity became more important, not less, as enormous segments of America's European population again became foreign-born. This happened slowly across the next decades. By 1850, for example, a quarter-million English-born immigrants, a half-million German-born immigrants, and almost a million Irish-born immigrants reshaped the immigrant communities of their colonial predecessors. The experience of America's German-speaking community was reasonably representative. What was "German" in America by the Civil War was not what remained from eighteenth-century Pennsylvania but what had been created by antebellum immigrants to America. These new immigrants overwhelmed descendants of colonial German immigrants and commanded "German" immigrant culture in antebellum America from Cincinnati and Memphis to Milwaukee.[15]

Merchants politicized old trading connections as colonial protests developed. The nonimportation agreements first made among merchants in Boston, New York, Philadelphia, and Charleston after passage of the Stamp Act in 1763 and reborn in the Townsend duty protests of 1767 hinged on local cooperation and exploited intercolonial ties made in earlier trade. Now merchants did not write merely about ships and goods, as Charleston's Robert Pringle had done in the 1740s. They filled letters with frank talk about politics, about political pressure, and about political principle. Their efforts at nonimportation were not easily made. Some merchants balked, and some supported the British. Yet far more supported the protests or acquiesced in them. Intercolonial trading connections developed in preceding decades between Massachusetts and South Carolina, Virginia and Pennsylvania— even if most merchant correspondence went to London—laid a ready foundation for coordinated protests and, ultimately, for revolutionary cooperation.[16]

Protest and revolution also drew upon and transformed early- and mid-eighteenth-century colonial associationalism. Charleston's Fire Company became the Sons of Liberty in 1766 and advertised the fact widely. Boston's "Loyal Nine" club directed the principal activities against the stamp distributor Andrew Oliver and made the effigies of Oliver it burned in August 1766. These clubs appropriated not only a generic name—the term "sons of" had been used previously—but the older tradition of fraternal, literary, and even ethnic organization evidenced in colonial Masonic groups, Annapolis's Tuesday Club, and Charleston's Fire Company or its St. Andrews Society of Scottish descendants. The clubs—British officials often called them mere "gangs" and "mobs"—reached across provincial boundaries seldom crossed before despite the transatlantic and international pretensions of some, such as the Masons. As Stamp Act opposition accelerated, New York protesters initiated correspondence with Sons of Liberty organizations in both Boston and Albany, then with New Hampshire and other Massachusetts towns. Sons of Liberty groups organized in Philadelphia and Maryland, explicitly following models in New York and Boston. The Charleston Sons of Liberty corresponded with Sons of Liberty groups in both North Carolina and Georgia to strengthen their organization and stimulate a wall of protest throughout the lower southern colonies.[17]

The continental congresses took intercolonial cooperation even farther. The only previous model, the Albany Congress of 1755, had been a notable failure, involving only seven colonies that never approved the work of their own delegates. In contrast, the Stamp Act Congress of October 1765 involved nine colonies, settled the important principle that Parliament could not tax the colonies at all (never mind any distinction between "internal" and "external" taxes), rejected the argument that the colonies were "virtually" represented in Parliament, yet acknowledged that the colonies owed Parliament "all due Subordination." Little wonder that when the colonies faced the Coercive Acts in 1774, the colonists' answer was another Continental Congress in Philadelphia that year.[18]

The language of the revolutionary protests descended directly from eighteenth-century British political culture in both the colonies and Great Britain. Paine's *Common Sense* trumped everything written before it, of course. Paine's clarity of expression ("Government, like dress, is the badge of lost innocence"), his succinct verdicts ("thirty kings and two minors" had produced "no less than eight civil wars and nineteen rebellions" for Britain), and his instinct for the jugular (Britain's monarchy rested on a "rascally original.—It certainly hath no divinity in it") drove readers to his bold revolutionary conclusion: "Independence is the only Bond that can tye and keep us together."[19]

But Paine's success also hinged on his cultivation of the colonial political dialogue created in the previous ninety years. By the time readers finished even fifteen pages of *Common Sense,* Paine had exposed the monarchy's self-possessed flatulence in language familiar to anyone who read even a few colonial political tracts. "Farcical," "absurdity," "ridiculous," "foolish," "delusion," "ridicule," "rogue," "worm," "fool," "superstition," "banditti," "sickly" gleefully assaulted every reader. Colonists knew this compilation of sarcasm, wit, and satire through British politics and through their own political invective dating back to Robert Hunter's 1714 scatological play *Androboros.* Now Paine used the same language to crush the monarchy that some colonists had hoped would save them against Parliament.[20]

The economy also shaped the nature and flow of colonial protest and the Revolution. The strength of the domestic and international trades became a major source for colonial confidence about their protests and, finally, their revolution in two contradictory yet interleaved ways. First, colonists seemed well aware that they had developed a strong economy and that they should be and perhaps already were increasingly important players in the growing British empire. The nonimportation agreements first broached in the Stamp Act crisis of 1764–1765 assumed the economic impact of colonial imports. Moreover, colonists before and after the Revolution, from Paine in *Common Sense* to Crèvecoeur in

Letters from an American Farmer, long pointed to standards of living among Europeans in America as remarkable in their substance and breadth. Indeed, cataloging them has been a major industry for commentators on eighteenth-century America.[21]

Second, the swings of colonial economic enterprise and the growing indebtedness of some colonists, especially in the free-spending, high-income, slavery-dominated southern colonies, inculcated resentment and bitterness. That this reaction was self-serving and narrow-minded never dislodged the bitterness itself or induced more realistic assessments of the colonists' position. After all, the indebted planters and merchants had asked for increased credit, usually from London merchants, and they enjoyed the splendid material goods bought by that credit on both sides of the Atlantic. Yet debt caused tension between Virginia planters and London merchants, who were seen as manipulating Parliament for favors in an expanding empire while sinking Virginians into greater obligation. Thus, while many colonists might see their economic achievements as a strong foundation for protest and independence, others might advance the same argument out of sullen convictions that Britain had saddled them with both taxes and debt.[22]

Colonial confidence in a vigorous, healthy economy also led patriots to exaggerate the ease of independence. This was not universally true. Philadelphia merchants looked on protest, much less independence, with considerable skepticism. If they knew anything, they knew how to calculate risk, and their calculations suggested serious, even disastrous, consequences from further trade disruptions within the empire, whether they involved nonimportation campaigns or actual independence.[23]

Protest and independence lived up to their expectations. The Revolutionary War reduced agricultural production in most colonies. It diminished domestic and international trade. Credit became more scarce and, thereby, more expensive. Money that would have gone to merchants went to speculators instead. The British market collapsed completely. Transatlantic merchants had to scramble for new markets and, often, for new credit sources. Loyalist merchants found themselves arrested or without either buyers or sellers. Patriot merchants who served the Continental army gained contracts that generated angry disputes about favoritism.[24]

Still, whatever its vagaries, the remarkably resilient domestic economy helped the colonies overcome shortages of food, clothing, even finished goods like furniture or implements. This would not have happened had colonial production been targeted more exclusively for British markets, especially if these were raw materials processed in Britain rather than America. Shortages of beef and wheat afflicted the Continental army troops, who had first call on much local production. But the troops as well as the residents of blockaded colonial cities survived because the remaining domestic production proved at least minimally sufficient and because the long-developed intercolonial trade was redirected to supply colonial troops and the blockaded cities, although the results were far from perfect.[25]

In addition, the colonists' constant trade with Dutch, Spanish, and French merchants—usually illegal under the British navigation acts—provided familiar non-English sources that could be exploited in the revolutionary crisis. France agreed to a commerce treaty with the independent states in 1778. Dutch and Spanish traders carried colonial grain and naval stores to Europe, largely from the southern colonies, and sold Chesapeake tobacco overseas. The successful British blockades against several American ports and their occupation of New York City through most of the Revolutionary War made the French, Dutch, and Spanish trade in the southern colonies all the more important.[26]

Slavery affected the Revolution in profoundly different ways. Slavery became a powerful metaphor for antiparliamentary protest. Metaphors about slavery had earlier informed British politics, especially in the Glorious Revolution of 1688. There they were often linked to English antiforeign and anti-Catholic sentiment, with English Protestants imagining themselves enslaved to the pope, intellectually and possibly even physically. But in colonial America of the 1760s and 1770s, with more than a half-million Africans enchained, enslavement became a powerful theme in antiparliamentary protest. Even in New England the theme dominated anti-British rhetoric. John Adams remembered that "the people were told weekly that the ministry had formed a plan to enslave them. . . . This perpetual incantation kept the people in continual alarm." When the town of Athol, Massachusetts, told the Boston Committee of Correspondence that evil men had put forward "avoritious Schums for enriching and agrandizing themselves . . . at the expence of Enslaving a free and Loyal People," the message hinged on direct knowledge of slaveholding that was commonplace by 1774 but rare a century earlier.[27]

In turn, Jefferson's original draft for the Declaration of Independence moved from metaphor to fact and blamed the king for both the slave trade and slaveholding in America. The king, Jefferson argued, "has waged cruel war against human nature itself" and created an "execreble commerce" in the slave trade, whose consequences were an "assemblage of horrors." Jefferson's outburst reflected growing colonial concern about slaveholding practice as well as principle. Even supporters of the institution of slavery blanched at actual slaveholding practices. George Whitefield demanded that Africans obey owners but bitterly criticized planter cruelty, especially the mistreatment of slave families. At mid-century a few colonists began rejecting slavery altogether. Pennsylvania Quakers removed slaveholders from their meetings in the 1750s and, led by the reformers Anthony Benezet and John Woolman, slowly began an open campaign against slaveholding generally. But the Continental Congress's committee of revision removed Jefferson's entire discussion. It raised dangerous, difficult issues, particularly when colonial patriots were about to declare, in the face of their own practice, that "all men are created equal."[28]

Africans saw immediate opportunities for freedom in revolution that the British quickly exploited. In 1775 Virginia's governor, Lord Dunmore, offered freedom to slaves who would support the British cause. Dunmore intended to undermine planter support, not to abolish slavery, so that Africans remained pawns in revolutionary politics. But freedom was freedom, especially after three to five generations inside slavery, and Dunmore and the British induced almost a thousand Africans to win it by deserting their masters and joining an "Ethiopian Brigade" despite overwhelming planter control of the countryside. Boston slaves audaciously delivered three petitions for freedom to General William Gage. Slaves rebelled in St. Andrew Parish in Georgia in 1774, killing several whites before they were captured and burned alive. The South Carolina Provincial Congress created three troop regiments "to keep those mistaken creatures in awe as well as to oppose any Troops that may be sent among us with coercive Orders."[29]

The specter of slaves running away to freedom terrified Virginia planters, particularly when they were employing metaphors about the "slavery" of America to Parliament and king. Edmund Pendleton heard rumors that "slaves flock to [Dunmore] in abundance" and hoped that the rumors were "magnified." The planter Landon Carter resolved deep fears about Africans in his reveries. In July 1776 he dreamed about "runaway people . . . most wretchedly meager and wan" who hid in a cave and then returned to seek Carter's pardon. Carter's actual runaways never returned, however much he dreamed they would. Better to starve free and die in the wilderness than submit again to planter captivity. Nor were Carter's slaves alone. By the end of the Revolution, several thousand slaves had fled from the colonies, some taking refuge in Canada, some escaping to the northern states, a few heading for the wilderness and life among the Indians. Most faced uncertain futures. But they were free.[30]

Women's roles in the Revolution strongly reflected their peculiar, often anomalous position in eighteenth-century colonial society and turned in important new directions after 1776. Locked out of formal politics, revolutionary-era women could not direct the protests of the colonial assemblies or the continental congresses. But women's strong roles in the family and farm economy and the literary and social activity of elite women dictated women's persistent presence in prerevolutionary protest and patriotic war activity. Women participated in anti-British rioting and managed nonimportation, giving them a minor yet unprecedented role in informal politics. Fifty-one women in Edenton, North Carolina, offered their own agreement to boycott British goods, although their sex won them both support and satirical ridicule. Several thousand women followed both the British and the American armies, sometimes to support husband-soldiers, sometimes to cook, launder, and nurse. More typically, women managed farms and businesses during the war, "making Cartridges, running Bullets, making Wallets, baking Biscuits, crying and bemoaning & at the same time animating their Husbands & Sons to fight for their liberties, tho not knowing whether they should ever see them again."[31]

Change in women's place in American society came after, not during, the Revolution, and then slowly and not always positively. A New Jersey change proved intriguing but short-lived. In 1790 the state adopted a new election law that termed voters "he or she" and enfranchised both women and African Americans. Rather than eschew the ballot, women and African Americans flocked to the polls and voted in New Jersey until 1807, when a disputed election resulted in the loss of the franchise for both women and African men. The episode demonstrated the potential for change in the revolutionary era as well as the enduring power of tradition.[32]

Developing notions about "republican womanhood" and "republican motherhood" proved far more significant, though not necessarily liberating. Colonial politicians and women writers themselves began to stress women's importance in inculcating civic virtue in the new republic. Women not only insisted on greater education but on their mastery of it. "Whatever you learn remember that you will receive no Benefit from it without making yourself Mistress of it," one New Yorker wrote in 1794. Revolutionary rhetoric and the republican emphasis on consent challenged traditional conceptions of women's subordination. A female writer in the *Lady's Magazine* of July 1792 wrote, "I object to the word 'obey' in the marriage service because it is a general word, without limitations or definition." It made the woman a *"slave"* to her husband. Ultimately these sentiments produced a new ideology of gender in the early Republic and antebellum era that emphasized the "women's sphere" of domestic activity.[33]

Yet this change, though important in the long run, meant little to many in the short run. Thousands of Revolutionary War widows were as devastated as widows in the earlier imperial wars. They became suddenly impoverished in a society where women remained subordinate to men, were frequently denigrated, lacked competitive economic skills they could pursue independently, and were denied formal political power. They could lose husbands in war, but they could not divorce except under the most horrendous circumstances. "Republican womanhood" may, in part, have been a reaction to the dangers posed by elite women's literary and even political activity of the 1760s and 1770s. It gave women a crucial role in shaping character in the new nation by stressing their domestic roles. It elevated only a few women, and the development of doctrines about women's "separate spheres" and "feminine domesticity" in the next decades only challenged men's political and economic power obliquely, not directly. Although Judith Sargeant Murray, the postrevolutionary reformer, believed the Revolution would bring a "new era of female history," the achievement took a long, tortured route.[34]

The Revolution proved devastatingly familiar to American Indians. Pressured on all sides, Indians divided during the conflict. The Revolution shattered the Iroquois Confederacy, most supporting the British, some supporting the Americans. Indian attacks on American targets seemingly confirmed the charge in the Declaration of Independence that the British had employed "merciless Indian savages, whose known rule of warfare is an undistinguished destruction of all ages, sexes, and condition." The war forced several thousand Oneidas to take refuge in miserable camps at Schenectady. Some Indians preserved or even extended their autonomy during the revolutionary crisis, especially the Abenakis in Maine, the Chickasaws in Mississippi, and the Seminoles in Florida. But the Revolution's political and military effects destroyed the independence of others, such as the Oquogans and other Iroquois groups in New York. Most ominously, the Revolution freed Americans to pursue further western settlement that forced all too familiar changes on ever-shrinking Indian societies, processes set in motion in the sixteenth century and continued relentlessly into the twentieth.[35]

Religion, available in such abundant, diverse forms, played subtle rather than direct and independent roles in the Revolution. Two controversies increased colonists' distrust of the Church of England and Tory politicians. Construction of an unusually large home for the Anglican minister in Cambridge, Massachusetts—the "bishop's palace," opponents charged—raised popular fears about the appointment of a Church of England bishop for the American colonies. In addition, British recognition of Roman Catholicism as the principal religion in Canada following the British conquest in the Seven Years' War, maintenance of French civil law, and Catholic eligibility for public office all sanctioned in the 1774 Quebec Act raised fears about Roman Catholic sympathies in Britain.[36]

Much colonial preaching in many denominations further reinforced Whig political ideology in its stress on morality and virtue. These broad moralizing points tumbled home in the 1770s. Harvard president Samuel Langdon criticized Britain in 1775 as a society and government driven to evil policies "by its public vices" that had "wage[d] a cruel war with its own children in these colonies, only to gratify the lust of power and demands of extravagance!" In Virginia, Landon Carter's local Anglican clergyman supported the Revolution and "cried out God Preserve all the Just rights and Liberties of America," not "God save the King."[37]

Yet religion's role in shaping the Revolution is easily exaggerated. In Boston, the bitter Loyalist and former stamp distributor Peter Oliver complained rightly about a seeming army of clergymen—a "black regiment" Oliver termed them—that used its pulpits against the Crown, and historians have argued that the criticisms of lethargic, unconverted ministers by revivalists like George Whitefield, Gilbert Tennent, and Virginia's Samuel Davies became models for revolutionary protest against parliamentary taxation and imperial authority.[38]

But clergymen who supported colonial protest, including the "black regiment" that Peter Oliver detested, supported causes initially made by politicians on overwhelmingly secular grounds. In addition, most New England ministers who backed protest and independence spoke from tax-supported pulpits invested with the authority of provincial government, as did pro-revolutionary Anglican ministers in Virginia. They represented the established legal order and were not hard-pressed, anti-authoritarian dissenters, although some were evangelicals. Even where revival preaching had prospered thirty and forty years earlier, the tumult of provincial politics and Whig political ideology determined the emerging contest with Britain more profoundly than did evangelical revivalism. The Synod of Philadelphia's 1775 pastoral letter assured Presbyterians that ministers had "not been instrumental in inflaming the minds of the people" and expressed concern for a civil war that might be "carried on with a rancour and spirit of revenge much greater than those between independent states."[39]

The Declaration of Independence offered remarkably nonreligious claims for independence. The Declaration referred to "the laws of nature and nature's God" and "the Supreme Judge of the world." The Declaration invoked a "Divine Providence" colonists might decipher individually, then moved to issues of common concern—taxes, troops, and tyranny. It never mentioned Christ and never cited Old or New Testament verses to support the American cause (ironically, the deist Thomas Paine had done exactly that in *Common Sense* six months earlier). Even the list of British offenses that closed the Declaration—the Crown's "history of repeated injuries and usurpations"—ignored religious issues, including the 1763 bishop controversy and the 1774 Quebec Act.[40]

Ultimately religion's greatest contribution to independence was its repose. Denominational differences played modest or even minor roles in the Revolution. Instead, the Revolution divided denominations, though not permanently. Virtually every colonial denomination found adherents on both sides of the contest, not merely the Church of England but Quakers, Presbyterians, Baptists, German Lutherans, and New England Congregationalists. No church could claim exclusive responsibility for the Revolution, and all could support the new government when Cornwallis surrendered in October 1781 and Britain and America signed the peace treaty in September 1783. Religion's place in the first sixteen words of the First Amendment—"Congress shall make no law respecting an establishment of religion, or prohibiting the free exercise thereof"—eloquently signaled not only crucial elements of the unique eighteenth-century colonial experience and religion's importance in the structure of society but quietly predicted the explosive religious activism that would turn antebellum America into the most spiritually creative society in nineteenth-century Western culture.[41]

The complex, sometimes elliptical relationship between the transformation of Britain's colonies after 1680 and the making of the American Revolution vividly points up the power of the Revolution and the uniqueness of the society in which it occurred. The economic, social, political, and material transformations that remade British America intersected in powerful ways with the protests against Britain after 1763 and then with the coming of independence in 1776. But they did not create the Revolution.

Similarly, the Revolution of 1776 did not sweep away the society that made it. It built on the immediate past and the transformations that re-created Britain's seventeenth-century colonies. It used a colonial politics to end Britain's colonial rule, mined domestic and transatlantic economies to support revolutionary armies, employed a rapidly advancing material culture in the service of independence, and took what support it could from a religion that was diverse and multifaceted, not uniform and homogeneous. After the revolutionary victory of 1783,

Americans transformed this very society in which the Revolution had been born, not by destroying the past but by transfiguring it once again in a politics, economics, religion, social milieu, and material culture whose deep roots in the eighteenth century seldom precluded newer changes and more powerful expressions. In this regard, the American Revolution proved even more revolutionary than its successors in France, Russia, or China, where revolution upended so much that had gone before. The American conflict demonstrated that the past could indeed be useful, particularly when it had itself been innovative.

WHEN Benjamin Franklin sat for a drawing by the French artist Charles Nicolas Cochin in Paris in 1777, Cochin sketched Franklin in what might have seemed a distinctively "American" attire— a plain coat and shirt, Franklin's seemingly quintessential round "spectacles," and a fur hat, unadorned yet obviously not inexpensive. The pose—especially the fur hat—was not entirely unique. A decade earlier, the French artist Allan Ramsay had painted Jean-Jacques Rousseau in a similar vein, although Rousseau wore a much finer coat and a fur hat with braids that draped across his shoulder and onto his chest.

Cochin's drawing ultimately served as the model for one of the most famous revolutionary-era portraits of Franklin, John Trumbull's 1778 oil on wood painting that also depicted Franklin in a simple fur hat. Trumbull's portrait revealed how thoroughly Franklin had come to represent America at the brink of political independence. In Allan Ramsay's painting of Rousseau, the fur hat linked Rousseau to nature, but also to the effete pleasures of European civilization. In Trumbull's portrait of Franklin, the fur hat represented Franklin's connection to a nature that was simple and direct, yet prosperous. It symbolized the often startling, aggressive society that remade itself between 1680 and 1770 from the original English colonies and that endured into, and beyond, the nineteenth century.[42]

Benjamin Franklin did not perfectly symbolize the transformation of the American colonies between 1680 and 1770. Franklin was thoroughly English in colonies where after 1680 most residents increasingly were not. He was an urban writer, editor, intellectual, scientist, philosopher, philanderer, and politician, not a farmer. Born in 1706 and dying

John Trumbull, *Benjamin Franklin*. Oil on wood, 1778.

in 1790, he was with Samuel Adams one of the "old revolutionaries" in a society that already seemed to worship youth.[43]

Yet more than many colonists, Benjamin Franklin personified the transformation of Britain's mainland colonies into the first modern society. Most of the major transformations that occurred in America between 1680 and 1770 unfolded before him—the colonies' massive population growth, the maturation of colonial politics, the creation of a slaveholding culture even outside the southern colonies, immense domestic and international economic expansion, the growth of a rich secular life and material culture, and the evolution of diverse, sometimes baffling modern religious pluralism.

The aphorisms of Franklin's *Poor Richard's Almanac* made sense of that transformation. In Franklin's hands and in the minds of many eager readers, life became something to be shaped, reshaped, then reshaped again—"Lost time is never found again"—"God helps them that helps themselves"—"He that's secure is not safe"—"Work as if you were to live a hundred years, Pray as if you were to die tomorrow"—"He that lives upon hope will die fasting." These aphorisms tamed and disciplined an expanding, aggressive, and calculating society. They did not guarantee a moral society or even a good society. But they channeled behavior that might drift toward pure greed, asserted the virtue of labor over status, and bypassed traditional European emphasis on family inheritance, political deference, and vengeful religious dogmatism. In *Poor Richard's Almanac,* many Americans could see what they were becoming and what they wanted to be.

Long before Franklin acquired his fur hat, he penned an epitaph that uncannily prefigured the transformation of prerevolutionary America. At age twenty-eight, thirty years before Maryland's Tuesday Club reveled in turning its own order upside down and "modelling the Club anew," the young Franklin composed an epitaph that hoped for "a new & more perfect Edition" of himself, "Corrected and amended By the Author."[44]

Franklin was writing about himself, not about America. But his sentiments well expressed what happened to Britain's mainland colonies across the next decades. Franklin articulated the drive and optimism that quietly underwrote the transformation of Britain's American colonies into the first modern society, unrolling an American history that epitomized the progress, for good or ill, of modernity itself.

The Body of
B. Franklin,
Printer;
Like the Cover of an old Book,
Its contents torn out,
And stript of its Lettering and Gilding,
Lies here, Food for Worms,
But the Work shall not be wholly lost:
For it will, as he believ'd, appear once more,
In a new & more perfect Edition,
Corrected and amended
By the Author.[45]

Notes · Acknowledgments · Index

NOTES

INTRODUCTION

1. What constitutes the "modern" is, of course, a matter of debate. A sophisticated attempt to trace the process of modernization in America before the Civil War is contained in Richard D. Brown, *Modernization: The Transformation of American Life, 1600–1865* (New York, 1976). For a controversial treatment of early-nineteenth-century "modernity," see Paul Johnson, *The Birth of the Modern: World Society, 1815–1830* (New York, 1991). The subject is treated in more sophisticated if indirect terms in Gordon S. Wood, *The Radicalism of the American Revolution* (New York, 1992). Anthony Giddens, *The Consequences of Modernity* (Stanford, Calif., 1990), Jean-François Lyotard, *The Post-Modern Condition* (Minneapolis, 1985), and other similar books unfortunately advance elliptical and elusive concepts of modernity that I found difficult to apply to eighteenth-century America.

2. For an older criticism of this habit, see Lawrence Leder, "A Neglected Aspect of New York's Forgotten Century," *New York History,* 37 (1956): 259–265, as well as Charles M. Andrews, *The Colonial Background of the American Revolution: Four Essays in American Colonial History* (New Haven, 1931), pp. 180–181, and Clinton Rossiter, *Seedtime of the Republic: The Origin of the American Tradition of Political Liberty* (New York: Harcourt, Brace, 1953). The historian Jack P. Greene has been especially critical of the focus on New England, most forcefully in his book, *Pursuits of Happiness: The Social Development of Early Modern British Colonies and the Formation of American Culture* (Chapel Hill, 1988). Criticism of the New England model in American religious history is contained in my own book, *Awash in a Sea of Faith: Christianizing the American People* (Cambridge, Mass., 1990). Text-

books with considerable interpretative significance in colonial American history include Clarence L. Ver Steeg, *The Formative Years, 1607–1763* (New York, 1964), and James A. Henretta, *The Evolution of American Society, 1700–1815* (Lexington, Mass., 1973), which was succeeded by James A. Henretta and Gregory H. Nobles, *Evolution and Revolution: American Society, 1600–1820* (Lexington, Mass., 1987).

3. Among the studies from the Chesapeake group that concentrated on economic and demographic issues are Lois Green Carr, Russell R. Menard, and Lorena S. Walsh, *Robert Cole's World: Agriculture and Society in Early Maryland* (Chapel Hill, 1991); Lois Green Carr et al., *Colonial Chesapeake Society* (Chapel Hill, 1989); Allan Kulikoff, *Tobacco and Slaves: The Development of Southern Cultures in the Chesapeake, 1680–1800* (Chapel Hill, 1986); Gloria L. Main, *Tobacco Colony: Life in Early Maryland, 1650–1720* (Princeton, 1982); Russell R. Menard, *Economy and Society in Early Colonial Maryland* (New York, 1985); and Darrett B. Rutman and Anita H. Rutman, *A Place in Time: Middlesex County, Virginia, 1650–1750* (New York, 1984). Other crucial studies on Maryland or Virginia include T. H. Breen, *Tobacco Culture: The Mentality of the Great Tidewater Planters on the Eve of the Revolution* (Princeton, 1985); Kathleen M. Brown, *Good Wives, Nasty Wenches, and Anxious Patriarchs: Gender, Race, and Power in Colonial Virginia* (Chapel Hill, 1996); Paul G. E. Clemens, *The Atlantic Economy and Colonial Maryland's Eastern Shore: From Tobacco to Grain* (Ithaca, N.Y., 1980); Richard Beale Davis, *Intellectual Life in the Colonial South, 1585–1763,* 3 vols. (Knoxville, 1978); Jack P. Greene, *The Quest for Power: The Lower Houses of Assembly in the Southern Royal Colonies, 1689–1776* (Chapel Hill, 1963); Joan R. Gundersen, *The Anglican Ministry in Virginia, 1723–1766: A Study of Social Class* (New York, 1989); Ronald Hoffman, *A Spirit of Dissension: Economics, Politics, and the Revolution in Maryland* (Baltimore, 1973); Rhys Isaac, *The Transformation of Virginia, 1740–1790* (Chapel Hill, 1982); Alan L. Karras, *Sojourners in the Sun: Scottish Migrants in Jamaica and the Chesapeake, 1740–1800* (Ithaca, N.Y., 1992); J. A. Leo Lemay, *Men of Letters in Colonial Maryland* (Knoxville, 1972); Kenneth A. Lockridge, *The Diary, and Life, of William Byrd II of Virginia, 1674–1744* (Chapel Hill, 1987); Edmund S. Morgan, *American Slavery, American Freedom: The Ordeal of Colonial Virginia* (New York, 1975); Jacob M. Price, *Capital and Credit in British Overseas Trade: The View from the Chesapeake, 1700–1776* (Cambridge, Mass., 1980); Jacob M. Price, *France and the Chesapeake: A History of the French Tobacco Monopoly, 1674–1791, and of Its Relationship to the British and American Tobacco Trades* (Ann Arbor, 1973); A. G. Roeber, *Faithful Magistrates and Republican Lawyers: Creators of Virginia Legal Culture, 1680–1810* (Chapel Hill, 1981); Michal J. Rozbicki, *The Complete Colonial Gentleman: Cultural Legitimacy in Plantation America* (Charlottesville, Va., 1998); Daniel Blake Smith, *Inside the Great House: Family Life in Eighteenth-*

Century Chesapeake Society (Ithaca, N.Y., 1980); Mechal Sobel, *The World They Made Together: Black and White Values in Eighteenth-Century Virginia* (Princeton, 1987).

4. See especially Randall H. Balmer, *A Perfect Babel of Confusion: Dutch Religion and English Culture in the Middle Colonies* (New York, 1989); Patricia U. Bonomi, *A Factious People: Politics and Society in Colonial New York* (New York, 1971); Patricia U. Bonomi, "The Middle Colonies: Embryo of the New Political Order," in *Perspectives in Early American History: Essays in Honor of Richard Morris*, ed. Alden T. Vaughn and George A. Billias (New York, 1973), pp. 63–92; Patricia U. Bonomi, *Under the Cope of Heaven: Religion, Society, and Politics in Colonial America* (New York, 1986); Patricia U. Bonomi, *The Lord Cornbury Scandal: The Politics of Reputation in British America* (Chapel Hill, 1998); Mary Maples Dunn, *William Penn: Politics and Conscience* (Princeton, 1967); Aaron S. Fogleman, *Hopeful Journeys: German Immigration, Settlement, and Political Culture in Colonial America, 1717–1775* (Philadelphia, 1996); J. William Frost, *A Perfect Freedom: Religious Liberty in Pennsylvania* (New York, 1990); Joyce D. Goodfriend, *Before the Melting Pot: Society and Culture in Colonial New York City, 1664–1730* (Princeton, 1991); Michael Kammen, *Colonial New York: A History* (Millwood, N.Y., 1975); Ned Landsman, *Scotland and Its First American Colony, 1683–1765* (Princeton, 1985); Gary B. Nash, *Quakers and Politics, Pennsylvania, 1681–1726* (Princeton, 1968); Gary B. Nash, *The Urban Crucible: Social Change, Political Consciousness, and the Origins of the American Revolution* (Cambridge, Mass., 1979); A. G. Roeber, *Palatines, Liberty, and Property: German Lutherans in British North America* (Baltimore, 1993); Alan Tully, "Englishmen and Germans: National-Group Contact in Colonial Pennsylvania," *Pennsylvania History*, 45 (1978): 237–256; and Alan Tully, *Forming American Politics: Ideals, Interests, and Institutions in Colonial New York and Pennsylvania* (Baltimore, 1994).

5. Peter A. Coclanis, *The Shadow of a Dream: Economic Life and Death in the South Carolina Low Country, 1670–1920* (New York, 1989); A. Roger Ekirch, *"Poor Carolina": Politics and Society in Colonial North Carolina, 1729–1776* (Chapel Hill, 1981); Rachel Klein, *Unification of a Slave State: The Rise of the Planter Class in the South Carolina Backcountry, 1760–1808* (Chapel Hill, 1990); James H. Merrell, *The Indians' New World: Catawbas and Their Neighbors from European Contact through the Era of Removal* (Chapel Hill, 1989); Jon F. Sensbach, *A Separate Canaan: The Making of an Afro-Moravian World in North Carolina, 1763–1840* (Chapel Hill, 1997); Daniel B. Thorp, *The Moravian Community in North Carolina: Pluralism on the Southern Frontier* (Knoxville, 1989); Peter H. Wood, *Black Majority: Negroes in Colonial South Carolina from 1670 through the Stono Rebellion* (New York, 1974); Peter H. Wood, Gregory A. Waselkov, and M. Thomas Hatley, eds., *Powhatan's Mantle: Indians in the Colonial Southeast* (Lincoln, 1989); and a

major original source that drew the attention of many historians to the Carolinas, Charles Woodmason, *The Carolina Backcountry on the Eve of the American Revolution: The Journal and Other Writings of Charles Woodmason, Anglican Itinerant,* ed. Richard J. Hooker (Chapel Hill, 1953). An important comparative study is found in Philip Morgan, *Slave Counterpoint: Black Culture in the Eighteenth-Century Chesapeake and Lowcountry* (Chapel Hill, 1998).

6. The literature on New England is enormous. Among studies that open new horizons on this society, especially after 1680, one might read Bernard Bailyn, "Religion and Revolution: Three Biographical Studies [Andrew Eliot, Jonathan Mayhew, Stephen Johnson]," *Perspectives in American History,* 4 (1970): 85–169; T. H. Breen, *The Character of the Good Ruler: A Study of Puritan Political Ideas in New England, 1630–1730* (New Haven, 1970); Richard L. Bushman, *From Puritan to Yankee: Character and the Social Order in Connecticut, 1690–1765* (Cambridge, Mass., 1967); John Demos, *The Unredeemed Captive: A Family Story from Early America* (New York, 1994); John Demos, *Entertaining Satan: Witchcraft and the Culture of Early New England* (New York, 1982); Norman Fiering, *Jonathan Edwards's Moral Thought and Its British Context* (Chapel Hill, 1981); Stephen Foster, *The Long Argument: English Puritanism and the Shaping of New England Culture, 1570–1700* (Chapel Hill, 1991); Charles S. Grant, *Democracy in the Connecticut Frontier Town of Kent* (New York, 1961); Philip J. Greven, Jr., *Four Generations: Population, Land, and Family in Colonial Andover, Massachusetts* (Ithaca, N.Y., 1970); David D. Hall, *World of Wonder, Days of Judgment: Popular Religious Belief in Early New England* (New York, 1989); Christine Leigh Heyrman, *Commerce and Culture: The Maritime Communities of Colonial Massachusetts, 1690–1750* (New York, 1984); James W. Jones, *The Shattered Synthesis: New England Puritanism before the Great Awakening* (New Haven, 1973); Jane Kamensky, *Governing the Tongue: The Politics of Speech in Early New England* (New York, 1998); Kenneth Lockridge, *Literacy in Colonial New England: An Enquiry into the Social Context of Literacy in the Early Modern West* (New York, 1974); Kenneth A. Lockridge, *A New England Town: The First Hundred Years* (New York, 1970); Paul R. Lucas, *Valley of Discord: Church and Society along the Connecticut River, 1636–1725* (Hanover, N.H., 1976); Jackson Turner Main, *Society and Economy in Colonial Connecticut* (Princeton, 1985); William G. McLoughlin, *New England Dissent, 1630–1833: The Baptists and the Separation of Church and State* (Cambridge, Mass., 1971); Edmund S. Morgan, *The Gentle Puritan: A Life of Ezra Stiles, 1727–1795* (New Haven, 1962); Mary Beth Norton, *Founding Mothers and Fathers: Gendered Power and the Forming of American Society* (New York, 1996), which provides important comparisons with the Chesapeake; William D. Piersen, *Black Yankees: The Development of an Afro-American Subculture in Eighteenth-Century New England* (Amherst, Mass., 1988); Dar-

rett B. Rutman, *Husbandmen of Plymouth: Farms and Villages in the Old Colony, 1620–1692* (Boston, 1967); Darrett B. Rutman, *Winthrop's Boston: Portrait of a Puritan Town, 1630–1649* (Chapel Hill, 1965); Harry S. Stout, *The New England Soul: Preaching and Religious Culture in Colonial New England* (New York, 1986); Laurel Thatcher Ulrich, *Good Wives: Image and Reality in the Lives of Women in Northern New England, 1650–1750* (New York, 1982); Laurel Thatcher Ulrich, *A Midwife's Tale: The Life of Martha Ballard Based on Her Diary, 1785–1812* (New York, 1990); Daniel Vickers, *Farmers and Fishermen: Two Centuries of Work in Essex County, Massachusetts, 1630–1830* (Chapel Hill, 1994); Robert Zemsky, *Merchants, Farmers, and River Gods: An Essay on Eighteenth-Century American Politics* (Boston, 1971); Michael Zuckerman, *Peaceable Kingdoms: New England Towns in the Eighteenth Century* (New York, 1970).

7. T. H. Breen has written a remarkable series of essays on Europeanization, including especially " 'Baubles of Britain': The American and Consumer Revolutions of the Eighteenth Century," in *Of Consuming Interests: The Style of Life in the Eighteenth Century,* ed. Cary Carson, Ronald Hoffman, and Peter J. Albert (Charlottesville, Va., 1994): 444–482; "An Empire of Goods: The Anglicization of Colonial America, 1690–1776," *Journal of British Studies,* 25 (1986): 467–499; and "Narrative of Commercial Life: Consumption, Ideology, and Community on the Eve of the American Revolution," *William and Mary Quarterly,* 3d ser., 50 (1993): 471–501. They are linked to an interpretation of the American Revolution in Breen, "Ideology and Nationalism on the Eve of the American Revolution: Revisions Once More in Need of Revising," *Journal of American History,* 84 (1997): 13–39. The argument, now much expanded, goes back to John M. Murrin, "Anglicizing an American Colony: The Transformation of Provincial Massachusetts" (Ph.D. diss., Yale University, 1966), which was partially summarized in Murrin, "The Legal Transformation: The Bench and Bar of Eighteenth-Century Massachusetts," in *Colonial America: Essays in Politics and Social Development,* ed. Stanley N. Katz (Boston, 1971): 415–449.

8. I have drawn this portrait in good part from Michael Zuckerman, "Tocqueville, Turner, and Turds: Four Stories of Manners in Early America," *Journal of American History,* 85 (1998): 13–42, which offers a critique of the "deference" thesis in colonial America. While I agree that early America was not a deferential society, I have not always joined Zuckerman in stressing the "bumptious egalitarianism and antiauthoritarianism" of prerevolutionary society (ibid., p. 42). Among the important works in establishing the theme of deference in the earlier literature, see Richard L. Bushman, *King and People in Provincial Massachusetts* (Chapel Hill, 1985); J. R. Pole, "Historians and the Problem of Early American Democracy," *American Historical Review,* 67 (1962): 626–646; Charles Sydnor, *Gentlemen Freeholders: Political Practices in Washington's Virginia* (Chapel Hill, 1952); and especially Gordon S. Wood,

The Radicalism of the American Revolution (New York, 1992). For an earlier evaluation of the theme of deference and its problems, see Joy B. Gilsdorf and Robert R. Gilsdorf, "Elites and Electorates: Some Plain Truths for Historians of Colonial America," in *Saints and Revolutionaries: Essays on Early American History* (New York, 1984), pp. 207–244. See also two important essays by Richard Beeman, "Robert Munford and the Political Culture of Frontier Virginia," *Journal of American Studies,* 12 (1978): 168–183, and "Deference, Republicanism, and the Emergence of Popular Politics in Eighteenth-Century America," *William and Mary Quarterly,* 3d ser., 49 (1992): 401–430.

9. The premier book on this topic is Charles Sellers, *The Market Revolution: Jacksonian America, 1815–1846* (New York, 1991). Readers might note that Sellers only briefly draws comparisons to the colonial era and does not actually provide a synoptic description of the "market revolution," preferring instead to attach the label to different aspects of "it." A sample of the debate on the "market revolution" and capitalism in the early Republic and antebellum eras can be found in *The Market Revolution in America: Social, Political, and Religious Expressions, 1800–1880,* ed. Melvyn Stokes and Stephen Conway (Charlottesville, 1996), especially the introduction, pp. 1–20. Other works on this topic include James T. Carson, "Native Americans, the Market Revolution, and Culture Change: The Choctaw Cattle Economy, 1690–1830," *Agricultural History,* 71 (1997): 1–18; Christopher Clark, *The Roots of Rural Capitalism, Western Massachusetts, 1780–1860* (Ithaca, N.Y., 1990); Douglas R. Egerton, "Markets without a Market Revolution: Southern Planters and Capitalism," *Journal of the Early Republic,* 16 (1996): 207–221; James A. Henretta, "The 'Market' in the Early Republic," *Journal of the Early Republic,* 18 (1998): 289–304; John D. Majewski, "Commerce and Community: Economic, Cultural, and Internal Improvements in Pennsylvania and Virginia, 1790–1860" (Ph.D. diss., University of California at Los Angeles, 1994); Allan Kulikoff, *The Agrarian Origins of American Capitalism* (Charlottesville, 1992); Michael Merrill, "Putting Capitalism in Its Place," *William and Mary Quarterly,* 3d ser., 52 (1995): 315–326; Winifred B. Rothenberg, *From Market-Places to a Market Economy: The Transformation of Rural Massachusetts, 1750–1850* (Chicago, 1992); Mark S. Schantz, "Religious Tracts, Evangelical Reform, and the Market Revolution in Antebellum America," *Journal of the Early Republic,* 17 (1997): 425–466; Samuel J. Watson III, "Flexible Gender Roles during the Market Revolution: Family, Friendship, Marriage, and Masculinity among U.S. Army Officers, 1815–1846," *Journal of Social History,* 29 (1995): 81–106; Thomas S. Wermuth, "New York Farmers and the Market Revolution: Economic Behavior in the Mid-Hudson Valley, 1780–1830," *Journal of Social History,* 32 (1998): 179–196; and Major L. Wilson, "The 'Country' versus the 'Court': A Republican Consensus and Party Debate in the Bank War," *Journal of the Early Republic,* 15 (1995): 619–647.

10. Among several interesting studies, see David Waldstreicher, *In the Midst of Perpetual Fetes: The Making of American Nationalism, 1776–1820* (Chapel

Hill, 1997); Simon P. Newman, *Parades and the Politics of the Street: Festive Culture in the Early American Republic* (Philadelphia, 1997); Linda Kerber, *Women of the Republic: Intellect and Ideology in Revolutionary America* (Chapel Hill, 1980); and Linda K. Kerber, "The Paradox of Women's Citizenship in the Early Republic: The Case of Martin vs. Massachusetts, 1805," *American Historical Review,* 97 (1992): 349–78.

1. PEOPLES

1. Coroner's Inquisition on William Asht, April 2, 1712, New-York Historical Society, Misc. Mss., New York City, Box 4, no. 12; Coroner's Inquisition on Augustus Grasset, April 9, 1712, ibid., no. 13. The only substantial historical study is by Kenneth Scott, "The Slave Insurrection in New York in 1712," *New-York Historical Society Quarterly,* 45 (1967): 43–74. The epigraphs in Chapters 1–5 are from Hector St. John de Crèvecoeur, *Letters from an American Farmer and Sketches of Eighteenth-Century America,* ed. Albert E. Stone (New York, 1981): 1, p. 68; 2, p. 81; 3, p. 69; 4, p. 87; 5, p. 73. The epigraph in Chapter 6 is from Thomas Paine, *Common Sense,* ed. Isaac Kramnick (Harmondsworth, 1976), p. 104.

2. Scott, "Slave Insurrection in New York in 1712," p. 57. On Hunter, see Lawrence H. Leder, ed., "Robert Hunter's Androboros," *New York Public Library Bulletin,* 68 (1964): 153–190, and Mary Lou Lustig, *Robert Hunter 1666–1734: New York's Augustan Statesman* (Syracuse, 1983).

3. Philip D. Curtin, *The Atlantic Slave Trade: A Census* (Madison, 1969), pp. 157–160. The lack of direct evidence about early New York makes it difficult to determine whether the distribution of slaves there in the late 1690s and early 1700s followed the broader patterns documented by Curtin.

4. The 1703 New York City census is printed in E. B. O'Callaghan, *The Documentary History of the State of New York,* 4 vols. (Albany, 1850), 1: 395–405, which names only heads of households. I have extrapolated the ethnic composition from the analysis of the New York City tax and census records found in Joyce D. Goodfriend, "'Too Great a Mixture of Nations': The Development of New York City Society in the Seventeenth Century" (Ph.D. diss., University of California at Los Angeles, 1975), p. 139; these figures are more full than those given in Goodfriend, *Before the Melting Pot: Society and Culture in Colonial New York City, 1664–1730* (Princeton, 1992), p. 62, which count only white men, not all adults or the full population. Crèvecoeur, *Letters from an American Farmer,* p. 68.

5. Crèvecoeur, *Letters from an American Farmer,* p. 68. The estimates are calculated from figures provided in Bureau of the Census, *Historical Statistics of the United States, Colonial Times to 1957* (Washington, D.C., 1961), p. 756.

6. On the question of the "middle colonies," see Wayne Bodle, "The 'Myth of the Middle Colonies' Reconsidered: The Process of Regionalization in Early America," *Pennsylvania Magazine of History and Biography,* 113 (1989): 527–548.

7. The startling rise of South Carolina's African population and its consequences is discussed in Peter H. Wood, *Black Majority: Negroes in Colonial South Carolina from 1670 through the Stono Rebellion* (New York, 1974).

8. Crèvecoeur, *Letters from an American Farmer*, pp. 120–124; quotations on pp. 120, 121, 122.

9. Jill Lepore, *The Name of War: King Philip's War and the Origins of American Identity* (New York, 1998), pp. xvi–xxi; Douglas E. Leach, *Flintlock and Tomahawk: New England in King Philip's War* (New York, 1966); Gary B. Nash, *Red, White, and Black: The Peoples of Early America* (Englewood Cliffs, N.J., 1982), pp. 116–121.

10. Russell Thornton, *American Indian Holocaust and Survival: A Population History since 1492* (Norman, 1987), pp. 65–90, for Nantucket, see table 4-2, p. 83; James Axtell, *The Invasion Within: The Conquest of Cultures in Colonial North America* (New York, 1985), pp. 190–191, 219–220; Neal Salisbury, *Manitou and Providence: Indians, Europeans, and the Making of New England, 1500–1643* (New York, 1982); Gary B. Nash, *Red, White, and Black: The Peoples of Early America*, 2d ed. (Englewood Cliffs, N.J., 1982), pp. 99–104.

11. T. J. Sugrue, "The Peopling and Depeopling of Early Pennsylvania: Indians and Colonists, 1680–1720," *Pennsylvania Magazine of History and Biography*, 116 (1992): 3–32; the Gabriel Thomas quotation is on p. 15.

12. The discussion of population change is based on descriptions given in John R. Swanton, *The Indians of the Southeastern United States* (Washington, D.C., 1946), pp. 82–216; Peter H. Wood, "The Changing Population of the Colonial South: An Overview by Race and Region, 1685–1790," in *Powhatan's Mantle: Indians in the Colonial Southeast,* ed. Peter H. Wood, Gregory A. Waselkov, and M. Thomas Hatley (Lincoln, 1989), pp. 35–103, see especially table 1, p. 38; and James H. Merrell, *The Indians' New World: Catawbas and Their Neighbors from European Contact through the Era of Removal* (Chapel Hill, 1989), pp. 47–48, 92–98. On California and Ishi, see Theodora Kroeber, *Ishi in Two Worlds: A Biography of the Last Wild Indian in North America* (Berkeley, 1961). The argument here is that a nonreproducing *culture* is extinct even if some of its adherents are living and its artifacts survive for centuries.

13. Merrell, *The Indians' New World*, pp. 92–95; Colin G. Calloway, *New Worlds for All: Indians, Europeans, and the Remaking of Early America* (Baltimore, 1997), pp. 142–143.

14. Merrell, *The Indians' New World*, pp. 117–133; the quotation from the German trader Conrad Weiser is in ibid., p. 112.

15. Ibid., pp. 49–91. For the picture of trade in the Ohio River valley, see Eric Hinderaker, *Elusive Empires: Constructing Colonialism in the Ohio Valley, 1673–1800* (New York, 1997), pp. 79–186.

16. Daniel K. Richter, *The Ordeal of the Longhouse: The Peoples of the Iroquois League in the Era of European Colonization* (Chapel Hill, 1992); Daniel K. Richter, "War and Culture: The Iroquois Experience," *William and Mary*

Quarterly, 3d ser., 40 (1983): 528–559; Rachel Wheeler, "Living upon Hope: Mahicans and Missionaries, 1730–1770" (Ph.D. diss., Yale University, 1998). For a record of steady dispossession in New England, see Jean M. O'Brien, *Dispossession by Degrees: Indian Land and Identity in Natick, Massachusetts, 1650–1790* (New York, 1997).

17. Crèvecoeur offers a highly ambivalent and openly contradictory account of Indians in America. See his *Letters from an American Farmer,* where Crèvecoeur is sometimes critical and contemptuous of Indians (pp. 119–124) and sometimes fearful and admiring (pp. 213–215).

18. Judith Giton's memoir is most dependably translated in "Early Manigault Records," ed. Slann L. G. Simmons, *Transactions of the Huguenot Society of South Carolina,* 59 (1954): 25–27. On the Huguenot flight from France, see Jon Butler, *The Huguenots in America: A Refugee People in New World Society* (Cambridge, Mass., 1983), pp. 13–40, and Miriam Yardeni, *Le Refuge Protestant* (Paris, 1985). On migration elsewhere in Europe, see Hans Fenske, "International Migration: Germany in the Eighteenth Century," *Central European History,* 13 (1980): 31–47; Marianne S. Wokeck, *Trade in Strangers: The Beginnings of Mass Migration to North America* (University Park, Pa., 1999), pp. 1–36; and Aaron S. Fogleman, *Hopeful Journeys: German Immigration, Settlement, and Political Culture in Colonial America, 1717–1775* (Philadelphia, 1996), pp. 15–35. On Peter Manigault's wealth in the 1770s, see Alice Hanson Jones, *American Colonial Wealth: Documents and Methods* (New York, 1978), 3: 1543–1559.

19. Nicholas P. Canny, *The Elizabethan Conquest of Ireland: A Pattern Established, 1565–76* (Sussex, 1976); Canny, *From Reformation to Restoration: Ireland, 1534–1660* (Dublin, 1987).

20. See Nicholas Canny, ed., *Europeans on the Move: Studies on European Migration, 1500–1800* (New York, 1994); Peter Clark, "Migration in England during the Late Seventeenth and Early Eighteenth Centuries," *Past and Present,* no. 83 (1979): 57–90; David Souden, "'East, West—Home's Best'? Regional Patterns in Migration in Early Modern England," in *Migration and Society in Early Modern England,* ed. Peter Clark and David Souden (London, 1987), pp. 292–332.

21. On the situation in Ireland, see Canny, *The Elizabethan Conquest of Ireland,* and Steven G. Ellis, *Tudor Ireland: Crown, Community, and the Conflict of Cultures, 1470–1603* (London, 1985). On the Huguenot refugees, see Bernard Cottret, *Huguenots in England: Immigration and Settlement, c. 1550–1700* (Cambridge, 1991); Anne Hartman Goldgar, "Gentlemen and Scholars: Conduct and Community in the Republic of Letters, 1680–1750" (Ph.D. diss., Harvard University, 1990); and Jon Butler, *The Huguenots in America: A Refugee People in New World Society* (Cambridge, Mass., 1983), chap. 1.

22. David Dobson, *Scottish Emigration to Colonial America, 1607–1785* (Athens, Ga., 1994), pp. 9–16; A. Francis Steuart, ed., *Papers Relating to the Scots in*

Poland, 1576–1793, vol. 59, Publications of the Scottish History Society (Edinburgh, 1915).

23. Bernard Bailyn discusses the relationship between migration in Europe and American emigration in *The Peopling of British North America: An Introduction* (New York, 1986), pp. 20–43. See James H. Kettner, *The Development of American Citizenship, 1608–1870* (Chapel Hill, 1978) on the difference between "subjectship" and "citizenship" in Europe and America before 1800, and David S. Katz, *The Jews in the History of England, 1485–1850* (Oxford, 1994) on discrimination against Jews.

24. Bernard Bailyn, *Voyagers to the West: A Passage in the Peopling of America on the Eve of the Revolution* (New York, 1986), pp. 256, 322–323; James T. Lemon, *The Best Poor Man's Country: A Geographical Study of Early Southeastern Pennsylvania* (Baltimore, 1972), pp. 29, 41.

25. Thomas Clifford quoted in Bailyn, *Voyagers to the West*, p. 318; Walter A. Knittle, *The Early Eighteenth Century Palatine Emigration: A British Government Redemptioner Project to Manufacture Naval Stores* (Philadelphia, 1936), pp. 32, 146–147.

26. Bailyn, *Voyagers to the West*, pp. 166–167; Abbot E. Smith, *Colonists in Bondage* (Chapel Hill, 1947); David W. Galenson, *White Servitude in Colonial America: An Economic Analysis* (New York, 1982).

27. There is no general study of European migration throughout the New World. The first comparative New World histories that discussed immigration were written in advance of specialized, systematic research—see Herbert E. Bolton, *History of the Americas: A Syllabus with Maps*, new ed. (Boston, 1935) and John Francis Bannon, *History of the Americas* (New York, 1952)—and no one has synthesized the specialized research that has been produced since 1950. Short overviews can be found in E. L. Jones, "The European Background," in *The Cambridge Economic History of the United States: The Colonial Era*, ed. Stanley L. Engerman and Robert E. Gallman (New York, 1996), pp. 95–134, and David W. Galenson, "The Settlement and Growth of the Colonies: Population, Labor, and Economic Development," in ibid., pp. 135–208.

28. Quoted in Richard Cook, "Lewis Morris—New Jersey's Colonial Poet-Governor," *Rutgers University Library Journal*, 24 (1960): 107.

29. Robert Mandrou et al., *Histoire des protestants en France* (Toulouse, 1977); Butler, *Huguenots in America*, pp. 13–40.

30. *Recueil de diverses pieces, concernant la Pensilvanie* (The Hague, 1684); *Description de la Caroline prés la Floride* (Geneva, 1684) [the copy at the William L. Clements Library, University of Michigan, contains material from South Carolina written in 1685 that was added to the original pamphlet without changing the publication date]; *Nouvelle relation de la Carolina* (The Hague, 1685); "Remarks on the New Account of Carolina by a French Gentleman—1686," *The Magnolia*, n.s., 1 (1842): 226–230; the original French edition no longer survives.

31. Butler, *Huguenots in America*, pp. 56–57.

32. Ibid., pp. 60–66.
33. Crèvecoeur, *Letters from an American Farmer*, pp. 69–70. Intriguingly, Crève-coeur was married to Mehetabel Tippet of Westchester County, by Rev. J. P. Tetârd, the minister of New York City's French Church, on Sept. 30, 1769.
34. The immigration figures are taken from Aaron Fogleman, "Migrations to the Thirteen British North American Colonies, 1700–1775: New Estimates," *Journal of Interdisciplinary History* 22 (1992), table 1.
35. Defoe quoted in Ned Landsman, *Scotland and Its First American Colony, 1683–1765* (Princeton, 1985), p. 18.
36. Wayland F. Dunaway, *The Scotch-Irish of Colonial Pennsylvania* (Chapel Hill, 1944), pp. 28–42.
37. The immigrant list is described in David Dobson, *Scottish Emigration to Colonial America, 1607–1785* (Athens, Ga., 1994), p. 161.
38. Bailyn, *Voyagers to the West*, pp. 112–113, 129–130, 160.
39. Dunaway, *The Scotch-Irish of Colonial Pennsylvania*, p. 32; Dobson, *Scottish Emigration to Colonial America*, pp. 97–99; quotation from Bailyn, *Voyagers to the West*, p. 173.
40. Landsman, *Scotland and Its First American Colony*, pp. 99–130; a variety of Scottish colonization efforts are discussed in Dobson, *Scottish Emigration to Colonial America*.
41. Landsman, *Scotland and Its First American Colony*, p. 250. Intermarriage is not discussed in either Dobson, *Scottish Emigration to Colonial America* or in Dunaway, *Scotch-Irish of Colonial Pennsylvania*, and I have inferred this argument from the attainment and rise of Scottish identity in the colonies, not from any systematic study of Scottish intermarriage, which is as yet nonexistent.
42. Landsman, *Scotland and Its First American Colony*, esp. chaps 8–9, offers a more sophisticated approach than Dunaway, *The Scotch-Irish of Colonial Pennsylvania* or Ian C. C. Graham, *Colonists from Scotland: Emigration to North America, 1707–1783* (Ithaca, N.Y., 1956).
43. Eli Faber, *A Time for Planting: The First Migration, 1654–1820* (Baltimore, 1992), pp. 27–33. A small group of Jews lived in Newport, Rhode Island, from 1658 forward but almost nothing is known about them until the 1680s. My discussion of Jews in colonial America greatly benefited from reading Jonathan Sarna's forthcoming study.
44. Faber, *A Time for Planting*, pp. 34, 36, 41, 111.
45. Ibid., pp. 28–29; Jeanette W. Rosenbaum, *Myer Myers, Goldsmith* (Philadelphia, 1954); Leo Hershkowitz, ed., *Wills of Early New York Jews (1704–1799)* (New York, 1967).
46. Leo Hershkowitz, "The Mill Street Synagogue Reconsidered," *American Jewish Historical Quarterly*, 53 (1964): 404–410; Faber, *A Time for Planting*.
47. Faber, *A Time for Planting*, pp. 58–66.
48. Faber, *A Time for Planting*, pp. 65, 93; Abigail Franks to Naphtali Franks, June 7, 1743, in *Letters of the Franks Family (1733–1748)*, ed. Leo Hershkowitz and Isidor S. Meyer (Waltham, Mass., 1968), p. 117. In 1744

Phila Franks's brother David Franks married a Philadelphia Anglican, Margaret Evans of Philadelphia; by the end of the colonial era the Franks family had become Christian. Malcolm H. Stern, "The Function of Genealogy in American Jewish History," in *Essays in American Jewish History to Commemorate the Tenth Anniversary of the Founding of the American Jewish Archives under the Direction of Jacob Rader Marcus* (Cincinnati, 1958), pp. 69–98. On colonial anti-Semitism, see Leonard Dinnerstein, *Antisemitism in America* (New York, 1994), pp. 3–12.

49. Petrus Iskenius to Johannes Peter Clements, April 26, 1732; Jorg Thomas Iskenius to Catharina Elisabetha Iskenius Clements et al., June 7, 1737, in F. J. Sypher, ed., "Voices in the Wilderness: Letters to Colonial New York from Germany (1726–1737)," *New York History* 67 (1986): 351, 352; John George Käsebier to Casimir, Count of Sayn-Wittgenstein-Berleburg, Nov. 7, 1724, in Donald F. Durnbaugh, "Two Early Letters from Germantown," *Pennsylvania Magazine of History and Biography*, 84 (1960): 225–226. For the origins of the phrase "the best poor man's country," see Lemon, *Best Poor Man's Country*, p. 229n1. Readers should also see Marianne S. Wokeck, *Trade in Strangers: The Beginnings of Mass Migration to North America* (University Park, Pa., 1999).

50. The figures are derived from Fogleman, "Migrations to the Thirteen British North American Colonies." Wokeck counts about 100,000 German immigrants to the mainland colonies; I have used Fogleman's lower estimate to remain consistent with his analysis of total immigration to the mainland colonies. See Marianne Wokeck, "Harnessing the Lure of the 'Best Poor Man's Country': The Dynamics of German-Speaking Immigration to British North America, 1683–1783," in *"To Make America": European Emigration in the Early Modern Period*, ed. Ida Altman and James Horn (Berkeley, 1991), p. 225, and Wokeck, "Patterns of German Settlements in the North American Colonies," unpublished paper, Philadelphia Center for Early American Studies (1994).

51. Hope Frances Kane, "Notes on Early Pennsylvania Promotion Literature," *Pennsylvania Magazine of History and Biography*, 63 (1939): 144–168; Wokeck, "Harnessing the Lure of the 'Best Poor Man's Country'"; Wokeck, "Patterns of German Settlements in the North American Colonies."

52. Wokeck, "Patterns of German Settlements in the North American Colonies"; Farley Grubb, "German Immigration to Pennsylvania, 1709 to 1820," *Journal of Interdisciplinary History*, 20 (1990): 417–436.

53. Grubb, "German Immigration to Pennsylvania, 1709 to 1820"; Grubb, "The Market Structure of Shipping German Immigrants to Colonial America," *Pennsylvania Magazine of History and Biography*, 111 (1987): 27–48; Farley Grubb, "Redemptioner Immigration to Pennsylvania: Evidence on Contract Choice and Profitability," *Journal of Economic History*, 46 (1986): 407–418.

54. A. G. Roeber, *Palatines, Liberty, and Property: German Lutherans in British North America* (Baltimore, 1993); Elizabeth W. Fisher, "'Prophecies and

Revelations': German Cabbalists in Early Pennsylvania," *Pennsylvania Magazine of History and Biography*, 109 (1985): 299–333; Julius Friedrich Sachse, *The German Pietists of Provincial Pennsylvania* (Philadelphia, 1895); Peter C. Erb, *Johann Conrad Beissel and the Ephrata Community* (New York, 1985); Gillian Lindt Gollin, *Moravians in Two Worlds: A Study of Changing Communities* (New York, 1967); Albert G. Hess, "Observations on *The Lamenting Voice of the Hidden Love*," *Journal of the American Musicological Society*, 5 (1952): 211–223; Stephen L. Longenecker, *Piety and Tolerance: Pennsylvania German Religion, 1700–1850* (Metuchen, N.J., 1994); F. Ernest Stoeffler, *Continental Pietism and Early American Christianity* (Grand Rapids, Mich., 1976); Daniel B. Thorp, *The Moravian Community in North Carolina: Pluralism on the Southern Frontier* (Knoxville, 1989); John D. Weaver, "Franz Daniel Pastorius (1651–c.1720): Early Life in Germany with Glimpses of His Removal to Pennsylvania" (Ph.D. diss., University of California at Davis, 1985).

55. Stephanie Grauman Wolf, *Urban Village: Population, Community, and Family Structure in Germantown, Pennsylvania, 1683–1800* (Princeton, 1976), p. 132.

56. Franklin, quoted in Wolf, *Urban Village*, pp. 138–139; William Smith quoted in Alan Tully, *Forming American Politics: Ideals, Interests, and Institutions in Colonial New York and Pennsylvania* (Baltimore, 1994), p. 111; Alan Tully, "Englishmen and Germans: National-Group Contact in Colonial Pennsylvania," *Pennsylvania History*, 45 (1978): 237–256.

57. Wolf, *Urban Village*, pp. 152–153; Samuel E. Weber, *The Charity School Movement in Colonial Pennsylvania* (Philadelphia, 1905).

58. For overviews, see James Horn, "British Diaspora: Emigration from Britain, 1680–1815," in *The Oxford History of the British Empire: The Eighteenth Century*, ed. P. J. Marshall, 5 vols. (New York, 1998), 2: 28–52, and J. Potter, "The Growth of Population in America, 1700–1860," in *Population in History*, ed. D. V. Glass and D. E. C. Eversley (London, 1965), pp. 631–688.

59. Barry Levy, *Quakers and the American Family: British Settlement in the Delaware Valley* (New York, 1988), pp. 110–118; quotation from the 1698 Yearly Meeting from Wales on p. 112.

60. A. Roger Ekirch, *Bound for America: The Transportation of British Convicts to the Colonies, 1718–1775* (Oxford, 1987), pp. 11–45, 166. Ekirch offered a detailed demographic profile of deported convicts in his article "Bound for America: A Profile of British Convicts Transported to the Colonies, 1718–1775," *William and Mary Quarterly*, 3d ser., 42 (1985): 184–200. See also Abbot E. Smith, *Colonists in Bondage: White Servitude and Convict Labor in America, 1607–1776* (Chapel Hill, 1947).

61. Ekirch, *Bound for America*, p. 125; table 12, p. 173.

62. Fogleman, "Migrations to the Thirteen British North American Colonies."

63. Bailyn, *Voyagers to the West*, pp. 126–134.

64. Ibid., pp. 147–166.

65. For information on English immigrants from 1760 to about 1776, see Potter, "The Growth of Population in America, 1700–1860," and Bailyn, *Voyagers to the West*, where they constitute the heart of Bailyn's study.

66. T. H. Breen and Stephen Innes, *"Myne Owne Ground": Race and Freedom on Virginia's Eastern Shore, 1640–1676* (New York, 1980).

67. See Ira Berlin, *Many Thousands Gone: The First Two Centuries of Slavery in North America* (Cambridge, Mass., 1998), for a superb synoptic account of the rise and experience of slavery in the British mainland colonies. On the labor demand in Virginia see both T. H. Breen, "A Changing Labor Force and Race Relations in Virginia 1660–1710," *Journal of Social History*, 7 (1973): 3–25, and Edmund S. Morgan, *American Slavery, American Freedom: The Ordeal of Colonial Virginia* (New York, 1975), p. 299. The question of the English institution of villeinage as a model for slavery is a vexed one. See Paul R. Hyams, *King, Lords, and Peasants in Medieval England: The Common Law of Villeinage in the Twelfth and Thirteenth Centuries* (Oxford, 1980), esp. part II: "The Villein and His Legal Rights," pp. 82–161. On colonial awareness of villeinage, see Thomas D. Morris, *Southern Slavery and the Law, 1619–1860* (Chapel Hill, 1996), pp. 52–55, and Morris, "'Villeinage . . . as It Existed in England, Reflects but Little Light on Our Subject': The Problem of Sources of Southern Slave Law," *American Journal of Legal History*, 32 (1988): 95–137. Morris's only example of colonial awareness of villeinage occurs in a 1736 case in which a Virginia slaveholder wished to distribute unborn children to specific heirs, the judge observing that "The Case of Villains comes the nearest to Slaves but I find nothing concerning them as to this matter" (the attempt was denied based on English property law: one could not convey what did not exist).

68. Steven Deyle, " 'By Farr the Most Profitable Trade': Slave Trading in British Colonial North America," *Slavery and Abolition*, 10 (1989): 107–125; Sarah Deutsch, "The Elusive Guineamen: Newport Slavers, 1735–1774," *New England Quarterly*, 55 (1982): 229–253; David Richardson, "The British Slave Trade to Colonial South Carolina," *Slavery and Abolition*, 12 (1991): 125–172; Daniel C. Littlefield, "The Slave Trade to Colonial South Carolina," *South Carolina Historical Magazine*, 91 (1990): 68–98.

69. On the concept and practice of early slavery, see Breen and Innes, *"Myne Owne Ground,"* and Winthrop D. Jordan, *White over Black: American Attitudes toward the Negro, 1550–1812* (Chapel Hill, 1968).

70. Merrell, *The Indians' New World*, pp. 36–37; Morgan, *American Slavery, American Freedom*, pp. 99–100, 233, 263–264; Theda Perdue, *Slavery and the Evolution of Cherokee Society, 1540–1866* (Knoxville, 1979).

71. Nash, *Red, White, and Black*, pp. 142–147; Philip D. Curtin, *The Atlantic Slave Trade: A Census* (Madison, 1969).

72. Even if Jordan's *White over Black* overemphasized the ubiquity of negative "racial" connotations about "blackness," in the seventeenth century, "black-

ness" scarcely enjoyed parity with the concept of "whiteness" among English men and women on either side of the Atlantic. On complexities in this issue, see the epilogue, "Making Race, Making Slavery," in Berlin, *Many Thousands Gone,* pp. 358–365.

73. Curtin, *The Atlantic Slave Trade,* p. 216; Berlin, *Many Thousands Gone,* pp. 18–20, 81–83, 100–104.

74. Curtin, *The Atlantic Slave Trade,* p. 119; Fogleman, "Migrations to the Thirteen British North American Colonies," pp. 691–709.

75. U.S. Bureau of the Census, *Historical Statistics of the United States, Colonial Times to 1957* (Washington, D.C., 1960), series Z, pp. 1–19; Russell R. Menard, *Economy and Society in Early Colonial Maryland* (New York, 1985), p. 245; Wood, *Black Majority,* table IV, p. 152; Philip Morgan, *Slave Counterpoint: Black Culture in the Eighteenth-Century Chesapeake and Lowcountry* (Chapel Hill, 1998), pp. 95–101.

76. Robert V. Wells, *The Population of the British Colonies in America before 1776* (Princeton, 1975), pp. 111–115, 143, 147.

77. Ibid., pp. 80–82, 89–91, 97–101.

78. Allan Kulikoff, *Tobacco and Slaves: The Development of Southern Cultures in the Chesapeake, 1680–1800* (Chapel Hill, 1986), pp. 67–69; William D. Piersen, "White Cannibals, Black Martyrs: Fear, Depression, and Religious Faith as Cause of Suicide among New Slaves," *Journal of Negro History* 62 (1977): 147–159.

79. For an example, see *Law for Regulating Negroes and Slaves in the Night Time City of New-York* (New York, 1731). The most encyclopedic treatment of this subject for the colonial period is A. Leon Higginbotham, Jr., *In the Matter of Color: Race and the American Legal Process, The Colonial Period* (New York, 1978); also see Berlin, *Many Thousands Gone,* pp. 68–69, 116, 117, 123–125, 186–188. Among others, also see Ernest J. Clark, Jr., "Aspects of the North Carolina Slave Code, 1715–1860," *North Carolina Historical Review,* 39 (1962): 148–164; Samuel J. Hurwitz and Edith F. Hurwitz, "A Token of Freedom: Private Bill Legislation for Free Negroes in Eighteenth-Century Jamaica," *William and Mary Quarterly,* 3d ser., 34 (1967): 423–431; Philip J. Schwarz, *Twice Condemned: Slaves and the Criminal Laws of Virginia, 1705–1865* (Baton Rouge, 1988). As Winthrop Jordan writes, "In America, the slaveholding gentry were coerced as individuals by the popularly elected legislatures toward maintenance of a private tyranny which was conceived to be in the community interest." Jordan, *White over Black,* p. 108.

80. Morgan, *Slave Counterpoint,* pp. 263–266.

81. Wood, *Black Majority,* p. 97. Barry Unsworth, *Sacred Hunger* (New York, 1992) offers a remarkable fictional account of the slave trade and its effects on both Africans and Europeans.

82. Francis Le Jau to the Society for the Propagation of the Gospel in Foreign Parts, Feb. 23, 1713, in *The Carolina Chronicle of Dr. Francis Le Jau 1706–1717,* ed.

Frank J. Klingberg (Berkeley, 1956), p. 130; Crèvecoeur, *Letters from an American Farmer*, pp. 177–178. Morgan, *Slave Counterpoint*, pp. 266–267, discusses the instruments used on slaves by owners.

83. On the question of the slaves' religions, see Butler, *Awash in a Sea of Faith: Christianizing the American People* (Cambridge, Mass., 1990), chap. 5, and a review essay, "Africans' Religions in British America, 1650–1840," *Church History*, 68 (1999), 118–127. For interpretations that stress greater continuities from African religion to America, see Sylvia R. Frey and Betty Wood, *Come Shouting to Zion: African American Protestantism in the American South and British Caribbean to 1830* (Chapel Hill, 1998), and Morgan, *Slave Counterpoint*, pp. 610–658. Berlin downplays progress in African Christianization; see *Many Thousands Gone*, pp. 60–61, 128–129, 138–140, 151, 159, 171–173, 189. Perhaps the disagreement is a classic example of the "half full, half empty" problem, whether to emphasize specific rituals and customs retained by Africans in British America or to stress the destruction of the African religious systems in the British mainland colonies, systems that created the traditional Old World meanings for the rituals and customs.

84. Much colonial legislation on Africans concerned itself with slave "marriages" and sexual relations between Europeans and Africans. See Higginbotham, *In the Matter of Color*, pp. 44–47, 108, 139, 251, 269, 286, 309; Berlin, *Many Thousands Gone*, pp. 44, 189; Morgan, *Slave Counterpoint*, pp. 498–558.

85. Kulikoff, *Tobacco and Slaves*, chap. 9; Morgan, *Slave Counterpoint*, pp. 530–558.

86. The watercolor is entitled *The Old Plantation* and is at the Abby Aldrich Rockefeller Folk Art Center, Williamsburg, Virginia. On New England, see William D. Piersen, *Black Yankees: The Development of an Afro-American Subculture in Eighteenth-Century New England* (Amherst, 1988), chaps. 9–11. For community among African seamen, see W. Jeffrey Bolster, *Black Jacks: African American Seamen in the Age of Sail* (Cambridge, Mass., 1997), and Bolster, "An Inner Diaspora: Black Sailors Making Selves," in *Through a Glass Darkly: Reflections on Personal Identity in Early America*, ed. Ronald Hoffman, Mechal Sobel, and Fredrika J. Teute (Chapel Hill, 1997), pp. 419–448.

87. Gerald W. Mullin, *Flight and Rebellion: Slave Resistance in Eighteenth-Century Virginia* (New York, 1972); Berlin, *Many Thousands Gone*, pp. 119–122. The connection between resistance, community, and the development of what Philip Morgan calls an "autonomous culture" among mainland colony Africans is explained in Morgan, *Slave Counterpoint*, p. xxii.

88. Mullin, *Flight and Rebellion*, pp. 33, 55, 58–59. Morgan, *Slave Counterpoint*, pp. 153–155, 183–184.

89. *The Poems of Charles Hansford*, ed. James A. Servies and Carl R. Dolmetsch (Chapel Hill, 1961).

90. Ibid., p. 47. Internal evidence suggests that Hansford wrote this poem in the 1750s.

91. Crèvecoeur, *Letters from an American Farmer*, p. 69.

2. ECONOMY

1. Hector St. John de Crèvecoeur, *Letters from an American Farmer and Sketches of Eighteenth-Century America*, ed. Albert E. Stone (New York, 1981), p. 67.

2. Edwin J. Perkins, *The Economy of Colonial America*, 2d ed. (New York, 1988), p. 9. The most comprehensive general view of the colonial economy is found in John J. McCusker and Russell R. Menard, *The Economy of British America, 1607–1789* (Chapel Hill, 1991). A recent brief history that stresses relationships with the British economy is found in Marc Egnal, *New World Economies: The Growth of the Thirteen Colonies and Early Canada* (New York, 1998). The vexed question of the origins of capitalism in America and its relationship to farming has produced an enormous scholarly literature in the past thirty years, much of which is effectively summarized in Allan Kulikoff, "The Transition to Capitalism in Rural America," *William and Mary Quarterly,* 3d ser., 46 (1989): 120–144, and Winifred B. Rothenberg, *From Market-Places to a Market Economy: The Transformation of Rural Massachusetts, 1750–1850* (Chicago, 1992). On the problem of consumption and consumers, see Carole Shammas, *The Pre-Industrial Consumer in England and America* (New York, 1990). A special issue of the *William and Mary Quarterly* for January 1999 (3d ser., vol. 56, no. 1) on "The Economy of British North America" contains many important articles that reflect current scholarship on this important topic, several of which are used elsewhere in this chapter. The focus of English historians on broad issues of commerce, international trade, and aristocracy has made comparisons difficult, but for beginnings see John Rule, *Albion's People: English Society, 1714–1815* (London, 1992); Charles Wilson, *England's Apprenticeship, 1603–1763*, 2d ed. (London, 1984); Neil McKendrick, John Brewer, and J. H. Plumb, eds., *The Birth of a Consumer Society: The Commercialization of Eighteenth-Century England* (Bloomington, Ind., 1982); G. E. Mingay, *English Landed Society in the Eighteenth Century* (London, 1963); and K. D. M. Snell, *Annals of the Labouring Poor: Social Change and Agrarian England, 1660–1900* (Cambridge, 1985).

3. Gloria L. Main, *Tobacco Colony: Life in Early Maryland, 1650–1720* (Princeton, 1982); T. H. Breen, *Tobacco Culture: The Mentality of the Great Tidewater Planters on the Eve of the Revolution* (Princeton, 1985).

4. Lois Green Carr, Russell R. Menard, and Lorena S. Walsh, *Robert Cole's World: Agriculture and Society in Early Maryland* (Chapel Hill, N.C., 1991), pp. 3–5.

5. Ibid., pp. 77–90. The problem of subsistence farming and the "market" is a difficult one. James A. Henretta, "Families and Farms: *Mentalité* in Pre-Industrial America," *William and Mary Quarterly,* 3d ser., 35 (1978): 3–32, argues that families approached the "market" question, or purely commercial agriculture, very gingerly, if at all. An extended discussion of this issue and its relationship to profits and exports is very usefully found in McCusker and Menard, *Economy of British America,* pp. 295–304.

6. Gloria L. Main and Jackson T. Main, "The Red Queen in New England?" *William and Mary Quarterly,* 3d ser., 56 (1999): 121–150; Darrett B. Rutman, "Governor Winthrop's Garden Crop: The Significance of Agriculture in the Early Commerce of Massachusetts Bay," ibid., 20 (1963): 396–415; Bernard Bailyn, *The New England Merchants in the Seventeenth Century* (Cambridge, Mass., 1955); Daniel Vickers, "Working the Fields in a Developing Economy: Essex County, Massachusetts, 1630–1675," in *Work and Labor in Early America,* ed. Stephen Innes (Chapel Hill, 1988), pp. 49–69, and Bettye Hobbs Pruitt, "Self-Sufficiency and the Agricultural Economy of Eighteenth-Century Massachusetts," *William and Mary Quarterly,* 3d ser., 41 (1984): 333–364. On the New Netherlands, see Oliver A. Rink, *Holland on the Hudson: An Economic and Social History of Dutch New York* (Ithaca, N.Y., 1986).

7. Carr, Menard, and Walsh, *Robert Cole's World,* pp. 71–75, offers an especially good description of women's labor in the mid-seventeenth-century Chesapeake farm. For descriptions of women's farm labor between 1750 and 1850, see Joan M. Jensen, *Loosening the Bonds: Mid-Atlantic Farm Women, 1750–1850* (New Haven, 1986), and Cynthia A. Kierner, *Beyond the Household: Women's Place in the Early South, 1700–1835* (Ithaca, N.Y., 1998), pp. 9–35. On New England women's labor, see especially Gloria L. Main, "Gender, Work, and Wages in Colonial New England," *William and Mary Quarterly,* 3d. ser., 51 (1994): 39–66, and Laurel Thatcher Ulrich, *Good Wives: Image and Reality in the Lives of Women in Northern New England, 1650–1750* (New York, 1982), pp. 37–38, 49–50. For a comparison with Britain, see Bridget Hill, *Women, Work, and Sexual Politics in Eighteenth-Century England* (Oxford, 1989), and for an urban study, see Patricia A. Cleary, " 'She Merchants' of Colonial America: Women and Commerce on the Eve of the Revolution" (Ph.D. diss., Northwestern University, 1989).

8. Stephanie Grauman Wolf, *As Various as Their Land: The Everyday Lives of Eighteenth-Century Americans* (New York, 1993), pp. 87–90. On the "female economy" of a late eighteenth-century Maine settlement, see Laurel Thatcher Ulrich, *A Midwife's Tale: The Life of Martha Ballard Based on Her Diary, 1785–1812* (New York, 1990), chap. 2.

9. Field Horne, ed., *The Diary of Mary Cooper: Life on a Long Island Farm, 1768–1773* (Oyster Bay, N.Y., 1981), p. 15.

10. Alice Hanson Jones, *Wealth of a Nation to Be: The American Colonies on the Eve of the Revolution* (New York, 1980), table 7.10, p. 229.

11. Main, *Tobacco Colony,* pp. 26–27; Russell Menard, "From Servants to Slaves: The Transformation of the Chesapeake Labor System," *Southern Studies,* 16 (1977): 360, 368–369; Allan Kulikoff, *Tobacco and Slaves: The Development of Southern Cultures in the Chesapeake, 1680–1800* (Chapel Hill, 1986), p. 157.

12. Peter H. Wood, *Black Majority: Negroes in Colonial South Carolina from 1670 through the Stono Rebellion* (New York, 1974), pp. 156–166. Varnod's

census is printed in Frank Klingberg, *An Appraisal of the Negro in Colonial South Carolina* (Washington, D.C., 1941), pp. 58–60. Of course, the situation in North Carolina was remarkably different, with fewer slaves than in South Carolina, Virginia, or Maryland.

13. The Varnod census can be compared with Philip D. Morgan, "A Profile of a Mid-Eighteenth Century South Carolina Parish: The Tax Return of St. James Goose Creek," *South Carolina Historical Magazine*, 81 (1980): 51–65.

14. Philip D. Morgan, "Work and Culture: The Task System and the World of Lowcountry Blacks 1700 to 1880," *William and Mary Quarterly*, 3d ser., 39 (1982): 563–599; Morgan, "Task and Gang Systems: The Organization of Labor on New World Plantations," in *Work and Labor in Early America*, ed. Innes, pp. 189–220. Gang labor had already become a feature of plantation life in the British Caribbean by the 1670s.

15. Louis Thibou [to Gabriel Bontefoy], Sept. 20, 1683, in *Description de la Caroline prés la Floride, ou La Nouvelle Angleterre, en l'Amerique* (Geneva, 1684), pp. 38–47. A manuscript version of the letter is in the Historical Society of South Carolina, Charleston, but it is not clear whether it is Thibou's original or a copy based on the printed pamphlet. On the promotion literature, see Hope Frances Kane, "Colonial Promotion and Promotion Literature of Carolina, 1660–1700" (Ph.D. diss., Brown University, 1930), and Bertrand Van Ruymbeke, "L'emigration huguenote en Caroline du Sud sous le régime des Siegneurs Propriétaires: étude d'une communauté du Refuge dans une province britannique d'Amerique du Nord (1680–1720)" (Ph.D. diss., Université de la Sorbonne Nouvelle, Paris III, 1995), pp. 184–281.

16. For an example of the diversity of enterprises and, especially, the emphasis on animal production, see the account book of the Huguenot Nicholas de Longuemare, who produced gold and silver goods in a Charleston shop and shepherded agriculture, especially animals, on acreage he owned on the Santee River: Samuel G. Stoney, "Nicholas de Longemare, Huguenot Goldsmith and Silk Dealer in Colonial South Carolina," *Transactions of the Huguenot Society of South Carolina*, 55 (1950): 38–69; Russell R. Menard, "Economic and Social Development of the South," in *The Cambridge Economic History of the United States: The Colonial Era*, ed. Stanley L. Engerman and Robert E. Gallman (New York, 1996), pp. 275–276; Menard, "Financing the Lowcountry Export Boom: Capital and Credit in Early South Carolina," *William and Mary Quarterly*, 3d ser., 51 (1994): 659–676.

17. The issue of African contributions to the technology of rice growing is discussed in Wood, *Black Majority*, pp. 59–62, from which the quotations from slave advertisements are taken, and in Menard, "Economic and Social Development of the South," p. 283.

18. Menard, "Economic and Social Development of the South," p. 275; for a contrary argument about rice prices in the 1720s, at least, see Peter A. Coclanis, "Rice Prices in the 1720s and the Evolution of the South Carolina Economy," *Journal of Southern History*, 48 (1982): 531–544.

19. The quotation and the figures are from Menard, "Economic and Social Development of the South," p. 281.

20. Ibid., pp. 281–282, table 6.6, p. 285, and James F. Shepherd and Gary M. Walton, *Shipping, Maritime Trade, and the Economic Development of Colonial North America* (Cambridge, 1972), tables 2–6, pp. 211–227. Philip Morgan, *Slave Counterpoint: Black Culture in the Eighteenth-Century Chesapeake and Lowcountry* (Chapel Hill, 1998), pp. 45–46, stresses the dependence on the rice trade in South Carolina. On the export economy of the South Carolina frontier, see George Johnson, *The Frontier in the Colonial South: South Carolina Backcountry, 1736–1800* (Westport, Conn., 1997), pp. 39–64.

21. Paul G. E. Clemens, *The Atlantic Economy and Colonial Maryland's Eastern Shore: From Tobacco to Grain* (Ithaca, N.Y., 1980), pp. 168–205; David C. Klingaman, *Colonial Virginia's Coastwise and Grain Trade* (New York, 1975); Kulikoff, *Tobacco and Slaves*, pp. 120–121.

22. Menard, "Economic and Social Development of the South," pp. 281–282, table 6.4, p. 267, and James F. Shepherd and Gary M. Walton, *Shipping, Maritime Trade, and the Economic Development of Colonial North America* (Cambridge, 1972), tables 2–6, pp. 211–227; Clemens, *Atlantic Economy*, pp. 176–177. On the early iron industry, see Robert B. Gordon, *American Iron, 1607–1900* (Baltimore, 1996), and Keach Johnson, "The Baltimore Company Seeks English Markets: A Study of the Anglo-American Iron Trade, 1731–1755," *William and Mary Quarterly*, 3d ser., 17 (1959): 37–60.

23. For overviews, see Daniel Vickers, "The Northern Colonies: Economy and Society, 1600–1755," in *Cambridge Economic History of the United States: Colonial Era*, ed. Engerman and Gallman, pp. 209–248, and Menard and McCusker, *Economy of British America*, pp. 91–116, 189–210. James T. Lemon, *The Best Poor Man's Country: A Geographical Study of Early Southeastern Pennsylvania* (Baltimore, 1972) remains the most systematic study of eighteenth-century Pennsylvania. On New England, see Howard S. Russell, *A Long, Deep Furrow: Three Centuries of Farming in New England* (Hanover, N.H., 1976) and Carolyn Merchant, *Ecological Revolutions: Nature, Gender, and Science in New England* (Chapel Hill, 1989).

24. Farley Grubb, "Redemptioner Immigration to Pennsylvania: Evidence on Contract Choice and Profitability," *Journal of Economic History*, 46 (1986): 407–418.

25. Samuel Swayne's hiring is discussed in Paul G. E. Clemens and Lucy Simler, "Rural Labor and the Farm Household in Chester County, Pennsylvania, 1750–1820," in *Work and Labor in Early America*, ed. Innes, pp. 106–143. Duane E. Ball and Gary M. Walton, "Agricultural Productivity Change in Eighteenth-Century Pennsylvania," *Journal of Economic History*, 36 (1976): 102–117, offer a preliminary view of changes in agricultural efficiency.

26. McCusker and Menard, *Economy of British America*, table 9.3, p. 199.

27. Kenneth P. Minkema, "Jonathan Edwards on Slavery and the Slave Trade," *William and Mary Quarterly*, 3d ser., 54 (1997): 823–834; Gloria L. Main,

"Gender, Work, and Wages in Colonial New England," *William and Mary Quarterly*, 3d ser., 51 (1994): 39–66; Vickers, "Working the Fields in a Developing Economy," pp. 49–69; Vickers, *Farmers and Fishermen: Two Centuries of Work in Essex County, Massachusetts, 1630–1830* (Chapel Hill, 1994), pp. 65–66, 173, 221.

28. Douglas R. McManis, *Colonial New England: A Historical Geography* (New York, 1975) pp. 86–102; Gloria L. Main and Jackson T. Main, "New England's Stable Economy," paper presented at the Economy of British North America: The Domestic Sector—A Conference, Huntington Library, San Marino, Calif., 1995; Thomas M. Truxes, *Irish-American Trade, 1660–1783* (New York, 1988), pp. 109–111. On New England ecology, see William Cronon, *Changes in the Land: Indians, Colonists, and the Ecology of New England* (New York, 1983), esp. chaps. 6–7; McCusker and Menard, *Economy of British America*, table 5.2, p. 108.

29. Vickers, *Farmers and Fishermen*, pp. 86–91.

30. Menard and McCusker, *Economy of British America*, pp. 108–109.

31. Vickers, "The Northern Colonies: Economy and Society, 1600–1755," pp. 231–233; Menard and McCusker, *Economy of British America*, pp. 97–100, 310–312.

32. For one effort at experimentation and modernization, see Christopher Grasso, "The Experimental Philosophy of Farming: Jared Eliot and the Cultivation of Connecticut," *William and Mary Quarterly*, 3d ser., 50 (1993): 502–528, and Grasso, *A Speaking Aristocracy: Transforming Public Discourse in Eighteenth-Century Connecticut* (Chapel Hill, 1998), pp. 190–229. See also Carl Raymond Woodward, *Ploughs and Politicks: Charles Read of New Jersey and His Notes on Agriculture, 1715–1741* (New Brunswick, N.J., 1941).

33. Rachel M. Wheeler, "Living upon Hope: Mahicans and Missionaries, 1730–1760" (Ph.D. diss., Yale University, 1998), pp. 19–22, 250; Jean M. O'Brien, *Dispossession by Degrees: Indian Land and Identity in Natick, Massachusetts, 1650–1790* (New York, 1997).

34. Daniel K. Richter, *The Ordeal of the Longhouse: The Peoples of the Iroquois League in the Era of European Colonization* (Chapel Hill, 1992), pp. 262–263, 270–271; James T. Carson, "Native Americans, the Market Revolution, and Culture Change: The Choctaw Cattle Economy, 1690–1830," *Agricultural History*, 71 (1997): 1–18; McCusker and Menard, *The Economy of British America*, pp. 312–313; James H. Merrell, *The Indians' New World: Catawbas and Their Neighbors from European Contact through the Era of Removal* (Chapel Hill, 1989), pp. 82–84, for the story of the Catawbas' 1729 departure from Christanna, see p. 131; George Johnson, *The Frontier in the Colonial South: South Carolina Backcountry, 1736–1800* (Westport, Conn., 1997), p.39. McCusker and Menard, in *The Economy of British America*, pp. 27–28, discuss problems in analyzing American Indian economies in the context of British colonial development.

35. Richard White, *The Middle Ground: Indians, Empires, and Republics in the*

Great Lakes Region, 1650–1815 (New York, 1991), pp. 132–141; quotation from Iroquois leaders in Richter, *The Ordeal of the Longhouse*, p. 272.

36. The "Paxton Boys" incidents of 1763–1764 are discussed in James H. Merrell, *Into the American Woods: Negotiators on the Pennsylvania Frontier* (New York, 1999), pp. 285–301, and the quotations are drawn from pp. 285 and 287.

37. The classic study of early New England merchants is Bernard Bailyn, *The New England Merchants in the Seventeenth Century* (Cambridge, Mass., 1955). There is no general study of merchants in the early Chesapeake nor for the eighteenth century generally, but see Jacob M. Price, *Capital and Credit in British Overseas Trade: The View from the Chesapeake, 1700–1776* (Cambridge, Mass., 1980), and Stuart Bruchey, "The Colonial Merchant: British," in *Encyclopedia of the North American Colonies,* ed. Jacob E. Cooke (New York, 1993), 1: 577–589. For the Keayne affair, see Bernard Bailyn, ed., *The Apologia of Robert Keayne* (New York, 1965), and Darrett B. Rutman, *Winthrop's Boston: Portrait of a Puritan Town, 1630–1649* (Chapel Hill, 1965), pp. 243–244.

38. Quotations are from the tables in James Glen, *A Description of South Carolina* (London, 1761) printed in Chapman J. Milling, ed., *Colonial South Carolina: Two Contemporary Descriptions by Governor James Glen and Doctor George Milligen-Johnston* (Columbia, S.C., 1951), where the introduction explains the tortured history behind the printing of Glen's report, originally written in 1749.

39. Thomas M. Doerflinger, *A Vigorous Spirit of Enterprise: Merchants and Economic Development in Revolutionary Philadelphia* (Chapel Hill, 1986), p. 17. Joyce D. Goodfriend, *Before the Melting Pot: Society and Culture in Colonial New York City, 1664–1730* (Princeton, 1991), table 8-1, pp. 156–157, can be compared with Thomas J. Archdeacon, *New York City, 1664–1710: Conquest and Change* (Ithaca, N.Y., 1976), pp. 58–77. I found it difficult to determine the number of merchants in Boston in 1700 and 1770, but see Carl Bridenbaugh, *Cities in the Wilderness: The First Century of Urban Life in America, 1625–1742* (New York, 1938), p. 38, and Bridenbaugh, *Cities in Revolt: Urban Life in America, 1743–1776* (New York, 1955), p. 77 for general estimates.

40. The description of Mingo Bottom is quoted from Bruchey, "The Colonial Merchant: British," p. 577, and the list of goods imported into South Carolina at mid-century is taken from Glen, *A Description of South Carolina*, pp. 45–47. Amy Smart Martin, "Common People and the Local Store: Consumerism in the Rural Virginia Backcountry," in *Common People and Their Material World: Free Men and Women in the Chesapeake, 1700–1830,* ed. David Harvey and Gregory Brown (Williamsburg, Va., 1995), pp. 39–54. On largely rural merchants in Connecticut, see Jackson Turner Main, *Society and Economy in Colonial Connecticut* (Princeton, 1985), pp. 278–316.

41. J. F. Bosher, "Huguenot Merchants and the Protestant International in the Sev-

enteenth Century," *William and Mary Quarterly*, 3d ser., 52 (1995): 77–103; Stanley F. Chyet, *Lopez of Newport: Colonial American Merchant Prince* (Detroit, 1970); see especially the letters from Isaac DeLyon of Savannah, Georgia, and Joseph Simon, of Lancaster, Pennsylvania, both dated 1760, in Jacob Rader Marcus, ed., *American Jewry: Documents; Eighteenth Century; Primarily Hitherto Unpublished Manuscripts*, Publications of the American Jewish Archives, no. 3 (Cincinnati, 1959), pp. 348–350.

42. Walter B. Edgar, ed., *The Letterbook of Robert Pringle*, 2 vols. (Columbia, S.C., 1972), pp. xv–xviii.

43. Ibid., pp. 81, 83, 96, 118, 129, 20, 204, 211, 26, 300, 263, 503.

44. Ibid. The letters for 1743 are found between pp. 472 and 628.

45. Doerflinger, *Vigorous Spirit of Enterprise*, pp. 77–122.

46. W. Robert Higgins, "Charleston Merchants and Factors Dealing in the External Negro Trade, 1735–1775," *South Carolina Historical Magazine*, 65 (1964): 205–217; Darold D. Wax, "Negro Import Duties in Colonial Pennsylvania," *Pennsylvania Magazine of History and Biography*, 97 (1973): 22–44; Wax, "Quaker Merchants and the Slave Trade in Colonial Pennsylvania," *Pennsylvania Magazine of History and Biography*, 86 (1962): 143–158; Wax, "Robert Ellis, Philadelphia Merchant and Slave Trader," *Pennsylvania Magazine of History and Biography*, 88 (1964): 52–69; Jay Coughtry, *The Notorious Triangle: Rhode Island and the African Slave Trade, 1700–1807* (Philadelphia: Temple University Press, 1981); Sarah Deutsch, "The Elusive Guineamen: Newport Slavers, 1735–1774," *New England Quarterly*, 55 (1982): 229–253.

47. Gary B. Nash, *The Urban Crucible: Social Change, Political Consciousness, and the Origins of the American Revolution* (Cambridge, Mass., 1979), p. 118.

48. Doerflinger, *Vigorous Spirit of Enterprise*, pp. 15–21; Patricia U. Bonomi, *A Factious People: Politics and Society in Colonial New York* (New York, 1971), pp. 60–68; M. Eugene Sirmans, *Colonial South Carolina: A Political History, 1663–1763* (Chapel Hill, 1966), pp. 227–228; Bridenbaugh, *Cities in Revolt*, pp. 70–72; Bernard Bailyn, *The Ordeal of Thomas Hutchinson* (Cambridge, Mass., 1974), pp. 10–12.

49. Bonomi, *Factious People*, pp. 60–69; Nash, *Urban Crucible*, pp. 340–341, 362, 363, 372, 378.

50. Doerflinger, *Vigorous Spirit of Enterprise*, is particularly suggestive on these points, though the issue awaits the more systematic study of the merchant trades in the other important cities of Boston, New York, and Charleston. The absence of these studies precluded systematic discussions of merchants in McCusker and Menard, *The Economy of British America*, and in Engerman and Gallman, *Cambridge Economic History of the United States: The Colonial Era*.

51. Ian M. G. Quimby, ed., *The Craftsman in Early America* (New York, 1984);

Carl Bridenbaugh, *The Colonial Craftsman* (New York, 1950); Nash, *Urban Crucible*, pp. 16–17.

52. Franklin describes his famous experience with Keimer in *The Autobiography of Benjamin Franklin,* ed. Leonard Labaree, Ralph L. Ketcham, Helen C. Boatfield, and Helene H. Fineman (New Haven, 1964), pp. 72–127.

53. Edward S. Cooke, Jr., *Making Furniture in Preindustrial America: The Social Economy of Newtown and Woodbury, Connecticut* (Baltimore, 1996), pp. 49–68.

54. Jean B. Russo, "Self-Sufficiency and Local Exchange: Free Craftsmen in the Rural Chesapeake Economy," in *Colonial Chesapeake Society,* ed. Lois Green Carr, Philip D. Morgan, and Jean B. Russo (Chapel Hill, 1989), table 1, p. 395.

55. Laurel Thatcher Ulrich, "Wheels, Looms, and the Gender Division of Labor in Eighteenth-Century New England," *William and Mary Quarterly,* 3d ser., 55 (1998): 3–38; Adrienne D. Hood, "The Gender Division of Labor in the Production of Textiles in Eighteenth-Century, Rural Pennsylvania (Rethinking the New England Model)," *Journal of Social History,* 27 (1994): 537–561. The importance of this issue is heightened by the large proportion of women among the region's immigrant servants (25%–45%), which is discussed in Farley Grubb, "Servant Auction Records and Immigration into the Delaware Valley, 1745–1831: The Proportion of Females among Immigrant Servants," *Proceedings of the American Philosophical Society,* 133 (1989): 154–169.

56. On the reward of work and its denial to late-twentieth-century African Americans, see William J. Wilson, *When Work Disappears: The World of the New Urban Poor* (New York, 1996). Under slavery, captured Africans had the work but were denied its reward.

57. John A. Schutz, *Thomas Pownall, British Defender of American Liberty: A Study of Anglo-American Relations in the Eighteenth Century* (Glendale, Calif., 1951), p. 28. For discussions of colonial housing and the use of log cabins, see Richard L. Bushman, *The Refinement of America: Persons, Houses, Cities* (New York, 1992), pp. 110–117, 425–431; C. A. Weslager, *The Log Cabin in America, from Pioneer Days to the Present* (New Brunswick, N.J., 1969), pp. 99–258; and Terry G. Jordan, *American Log Buildings: An Old World Heritage* (Chapel Hill, 1985).

58. On books in colonial estates, see Jon Butler, "Thomas Teackle's 333 Books: A Great Library on Virginia's Eastern Shore," *William and Mary Quarterly,* 3d ser., 49 (1992): 449–491. Crèvecoeur, *Letters from an American Farmer,* p. 67.

59. The debate is extensive and is well summarized in both David W. Galenson, "Settlement and Growth of the Colonies," in *Cambridge Economic History of the United States,* pp. 205–207, and McCusker and Menard, *Economy of British America,* chap. 12.

60. James A. Henretta, "Economic Development and Social Structure in Colonial Boston," *William and Mary Quarterly,* 3d ser., 32 (1965): 75–92; Allan Kulikoff, "The Progress of Inequality in Revolutionary Boston," *William and Mary*

Quarterly, 3d ser., 38 (1971): 375–412; Jones, *Wealth of a Nation to Be,* chap. 6; Jeffrey G. Williamson and Peter H. Lindert, "Long-Term Trends in American Wealth Inequality," in *Modeling the Distribution and Intergenerational Transmission of Wealth,* ed. James D. Smith (Chicago, 1980), pp. 9–93.

61. Galenson, "Settlement and Growth of the Colonies," table 4.9, p. 195.

62. Jones, *Wealth of a Nation to Be,* pp. 170–189; Peter Manigault's estate inventory is found in Alice Hanson Jones, *American Colonial Wealth: Documents and Methods* (New York, 1978), 3: 1543–1559.

63. Jones, *Wealth of a Nation to Be,* pp. 170–189.

64. Ibid., pp. 214–216, table 7.32, pp. 248–249; the figures for average estates for each region are on pp. 181–183. Elaine Forman Crane, *Ebb Tide in New England: Women, Seaports, and Social Change, 1630–1800* (Boston, 1998), pp. 109–112. There may well be complicated explanations for other aspects of these patterns; for example, northern families may have kept assets, especially land, away from widowed women. For women's problems in retaining wealth, and for evidence that jealousy of wealthy women may have played into witch accusations in seventeenth-century New England, see Carol F. Karlsen, *The Devil in the Shape of a Woman: Witchcraft in Colonial New England* (New York, 1987).

65. Abigail Franks to Naphtali Franks, June 7, 1743, in *The Lee Max Friedman Collection of American Jewish Colonial Correspondence: Letters of the Franks Family (1733–1748),* ed. Leo Hershkowitz and Isidor S. Meyer (Waltham, Mass., 1968), pp. 116–122.

66. Paul Slack, *Poverty and Policy in Tudor and Stuart England* (London, 1988); George R. Boyer, *An Economic History of the English Poor Law, 1750–1850* (Cambridge, 1990). These supersede the widely cited M. Dorothy George, *London Life in the Eighteenth Century* (New York, 1925). Most scholarship on British poverty deals with the nineteenth century.

67. Nash, *Urban Crucible,* pp. 22, 65; on the poor in 1774, see Jones, *Wealth of a Nation to Be,* chap. 6.

68. Nash, *Urban Crucible,* pp. 124–127.

69. Ibid., pp. 253–254.

70. Ibid., pp. 254–255; William H. Williams, "The 'Industrious Poor' and the Founding of the Pennsylvania Hospital," *Pennsylvania Magazine of History and Biography,* 97 (1973): 431–443.

71. Morgan, *Slave Counterpoint,* pp. 358–376; Orlando Patterson quoted on p. 358.

72. Ibid., pp. 373–376.

73. T. H. Breen and Stephen Innes, *"Myne Owne Ground": Race and Freedom on Virginia's Eastern Shore, 1640–1676* (New York, 1980), pp. 72–73.

74. *The Old Plantation,* artist unknown, c. 1800, Abby Aldrich Rockefeller Folk Art Center, Williamsburg; Main, *Tobacco Colony,* pp. 134–135; Morgan, *Slave Counterpoint,* pp. 358–376.

3. POLITICS

1. Hector St. John de Crèvecoeur, *Letters from an American Farmer and Sketches of Eighteenth-Century America,* ed. Albert E. Stone (New York, 1981), p. 69. For a brief general account of colonial political development, see Michael Schudson, *The Good Citizen: A History of American Civic Life* (New York, 1998), pp. 11–47.

2. Crèvecoeur, *Letters from an American Farmer and Sketches of Eighteenth-Century America,* p. 227.

3. By "local politics," I mean the politics of the immediate governing unit, usually the town, township, or county. On New England, see Edward M. Cook, Jr., *The Fathers of the Towns: Leadership and Community Structure in Eighteenth-Century New England* (Baltimore, 1976); Robert E. Brown, *Middle Class Democracy and the Revolution in Massachusetts, 1691–1780* (Ithaca, N.Y., 1955); Bruce C. Daniels, *The Connecticut Town: Growth and Development, 1635–1790* (Middletown, Conn., 1979); Charles S. Grant, *Democracy in the Connecticut Frontier Town of Kent* (New York, 1961); Kenneth A. Lockridge, *A New England Town: The First Hundred Years* (New York, 1970); Kenneth A. Lockridge and Alan Kreider, "The Evolution of Massachusetts Town Government, 1640 to 1740," *William and Mary Quarterly,* 3d ser., 33 (1966): 549–574; Michael Zuckerman, *Peaceable Kingdoms: New England Towns in the Eighteenth Century* (New York, 1970). Obviously, the New England town has received much more substantial study than has local government in other mainland colonies.

4. Patricia U. Bonomi, *A Factious People: Politics and Society in Colonial New York* (New York, 1971), pp. 31–34, 188–190; Jessica Kross, *The Evolution of an American Town: Newtown, New York, 1642–1775* (Philadelphia, 1983); Bruce M. Wilkenfeld, "The New York City Common Council, 1689–1800," *New York History,* 52 (1971): 249–273; Sung Bok Kim, *Landlord and Tenant in Colonial New York: Manorial Society, 1664–1775* (Chapel Hill, 1978), pp. 89–91.

5. Wayne L. Bockelman, "Local Government in Colonial Pennsylvania," in *Town and County: Essays on the Structure of Local Government in the American Colonies,* ed. Bruce C. Daniels (Middletown, Conn., 1978), pp. 216–237; A. Roger Ekirch, *"Poor Carolina": Politics and Society in Colonial North Carolina, 1729–1776* (Chapel Hill, 1981), p. 52. M. Eugene Sirmans, *Colonial South Carolina: A Political History, 1663–1763* (Chapel Hill, 1966), pp. 142, 250–252.

6. Cook, *The Fathers of the Towns,* pp. 95–118.

7. Ibid., pp. 143–163.

8. Sudbury freemen quoted in Sumner Chilton Powell, *Puritan Village: The Formation of a New England Town* (Middletown, Conn., 1963), p. 125; Charles S. Grant, *Democracy in the Connecticut Frontier Town of Kent* (New York, 1961), p. 132.

9. Darrett B. Rutman and Anita H. Rutman, *A Place in Time: Middlesex County, Virginia, 1650–1750* (New York, 1984), pp. 147, 149.

10. Lorena S. Walsh, "The Development of Local Power Structures: Maryland's Lower Western Shore in the Early Colonial Period," in *Power and Status: Office-holding in Colonial America*, ed. Bruce C. Daniels (Middletown, Conn., 1986), pp. 53–74; quotation about Roman Catholic freeholders is from note 52, p. 287.

11. Ibid.; John M. Murrin, "The Legal Transformation: The Bench and Bar of Eighteenth-Century Massachusetts," in *Colonial America: Essays in Politics and Social Development*, ed. Stanley N. Katz (Boston, 1971), pp. 415–449; A. G. Roeber, *Faithful Magistrates and Republican Lawyers: Creators of Virginia Legal Culture, 1680–1810* (Chapel Hill, 1981), pp. 32–111.

12. Peter Charles Hoffer, *Law and People in Colonial America* (Baltimore, 1992), pp. 50–51. Criminal prosecutions also changed from pursuing moral offenses to regulating social crimes like assault and battery. See Peter C. Hoffer and William B. Scott, eds., *Criminal Court Proceedings in Colonial Virginia: Richmond County, 1710/11–1754* (Athens, Ga., 1984), table 5, p. lvi.

13. Hoffer, *Law and People in Colonial America*, p. 65; C. Bradley Thompson, "Young John Adams and the New Philosophic Rationalism," *William and Mary Quarterly*, 3d ser., 55 (1998): 259–280. See the extensive discussion of the rise of the law and of lawyers in Christopher Grasso, *A Speaking Aristocracy: Transforming Public Discourse in Eighteenth-Century Connecticut* (Chapel Hill, 1998).

14. John M. Murrin, "The Legal Transformation: The Bench and Bar of Eighteenth-Century Massachusetts," in *Colonial America*, ed. Katz, pp. 415–449; A. G. Roeber, *Faithful Magistrates and Republican Lawyers: Creators of Virginia Legal Culture, 1680–1810* (Chapel Hill, 1981), p. 123; quotation from *Virginia Almanac* is from Roeber, *Faithful Magistrates and Republican Lawyers*, p. 126.

15. Gary B. Nash, *The Urban Crucible: Social Change, Political Consciousness, and the Origins of the American Revolution* (Cambridge, Mass., 1979), pp. 129–136.

16. Ibid., pp. 143, 148–151. Myrmidons were Thessalian warriors who followed Achilles in his expedition to Troy and obeyed orders without question.

17. Cornelia Hughes Dayton, *Women before the Bar: Gender, Law, and Society in Connecticut, 1639–1789* (Chapel Hill, 1995), esp. chap. 4.

18. Marilyn Salmon, *Women and the Law of Property in Early America* (Chapel Hill, 1986).

19. Chilton Williamson, *American Suffrage, from Property to Democracy, 1760–1860* (Princeton, 1960); Robert J. Dinkin, *Voting in Provincial America: A Study of Elections in the Thirteen Colonies, 1689–1776* (Westport, Conn., 1977), pp. 37–40. Compare the colonial patterns with evidence in H. T. Dickinson, *The Politics of the People in Eighteenth-Century Britain* (New York,

1995), pp. 13–55. On political mobilization in eighteenth-century Britain, see Kathleen Wilson, *The Sense of the People: Politics, Culture, and Imperialism in England, 1715–1785* (New York, 1995). For a general account, see Frank O'Gorman, *The Long Eighteenth Century: British Political and Social History, 1688–1832* (London, 1997).

20. Dinkin, *Voting in Provincial America,* pp. 144–180. In South Carolina, the parish served as the election district for assembly elections. These percentages probably remained relatively constant throughout the prerevolutionary period except in the colonial cities, where the rise of poverty and frequent rental of housing probably constricted the urban electorate.

21. Douglas Hay and Nicholas Rogers, *Eighteenth-Century English Society: Shuttles and Swords* (New York, 1997), p. 58; John Gilman Kolp, *Gentlemen and Freeholders: Electoral Politics and Political Commentary in Colonial Virginia* (Baltimore, 1998), pp. 59–80.

22. Dinkin, *Voting in Provincial America,* pp. 162–163, 176. Cf. Alan Tully, *Forming American Politics: Ideals, Interests, and Institutions in Colonial New York and Pennsylvania* (Baltimore, 1994), p. 329.

23. Dinkin, *Voting in Provincial America,* pp. 93–119, surveys the range of election practices. *New York Gazette,* Feb. 5, 1761, quoted in Williamson, *American Suffrage,* p. 46.

24. Dinkin, *Voting in Provincial America,* p. 102. For a classic account of "treating" in Virginia, see Charles Sydnor, *Gentlemen Freeholders: Political Practices in Washington's Virginia* (Chapel Hill, 1952), quotation from p. 55; Tully, *Forming American Politics,* pp. 201, 328, 343.

25. John A. Phillips, *Electoral Behavior in Unreformed England: Plumpers, Splitters, and Straights* (Princeton, 1982), pp. 77–78; Hay and Rogers, *Eighteenth-Century English Society,* p. 57; Ian Gilmour, *Riot, Risings, and Revolution: Governance and Violence in Eighteenth-Century England* (London, 1992), pp. 207–223.

26. Nash, *Urban Crucible,* pp. 129–148.

27. Phillips, *Electoral Behavior in Unreformed England,* pp. 159–168, 286–305. For instances of religion in colonial politics, many of which occur in the late stages of the colonial era, see Bonomi, *A Factious People,* pp. 237–238, 248–254, 264–265; Rhys Isaac, "Evangelical Revolt: The Nature of the Baptists' Challenge to the Traditional Order in Virginia, 1765 to 1775," *William and Mary Quarterly,* 3d ser., 31 (1974): 345–368; Isaac, "Religion and Authority: Problems of the Anglican Establishment in Virginia in the Era of the Great Awakening and the Parsons' Cause," *William and Mary Quarterly,* 3d ser., 30 (1973): 3–36; Tully, *Forming American Politics,* pp. 136–142, 195–196, 205–209, 254; Deborah M. Gough, "Pluralism, Politics, and Power Struggles: The Church of England in Colonial Philadelphia, 1695–1789" (Ph.D. diss., University of Pennsylvania, 1978).

28. There is a wide literature on Whigs in eighteenth-century British politics. As a start, see Linda Colley, *Britons: Forging the Nation, 1707–1837* (New Haven,

1992), pp. 110, 202, 344–349; Phillips, *Electoral Behavior in Unreformed England;* Lewis Namier, *The Structure of Politics at the Accession of George III,* 2d ed. (London, 1957); Frank O'Gorman, *Voters, Patrons, and Parties: The Unreformed Electoral System of Hanoverian England, 1734–1832* (New York, 1989); Linda Colley, *In Defiance of Oligarchy: The Tory Party, 1714–1760* (Cambridge, 1982).

29. Gary B. Nash, *Quakers and Politics, Pennsylvania, 1681–1726* (Princeton, 1968); Sally Schwartz, *A Mixed Multitude: The Struggle for Toleration in Colonial Pennsylvania* (New York, 1987); Roy Norman Lokken, *David Lloyd, Colonial Lawmaker* (Seattle, 1959); Alan Tully, *Forming American Politics: Ideals, Interests, and Institutions in Colonial New York and Pennsylvania* (Baltimore, 1994), pp. 68–85; Benjamin H. Newcomb, *Political Partisanship in the American Middle Colonies, 1700–1776* (Baton Rouge, 1995).

30. Quoted in Tully, *Forming American Politics,* p. 145.

31. Ibid., pp. 145–150. William Allen claimed that in Philadelphia, Quakers won support from "about 400 Germans who hardly ever came to elections formerly, perhaps never 40 of them having voted" previously. Quoted in ibid., p. 149.

32. Ibid., pp. 150–159. On the origins of the Quaker "withdrawal" from politics, see Jack D. Marietta, *The Reformation of American Quakerism, 1748–1783* (Philadelphia, 1984).

33. Tully, *Forming American Politics,* pp. 51–60, and Bonomi, *A Factious People,* pp. 66, 204. For doubts about the accusation against Cornbury and a revisionist view of his career, see Patricia U. Bonomi, *The Lord Cornbury Scandal: The Politics of Reputation in British America* (Chapel Hill, 1998), pp. 1–26; for one of the specific charges made by the New York Huguenot refugee and Anglican catechist Elias Neau, see pp. 71, 75, 146, 148, 158–164, 179. An eighteenth-century view of New York politics from the 1690s to the 1740s is found in William Smith, Jr., *The History of the Province of New York,* ed. Michael Kammen, 2 vols. (Cambridge, Mass., 1972).

34. Tully, *Forming American Politics,* p. 53; Beverly McAnear, *The Income of the Colonial Governors of British North America* (New York, 1967), pp. 21–25; Bellomont quoted in Dixon Ryan Fox, *Caleb Heathcote, Gentleman Colonist: The Story of a Career in the Province of New York, 1692–1721* (New York, 1926), p. 116. For a positive view of tenant farming, see Sung Bok Kim, *Landlord and Tenant in Colonial New York: Manorial Society, 1664–1775* (Chapel Hill, 1978). Many of Governor Benjamin Fletcher's land grants were subsequently voided.

35. Michael Kammen, *Colonial New York: A History* (Millwood, N.Y., 1975), p. 210; Clinton quoted in Tully, *Forming American Politics,* p. 245.

36. A now classic introduction to the general topic of Whig ideology is found in Bernard Bailyn, *The Ideological Origins of the American Revolution* (Cambridge, Mass., 1967). Tully explains the differences between New York's "popular Whigs" and "provincial Whigs" in *Forming American Politics,* pp. 213–256.

37. Robert M. Weir, "'The Harmony We Were Famous For': An Interpretation of Pre-Revolutionary South Carolina Politics," *William and Mary Quarterly*, 3d ser., 26 (1969): 473–501; Sirmans, *Colonial South Carolina*; Rebecca Starr, *A School for Politics: Commercial Lobbying and Political Culture in Early South Carolina* (Baltimore, 1998), pp. 11–43.

38. Nash, *Urban Crucible*, pp. 271–282.

39. Robert M. Zemsky, "Power, Influence, and Status: Leadership Patterns in the Massachusetts Assembly, 1740–1755," *William and Mary Quarterly*, 3d ser., 36 (1969): 502–520; Robert Zemsky, *Merchants, Farmers, and River Gods: An Essay on Eighteenth-Century American Politics* (Boston, 1971).

40. Michael Kammen, *Deputyes & Libertyes: The Origins of Representative Government in Colonial America* (New York, 1969), p. 11.

41. Jack P. Greene, *The Quest for Power: The Lower Houses of Assembly in the Southern Royal Colonies, 1689–1776* (Chapel Hill, 1963), pp. 206–207.

42. Tully, *Forming American Politics*, pp. 57, 70–78, 147, 149, 155, 291–295.

43. George Edward Frakes, *Laboratory for Liberty: The South Carolina Legislative Committee System, 1719–1776* (Lexington, Ky., 1970), pp. 4–5, 21–39, 68–70, 89–91, 144–145, 148; Greene, *Quest for Power*, pp. 24–47; Kammen, *Colonial New York*, pp. 184–185. On the development of committees in Virginia, see Raymond C. Bailey, *Popular Influence upon Public Policy: Petitioning in Eighteenth-Century Virginia* (Westport, Conn., 1979), pp. 18, 28–29.

44. Greene, *Quest for Power*, pp. 24–47; Zemsky, "Power, Influence, and Status," pp. 504–508; Sydnor, *Gentlemen Freeholders*, pp. 97–101; Thomas L. Purvis, "'High-Born, Long-Recorded Families': Social Origins of New Jersey Assemblymen, 1703 to 1776," *William and Mary Quarterly*, 3d ser., 37 (1980): 592–615.

45. Greene, *Quest for Power*, pp. 143–148; David J. Mays, *Edmund Pendleton, 1721–1803*, 2 vols. (Cambridge, Mass., 1952), 1: 174–208, 358–385.

46. Jackson Turner Main, *The Upper House in Revolutionary America, 1763–1788* (Madison, 1967), pp. 3–4.

47. The story of the loss of power by councils in the southern colonies is woven throughout Greene, *Quest for Power*. For their reincarnation after the Revolution, see Main, *The Upper House in Revolutionary America*, pp. 230–238.

48. Charles E. Clark, *The Public Print: The Newspaper in Anglo-American Culture, 1665–1740* (New York, 1994); A. G. Roeber, *Palatines, Liberty, and Property: German Lutherans in British North America* (Baltimore, 1993), p. 175; Jürgen Habermas, *The Structural Transformation of the Public Sphere*, trans. Thomas Burger (Cambridge, Mass., 1989). On taverns, see David W. Conroy, *In Public Houses: Drink and the Revolution of Authority in Colonial Massachusetts* (Chapel Hill, 1995), pp. 177–178, 187–188, 233–235, 241–242, 275–277, 281–287, a subject further discussed in Chapter 4.

49. Kenneth Lockridge, *Literacy in Colonial New England: An Enquiry into the Social Context of Literacy in the Early Modern West* (New York, 1974).

50. Kammen, *Colonial New York*, pp. 184-185.

51. Greene, *Quest for Power*, pp. 348-352; Glenn C. Smith, "The Parson's Cause, 1755-1765," *Tyler's Quarterly Historical and Genealogical Magazine*, 21 (1940): 140-171, 291-306. Thad W. Tate, "The Coming of the Revolution in Virginia: Britain's Challenge to Virginia's Ruling Class, 1763-1776," *William and Mary Quarterly*, 3d ser., 19 (1962): 323-343; Patrick Henry quoted in Rhys Isaac, "Religion and Authority: Problems of the Anglican Establishment in Virginia in the Era of the Great Awakening and the Parsons' Cause," *William and Mary Quarterly*, 3d ser., 30 (1973): 20; quotation on Patrick Henry's speaking style in Rhys Isaac, *The Transformation of Virginia, 1740-1790* (Chapel Hill, 1982), p. 268. The Virginia governor won the right to levy the fee on land grants, although the Burgesses won an admission from London that such fees were limited by the original charter, and the Virginia clergy succeeded in getting the Privy Council in England to veto the Two-Penny Act.

52. Lawrence H. Leder, ed., "Robert Hunter's Androboros," *New York Public Library Bulletin*, 68 (1964): 153-190; Peter Davis, "The Writing of 'Androboros': A Historical Study and Annotation of America's Earliest Extant Play" (Ph.D. diss., University of Southern California, 1981); "Dinwiddianæ Poems," quoted in Richard Beale Davis, "The Colonial Virginia Satirist: Mid-Eighteenth-Century Commentaries on Politics, Religion, and Society," *Transactions of the American Philosophical Society*, n.s., 57, pt. 1 (1967), p. 18. For additional work on colonial satire, see Elaine G. Breslaw, "Wit, Whimsy, and Politics: The Uses of Satire by the Tuesday Club of Annapolis, 1744 to 1756," *William and Mary Quarterly*, 3d ser., 32 (1975): 295-306; Bruce I. Granger, *Political Satire in the American Revolution, 1763-1783* (Ithaca, N.Y., 1960); Carl R. Kropf, "Libel and Satire in the Eighteenth Century," *Eighteenth-Century Studies*, 8 (1974): 153-168; E. T. Shields, "A Modern Poem by the Mecklenburg Censor: Politics and Satire in Revolutionary North Carolina," *Early American Literature* (1994): 205-233.

53. Milton M. Klein, ed., *The Independent Reflector, or Weekly Essays on Sundry Important Subjects More Particularly Adapted to the Province of New-York* (Cambridge, Mass., 1963), pp. 1-50. For example, see the essay on the sale of public offices, published in January 1753 and printed in ibid., pp. 111-117.

54. Paul Finkelman, "The Zenger Case: Prototype of a Political Trial," in *American Political Trials*, ed. Michal R. Belknap (Westport, Conn., 1981), pp. 21-42; Leonard W. Levy, *Emergence of a Free Press* (New York, 1985), pp. 37-45; Charles E. Clark, "The Newspapers of Provincial America," *American Antiquarian Society Proceedings*, 100 (1990): 367-389. The offending issues of Zenger's newspaper are conveniently reproduced in Stephen Botein, ed., *'Mr. Zenger's Malice and Falshood': Six Issues of the New-York Weekly Journal, 1733-34* (Worcester, 1985).

55. James Alexander, *A Brief Narrative of the Case and Trial of John Peter Zenger, Printer of the New York Weekly Journal*, ed. Stanley N. Katz (Cambridge,

Mass., 1963), quotation from Andrew Hamilton on Moses, p. 95; quotation from John Peter Zenger on p. 101.

56. Klein, ed., *The Independent Reflector,* pp. 341–342.

57. See examples from the *New-England Courant, South Carolina Gazette,* and *Virginia Gazette* in *Colonial and Federalist American Writing,* ed. George F. Horner and Robert A. Bain (New York, 1966), pp. 284–300.

58. Quotation from Patricia U. Bonomi, *Under the Cope of Heaven: Religion, Society, and Politics in Colonial America* (New York, 1986), p. 194.

59. Klein, ed., *The Independent Reflector,* pp. 23–28; Michael Warner, *Letters of the Republic: Publication and the Public Sphere in Eighteenth-Century America* (Cambridge, Mass., 1990), pp. 34–72; Bailyn, *The Ideological Origins of the American Revolution,* pp. 22–54; Henry F. May, *The Enlightenment in America* (New York, 1976), pp. 26–41.

60. For a recent overview, see Bruce Lenman, "Colonial Wars and Imperial Instability, 1688–1793," in *The Oxford History of the British Empire: The Eighteenth Century,* ed. P. J. Marshall, 5 vols. (New York, 1998), 2: 151–168.

61. Nicholas Canny, "The Origins of Empire: An Introduction," in *The Oxford History of the British Empire: The Eighteenth Century,* ed. Marshall, 2: 1–33; Jack P. Greene, *Peripheries and Center: Constitutional Development in the Extended Polities of the British Empire and the United States, 1607–1788* (Athens, Ga., 1986), pp. 7–18; Charles McLean Andrews, *The Colonial Period of American History,* 4 vols. (New Haven, 1934–1938), vol. 4, pp. 272–317, discusses the Board of Trade; an especially succinct view of imperial development is found in Greene, ed., *Great Britain and the American Colonies, 1606–1763* (New York, 1970), pp. xi–xlvii.

62. Michael G. Hall, *Edward Randolph and the American Colonies, 1676–1703* (Chapel Hill, 1960), pp. 154–178.

63. The wars are summarized in Howard H. Peckham, *The Colonial Wars, 1689–1762* (Chicago, 1964), and in Douglas Edward Leach, *The Northern Colonial Frontier, 1607–1763* (New York, 1966).

64. On the effects of the wars in the cities, see Nash, *Urban Crucible,* pp. 54–75, 161–197, 233–263.

65. Kenneth M. Morrison, "Native Americans and the American Revolution: Historic Stories and Shifting Frontier Contact," in *Indians in American History: An Introduction,* ed. Frederick E. Hoxie (Arlington Heights, Ill., 1988), pp. 95–116.

66. John Demos, *The Unredeemed Captive: A Family Story from Early America* (New York, 1994); Richard I. Melvoin, *New England Outpost: War and Society in Colonial Deerfield* (New York, 1989); Sally Schwartz, *A Mixed Multitude: The Struggle for Toleration in Colonial Pennsylvania* (New York, 1987), pp. 225–232; James H. Merrell, *Into the American Woods: Negotiators on the Pennsylvania Frontier* (New York, 1999), pp. 286–287.

67. Bernard Bailyn, *The Ordeal of Thomas Hutchinson* (Cambridge, Mass., 1974).

68. William Smith, Jr., *The History of the Province of New York,* ed. Michael Kammen (Cambridge, Mass., 1972), 1: 128. Milton M. Klein, "Corruption in Colonial America," *South Atlantic Quarterly,* 78 (1979): 57–72.

69. The careers of the New York governors are discussed extensively throughout Kammen, *Colonial New York,* and the governors' terms are digested in Smith, *History of the Province of New York,* 2: 277–282.

70. Bernard Bailyn, *The Origins of American Politics* (New York, 1968), pp. 66–71; Leonard Woods Labaree, *Royal Government in America: A Study of the British Colonial System before 1783* (New Haven, 1930), p. 279.

71. Bailyn, *Origins of American Politics,* pp. 69–85, where Bailyn stresses the loss of the governors' power. On the patronage system in one colony, see Richard Bushman's superb study, *King and People in Provincial Massachusetts* (Chapel Hill, 1985).

72. Anthony Stokes quoted in Bailyn, *Origins of American Politics,* pp. 72–73; Greene, *Quest for Power,* pp. 243–248, 344–354; Sirmans, *Colonial South Carolina,* p. 107; Governor James Glen to Board of Trade, Oct. 10, 1748, in Greene, ed., *Great Britain and the American Colonies, 1606–1763,* p. 262.

73. Bailyn, *Origins of American Politics,* 71–72; Greene, *Quest for Power,* pp. 13–14; Labaree, *Royal Government in America,* pp. 420–448.

74. The suicide of Sir Danvers Osborne is discussed in Smith, *The History of the Province of New York,* 2: 133–134. In the *History,* Smith is referring to the behavior of his father, William Smith, Sr.

75. Joseph J. Malone, *Pine Trees and Politics: The Naval Stores and Forest Policy in Colonial New England, 1691–1775* (Seattle, 1964); Greene, *Peripheries and Center,* pp. 46–47.

76. Hall, *Edward Randolph and the American Colonies, 1676–1703,* 183–186; Malone, *Pine Trees and Politics,* pp. 64, 68, 103, 105, 106–107.

77. Michael C. Batinski, *Jonathan Belcher, Colonial Governor* (Lexington, Ky., 1996), pp. 92–93, 129–130, 136–137; Nash, *Urban Crucible,* p. 131; Bushman, *King and People in Provincial Massachusetts,* pp. 72–82.

78. T. H. Breen, *The Character of the Good Ruler: A Study of Puritan Political Ideas in New England, 1630–1730* (New Haven, 1970), p. 225; Carl Ubbelohde, *The Vice-Admiralty Courts and the American Revolution* (Chapel Hill, 1960), pp. 16–21.

79. Michael G. Kammen, *A Rope of Sand: The Colonial Agents, British Politics, and the American Revolution* (Ithaca, N.Y., 1968); Alison Gilbert Olson, *Making the Empire Work: London and American Interest Groups, 1690–1790* (Cambridge, Mass., 1992); Olson, "The Virginia Merchants of London: A Study in Eighteenth-Century Interest-Group Politics," *William and Mary Quarterly,* 3d ser., 40 (1983): 363–388; Olson and Richard Maxwell Brown, *Anglo-American Political Relations, 1675–1775* (New Brunswick, N.J., 1970).

80. Hall, *Edward Randolph and the American Colonies, 1676–1703;* Greene, ed., *Great Britain and the American Colonies, 1606–1763,* pp. 135–139, 272–291.

81. Ronald W. Clark, *Benjamin Franklin: A Biography* (New York, 1983),

pp. 102–107; Carl Ubbelohde, *The American Colonies and the British Empire, 1607–1763* (New York, 1968), pp. 77, 103; Greene, *Peripheries and Center*, pp. 154, 157–158, 168.

82. The Pownall quotation is in John A. Schutz, *Thomas Pownall, British Defender of American Liberty: A Study of Anglo-American Relations in the Eighteenth Century* (Glendale, Calif., 1951), p. 185.

83. Ibid., pp. 181–194.

84. Kammen, *Colonial New York*, p. 326.

85. Fred Anderson, *A People's Army: Massachusetts Soldiers and Society in the Seven Years' War* (Chapel Hill, 1984), pp. 111–141. The quotation from Rev. John Cleaveland is in Christopher M. Jedrey, *The World of John Cleaveland: Family and Community in Eighteenth-Century New England* (New York, 1979), p. 127. See also Harold E. Selesky, *War and Society in Colonial Connecticut* (New Haven, 1990), pp. 216–227. Unfortunately, scholarship on the soldiers' experience of the Seven Years' War in the middle and southern colonies is lacking.

4. THINGS MATERIAL

1. The literature on Edwards is enormous. The definitive Yale University Press edition of Edwards's writings, *The Works of Jonathan Edwards* (New Haven, 1957—) has now reached seventeen volumes. Regrettably, there is no adequate biography. Ola Elizabeth Winslow, *Jonathan Edwards, 1703–1758: A Biography* (New York, 1940) is charming but thoroughly superseded by modern scholarship, and Perry Miller, *Jonathan Edwards* (New York, 1949) is an almost wholly intellectual biography that adopts a highly idiosyncratic view of Edwards's thought. More satisfactory but now dated is Alfred Owen Aldridge, *Jonathan Edwards* (New York, 1964). Norman Fiering, *Jonathan Edwards's Moral Thought and Its British Context* (Chapel Hill, 1981) is a model account of both Edwards and the eighteenth-century transatlantic intellectual world. Two books sample more recent work on Edwards: Barbara B. Oberg and Harry S. Stout, eds., *Benjamin Franklin, Jonathan Edwards, and the Representation of American Culture* (New York, 1993), and Stephen Stein, ed., *Jonathan Edwards's Writings: Text, Context, Interpretation* (Bloomington, 1996). For a bibliographical guide to this literature, see M. X. Lesser, *Jonathan Edwards: An Annotated Bibliography, 1979–1993* (Westport, Conn., 1994).

2. Jonathan Edwards to the Trustees of the College of New Jersey, October 19, 1757, in John E. Smith, Harry S. Stout, and Kenneth P. Minkema, *A Jonathan Edwards Reader* (New Haven, 1995), p. 321. The letter was sent from Stockbridge, Mass., and explained Edwards's reluctance to assume the presidency of the college.

3. Kenneth Minkema, "Jonathan Edwards and 'The Refinement of America,' " unpublished paper, Yale Art Gallery, April 17, 1996. Although the lack of

information about the descent of the so-called Edwards desk at Yale induces doubt about Edwards's actual ownership, anecdotal information tends to confirm it. Edwards's estate inventory lists a "Desk and Book Case," valued at £2, but lists other study furniture valued at considerably less—a "small book case," a "book table," and a "Writing Table" separately; the division of the drawers fits Edwards's known writing papers exactly; the sliding-drawer bookcases were reasonably uncommon and match those of a desk at the Mission House in Stockbridge, where his predecessor and friend, John Sargent, lived. Minkema believes that a local carpenter, a "Mr. Bush," might have made the bookshelves, although the maker of the desk itself and the attached cupboards remains a mystery. As Minkema points out, the bookcases could be loaded into a wagon quickly for transport since the books were packed inside the closed sliding doors, perhaps an important consideration in Stockbridge, where the danger from both Indians and the French was more than imaginary.

4. Kenneth L. Sokoloff and Georgia C. Villaflor, "The Early Achievement of Modern Stature in America," *Social Science History*, 6 (1982): 453–481. The debate about food really goes back to the debate about capitalism, which is discussed briefly in note 2 of Chapter 2.

5. On the eighteenth-century colonial diet generally, see Stephanie Grauman Wolf, *As Various as Their Land: The Everyday Lives of Eighteenth-Century Americans* (New York, 1993), pp. 88–94.

6. Henry M. Miller, "An Archaeological Perspective on the Evolution of Diet in the Colonial Chesapeake, 1620–1745," in *Colonial Chesapeake Society*, ed. Lois Green Carr, Philip D. Morgan, and Jean B. Russo (Chapel Hill, 1988), pp. 176–199. For an example of branding marks, see A. S. Salley, ed., "Stock Marks Recorded in South Carolina, 1695–1721," *South Carolina Historical and Genealogical Magazine*, 13 (1912): 126–131, 224–228; ms. autobiography of John Craig, Historical Foundation of the Presbyterian and Reformed Churches, Montreat, N.C. Ironically, when Craig accused some neighbors of poisoning his animals, the neighbors accused him of using occult "Charms" to identify the offenders.

7. David Hackett Fisher, *Albion's Seed: Four British Folkways in America* (New York, 1989), pp. 134–139, 349–354, 538–544, 814. Also see Jane Carson, *Colonial Virginia Cookery: Procedures, Equipment, and Ingredients in Colonial Cooking* (Williamsburg, Va., 1985).

8. Diana C. Crader, "Slave Diet at Monticello," *American Antiquity*, 55 (1990): 690–717. There has been considerable debate, some of it acrimonious, about slave conditions and diet in the antebellum period from 1810 to 1860, much of which is not especially relevant to understanding diet between 1680 and 1770 given the substantial technical differences in food production, distribution, and consumption after the Revolution. For an introduction, see the books that started the debate: Robert William Fogel and Stanley L. Engerman, *Time on the Cross: The Economics of American Negro Slavery* (Boston, 1974); George

Herbert Gutman, *Slavery and the Numbers Game: A Critique of 'Time on the Cross'* (Urbana, 1975); and Paul A. David et al., *Reckoning with Slavery: A Critical Study in the Quantitative History of American Negro Slavery* (New York, 1976). Gloria L. Main, *Tobacco Colony: Life in Early Maryland, 1650–1720* (Princeton, 1982), p. 136; Philip Morgan, *Slave Counterpoint: Black Culture in the Eighteenth-Century Chesapeake and Lowcountry* (Chapel Hill, 1998), pp. 134–143.

9. Daniel K. Richter, *The Ordeal of the Longhouse: The Peoples of the Iroquois League in the Era of European Colonization* (Chapel Hill, 1992), pp. 18–22, 294–295n; James H. Merrell, *The Indians' New World: Catawbas and Their Neighbors from European Contact through the Era of Removal* (Chapel Hill, 1989), pp. 2–3, 37, 130–131.

10. Merrell, *The Indians' New World,* pp. 138, 153; Richter, *The Ordeal of the Longhouse,* p. 267; Peter C. Mancall, *Deadly Medicine: Indians and Alcohol in Early America* (Ithaca, N.Y., 1995), pp. 91–93, 96–100.

11. Richter, *The Ordeal of the Longhouse,* pp. 263–280; Mancall, *Deadly Medicine,* pp. 96–100.

12. See Chapter 2.

13. Billy G. Smith, "The Material Lives of Laboring Philadelphians 1750 to 1800," *William and Mary Quarterly,* 3d ser., 38 (1981): 163–202.

14. Main, *Tobacco Colony,* pp. 183–184.

15. Carole Shammas, "How Self-Sufficient Was Early America?" *Journal of Interdisciplinary History,* 13 (1982), table 5, p. 267.

16. Laurel Thatcher Ulrich, "Wheels, Looms, and the Gender Division of Labor in Eighteenth-Century New England," *William and Mary Quarterly,* 3d ser., 55 (1998): 3–38; Shammas, "How Self-Sufficient Was Early America?" pp. 255–259.

17. Adrienne D. Hood, "The Gender Division of Labor in the Production of Textiles in Eighteenth-Century, Rural Pennsylvania (Rethinking the New England Model)," *Journal of Social History,* 27 (1994): 537–561; Ulrich, "Wheels, Looms, and the Gender Division of Labor," pp. 3–15, 34–36.

18. Morgan, *Slave Counterpoint,* pp. 125–133, quotation from Surry County court on p. 14; Main, *Tobacco Colony,* pp. 186–188, quotation about "Negro clothing" on p. 112.

19. Quoted in Morgan, *Slave Counterpoint,* p. 128. Morgan's discussion of African clothing supersedes earlier available accounts. The vivid colors in slave clothing do not necessarily show well in the few examples surviving into the early twenty-first century.

20. Fischer, *Albion's Seed,* pp. 354–360, 544–552; Fischer's discussion of Puritan clothing do not take the discussion past 1680.

21. Eric Hinderaker, "The 'Four Indian Kings' and the Imaginative Construction of the First British Empire," *William and Mary Quarterly,* 3d ser., 53 (1996): 487–526.

22. James Axtell, *The Indians' New South: Cultural Change in the Colonial South-*

east (Baton Rouge, 1997), pp. 61–62. Virginia quotation from Colin G. Calloway, *New Worlds for All: Indians, Europeans, and the Remaking of Early America* (Baltimore, 1997), p. 67; Philipp Georg Friedrich von Reck, *Von Reck's Voyage: Drawings and Journal of Philip Georg Friedrich von Reck,* ed. Kristian Hvidt (Savannah, 1990), p. 115, quotation on p. 114. See also Colin G. Calloway, ed., *Dawnland Encounters: Indians and Europeans in Northern New England* (Hanover, 1991), and Merrell, *The Indians' New World,* pp. 125–126.

23. Abbott Lowell Cummings, *The Framed Houses of Massachusetts Bay, 1625–1725* (Cambridge, Mass., 1979), and Cary Carson et al., "Impermanent Architecture in the Southern American Colonies," *Winterthur Portfolio,* 16 (1981): 135–196, offer superb introductions to seventeenth-century houses and the difficulty of comprehending and interpreting them.

24. Quotation from Carson et al., "Impermanent Architecture," p. 140.

25. Carson et al., "Impermanent Architecture." The evidence, if not the argument, advanced in David H. Flaherty, *Privacy in Colonial New England* (Charlottesville, Va., 1972), suggests a sharp divide between seventeenth-century and nineteenth- or twentieth-century notions of physical privacy as a condition for sexual relations.

26. Carson et al., "Impermanent Architecture," pp. 149–151.

27. Cummings, *The Framed Houses of Massachusetts Bay, 1625–1725,* p. 36.

28. Quoted in Carson et al., "Impermanent Architecture," p. 123.

29. On vernacular architecture, see the important work by Dell Upton, including "The Power of Things: Recent Studies in American Vernacular Architecture," *American Quarterly,* 35 (1983); "Toward a Performance Theory of Vernacular Architecture in Tidewater Virginia," *Folklore Forum,* 12, no. 2–3 (1979): 173–196; and Upton and John M. Vlach, *Common Places: Readings in American Vernacular Architecture* (Athens, Ga., 1986).

30. Billy G. Smith, "The Material Lives of Laboring Philadelphians 1750 to 1800," *William and Mary Quarterly,* 3d ser., 38 (1981): 163–202. For the example of the Fight and Nail families, see p. 177.

31. Morgan, *Slave Counterpoint,* p. 46. Morgan argues that "as colonial societies became more settled, planters built more secure housing, displayed their wealth through their plantation establishment, and in general regularized the material conditions of their laborers" (ibid., p. 103). The form of housing indeed changed, as Morgan suggests, but I have emphasized the low quality of that housing, especially when compared with housing for modest and poorer Europeans. See Chapter 4. Also see John M. Vlach, *The Afro-American Tradition in Decorative Arts* (Cleveland, 1978); Dell Upton, "White and Black Landscapes of Eighteenth-Century Virginia," *Places,* 2 (1985): 59–72.

32. Morgan, *Slave Counterpoint,* quotation on slave quarter construction on p. 106, quotation on beds on p. 114.

33. Visitor's observation about George Washington and Mount Vernon is quoted in Ronald L. Hurst and Jonathan Prown, *Southern Furniture, 1680–1830: The*

Colonial Williamsburg Collection (Williamsburg, Va., and New York, 1997), p. 19. Edward A. Chappell, "Housing a Nation: The Transformation of Living Standards in Early America," in *Of Consuming Interests: The Style of Life in the Eighteenth Century,* ed. Cary Carson, Ronald Hoffman, and Peter J. Albert (Charlottesville, Va., 1994), p. 192; Darrett B. Rutman and Anita H. Rutman, *A Place in Time: Middlesex County, Virginia, 1650–1750* (New York, 1984), pp. 166–167; Main, *Tobacco Colony,* pp. 133–137. See the late-eighteenth- and early-nineteenth-century slave quarters, also often lacking windows and wood floors, illustrated in Mechal Sobel, *The World They Made Together: Black and White Values in Eighteenth-Century Virginia* (Princeton, 1987), pp. 112, 130. Margaret Bayard Smith's comments on Jefferson's Monticello are quoted in William M. Kelso, "Archaeology of Chesapeake Common Folks: Artifacts of Definition and Change among the Rich and Poor at Kingsmill and Monticello, 1650–1810," in *Common People and Their Material World: Free Men and Women in the Chesapeake, 1700–1830,* ed. David Harvey and Gregory Brown (Williamsburg, Va., 1995), p. 86. Like so much in the study of early American material culture, this subject is made all the more difficult by problems in dating buildings and in the penchant of well-meaning partisans to assign earlier dates than the evidence permits in order to make the buildings "older."

34. Richter, *The Ordeal of the Longhouse,* p. 260; Merrell, *The Indians' New World,* pp. 125, 229–230.

35. Richter, *The Ordeal of the Longhouse,* pp. 257–262; Clark quotation on p. 260; Richter quotation on p. 261.

36. Richard L. Bushman, *The Refinement of America: Persons, Houses, Cities* (New York, 1992), pp. 100–139.

37. On the "vernacular," see Dell Upton, *Holy Things and Profane: Anglican Parish Churches in Colonial Virginia* (Cambridge, Mass., 1986), p. 11. Both the William Hancock house and the so-called Rochester House are discussed in Kevin M. Sweeney, "High-Style Vernacular: Lifestyles of the Colonial Elite," in *Of Consuming Interests: The Style of Life in the Eighteenth Century,* ed. Cary Carson, Ronald Hoffman, and Peter J. Albert (Charlottesville, Va., 1994), pp. 1–58.

38. Walter M. Whitehill, *Boston, A Topographical History* (Cambridge, Mass., 1968), p. 35.

39. James Thomas Flexner, *Washington, The Indispensable Man* (Boston, 1974), pp. 4, 6, 19, 43–49; Sweeney, "High-Style Vernacular," p. 39.

40. Sweeney, "High-Style Vernacular," pp. 12, 13; Nathaniel W. Alcock, "Vernacular Architecture: Historical Evidence and Historical Problems," in *Material Culture and the Study of American Life,* ed. Ian M. G. Quimby (New York, 1978), pp. 109–120; Dell Upton, "Vernacular Domestic Architecture in Eighteenth-Century Virginia," *Winterthur Portfolio,* 17 (1982): 95–119.

41. Hurst and Prown, *Southern Furniture,* pp. 23–33; quotation on p. 27.

42. By its nature, the material range of poverty in the colonies is exceptionally difficult to study, since fine homes and furniture survive while small cabins and crude furniture seldom do. For interesting approaches to consumer habits and the archaeology of consumption, see Amy Smart Martin, "Common People and the Local Store: Consumerism in the Rural Virginia Backcountry," in *Common People and Their Material World*, ed. Harvey and Brown, pp. 39–54, and William M. Kelso, "Archaeology of Chesapeake Common Folks: Artifacts of Definition and Change among the Rich and Poor at Kingsmill and Monticello, 1650–1810," in ibid., pp. 74–94.

43. Neil McKendrick, John Brewer, and J. H. Plumb, eds., *The Birth of a Consumer Society: The Commercialization of Eighteenth-Century England* (Bloomington, Ind., 1982); Carole Shammas, *The Pre-Industrial Consumer in England and America* (New York, 1990), and Cary Carson, Ronald Hoffman, and Peter J. Albert, eds., *Of Consuming Interests: The Style of Life in the Eighteenth Century* (Charlottesville, Va., 1994) offer important guides to the larger literature on this topic.

44. On the subject of the consumer revolution, see McKendrick, Brewer, and Plumb, eds., *The Birth of a Consumer Society.* The quotation about London furniture for sale by Richard Baker of Charleston is from John Bivins, *The Furniture of Coastal North Carolina, 1700–1820* (Winston-Salem, N.C., 1988), p. 95, and Bivins has an excellent and detailed account of the furniture import trade in colonial North Carolina. On imports in South Carolina's low country, see Hurst and Prown, *Southern Furniture*, p. 28. On the pewter trade, see Peter Hornsby, "Britain and the Growth of the American Pewter Industry," *Bulletin of the Pewter Collector's Club of America*, 86 (1983): 253–256.

45. T. H. Breen, "'Baubles of Britain': The American and Consumer Revolutions of the Eighteenth Century," in *Of Consuming Interests: The Style of Life in the Eighteenth Century*, ed. Cary Carson, Ronald Hoffman, and Peter J. Albert (Charlottesville, Va., 1994), pp. 444–482; the quotation is on p. 456. Francis J. Puig and Michael Conforti, *The American Craftsman and the European Tradition* (Minneapolis, 1989). Also see Bushman, *The Refinement of America*, pp. 3–29.

46. Carl R. Lounsbury, *An Illustrated Glossary of Early Southern Architecture and Landscape* (New York, 1994), p. 221; the Henry Laurens quotation is on p. 347.

47. Christopher Hartop, *The Huguenot Legacy: English Silver, 1680–1760, from the Alan and Simone Hartman Collection* (London, 1996); Jon Butler, *The Huguenots in America: A Refugee People in New World Society* (Cambridge, Mass., 1983), pp. 177–180.

48. Butler, *The Huguenots in America*, pp. 86, 131–132; Kathryn Buhler, *Colonial Silversmiths, Masters and Apprentices* (Boston, 1956).

49. George Kubler, "Time's Perfection and Colonial Art," in *Spanish, French, and*

English Traditions in the Colonial Silver of North America (Winterthur, Del., 1968), pp. 7–12; Michael Conforti, "The Transfer and Adaptation of European Culture in North America," in *The American Craftsman and the European Tradition, 1620–1820,* ed. Francis J. Puig and Michael Conforti (Hanover, N.H., 1989), pp. xii–xxi.

50. Jeanette W. Rosenbaum, *Myer Myers, Goldsmith* (Philadelphia, 1954). I am indebted for the information on Myer Myers's clientele to David Barquist of the Yale Art Gallery.

51. Thomas J. Schlereth, "Artisans and Craftsmen: A Historical Perspective," in *The Craftsman in Early America,* ed. Ian M. G. Quimby (New York, 1984), pp. 57–58; *Paul Revere: Artisan, Businessman, and Patriot—The Man behind the Myth* (Boston, 1988); Jayne E. Triber, *A True Republican: The Life of Paul Revere* (Amherst, 1998).

52. Sweeney, "High-Style Vernacular," p. 43. Peter Manigault quotation in Hurst and Prown, *Southern Furniture,* p. 28; Jonathan Prown and Richard Miller, "The Rococo, the Grotto, and the Philadelphia High Chest," *American Furniture,* 4 (1996): 105–136.

53. Sweeney, "High-Style Vernacular," p. 42; John Bivins, Jr., and Alexander Forsyth, *The Regional Arts of the Early South: A Sampling from the Collection of the Museum of Early Southern Decorative Arts* (Chapel Hill, 1991), pp. 94–95. Bivins and Forsyth speculate that the library bookcase was part of a set that included a double chest of drawers.

54. John T. Kirk, *American Furniture and the British Tradition to 1830* (New York, 1982), pp. 144–158.

55. Ibid.

56. Bivins and Forsyth, *The Regional Arts of the Early South,* p. 22; Kevin M. Sweeney, "Furniture and the Domestic Environment in Wethersfield, Connecticut, 1639–1800," in *Material Life in America, 1600–1860,* ed. Robert Blair St. George (Boston, 1988), p. 273; David Knell, *English Country Furniture: The National and Regional Vernacular, 1500–1900* (London, 1992), pp. 47–60.

57. Wolf, *As Various as Their Lands,* plate 8.4; Hurst and Prown, *Southern Furniture,* pp. 337–343. For an exploration of gender, see Laurel Thatcher Ulrich, "Hannah Bernard's Cupboard: Female Property and Identity in Eighteenth-Century New England," in *Through a Glass Darkly: Reflections on Personal Identity in Early America,* ed. Ronald Hoffman, Mechal Sobel, and Fredrika J. Teute (Chapel Hill, 1997), pp. 238–273.

58. There is no study of "cheap" furniture in early America, but for an analysis of the range of furniture in two New England towns, see Edward S. Cooke, Jr., *Making Furniture in Preindustrial America: The Social Economy of Newtown and Woodbury, Connecticut* (Baltimore, 1996), chap. 5.

59. Ibid., chaps. 6 and 7; Kevin M. Sweeney, "Furniture and the Domestic Environment in Wethersfield, Connecticut." Bivins and Forsyth, *Regional Arts of the Early South,* pp. 21, 29, 32, 34, 39.

60. For eighteenth-century English chairs, see Bernard D. Cotton, *The English Regional Chair* (Woodbridge, Engl., 1990).

61. Peter Benes and Philip D. Zimmerman, eds., *New England Meeting House and Church, 1630–1850* (Boston, 1979), pp. 3–27. In New England, the tax-supported meeting house used by the tax-supported congregation continued to serve as the principal place where selectmen gathered to conduct public business—despite growing numbers of dissenting church buildings. Carl Lounsbury of Colonial Williamsburg furnished the information on construction of Hingham's Old Ship Meeting House.

62. John O. Peters and Margaret T. Peters, *Virginia's Historic Courthouses* (Charlottesville, Va., 1995), pp. 7–18; Jay B. Hubbell and Douglass Adair, "Robert Munford's The Candidates," *William and Mary Quarterly,* 3d ser., 5 (1948): 233. For a discussion of the construction process in a single Virginia courthouse building, see Carl R. Lounsbury, "'An Elegant and Commodious Building': William Buckland and the Design of the Prince William County Courthouse," *Journal of the Society of Architectural Historians,* 16 (1987): 227–240. Also see Lounsbury, "The Structure of Justice: The Courthouses of Colonial Virginia," *Perspectives in Vernacular Architecture,* 3 (1989): 214–226. All of the surviving eighteenth-century Virginia courthouses have undergone numerous and extensive interior remodeling; none has its original interior.

63. Butler, *Huguenots in America,* p. 178; Hollis French, *Jacob Hurd and His Sons Nathaniel and Benjamin, Silversmiths, 1702–1781* ([Cambridge, Mass.], 1939), p. 40; Lounsbury, *An Illustrated Glossary of Early Southern Architecture and Landscape,* pp. 99–100; A. G. Roeber, "Authority, Law, and Custom: The Rituals of Court Day in Tidewater Virginia, 1720–1750," *William and Mary Quarterly,* 3d ser., 37 (1980): 29–53.

64. Whitehill, *Boston: A Topographical History,* pp. 9, 13–15, 41–44; Carl Bridenbaugh, *Cities in Revolt: Urban Life in America, 1743–1776* (New York, 1955), pp. 19–22, 228–230; Walter J. Fraser, Jr., *Charleston! Charleston! The History of a Southern City* (Columbia, S.C., 1989), pp. 78, 88; Peter A. Coclanis, "The Sociology of Architecture in Colonial Charleston: Pattern and Process in an Eighteenth-Century Southern City," *Journal of Social History,* 18 (1985): 607–624.

65. Graham Hood, *The Governor's Palace in Williamsburg: A Cultural Study* (Chapel Hill, 1991); Marcus Whiffen, *Public Buildings of Williamsburg* (Williamsburg, Va., 1958); Barbara G. Carson, *The Governor's Palace: The Williamsburg Residence of Virginia's Royal Governor* (Williamsburg, Va., 1987).

66. David W. Conroy, *In Public Houses: Drink and the Revolution of Authority in Colonial Massachusetts* (Chapel Hill, 1995), pp. 12–56. On drinking at Maryland funerals, see Main, *Tobacco Colony,* pp. 210–211.

67. Conroy, *In Public Houses,* p. 171. The quotation from Robert Breck, *The Only Method to Promote the Happiness of a People and their Property* (Boston, 1728), is in Conroy, *In Public Houses,* pp. 79–80.

68. Conroy, *In Public Houses*, pp. 189–240; the quotation from John Adams is on p. 196.

69. Ibid., pp. 87–98, 130–147; Carl Bridenbaugh, *Cities in the Wilderness: The First Century of Urban Life in America, 1625–1742* (New York, 1938), p. 437.

70. Conroy, *In Public Houses*, pp. 181–188, 241–242, 308–309; Bridenbaugh, *Cities in the Wilderness*, pp. 267–268, 426–428.

71. Bridenbaugh, *Cities in the Wilderness*, p. 369; Ronald W. Clark, *Benjamin Franklin: A Biography* (New York, 1983), p. 52. I am especially indebted to Benjamin Carp for his 1998 Yale senior essay, "Fire of Liberty: Fire Fighters and the American Revolution."

72. Clark, *Benjamin Franklin*, pp. 51–53; Bridenbaugh, *Cities in Revolt*, p. 178; Raymond Phineas Stearns, *Science in the British Colonies of America* (Urbana, 1970), pp. 502–674.

73. Steven C. Bullock, *Revolutionary Brotherhood: Freemasonry and the Transformation of the American Social Order, 1730–1840* (Chapel Hill, 1996), pp. 68–69.

74. Carl Bridenbaugh, *Myths and Realities: Societies of the Colonial South* (Baton Rouge, 1952), p. 104; Bridenbaugh, *Cities in Revolt*, p. 181.

75. David S. Shields, *Civil Tongues and Polite Letters in British America* (Chapel Hill, 1997), pp. 120–140, 284.

76. Catherine La Courreye Blecki and Karin A. Wulf, eds., *Milcah Martha Moore's Book: A Commonplace Book from Revolutionary America* (University Park, Pa., 1997), quotation from Griffitts's "Essay on Friendship" from p. 115.

77. Esther Edwards Burr, *The Journal of Esther Edwards Burr, 1754–1757*, ed. Carol Karlsen and Laurie Crumpacker (New Haven, 1984), p. 107; the quotation is from a letter to Sarah Prince of April 7, 1755. Eliza L. Pinckney, *The Letterbook of Eliza Lucas Pinckney, 1739–1762*, ed. Elise Pinckney and Marvin R. Zahniser (Chapel Hill, 1972); Darcy R. Fryer, "The Mind of Eliza Pinckney: An Eighteenth-Century Woman's Construction of Herself," *South Carolina Historical Magazine*, 99 (1998): 215–237; Phyllis Wheatley, *The Poems of Phyllis Wheatley*, ed. Julian D. Mason, Jr. (Chapel Hill, 1989).

78. Shields, *Civil Tongues and Polite Letters*, Joseph Shippen poem quoted on pp. 150–151, and William Franklin poem quoted on p. 158.

79. David Shields, *Oracles of Empire: Poetry, Politics, and Commerce in British America, 1690–1750* (Chicago, 1990), quotation from Androboros on p. 145; Shields, *Civil Tongues and Polite Letters*, pp. 194–195, 302–303; William Spengemann, "Discovering the Literature of British America," *Early American Literature*, 8 (1983): 3–16.

80. The College of William and Mary remained a private institution until 1906, and Rutgers remained a private institution until 1945, although it had become New Jersey's land grant college in the nineteenth century, just as Cornell became New York's land grant college. On the colonial colleges and their purposes, see Lawrence A. Cremin, *American Education: The Colonial Experience, 1607–1783* (New York, 1970), pp. 321–330, 335–338, 379–386,

404–406, 429–431, 460–468, 509–516. Since there are disagreements about the "founding" dates of some of the colleges, I have used the founding dates currently claimed by the colleges in their promotional literature.

81. On the problem of secrets in modern times, see Sissela Bok, *Secrets: On the Ethics of Concealment and Revelation* (New York, 1982).

82. See Bullock, *Revolutionary Brotherhood*, pp. 13, 14, 19–20, 59–63; Bullock's study supersedes all previous studies of early American Freemasonry. Freemasonry's origins and early history, too complicated to be digested here, are described by Bullock on pp. 9–49. See also Margaret C. Jacob, *The Radical Enlightenment: Pantheists, Freemasons, and Republicans* (London, 1981), on Masonic philosophy and politics. On diverse aspects of colonial Freemasonry, see J. A. Leo Lemay, *Deism, Masonry, and the Enlightenment: Essays Honoring Alfred Owen Aldridge* (Newark, Del., 1987).

83. Bullock, *Revolutionary Brotherhood*, pp. 15–18.

84. Ibid., pp. 46–55; quotation from the *Pennsylvania Gazette* on pp. 53–55; Wallace B. Gusler, "Anthony Hay, A Williamsburg Tradesman," in *Common People and Their Material World*, ed. Harvey and Brown, pp. 23–32.

85. Bullock, *Revolutionary Brotherhood*, pp. 46–55.

86. Alexander Hamilton, *The History of the Ancient and Honorable Tuesday Club,* ed. Robert Micklus, 2 vols. (Chapel Hill, 1990), 1: xviii–xix. This Alexander Hamilton, a physician, was not related to *the* Alexander Hamilton. There is a large literature on the Tuesday Club. Among additional important sources and studies are Elaine Breslaw, ed., *Records of the Tuesday Club of Annapolis, 1745–56* (Urbana, 1988); and Robert Micklus, *The Comic Genius of Dr. Alexander Hamilton* (Knoxville, 1990). The club's music is discussed in John Barry Talley, *Secular Music in Colonial Annapolis: The Tuesday Club, 1745–56* (Urbana, 1988).

87. Hamilton, *History of the Ancient and Honorable Tuesday Club,* 1: xix–xx, 3: 215.

88. Elaine G. Breslaw, "Wit, Whimsy, and Politics: The Uses of Satire by the Tuesday Club of Annapolis, 1744 to 1756," *William and Mary Quarterly,* 3d ser., 32 (1975): 295–306. The quotation from the Tuesday Club record book, Dec. 1749, is in ibid., p. 299.

89. Hamilton, *History of the Ancient and Honorable Tuesday Club,* 1: 45–46, 92, 147, 216, 282, 411; 2: 93.

90. Ibid., 1: 240–242.

91. I first noticed this quotation in Breslaw, "Wit, Whimsy, and Politics," p. 305. I have quoted the original in Hamilton, *History of the Ancient and Honorable Tuesday Club,* 3: 121.

5. THINGS SPIRITUAL

1. "Governor Thomas Dongan's Report to the Committee of Trade on the Province of New York, dated 22d February, 1687," in *Documentary History of the*

State of New York, ed. E. B. O'Callahan, 4 vols. (Albany, 1849–1851), 1: 186. For a view of these conditions, see Jon Butler, *Awash in a Sea of Faith: Christianizing the American People* (Cambridge, Mass., 1990), chap. 2.

2. Portions of this chapter are drawn from Butler, *Awash in a Sea of Faith,* chaps. 4, 5, and 6.

3. John Hammond, *Leah and Rachel; or, The Two Fruitful Sisters Virginia, and Maryland* (London, 1656) in *Tracts and Other Papers Relating Principally to the Origin, Settlement, and Progress of the Colonies of North America, from the Discovery of the Country to the Year 1776,* ed. Peter Force (Washington, D.C., 1844), 3, no. 14, p. 9.

4. John Bossy, "Reluctant Colonists: The English Catholics Confront the Atlantic," in *Early Maryland in a Wider World,* ed. David Quinn (Detroit, 1982), pp. 149–166; Gloria L. Main, *Tobacco Colony: Life in Early Maryland, 1650–1720* (Princeton, 1982), pp. 9–16; Jay P. Dolan, *The American Catholic Experience: A History from Colonial Times to the Present* (Garden City, N.Y., 1985), pp. 17–86. For a list of known Anglican ministers in the colony, see Nelson W. Rightmyer, *Maryland's Established Church* (Philadelphia, 1956), pp. 153–221. For some expression of faith at death in Maryland, see Jon Butler, "Thomas Teackle's 333 Books: A Great Library on Virginia's Eastern Shore," *William and Mary Quarterly,* n.s., 49 (1992): 490–491. Historians have tended to exaggerate the size, importance, or even continuing existence of early Baptist and Presbyterian congregations in Virginia and Maryland.

5. Bruce C. Daniels, *The Connecticut Town: Growth and Development, 1635–1790* (Middletown, Conn., 1979), pp. 94–118. The progress of the renewed establishment in eighteenth-century New England scarcely was peaceful. For examples of the difficulties, see C. C. Goen, *Revivalism and Separatism in New England, 1740–1800: Strict Congregationalists and Separate Baptists in the Great Awakening* (New Haven, 1962).

6. Park Rouse, *James Blair of Virginia* (Chapel Hill, 1971), pp. 63–79, 137–151; G. MacLaren Brydon, *Virginia's Mother Church and the Political Conditions under Which It Grew* (Philadelphia, 1947), 1: 225–240, 309–326.

7. Rightmyer, *Maryland's Established Church,* pp. 14–54; John W. Pratt, *Religion, Politics, and Diversity: The Church-State Theme in New York History* (Ithaca, N.Y., 1967), pp. 40–52; M. Eugene Sirmans, *Colonial South Carolina: A Political History, 1663–1763* (Chapel Hill, 1966), pp. 88–89; Stephen Beauregard Weeks, *The Religious Development in the Province of North Carolina* (Baltimore, 1892), pp. 36–37, 46–47; Hugh T. Lefler and William S. Powell, *Colonial North Carolina: A History* (New York, 1973), pp. 194–198.

8. H. P. Thompson, *Thomas Bray* (London, 1954).

9. Nicholas Trott, *The Laws of the British Plantations in America Relating to the Church and to the Clergy* (London, 1721), pp. 231–243; Carl Zollman, *American Church Law* (St. Paul, 1933), pp. 2–6; Anson Phelps Stokes, *Church and State in the United States* (New York, 1950), 1: 168.

10. Jon Butler, *Power, Authority, and the Origins of American Denominational Order: The English Churches in the Delaware Valley, 1680–1730,* American Philosophical Society Transactions, 68, part 2 (Philadelphia, 1978).

11. The 1690 gatherings in Cambridge preceded the better-known meeting in 1708 that produced the Saybrook Platform that settled doctrinal issues and produced what Sydney Ahlstrom has called a "semipresbyterian structure" in church government. Sydney Ahlstrom, *A Religious History of the American People* (New Haven, 1972), p. 163. Robert F. Scholz, "Clerical Consociation in Massachusetts Bay: Reassessing the New England Way and Its Origins," *William and Mary Quarterly,* 3d ser., 29 (1972): 391–414. "Records of the Cambridge Association," *Proceedings of the Massachusetts Historical Society,* 17 (1879–80): 254–281; J. William T. Youngs, *God's Messengers: Religious Leadership in Colonial New England, 1700–1750* (Baltimore, 1976), and on Lutherans, Leonard R. Riforgiato, *Missionary of Moderation: Henry Melchior Muhlenberg and the Lutheran Church in English America* (Lewisburg, Pa., 1980); Frederick V. Mills, Sr., "Anglican Expansion in Colonial America," *Historical Magazine of the Protestant Episcopal Church,* 39 (1970): 315–324; John F. Woolverton, *Colonial Anglicanism in North America* (Detroit, 1984), pp. 27–30.

12. Butler, *Awash in a Sea of Faith,* pp. 116–128.

13. Information in the next three paragraphs is based on calculations drawn from Frederick L. Weis, *The Colonial Churches and the Colonial Clergy of the Middle and Southern Colonies, 1607–1776* (Boston, 1938); Frederick L. Weis, *The Colonial Clergy and the Colonial Churches of New England* (Boston, 1936); Charles O. Paullin, *Atlas of the Historical Geography of the United States* (Washington, D.C., 1932); and Rodney Stark and Roger Finke, "American Religion in 1776: A Statistical Portrait," *Sociological Analysis,* 49 (1988): 39–51. Paullin especially exaggerated the number of congregations, so that where he estimates more than 3,000 congregations on the eve of the Revolution, I have reduced that number to about 2,500. See also Jon Butler, "Church Formation in Colonial America: Era of Expansion, 1680–1770," in *Mapping America's Past: A Historical Atlas,* ed. Mark C. Carnes and John A. Garraty (New York, 1996), pp. 46–47.

14. Dolan, *The American Catholic Experience,* pp. 84–97; Eli Faber, *A Time for Planting: The First Migration, 1654–1820* (Baltimore, 1992), pp. 27–51; Hector St. John de Crèvecoeur, *Letters from an American Farmer and Sketches of Eighteenth-Century America,* ed. Albert E. Stone (New York, 1981), p. 76.

15. For discussions of post-1680 church construction in the colonies see Butler, *Awash in a Sea of Faith,* pp. 107–116, and Richard L. Bushman, *The Refinement of America: Persons, Houses, Cities* (New York, 1992), pp. 169–180.

16. Butler, *Awash in a Sea of Faith,* pp. 113–115; Bushman, *The Refinement of America,* pp. 173–176.

17. Albert Simons and Samuel Lapham, Jr., *The Early Architecture of Charleston*

(Columbia, S.C., 1970); Samuel G. Stoney, *The Plantations of the Carolina Low Country,* ed. Albert Simons and Samuel Lapham, Jr. (Charleston, n.d.).

18. Abbott L. Cummings, "Meeting and Dwelling House: Interrelationships in Early New England," in *New England Meeting House and Church, 1630–1850,* ed. Peter Benes (Boston, 1980), pp. 4–17.

19. Peter Benes, "Sky Colors and Scattered Clouds: The Decorative and Architectural Painting of New England Meeting Houses, 1738–1834," in *New England Meeting House and Church, 1630–1850,* ed. Benes, pp. 51–69, quotation from Pomfret, Massachusetts, on p. 54. Also see *New England Meeting House and Church, 1630–1850: A Loan Exhibition at the Currier Gallery of Art, Manchester, New Hampshire,* ed. Peter Benes and Philip D. Zimmerman (Boston, 1979).

20. Robert Ellingwood, *The History of American Church Music* (New York, 1953), chap. 7; Gottlieb Mittelberger, *Journey to Pennsylvania,* ed. and trans. Oscar Handlin and John Clive (Cambridge, Mass., 1960), pp. 91–92; Francis Wallett, ed., *Diary of Ebenezer Parkman* (Worcester, Mass., 1982), p. 126. Guilford, Connecticut, town records quoted in *New England Meeting House and Church, 1630–1850: A Loan Exhibition,* ed. Benes and Zimmerman, p. 61.

21. See the painting by Bishop Roberts, *A View of Charleston,* c. 1739, owned by Colonial Williamsburg, Williamsburg, Virginia.

22. For material on church interiors, see Morgan Dix et al., *A History of the Parish of Trinity Church in the City of New York,* 7 vols. (New York, 1898), 1: 154, 222; Henry Wilder Foote, *Annals of King's Chapel from the Puritan Age of New England to the Present Day* (Boston: Little, 1882), 1: 211, 214, 421, 2: 102, 170. Organ building, however, remained dominated by European-trained craftsmen down to the Revolution. For examples, see M. K. D. Babcock, "The Organs and Organ Builders of Christ Church, Boston, 1736–1945," *Historical Magazine of the Protestant Episcopal Church,* 14 (1945): 241–263; Leonard Ellinwood, *A History of American Church Music* (New York, 1953), chap. 4. On Myer Myers's religious production of silver, see Jeanette W. Rosenbaum, *Myer Myers, Goldsmith* (Philadelphia, 1954) and Faber, *A Time for Planting,* pp. 150–151.

23. W. R. Ward, *The Protestant Evangelical Awakening* (Cambridge, 1992), pp. 115–169, 296–352. Historians have debated the character and significance of eighteenth-century colonial revivalism and "the Great Awakening" for several decades. Two of the principal contesting views can be found in two articles: Harry S. Stout, "Religion, Communication, and the Ideological Origins of the American Revolution," *William and Mary Quarterly,* 3d ser., 34 (1977): 519–541, and Jon Butler, "Enthusiasm Described and Decried: The Great Awakening as Interpretative Fiction," *Journal of American History,* 69 (1982): 305–325. Recent additions to this debate can be found in Joseph H. Conforti, "The Invention of the Great Awakening, 1795–1842," *Early American Litera-*

ture, 26 (1991): 99–118; Joseph H. Conforti, *Jonathan Edwards, Religious Tradition, and American Culture* (Chapel Hill, 1995); and Frank Lambert, *Inventing the "Great Awakening"* (Princeton, 1999).

24. Goen, *Revivalism and Separatism in New England, 1740–1800*, p. 6; Paul R. Lucas, *Valley of Discord: Church and Society along the Connecticut River, 1636–1725* (Hanover, N.H., 1976), pp. 199–202; Edwin S. Gaustad, *The Great Awakening in New England* (New York, 1957), pp. 16–20; Ahlstrom, *A Religious History of the American People*, pp. 314–329.

25. Alexander Garden, *Take Heed How Ye Hear* (Charleston, S.C., 1741); [Charles Chauncy?], *The Wonderful Narrative: or, A Faithful Account of the French Prophets, . . .* (Boston, 1742); Hillel Schwartz, *The French Prophets: The History of a Millenarian Group in Eighteenth-Century England* (Berkeley, 1980); Jonathan Edwards, "Some Thoughts concerning the Present Revival" (1742), in *The Great Awakening*, ed. C. C. Goen, in *The Works of Jonathan Edwards* (New Haven, 1972), 4: 313, 330, 341; David Lovejoy, *Religious Enthusiasm in the New World: Heresy to Revolution* (Cambridge, Mass., 1985), pp. 178–194; John Bumsted and Van de Wetering, *What Must I Do to Be Saved?: The Great Awakening in Colonial America* (Hinsdale, Ill., 1976), pp. 40–53; James Tanis, *Dutch Calvinistic Pietism in the Middle Colonies: A Study in the Life and Theology of Theodorus Jacobus Frelinghuysen* (The Hague, 1967).

26. Gaustad, *Great Awakening in New England*, p. 111; John B. Frantz, "The Awakening of Religion among the German Settlers in the Middle Colonies," *William and Mary Quarterly*, 3d ser., 33 (1976): 266–288; Charles H. Maxson, *The Great Awakening in the Middle Colonies* (Chicago, 1920), pp. 1–10, 28, 32; Wesley M. Gewehr, *The Great Awakening in Virginia, 1740–1790* (Durham, N.C., 1930), p. 254; Christine Leigh Heyrman, *Commerce and Culture: The Maritime Communities of Colonial Massachusetts, 1690–1750* (New York, 1984), pp. 182–208, 366–405.

27. Richard L. Bushman, *From Puritan to Yankee: Character and the Social Order in Connecticut, 1690–1765* (Cambridge, Mass., 1967), pp. 135–143, 183–220; Ned Landsman, *Scotland and Its First American Colony, 1683–1765* (Princeton, 1985), pp. 227–255; Rhys Isaac, *The Transformation of Virginia, 1740–1790* (Chapel Hill, 1982), pp. 161–205.

28. Susan O'Brien, "A Transatlantic Community of Saints: The Great Awakening and the First Evangelical Network, 1735–1755," *American Historical Review*, 91 (1985): 811–832; *George Whitefield's Journals* [ed. Iain Murray] (London, 1960), p. 476; Timothy D. Hall, *Contested Boundaries: Itinerancy and the Reshaping of the Colonial American Religious World* (Durham, N.C., 1994).

29. Eliza Pinckney to George Lucas, [June 1742], in *The Letterbook of Eliza Lucas Pinckney, 1739–1762*, ed. Elise Pinckney and Marvin R. Zahniser (Chapel Hill, 1972), pp. 29–30; *A Letter to the Negroes Lately Converted to Christ in America. And Particularly to Those, Lately Called Out of Darkness into God's Marvellous Light, at Mr. Jonathan Bryan's in South Carolina; or, A Welcome to*

the Believing Negroes, into the Household of God. By a Friend and Servant of Theirs in England (London, 1743); Hugh Bryan and Mary Hutson, *Living Christianity Delineated, in the Diaries and Letters of Two Eminently Pious Persons Lately Deceased: viz. Mr. Hugh Bryan, and Mrs. Mary Hutson, both of South-Carolina* (London, 1760); Alan Gallay, "Jonathan Bryan's Plantation Empire: Land Politics and the Formation of a Ruling Class in Colonial Georgia," *William and Mary Quarterly,* 3d ser., 45 (1988): 253–279; Harvey H. Jackson, "Hugh Bryan and the Evangelical Movement in Colonial South Carolina," *William and Mary Quarterly,* 3d ser., 43 (1986): 594–614.

30. Ned Landsman, "Revivalism and Nativism in the Middle Colonies," *American Quarterly,* 34 (1982): 155–156; De Benneville K. Ludwig, "Memorabilia of the Tennents," *Journal of Presbyterian History,* 1 (1902): 344–354. Gilbert Tennent did have a mutually unsatisfactory one-year residence at New Castle, Delaware, when he began his ministry in 1726. William Tennent [Sr.] manuscript sermons, Presbyterian Historical Society, Philadelphia; Thomas C. Pears, Jr., ed., "William Tennent's Sacramental Sermon," *Journal of Presbyterian History,* 19 (1940): 76–84. In general, the Tennents eschewed millennialism, which occupied a much larger place in the theology of other revivalists. In Alan Heimert, *Religion and the American Mind from the Great Awakening to the Revolution* (Cambridge, Mass., 1966), Gilbert Tennent figures prominently as an evangelical but not as a millennialist.

31. Gilbert Tennent, "Prefatory Discourse," in John Tennent, *The Nature of Regeneration Opened* (Boston, 1735), pp. i–ix; Thomas Henderson to Elias Boudinot, n.d. [ca. 1805], no. 11M7, ms. group I, New Jersey Historical Society, Trenton, N.J.; Archibald Alexander, *Biographical Sketches of the Founder and Principal Alumni of the Log College* (Philadelphia, 1851), pp. 127–134, 150–152; Elias Boudinot, *The Life of William Tennent, Late Pastor of the Presbyterian Church at Freehold, N.J.,* improved ed. (Trenton, N.J., 1833), pp. 20–24. Boudinot based his sketch on letters he received from members of William Tennent, Jr.'s Freehold, New Jersey, congregation. Alexander offered a naturalistic explanation for the loss of Tennent's toes to deflate what he regarded as the embarrassing claims about supernatural intervention made by Tennent and his congregants. On missing body parts, see Douglas B. Price, "Miraculous Restoration of Lost Body Parts: Relationship to the Phantom Limb Phenomenon and to Limb Burial Superstitions and Practices," in *American Folk Medicine: A Symposium,* ed. Wayland D. Hand (Berkeley, 1976), pp. 49–72.

32. *The Querists, Part III* (Philadelphia, 1741), p. 91; "The Wonderful Wandering Spirit," in *The Great Awakening,* ed. Alan Heimert and Perry Miller (Indianapolis, 1967), pp. 147–151; also see *The Querists; or, An Extract of Sundry Passages Taken Out of Mr. Whitefield's Printed Sermons, Journals and Letters* (Philadelphia, 1740), p. 44. On miracles both before and after the Tennents, see Howard Clark Kee, *Miracle in the Early Christian World: A Study in*

Sociohistorical Method (New Haven: Yale University Press, 1983); Ramsay MacMullen, *Christianizing the Roman Empire, 100 A.D.–400 A.D.* (New Haven, 1984); Henry J. Cadbury, ed., *George Fox's 'Book of Miracles'* (Cambridge, 1948); Richard L. Bushman, *Joseph Smith and the Beginnings of Mormonism* (Urbana, 1984); David E. Harrell, Jr., *All Things Are Possible: The Healing and Charismatic Revivals in Modern America* (Bloomington, Ind., 1975).

33. The best biographies are Harry S. Stout, *The Divine Dramatist: George Whitefield and the Rise of Modern Evangelicalism* (Grand Rapids, Mich., 1991), and Frank Lambert, *"Pedlar in Divinity": George Whitefield and the Transatlantic Revivals, 1737–1770* (Princeton, 1994).

34. Stuart C. Henry, *George Whitefield: Wayfaring Witness* (Nashville, 1957), pp. 95–114.

35. Quotation from "The Spiritual Travels of Nathan Cole," in *The Great Awakening: Event and Exegesis,* ed. Darrett B. Rutman (New York, 1970), p. 44.

36. Historians generally homogenize evangelical revivalist style. For a general introduction to evangelicalism, see Leonard I. Sweet, "The Evangelical Tradition in America[: Introduction]," in *The Evangelical Tradition in America,* ed. Leonard I. Sweet (Macon, Ga., 1984), pp. 1–86; George Marsden, ed., *Evangelicalism and Modern America* (Grand Rapids, Mich., 1984); and Mark Noll, David W. Bebbington, and George A. Rawlyk, eds., *Evangelicalism: Comparative Studies of Popular Protestantism in North America, the British Isles, and Beyond, 1700–1990* (New York, 1994).

37. Patricia U. Bonomi, *Under the Cope of Heaven: Religion, Society, and Politics in Colonial America* (New York, 1986), p. 125; Philip J. Greven, Jr., "Youth, Maturity, and Religious Conversion: A Note on Ages of Converts in Andover, Massachusetts, 1711–1749," *Essex Institute Historical Collections,* 108 (1972): 126–134; *The Autobiography of Benjamin Franklin,* ed. Leonard W. Labaree et al. (New Haven, 1964), pp. 175–176.

38. Charles Woodmason, *The Carolina Backcountry on the Eve of the American Revolution: The Journal and Other Writings of Charles Woodmason, Anglican Itinerant,* ed. Richard J. Hooker (Chapel Hill, 1953), pp. 6–7, 15, 16, 22, 23.

39. Ibid., p. 13.

40. Hector St. John de Crèvecoeur, *Letters from an American Farmer and Sketches of Eighteenth-Century America,* ed. Albert E. Stone (New York, 1981), pp. 73, 76.

41. Mary Maples Dunn, "Saints and Sisters: Congregational and Quaker Women in the Early Colonial Period," *American Quarterly,* 30 (1978): 582–601; Richard D. Shiels, "The Feminization of American Congregationalism, 1735–1835," *American Quarterly,* 33 (1981): 46–62; Bonomi, *Under the Cope of Heaven,* pp. 107–108; Elaine Forman Crane, *Ebb Tide in New England: Women, Seaports, and Social Change, 1630–1800* (Boston, 1998), pp. 62–64; Laurel Thatcher Ulrich, *Good Wives: Image and Reality in the Lives of Women*

in Northern New England, 1650–1750 (New York, 1982), pp. 115–116; Greven, "Youth, Maturity, and Religious Conversion"; Joyce D. Goodfriend, "The Social Dimensions of Congregational Life in Colonial New York City," *William and Mary Quarterly,* 3d ser., 46 (1989): 252–278; Janet Moore Lindman, "A World of Baptists: Gender, Race, and Religious Community in Pennsylvania and Virginia, 1689–1825" (Ph.D. diss., University of Minnesota, 1994), pp. 110–119; Barbara E. Lacey, "Gender, Piety, and Secularization in Connecticut Religion, 1720–1775," *Journal of Social History,* 24 (1991): 799–821.

42. Ulrich, *Good Wives,* pp. 115–118; H. R. McIlwaine, ed., *Minutes of the Council and General Court of Colonial Virginia, 1622–1632, 1670–1676* (Richmond, 1924), pp. 15, 17, 89, 107, 159, 167; Mary Beth Norton, *Founding Mothers and Fathers: Gendered Power and the Forming of American Society* (New York, 1996), pp. 335–347. It is important to point out that among English Calvinists, women had been extraordinarily active in church matters and religion generally in the seventeenth century. For a brief summary, see Richard L. Greaves, "Women in Early English Nonconformity," in *Triumph over Silence: Women in Protestant History,* ed. Richard L. Greaves (Westport, Conn., 1985), pp. 75–92.

43. Ulrich, *Good Wives,* pp. 215–226; Crane, *Ebb Tide in New England,* pp. 62–79. On the broad changes for women in eighteenth-century colonial society, see Mary Beth Norton, "The Evolution of White Women's Experience in Early America," *American Historical Review,* 89 (1984): 593–619; Cornelia Hughes Dayton, *Women before the Bar: Gender, Law, and Society in Connecticut, 1639–1789* (Chapel Hill, 1995); Kathleen M. Brown, "Brave New Worlds: Women's and Gender History," *William and Mary Quarterly,* 3d ser., 50 (1993): 311–328; Brown, *Good Wives, Nasty Wenches, and Anxious Patriarchs: Gender, Race, and Power in Colonial Virginia* (Chapel Hill, 1996); Carol Berkin, *First Generations: Women in Colonial America* (New York, 1996); and Joan R. Gundersen, *To Be Useful to the World: Women in Revolutionary America, 1740–1790* (New York, 1996).

44. Benjamin Colman and Increase Mather quoted in Crane, *Ebb Tide in New England,* p. 70.

45. Susan Juster, *Disorderly Women: Sexual Politics and Evangelicalism in Revolutionary New England* (Ithaca, N.Y., 1994), pp. 41–43; Lindman, "A World of Baptists," pp. 140–182; Greaves, "Women in Early English Nonconformity."

46. A. D. Gillette, ed., *Minutes of the Philadelphia Baptist Association, from* A.D. *1707 to* A.D. *1807: Being the First One Hundred Years of Its Existence* (Philadelphia, 1851), p. 53; Lindman, "A World of Baptists," pp. 148–151.

47. Joanna Anthony, letter to Philadelphia Baptist Church, May 1764, quoted in Lindman, "A World of Baptists," pp. 162–163. Edwards later discussed female voting in Morgan Edwards, *The Customs of Primitive Churches; or, A Set of Propositions: Relative to the Name, Matterials* [sic], *Constitution, Power,*

Officers, Ordinances, Rites, Business, Worship, Discipline, Government, &c. of a Church (Philadelphia, 1768), p. 102.

48. Juster, *Disorderly Women,* pp. 122–135; also see William Lumpkin, "The Role of Women in Eighteenth Century Virginia Baptist Life," *Baptist History and Heritage,* 8 (1973): 158–167, which can be compared with Anglicans through the study by Joan R. Gundersen, "The Non-Institutional Church: The Religious Role of Women in Eighteenth-Century Virginia," *Historical Magazine of the Protestant Episcopal Church,* 51 (1982): 347–357.

49. Barry Levy, *Quakers and the American Family: British Settlement in the Delaware Valley* (New York, 1988), pp. 70–80. George Fox, 1672, quoted in Jean R. Soderlund, "Women's Authority in Pennsylvania and New Jersey Quaker Meetings 1680–1760," *William and Mary Quarterly,* 3d ser., 44 (1987): 726. Soderlund points out (p. 726) that Fox shifted the emphasis in Genesis 2:18, 20 from the point that God created women as "a helpmeet to man, to urge that men and women help each other."

50. Soderlund, "Women's Authority in Pennsylvania and New Jersey Quaker Meetings," pp. 722–749.

51. Nancy Cott, "Young Women in the Second Great Awakening in New England," *Feminist Studies,* 3 (1975): 15–29; Mary Ryan, *Cradle of the Middle Class: The Family in Oneida County, New York, 1790–1865* (New York, 1981), pp. 60–104; Ann Braude, *Radical Spirits: Spiritualism and Women's Rights in Nineteenth-Century America* (Boston, 1989), and Braude, "Women's History *Is* American Religious History," in *Retelling U.S. Religious History,* ed. Thomas A. Tweed (Berkeley, 1996), pp. 87–107.

52. Phyllis Mack, *Visionary Women: Ecstatic Prophecy in Seventeenth-Century England* (Berkeley, Calif., 1993); William C. Braithwaite, *The Beginnings of Quakerism,* ed. Henry J. Cadbury, 2d ed. (Cambridge, 1961), pp. 401–433. On female Public Friends in colonial America, see Cristine Levenduski, *Peculiar Power: A Quaker Woman Preacher in Eighteenth-Century America* (Washington, D.C., 1996); Daniel B. Shea, "Elizabeth Ashbridge and the Voice Within," in *Journeys in New Worlds: Early American Narratives,* ed. Shea (Madison, 1990), pp. 119–146; and Rebecca Larson, *Daughters of Light: Quaker Women Preaching and Prophesying in the Colonies and Abroad, 1700–1775* (New York, 1999).

53. Charles Chauncy quoted in *The Great Awakening,* ed. Goen, 4: 473n. It is intriguing that Edwards did not pursue Chauncy's point in Edwards's *Some Thoughts concerning the Revival of Religion in New England* (Boston, 1742), which cautioned ministers against overemotional revivals.

54. *The Great Awakening,* ed. Goen, pp. 69–70, 331–341. Quotations regarding Mary Reed from Ulrich, *Good Wives,* pp. 225–226. Ruth H. Bloch, "Women, Love, and Virtue in the Thought of Edwards and Franklin," in *Benjamin Franklin, Jonathan Edwards, and the Representation of American Culture,* ed. Barbara B. Oberg and Harry S. Stout (New York, 1993), pp. 134–151.

55. Bryan and Hutson, *Living Christianity Delineated*. The quotation about the four female popes is from Esther Edwards Burr, *The Journal of Esther Edwards Burr, 1754–1757*, ed. Carol Karlsen and Laurie Crumpacker (New Haven, 1984), p. 74.

56. Sarah Osborne quoted in Mary Beth Norton, "'My Resting Reaping Times': Sarah Osborne's Defense of Her 'Unfeminine Activities,'" *Signs*, 2 (1976): 515–529; Charles E. Hambrick-Stowe, "The Spiritual Pilgrimage of Sarah Osborn (1714–1796)," *Church History*, 61 (1992): 408–421.

57. Fortunately or unfortunately, two of the most vigorous books on gender relations in colonial America concentrate on the seventeenth century: Norton, *Founding Mothers and Fathers*, and Brown, *Good Wives, Nasty Wenches, and Anxious Patriarchs*. Carol Berkin, *First Generations: Women in Colonial America* (New York, 1996), emphasizes secular issues.

58. James Axtell, *The Indians' New South: Cultural Change in the Colonial Southeast* (Baton Rouge, 1997), p. 48; Calvin Martin, "The European Impact on the Culture of a Northeastern Algonquin Tribe: An Ecological Interpretation," *William and Mary Quarterly*, 3d ser., 31 (1974): 3–26.

59. Father Chrestien Le Clercq quoted on Micmac medicine woman, in *The Indian Peoples of Eastern America: A Documentary History of the Sexes*, ed. James Axtell (New York, 1981), p. 193; Field Horne, ed., *The Diary of Mary Cooper: Life on a Long Island Farm, 1768–1773* (Oyster Bay, N.Y., 1981), p. 17.

60. Ned Bearskin quoted in James H. Merrell, *The Indians' New World: Catawbas and Their Neighbors from European Contact through the Era of Removal* (Chapel Hill, 1989), pp. 131–133.

61. Quotations drawn from Gregory E. Dowd, *A Spirited Resistance: The North American Indian Struggle for Unity, 1745–1815* (Baltimore, 1992), pp. 30–32.

62. Ibid., pp. 33–34. Also see Anthony F. C. Wallace, "New Religions among the Delaware," *Southwestern Journal of Anthropology*, 12 (1956): 1–21.

63. James Axtell, *The Invasion Within: The Conquest of Cultures in Colonial North America* (New York, 1985), pp. 131–217.

64. Melville Herskovits, *The Myth of the Negro Past* (Boston, 1941). The quotation is from Eugene Genovese, *Roll, Jordan, Roll: The World the Slaves Made* (New York, 1975), p. 210. For more recent debate, see Butler, *Awash in a Sea of Faith*, pp. 129–163, which is disputed directly by Philip Morgan, *Slave Counterpoint: Black Culture in the Eighteenth-Century Chesapeake and Lowcountry* (Chapel Hill, 1998), esp. pp. 610–658, and Sylvia R. Frey and Betty Wood, *Come Shouting to Zion: African American Protestantism in the American South and British Caribbean to 1830* (Chapel Hill, 1998), pp. xi, 35.

65. Lorenzo J. Greene, *The Negro in Colonial New England, 1620–1776* (New York, 1942); Albert J. Raboteau, *Slave Religion: The "Invisible Institution" in the Antebellum South* (New York, 1978), pp. 108–110; William D. Piersen, *Black Yankees: The Development of an Afro-American Subculture in Eighteenth-Century New England* (Amherst, 1988).

66. Kenneth Scott, "The Slave Insurrection in New York in 1712," *New-York*

Historical Society Quarterly, 45 (1961): 43–74; Winthrop D. Jordan, *White over Black: American Attitudes toward the Negro, 1550–1812* (Chapel Hill, 1968), pp. 20–24, 180–187.

67. William Byrd II, *The Secret Diary of William Byrd of Westover, 1709–1712*, ed. Marion Tinling (Richmond, Va., 1941); William Byrd, *Another Secret Diary of William Byrd of Westover, 1739–1741, with Letters and Literary Exercises, 1696–1726* (Richmond, Va., 1942); Kenneth A. Lockridge, *The Diary, and Life, of William Byrd II of Virginia, 1674–1744* (Chapel Hill, 1987); Jack P. Greene, ed., *The Diary of Colonial Landon Carter of Sabine Hall, 1752–1778*, 2 vols. (Charlottesville, Va., 1965). Robert Beverley, *History and Present State of Virginia*, ed. David Freeman (Indianapolis, 1971), pp. 102–111; Thomas Jefferson, *Notes on the State of Virginia* (New York, 1964), pp. 150–155.

68. Daniel Horsmanden, *The New York Conspiracy*, ed. Thomas J. Davis (Boston, 1971), pp. 369–370, 421–431; Peter H. Wood, *Black Majority: Negroes in Colonial South Carolina from 1670 through the Stono Rebellion* (New York, 1974), pp. 308–317. On slave revolts generally, see Eugene Genovese, *From Rebellion to Revolution: Afro-American Slave Revolts in the Making of the Modern World* (Baton Rouge, 1980).

69. Charles Ball, *Fifty Years in Chains; or, The Life of an American Slave* (New York, 1858), pp. 9, 15. Allan Kulikoff kindly brought Ball's narrative to my attention.

70. On suicides, see William D. Piersen, "White Cannibals, Black Martyrs: Fear, Depression, and Religious Faith as Causes of Suicide among New Slaves," *Journal of Negro History*, 62 (1977): 147–159.

71. Francis Le Jau to SPG, October 20, 1709, and June 13, 1710, in Frank J. Klingberg, ed., *The Carolina Chronicle of Dr. Francis Le Jau, 1706–1717* (Berkeley, 1956), pp. 61, 77.

72. "Thomas Walduck's Letters from Barbados, 1710–11," *Barbados Museum and Historical Society*, 15 (1947): 148–149; Mechal Sobel, *Trabelin' On: The Slave Journey to an Afro-Baptist Faith* (Westport, Conn., 1979), p. 43; Philip D. Morgan, "Black Society in the Lowcountry, 1760–1810," in *Slavery and Freedom in the Age of the American Revolution*, ed. Ira Berlin and Ronald Hoffman (Charlottesville, Va., 1983), p. 138. The information on healing and on the magical significance of African words is taken from Morgan, *Slave Counterpoint*, p. 622. See Morgan's general discussion of this issue on pp. 615–631.

73. John Noble Wilford, "Slave Artifacts under the Hearth," *New York Times*, Aug. 27, 1996, pp. C1, C7. Morgan, *Slave Counterpoint*, pp. 621, 633. On archaeology and religious practice among antebellum Africans, see Charles E. Orser, "The Archaeology of African-American Slave Religion in the Antebellum South," *Cambridge Archaeological Journal*, 4 (1994): 33–45; Laurie Wilkie, "Magic and Empowerment on the Plantation: An Archaeological Consideration of the African-American World View," *Southeastern Archaeology*,

14 (1995): 136–148; Aaron E. Russell, "Material Culture and African-American Spirituality at the Hermitage," *Historical Archaeology*, 31 (1997): 63–80.

74. Jerome Handler and Frederick Lange, *Plantation Slavery in Barbados: An Archaeological and Historical Investigation* (Cambridge, Mass., 1978), pp. 171–215. The Ligon quotation is found in ibid., p. 182.

75. Sobel, *Trabelin' On*, pp. 44, 197–200; Mechal Sobel, *The World They Made Together: Black and White Values in Eighteenth-Century Virginia* (Princeton, 1987), pp. 214–225; Morgan, *Slave Counterpoint*, pp. 640–646; Albert J. Raboteau, *Slave Religion: The "Invisible Institution" in the Antebellum South* (New York, 1978), pp. 84–85.

76. Francis Le Jau to SPG, October 20, 1709, in *Carolina Chronicle of Dr. Francis Le Jau,* ed. Klingberg, 60.

77. On Church of England proselytizing, see Frank Klingberg, *An Appraisal of the Negro in Colonial South Carolina* (Washington, D.C., 1941); Edgar Legare Pennington, *Thomas Bray's Associates and Their Work among the Negroes* (Worcester, Mass., 1939); John C. Van Horne, *Religious Philanthropy and Colonial Slavery: The American Correspondence of the Associates of Dr. Bray, 1717–77* (Urbana, 1985); David Brion Davis, *The Problem of Slavery in Western Culture* (Ithaca, N.Y., 1966), p. 219; J. H. Bennett, *Bondsmen and Bishops: Slavery and Apprenticeship on the Codrington Plantation of Barbados, 1710–1838* (Berkeley, 1958).

78. Albert J. Raboteau, *Slave Religion: The "Invisible Institution" in the Antebellum South* (New York, 1978), pp. 129–130.

79. The quotations are found in ibid., p. 131. On the Baptists, see Mechal Sobel, *Trabelin' On.*

80. Sobel, *The World They Made Together,* pp. 178–203; John B. Boles, ed., *Masters and Slaves Together: Race and Religion in the American South, 1740–1870* (Lexington, Ky., 1988).

81. George E. Simpson, *Black Religions in the New World* (New York, 1978); Roger Bastide, *African Civilisations in the New World,* trans. Peter Green (New York, 1971).

6. 1776

1. Thomas Paine, *Common Sense,* ed. Isaac Kramnick (New York, 1976), pp. 8–9, 84, 89, 100, 104. The press runs for *Common Sense* were unprecedented. Paine's intimations about providence strongly parallel the millennialist thought discussed in Ruth H. Bloch, *Visionary Republic: Millennial Themes in American Thought, 1756–1800* (New York, 1985).

2. On these broad themes, see, among others, Bernard Bailyn, *The Ideological Origins of the American Revolution* (Cambridge, Mass., 1967), esp. pp. 22–54; Pauline Maier, *From Resistance to Revolution: Colonial Radicals and the Development of American Opposition to Britain, 1765–1776* (New York,

1972); and H. Trevor Colbourn, *The Lamp of Experience: Whig History and the Intellectual Origins of the American Revolution* (Chapel Hill, 1965). For an older but still interesting comparison of the French and American Revolutions, see R. R. Palmer, *The Age of the Democratic Revolution: A Political History of Europe and America, 1760–1800*, 2 vols. (Princeton, N.J., 1959–1964). For interpretations that place greater stress on issues of class, or at least of discontent among laboring people, see Gary B. Nash, *The Urban Crucible: Social Change, Political Consciousness, and the Origins of the American Revolution* (Cambridge, Mass., 1979); Edward Countryman, *A People in Revolution: The American Revolution and Political Society in New York, 1760–1790* (Baltimore, 1981); Edward Countryman, *The American Revolution* (New York, 1985), in which the excellent bibliographical essay is especially helpful; Dirk Hoerder, *Crowd Action in Revolutionary Massachusetts, 1765–1780* (New York, 1977); Jesse Lemisch and John K. Alexander, "The White Oaks, Jack Tar, and the Concept of the 'Inarticulate,' " *William and Mary Quarterly,* 3d ser., 29 (1972): 109–142; Jesse Lemisch, "Jack Tar in the Streets: Merchant Seamen in the Politics of Revolutionary America," *William and Mary Quarterly,* 3d ser., 25 (1968): 371–407.

3. The literature on these topics is enormous. Among other excellent books, see Bailyn, *Ideological Origins of the American Revolution*; Edmund S. Morgan, *Inventing the People: The Rise of Popular Sovereignty in England and America* (New York, 1988); Gordon S. Wood, *The Creation of the American Republic, 1776–1787* (Chapel Hill, 1969); Gordon S. Wood, *The Radicalism of the American Revolution* (New York, 1992). On the American Revolution as a model for other revolutions, see David Brion Davis, *Revolutions: Reflections on American Equality and Foreign Liberations* (Cambridge, Mass., 1989).

4. Edmund S. Morgan and Helen M. Morgan, *The Stamp Act Crisis: Prologue to Revolution* (Chapel Hill, 1953); Countryman, *The American Revolution,* pp. 43–56.

5. These events are recounted succinctly in Countryman, *The American Revolution,* and in Edmund S. Morgan, *The Birth of the Republic* (Chicago, 1956).

6. Quotations from John Adams's resolution in the First Continental Congress are from Morgan, *Birth of the Republic,* p. 66. On British nationalism and the American Revolution, see the important article by T. H. Breen, "Ideology and Nationalism on the Eve of the American Revolution: Revisions Once More in Need of Revising," *Journal of American History,* 84 (1997): 13–39.

7. Quotations from the Declaration of Independence are from Pauline Maier, *American Scripture: Making the Declaration of Independence* (New York, 1997), pp. 236–241. See also pp. 225–234 for samples of instructions on independence from local governments and agencies.

8. The resolves of the colonial assemblies are printed in *Prologue to Revolution: Sources and Documents on the Stamp Act Crisis, 1764–1766,* ed. Edmund S. Morgan (Chapel Hill, 1959), pp. 44–62.

9. Michael Kammen, *Colonial New York: A History* (Millwood, N.Y., 1975), pp. 356, 366; David Ammerman, *In the Common Cause: American Response to the Coercive Acts of 1774* (Charlottesville, Va., 1974), pp. 10–12, 66, 67.

10. James Kirby Martin, *Men in Rebellion: Higher Governmental Leaders and the Coming of the American Revolution* (New Brunswick, N.J., 1973), p. 191.

11. The incident involving Jared Ingersol is described in Robert M. Calhoun, *Revolutionary America: An Interpretive Overview* (New York, 1976), p. 74. On the placemen, see Richard L. Bushman, *King and People in Provincial Massachusetts* (Chapel Hill, 1985), pp. 55–57. On the Loyalists, see Wallace Brown, *The Good Americans* (New York, 1969); Robert M. Calhoon, *The Loyalists in Revolutionary America, 1760–1781* (New York, 1973); and Robert M. Calhoon, Timothy M. Barnes, and George A. Rawlyk, eds., *Loyalists and Community in North America* (Westport, Conn., 1994).

12. Alfred Young, "George Robert Twelves Hughes (1742–1840): A Boston Shoemaker and the Memory of the American Revolution," *William and Mary Quarterly*, 3d ser., 38 (1981): 561–623; Countryman, *The American Revolution*, p. 103. An impressive literature developed in the 1970s examined popular participation in the Revolution. Among the important works are Maier, *From Resistance to Revolution;* Dirk Hoerder, *Crowd Action in Revolutionary Massachusetts, 1765–1780* (New York, 1977); Richard Alan Ryerson, *The Revolution Is Now Begun: The Radical Committees of Philadelphia, 1765–1776* (Philadelphia, 1978); Edward Countryman, *A People in Revolution: The American Revolution and Political Society in New York, 1760–1790* (Baltimore, 1981); and Jesse Lemisch, "Jack Tar in the Streets: Merchant Seamen in the Politics of Revolutionary America," *William and Mary Quarterly*, 3d ser., 25 (1968): 371–407.

13. One supposes that the influence of eighteenth-century Scottish philosophy in colonial political thinking or, more specifically, in American constitutional thinking could be treated as an ethnic issue, but it is not. On intellectual issues, see Garry Wills, *Explaining America: The Federalist* (Garden City, N.Y., 1981), and *Inventing America: Jefferson's Declaration of Independence* (New York, 1978).

14. On the Regulator movement, see the fascinating documents in Charles Woodmason, *The Carolina Backcountry on the Eve of the American Revolution: The Journal and Other Writings of Charles Woodmason, Anglican Itinerant,* ed. Richard J. Hooker (Chapel Hill, 1953), pp. 165–298; Richard Maxwell Brown, *The South Carolina Regulators* (Cambridge, Mass., 1963); and Marvin L. Michael Kay, "The North Carolina Regulation, 1766–1776," in *The American Revolution: Explorations in the History of American Radicalism,* ed. Alfred F. Young (DeKalb, Ill., 1976), pp. 71–123.

15. U.S. Bureau of the Census, *Historical Statistics of the United States, Colonial Times to 1957* (Washington, D.C., 1960), 66; Roger Daniels, *Coming to America: A History of Immigration and Ethnicity in American Life* (New York, 1990), pp. 121–126. An interesting comparison of pre- and postrevolutionary

German participation in Pennsylvania politics is found in Wolfgang Splitter, "The Germans in Pennsylvania Politics, 1758–1790: A Quantitative Analysis," *Pennsylvania Magazine of History and Biography,* 122 (1998): 39–76. Ironically, the nineteenth-century German immigration to America has yet to receive a worthy synoptic study, but see Daniels, *Coming to America,* pp. 145–164, for a brief introduction. For a study of an antebellum immigrant city, see Kathleen Neils Conzen, *Immigrant Milwaukee, 1836–1860* (Cambridge, Mass., 1976). On English and Scottish immigrants to America, see Charlotte Erickson, *Invisible Immigrants: The Adaptation of English and Scottish Immigrants in Nineteenth-Century America* (London, 1972), and Erickson, *Leaving England: Essays on British Emigration in the Nineteenth Century* (Ithaca, N.Y., 1994).

16. Thomas M. Doerflinger, *A Vigorous Spirit of Enterprise: Merchants and Economic Development in Revolutionary Philadelphia* (Chapel Hill, 1986); Jack M. Sosin, *Agents and Merchants: British Colonial Policy and the Origins of the American Revolution, 1763–1775* (Lincoln, 1965); Arthur Meier Schlesinger, *The Colonial Merchants and the American Revolution, 1763–1776* (New York, 1918). The merchant involvement was not uniform, as Doerflinger especially demonstrates in his study of Philadelphia, where merchants frequently proved to be reluctant revolutionaries.

17. Steven C. Bullock, *Revolutionary Brotherhood: Freemasonry and the Transformation of the American Social Order, 1730–1840* (Chapel Hill, 1996), pp. 68–71; James H. Easterby, *History of the St. Andrews Society of Charleston, South Carolina, 1729–1929* (Charleston, 1929); Maier, *From Resistance to Revolution,* pp. 78–81; also see Roger Champagne, "The Military Association of the Sons of Liberty," *New-York Historical Quarterly,* 41 (1957): 338–350.

18. Morgan, ed., *Prologue to Revolution,* quotation from Stamp Act Congress on p. 62.

19. Paine, *Common Sense,* pp. 65, 78, 121. On Paine and his tract *Common Sense,* see especially Eric Foner, *Tom Paine and Revolutionary America* (New York, 1976), and Jack Fruchtman, Jr., *Thomas Paine and the Religion of Nature* (Baltimore, 1994).

20. Paine, *Common Sense,* pp. 69, 71, 72, 73, 77, 78, 79, 81. The predicament of Paine's adversaries is revealed in the first substantial answer to *Common Sense,* which was a pamphlet entitled *Plain Truth; Address to the Inhabitants of America, Containing, Remarks on a Late Pamphlet, entitled Common Sense* (Philadelphia, 1776), now known to be written by James Chalmers, a leaden answer that galvanized no one. On its authorship, see Thomas R. Adams, "The Authorship and Printing of Plain Truth by 'Candidus,'" *Papers of the Bibliographical Society of America,* 49 (1955): 230–248.

21. For a discussion of the colonial economy in the revolutionary period, see John J. McCusker and Russell R. Menard, *The Economy of British America, 1607–1789* (Chapel Hill, 1985), pp. 351–377, and Cathy Matson, "The Revolution, the Constitution, and the New Nation," in *The Cambridge Economic History*

of the United States: The Colonial Era, ed. Stanley L. Engerman and Robert E. Gallman (New York, 1996), pp. 337–362.

22. The most extensive discussion of indebtedness in a single colony is found in T. H. Breen, *Tobacco Culture: The Mentality of the Great Tidewater Planters on the Eve of the Revolution* (Princeton, 1985). The general issue of indebtedness is discussed in McCusker and Menard, *Economy of British America,* pp. 353–354, and Menard, "Economic and Social Development of the South," in *The Cambridge Economic History of the United States: The Colonial Era,* ed. Engerman and Gallman, p. 294.

23. Doerflinger, *A Vigorous Spirit of Enterprise,* pp. 167–196.

24. Matson, "The Revolution, the Constitution, and the New Nation," pp. 337–362. Doerflinger, *A Vigorous Spirit of Enterprise,* is the best case study of the Revolution and its economic consequences, in this case in Philadelphia.

25. Ibid., pp. 203–204; E. Wayne Carp, *To Starve the Army at Pleasure: Continental Army Administration and American Political Culture, 1775–1783* (Chapel Hill, 1984); Charles Royster, *A Revolutionary People at War: The Continental Army and American Character, 1775–1783* (Chapel Hill, 1979), pp. 270–272.

26. Matson, "The Revolution, the Constitution, and the New Nation," p. 365.

27. John Locke, *Two Treatises of Government: A Critical Edition with an Introduction and Apparatus Criticus,* ed. Peter Laslett (Cambridge, 1960), pp. 325–326; David Brion Davis, *The Problem of Slavery in Western Culture* (Ithaca, N.Y., 1966), pp. 118–121. Also see Jennifer Welchman, "Locke on Slavery and Inalienable Rights," *Canadian Journal of Philosophy,* 25 (1995): 67–71; Wayne Glausser, "Three Approaches to Locke and the Slave Trade," *Journal of the History of Ideas,* 51 (1990): 199–216. Quotations from John Adams and the Athol town meeting as well as the Samuel Webster reference are from Richard L. Bushman, *King and People in Provincial Massachusetts* (Chapel Hill, 1985), pp. 183, 191, 192.

28. Maier, *American Scripture,* p. 147; Maier prints Jefferson's original draft of the Declaration of Independence with the excisions and additions made to Jefferson's text in an appendix on pp. 235–241. Davis, *The Problem of Slavery in Western Culture,* pp. 291–332; Jean R. Soderlund, *Quakers and Slavery: A Divided Spirit* (Princeton, 1985); Gary B. Nash and Jean R. Soderlund, *Freedom by Degrees: Emancipation in Pennsylvania and Its Aftermath* (New York, 1991); Jack D. Marietta, *The Reformation of American Quakerism, 1748–1783* (Philadelphia, 1984), pp. 111–127; Stephen Stein, "George Whitefield on Slavery: Some New Evidence," *Church History,* 42 (1973): 243–256.

29. Benjamin Quarles, "Lord Dunmore as Liberator," *William and Mary Quarterly,* 3d ser., 15 (1958): 494–507; Sylvia R. Frey, *Water from the Rock: Black Resistance in a Revolutionary Age* (Princeton, 1991), pp. 45–80, quotation from South Carolina Provincial Assembly on p. 57.

30. Edmund Pendleton quoted in *American Negro Slavery,* ed. Michael Mullin (New York, 1976), p. 118; Landon Carter quoted in Mechal Sobel, *The World*

They Made Together: Black and White Values in Eighteenth-Century Virginia (Princeton, 1987), pp. 131–132.

31. Carol Berkin, *First Generations: Women in Colonial America* (New York, 1996), pp. 165–194, quotation on pp. 178–179.

32. Mary Beth Norton, *Liberty's Daughters: The Revolutionary Experience of American Women, 1750–1800* (Boston, 1980), pp. 191–193; also see important articles by Ruth H. Bloch, "The Gendered Meanings of Virtue in Republican America," *Signs: Journal of Women in Culture and Society,* 13 (1987–88): 37–58, and Joan R. Gundersen, "Independence, Citizenship, and the American Revolution," ibid., 59–77.

33. Norton, *Liberty's Daughters,* quotations on pp. 235, 276; Linda Kerber, *Women of the Republic: Intellect and Ideology in Revolutionary America* (Chapel Hill, 1980). For an exploration of developing patterns in sexuality, see Clare A. Lyons, "Sex among the 'Rabble': Gender Transitions in the Age of Revolution, Philadelphia, 1750–1830" (Ph.D. diss., Yale University, 1996).

34. Judith Sargeant Murray quoted in Norton, *Liberty's Daughters,* p. 295. Nancy F. Cott, *The Bonds of Womanhood: "Woman's Sphere" in New England, 1780–1835* (New Haven, 1977).

35. Colin G. Calloway, *The American Revolution in Indian Country: Crisis and Diversity in Native American Communities* (New York, 1995); Eric Hinderaker, *Elusive Empires: Constructing Colonialism in the Ohio Valley, 1673–1800* (New York, 1997), pp. 187–270.

36. Bridenbaugh, Carl, *Mitre and Sceptre: Transatlantic Faiths, Ideas, Personalities, and Politics, 1689–1775* (New York: Oxford University Press, 1962), pp. 333–334. For a vigorous recent argument about religion's importance in the revolutionary contest, see Kevin Phillips, *The Cousins' Wars: Religion, Politics, and the Triumph of Anglo-America* (New York, 1999).

37. Christopher M. Jedrey, *The World of John Cleaveland: Family and Community in Eighteenth-Century New England* (New York, 1979), pp. 126–127; John Gordon, *A Sermon on the Late Rebellion* (Williamsburg, 1746); Samuel Langdon, *Government Corrupted by Vice, and Recovered by Righteousness* (Boston, 1775), in *Religion and the Coming of the American Revolution,* ed. Peter Carroll (Waltham, Mass., 1970), pp. 128–142; quotation from Langdon Carter's diary in Patricia U. Bonomi, *Under the Cope of Heaven: Religion, Society, and Politics in Colonial America* (New York, 1986), p. 210.

38. Bridenbaugh, *Mitre and Sceptre;* Alan Heimert, *Religion and the American Mind from the Great Awakening to the Revolution* (Cambridge, Mass., 1966); Harry S. Stout, *The New England Soul: Preaching and Religious Culture in Colonial New England* (New York, 1986); Harry S. Stout, "Religion, Communication, and the Ideological Origins of the American Revolution," *William and Mary Quarterly,* 3d ser., 34 (1977): 519–541; Harry S. Stout, *The Divine Dramatist: George Whitefield and the Rise of Modern Evangelicalism* (Grand Rapids, Mich., 1991); Rhys Isaac, "Evangelical Revolt: The Nature of the

Baptists' Challenge to the Traditional Order in Virginia, 1765–1775," *William and Mary Quarterly,* 3d ser., 31 (1974): 345–368; Patricia U. Bonomi, *Under the Cope of Heaven,* pp. 187–216; Timothy D. Hall, *Contested Boundaries: Itinerancy and the Reshaping of the Colonial American Religious World* (Durham, N.C., 1994); Frank Lambert, *"Pedlar in Divinity": George Whitefield and the Transatlantic Revivals* (Princeton, 1994); T. H. Breen and Timothy Hall, "Structuring Provincial Imagination: The Rhetoric and Experience of Social Change in Eighteenth-Century New England," *American Historical Review,* 103 (1998): 1411–1439. Phillips, *The Cousins' Wars,* pp. 91–100, 158–159, 161–232, makes much of religious and ethnic antagonisms that prompted support for the Revolution.

39. This argument is developed at greater length in Jon Butler, *Awash in a Sea of Faith: Christianizing the American People* (Cambridge, Mass., 1990), pp. 194–224. *Records of the Presbyterian Church in the United States of America . . . , 1706–1788* (Philadelphia, 1904), 466–469; Mark A. Noll, *Christians in the American Revolution* (Washington, D.C., 1977), pp. 65–68; Nathan Hatch, *The Sacred Cause of Liberty: Republican Thought and the Millennium in Revolutionary New England* (New Haven, 1977), pp. 22, 61. Four Presbyterian ministers endorsed the view of the Anglican clergyman George Mickeljohn, whose sermon *On the Important Duty of Subjection to the Civil Powers* (Newbern, N.C., 1768), is reprinted in *Some Eighteenth-Century Tracts concerning North Carolina,* ed. William K. Boyd (Raleigh, N.C., 1927), pp. 393–412.

40. On the Declaration itself and the process from which it emerged, see Maier, *American Scripture.* The American spiritualist leader Andrew Jackson Davis published a new version of the Declaration of Independence in 1851 that emphasized religious rather than political issues, as if to underscore the overwhelming secularism of the 1776 Declaration. See Bret E. Carroll, *Spiritualism in Antebellum America* (Bloomington, 1997), p. 35.

41. For an excellent introduction to religious creativity in early national and antebellum America, see Nathan O. Hatch, *The Democratization of American Christianity* (New Haven, 1989).

42. Charles Coleman Sellers, *Benjamin Franklin in Portraiture* (New Haven, 1962), pp. 9, 10, 231; Ronald W. Clark, *Benjamin Franklin: A Biography* (New York, 1983), p. 315.

43. Pauline Maier, *The Old Revolutionaries: Political Lives in the Age of Samuel Adams* (New York, 1980).

44. Benjamin Franklin, *The Autobiography of Benjamin Franklin,* ed. Leonard Labaree, Ralph L. Ketcham, Helen C. Boatfield, and Helene H. Fineman (New Haven, 1964), p. 44.

45. In writing this epitaph, Franklin reshaped a crabbed seventeenth-century idea about the transmigration of souls after death, a notion circulating among an eclectic mix of European and American religious radicals, into an affirmation of near-modern optimism. In the 1720s Franklin may have been especially

intrigued by the transmigration of souls and occult Masonic and Hermetic notions. Some of these interests may have come from Franklin's original printing master in Philadelphia, the eccentric Samuel Keimer, who later became his nemesis. Keimer and his wife worked with millennial and apocalyptic groups in London, including London's infamous French Prophets, before leaving for the New World. Franklin biographers generally dismiss Keimer as a crank and do not explore a possible momentary influence on Franklin, and only a few older articles treat Keimer seriously, among them Chester E. Jorgenson, "A Brand Flung at Colonial Orthodoxy: Samuel Keimer's 'Universal Instructor in All Arts and Sciences,' " *Journalism Quarterly*, 12 (1935): 272–277. The Quaker schismatic George Keith entertained beliefs in the transmigration of souls in correspondence with Lady Ann Conway in the 1680s; see Marjorie Nicolson, "George Keith and the Cambridge Platonists," *Philosophical Review*, 39 (1930): 51. Jeremiah Dummer, the first American to earn a Ph.D., wrote a dissertation on the transmigration of souls at Utrecht, published in 1703; see Calhoun Winton, "Jeremiah Dummer: The 'First American'?" *William and Mary Quarterly*, 3d ser., 26 (1969): 105–108. In 1801 Rev. Isaac Story suggested that Jefferson might investigate the doctrine of the transmigation of souls but Jefferson replied that one could never determine the truth of such a notion; see William D. Gould, "The Religious Opinions of Thomas Jefferson," *Mississippi Valley Historical Review*, 20 (1933): 200. The eighteenth-century New England minister Jonathan Mayhew discussed the possibility of the transmigration of souls; see John Corrigan, *The Hidden Balance: Religion and the Social Theories of Charles Chauncy and Jonathan Mayhew* (New York, 1987), pp. 101–103. Older surveys of views on the transmigration of souls can be found in J. Gibbons, *Theories of the Transmigration of Souls* (London, 1907), and D. Alfred Bertholet, *The Transmigration of Souls*, trans. H. J. Chaytor (New York, 1909). The idea of migrating souls encouraged an optimism closely related to the notion of progress, which is itself discussed with important implications for the history of slavery in David Brion Davis, *Slavery and Human Progress* (New York, 1984).

ACKNOWLEDGMENTS

My greatest immediate debts are to the historians cited in the notes. Over the past quarter century they have thoroughly transformed the study of colonial American history. Anyone who writes about early America will appreciate my immense debt to each person whose work I have cited. This book could never have been written without their scholarship.

My long-term intellectual debts begin with three mentors—Anita Rutman, Darrett Rutman, and John R. Howe, Jr. The Rutmans' untimely deaths in 1997 and 1998 took from the ranks of early American historians two of the most original and demanding voices who ever practiced the craft. To study with them at the University of Minnesota was a privilege. They would have told me *exactly* what was wrong with this book. They also would have appreciated what might be right about it. John Howe has been a wonderful teacher and friend for thirty years. He patiently allowed me to write a Ph.D. dissertation on a topic far from his own specialty, gave sage advice, and has been warmly supportive ever since. He was the perfect adviser.

Many friends provided advice as I worked. At Yale, Skip Stout not only read the entire manuscript but has been a remarkable partner in fifteen years of endeavors from the Works of Jonathan Edwards, which he directs, to the Pew Program in Religion and American History and now the Institute for the Advanced Study of Religion at Yale, which we have directed jointly. I can't thank him enough. David Brion Davis has been a colleague, critic, and friend of great generosity. Ned Cooke and John Demos read chapters and offered succinct criticisms and keen suggestions. Ken Minkema, Executive Editor of the Works of Jonathan

Edwards, furnished the picture of Jonathan Edwards's desk and lent his scholarship on the subject, as well as savvy help on other matters. Jean-Christophe Agnew, Richard Brodhead, Linda Colley, Nancy Cott, Johnny Faragher, George Miles, David Montgomery, Jules Prown, Alan Trachtenberg, Frank Turner, David Waldstreicher, John Harley Warner, and Bryan Wolf answered questions large and small, sometimes even when they did not realize they were doing so. Similarly, Richard Brodhead, Susan Hockfield, Richard Levin, Charles Long, Alison Richard, and my terrific colleagues on Yale's Humanities Advisory Committee may not realize how fully our discussions of higher education affected this book.

Historians on both sides of the Atlantic have offered important suggestions over many years about problems discussed in this book, including good advice about evidence and sources. These include Joyce Appleby, Patricia Bonomi, T. H. Breen, Richard D. Brown, Richard Bushman, Ted Cook, Roger Daniels, Peter Davis, Stephen Foster, Aaron Fogleman, J. William Frost, Nathan Hatch, Christine Heyrman, Ronald Hoffman, Ned Landsman, Hartmut Lehmann, Janet Moore Lindman, Russell Menard, John Murrin, Gary Nash, Alison Olson, Gregg Roeber, Jonathan Sarna, Robert Scholz, Stephen Stein, Hermann Wellenreuther, and Marianne Wokeck, as well as former colleagues at the University of Illinois at Chicago including Carolyn Edie, Robert Messer, Michael Perman, James Sack, and Daniel Scott Smith.

Richard Dunn and Michael Zuckerman at the University of Pennsylvania provided many kindnesses, not the least being an invitation to address the 1994 year-end picnic for what now is the McNeill Center for Early American Studies. Gloria Main of the University of Colorado and Alan Tully of the University of British Columbia generously read chapters with critical empathy. Cary Carson and Catherine Grosfils of Colonial Williamsburg retrieved the picture of Samuel Harrison's plantation, and Sarah J. Rittgers rescued the powder horn photograph from the bowels of the Smithsonian Institution. Carl Lounsbury of Colonial Williamsburg provided important information on colonial architecture and secured the Virginia courthouse picture. William Reese of New Haven kindly furnished the picture by Thomas Pownall. Fredrika Teute, Philip Morgan, and Michael McGiffert of the Omohundro Institute of Early American History and Culture gave me good advice about widely different aspects of this book. Laurel Thatcher Ulrich provided a penetrating critique. My dear friend Eric Monkkonen always tells me what's right. John Hench of the American Antiquarian Society and the Department of History at the University of Minnesota sponsored vigorous discussions of the principal themes in this book that improved the final draft. Students helped with research at different points, including Jim Bennett, Catherine Brekus, Scott Casper, Scott Cormode, Stewart Davenport, Christopher Grasso, Joseph Kosek, and Andrew Lewis. Genevieve Ko helped assemble the final manuscript.

How I wish my friend Paul Lucas were here to read this; he would have laughed, just as he did when we were in graduate school.

Staff members at several institutions were exceptionally helpful in arranging illustrations. These include the Abby Aldrich Rockefeller Folk Art Center; Albany Institute of History and Art; American Jewish Historical Society; British Museum; Colonial Williamsburg; Congregation Mikveh Israel of Philadelphia; Gibbes Museum of Art; Henry Francis du Pont Winterthur Museum; Milton S. Eisenhower Library at The Johns Hopkins University; Museum of Early Southern Decorative Arts; Museum of Fine Arts, Boston; McCord Museum of Canadian History; New Haven Colony Historical Society; New-York Historical Society; Old Sturbridge Village; Philadelphia Historical Commission; Philadelphia Museum of Art; Society for the Preservation of New England Antiquities; and the Yale University Art Gallery. Some portions of Chapter 5 appeared in a different form in *Awash in a Sea of Faith: Christianizing the American People* (Harvard University Press, 1990). At Harvard University Press, Aida Donald was extraordinarily patient and wise, Elizabeth Suttell again advised on manuscript preparation to my great benefit, and Elizabeth Gilbert smoothed the final text, once more correcting prose that might sometimes have been called remarkable. The usual caveat applies: these people have helped me write the book, but every mistake is my own.

Some acknowledgments are personal. Roxanne, Ben, and Peter make my life, including outings from the basketball courts of Massachusetts to the baseball diamond at Minneapolis's Hubert H. Humphrey Metrodome, always filled with laughter and fun.

The book is dedicated to my parents, who had the grace to raise their three children in the rural Midwest—Hector, Minnesota, in Renville County on U.S. Highway 212—an upbringing that has supported everything good in my life for more than a half century.

INDEX